An Invention without a Future

BY JAMES NAREMORE

The World without a Self: Virginia Woolf and the Novel
Filmguide to Psycho
The Magic World of Orson Welles
Acting in the Cinema
The Films of Vincente Minnelli
More Than Night: Film Noir in Its Contexts
On Kubrick
Sweet Smell of Success

An Invention without a Future

Essays on Cinema

JAMES NAREMORE

University of California *Press*

BERKELEY   LOS ANGELES   LONDON

University of California Press, one of the most distinguished university presses in the United States, enriches lives around the world by advancing scholarship in the humanities, social sciences, and natural sciences. Its activities are supported by the UC Press Foundation and by philanthropic contributions from individuals and institutions. For more information, visit www.ucpress.edu.

University of California Press
Berkeley and Los Angeles, California

University of California Press, Ltd.
London, England

© 2014 by The Regents of the University of California

Library of Congress Cataloging-in-Publication Data

Naremore, James.
   An invention without a future : essays on cinema / James Naremore.
     pages   cm
   Includes bibliographical references and index.
   ISBN 978-0-520-27973-5 (cloth : alk. paper)—ISBN 978-0-520-27974-2 (pbk. : alk. paper)—ISBN 978-0-520-95794-7 (ebook)
   1. Motion pictures.   I. Title.
   PN1995.N3395   2014
   791.43—dc23
                        2013032932

23 22 21 20 19 18 17 16 15 14
10 9 8 7 6 5 4 3 2 1

For Darlene, as always

Contents

Acknowledgments	ix
Introduction: An Invention without a Future	1

PART I. ISSUES

Authorship, Auteurism, and Cultural Politics	15
The Reign of Adaptation	33
Notes on Acting in Cinema	49
Imitation, Eccentricity, and Impersonation in Movie Acting	58
The Death and Rebirth of Rhetoric	77

PART II. AUTHORS, ACTORS, ADAPTATIONS

Hawks, Chandler, Bogart, Bacall: *The Big Sleep*	87
Uptown Folk: Blackness and Entertainment in *Cabin in the Sky*	104
Hitchcock and Humor	124
Hitchcock at the Margins of Noir	139
Spies and Lovers: *North by Northwest*	156
Welles, Hollywood, and *Heart of Darkness*	172
Orson Welles and Movie Acting	187
Welles and Kubrick: Two Forms of Exile	198

The Treasure of the Sierra Madre	215
The Return of *The Dead*	231

PART III. IN DEFENSE OF CRITICISM

James Agee	247
Manny Farber	264
Andrew Sarris	275
Jonathan Rosenbaum	289
Four Years as a Critic: 2007–2010	305
Works Cited	327
Index	337

Acknowledgments

Different versions of several essays in this book were published elsewhere or were commissioned as public lectures. I am grateful to the following publishers and institutions:

"Authorship, Auteurism, and Cultural Politics" derives from "Authorship and the Cultural Politics of Film Criticism," in *Film Quarterly* (Fall 1990) and "Authorship," in *A Companion to Film Theory*, ed. Toby Miller and Robert Stam (Oxford: Blackwell, 1999).

"The Reign of Adaptation," in a different form, appeared in *Distinguished Lecturer Series* (Indiana University Institute for Advanced Study, no. 10) and as the Introduction to *Film Adaptation*, ed. James Naremore (New Brunswick, NJ: Rutgers, 2000).

"Notes on Acting in Cinema" was originally published as "Acting in the Cinema," in *The Cinema Book*, ed. Pam Cook (London: BFI, 2005).

"Imitation, Eccentricity, and Impersonation in Movie Acting" is a revised and expanded version of a lecture entitled "Film Acting and the Arts of Imitation," presented to the conference of the Group for the Study of the Actor in Cinema at the Cinémathèque de Nice, France; the lecture was later published in the proceedings of the conference and in *Film Quarterly* (Summer 2012).

"The Death and Rebirth of Rhetoric," in a shorter version, was a conference paper in a panel organized at the Society of Cinema Studies in 2000 and later published in the online journal *Senses of Cinema* (April 2000).

"Hawks, Chandler, Bogart, Bacall: *The Big Sleep*" originated as the keynote address for the Noir Festival at the New School in New York, 2011. It was also delivered at the Key Figures in Film Studies lectures sponsored by King's College London and the British Film Institute; at

Middlebury College; and at the University of Iowa Annual Film Studies Lecture in 2011.

"Uptown Folk: Blackness and Entertainment in *Cabin in the Sky*," in a slightly different form, was published in *Arizona Quarterly* (Winter 1992).

"Hitchcock and Humor" originally appeared in *Strategies* (May 2001).

"Hitchcock at the Margins of Noir" was published in *Alfred Hitchcock Centenary Essays*, ed. Richard Allen and S. Ishii Gonzales (London: BFI 1999).

"Spies and Lovers: *North by Northwest*" was the Introduction to *North by Northwest*, ed. James Naremore (New Brunswick, NJ: Rutgers University Press, 1993).

"Welles, Hollywood, and *Heart of Darkness*," under a different title, was a lecture at the University of Pittsburgh in 2007 and later published in *True to the Spirit: Film Adaptation and the Question of Fidelity*, ed. Colin McCabe, Kathleen Murray, and Rick Warner (New York: Oxford University Press, 2011).

"Orson Welles and Movie Acting" is derived from "Orson Welles and the Direction of Actors," in *Action!*, ed. Paolo Bertetto (Rome: Fondazione Cinema per Roma, 2007) and "The Actor as Director," in *Perspectives on Orson Welles*, ed. Morris Beja (Boston: G.K. Hall, 1995).

"Welles and Kubrick: Two Forms of Exile" was a lecture in the Symposium on Orson Welles and International Cinema at Yale University in 2007.

"*The Treasure of the Sierra Madre*" is a revised version of my introduction to John Huston's screenplay of the film (Madison: University of Wisconsin Press, 1979).

"The Return of *The Dead*" was published in *Perspectives on John Huston*, ed. Stephen Cooper (Boston: G.K. Hall, 1994).

"Andrew Sarris" is a revised version of "An ABC of Reading Andrew Sarris," in *Citizen Sarris*, ed. Emmanuel Levy (Lanham, MD: Scarecrow Press, 2001).

"James Agee," in a shorter version, was presented as a lecture for the Graduate Colloquium in Cinema and Media Studies, UCLA, 2012.

At the University of California Press I owe thanks to my editor, Mary Francis, for her patience, promptness, and wise responsiveness; to Lea Jacobs and the anonymous readers of the manuscript for their useful suggestions; to Rose Vekony for gracefully shepherding the book through production; and to copy editor Sharron Wood for her care and expertise, which saved me from many embarrassing errors.

The following individuals were instrumental in giving me information or opportunities to publish essays and present lectures: Charles Affron, Mirella Affron, Richard Allen, Dudley Andrew, Sarah Cooper, Corey Creekmur, Christophe Damour, Rhidian Davis, Richard Dyer, Christian Keathley, Robert Lupone, Robert Lyons, Colin MacCabe, Kathleen McHugh, Jim Miller, Michael Morgan, Chon Noriega, Gilberto Perez, Robert Polito, Jonathan Rosenbaum, Robert Stam, Steven Ungar, Helene Valmary, Ginette Vincendeau, Christian Viviani, Rob White, and Susan White.

Introduction
An Invention without a Future

> The cinema is an invention without a future.
> Attributed to LOUIS LUMIÈRE, 1895

> In twenty-five years there will be very few scoffers at the movies; in fifty years the most cultivated men will be reading movie literature; in a hundred years such men as von Stroheim and Murnau will be spoken of as reverently as Mozart or Dickens are today, and *The Last Laugh* will be as enduring a work of Art as *Vanity Fair*.
> JAMES AGEE, "The Moving Picture," Bulletin of the Phillips Exeter Academy, 1926

> Until such time as there is a past of some sort . . . a past which has been examined, has been subjected to a critical, a theoretical analysis, there can be no future. . . . This body of material, whatever it is, then imposes upon us the responsibility of inventing it.
> HOLLIS FRAMPTON, "The Invention without a Future," 1979

In the past seventy-five years we have seen the end of Hollywood's classic studio system, the rise and decline of network television, the development of tent-pole exhibitions and huge marketing campaigns, the emergence of digital cinema, and a variety of ups and downs in the world of independent and international art films. As the millennium arrived, the U.S. film industry found new ways of controlling production and exhibition, digital technology altered the look and even the physical basis of cinema, most people watched movies at home, and the Internet was on the verge of supplanting all delivery systems for words, sound, and images. Film study in the academy had grown significantly, but universities were replacing aesthetics with sociology or anthropology and had become preoccupied with "new media." The deaths of Michelangelo Antonioni and Ingmar Bergman in 2007 seemed to put a full stop to what had been a period of intense cinephilia, and there was widespread discussion of "postcinema" or the death of cinema, as if feature-length movies were going the way of God and the novel (whose obituaries were premature).

The titles of several recent essay collections—David Denby's *Do the Movies Have a Future?*, J. Hoberman's *Film after Film: Or, What Became of 21st Century Cinema?*, Dave Kehr's *When Movies Mattered*, and Jonathan

Rosenbaum's *Goodbye Cinema, Hello Cinephilia*—are symptomatic of the times. Also symptomatic was the 2013 symposium sponsored by the Slough Foundation entitled "The End of Cinema and the Future of Cinema Studies." Jonathan Rosenbaum, one of the featured speakers, offered a sort of counter-lecture entitled "The Future of Cinema and the End of Cinema Studies." I'm in sympathy with him: cinema isn't ending, but academic specialists sometimes appear to be trying to kill off both it and themselves.

In recognition of such events, this book, which is preoccupied at various points with themes of death, takes its title from a remark supposedly made by Louis Lumière in reference to the motion pictures he and his brother exhibited in Paris at the end of the nineteenth century. Many cinephiles, among them Jean-Luc Godard, have attributed the statement to Lumière, but there's no evidence he actually said it. The attribution nevertheless persists, linking cinema from its beginnings with death (for commentary on the phenomenon, see Cahill, 19). And yet the statement has a proleptic and ambiguous quality: it suggests that a work in progress was already accomplished, and its definition of cinema is unclear. Does it refer to the cinematograph, which indeed had a relatively short life-span, or to moving images in general? If the latter, history has proved its author laughably wrong. By 1926, thirty-one years after the first Lumière films, motion-picture technology and its various uses had developed to such an extent that a movie-mad, sixteen-year-old James Agee, quoted in the second epigraph above, could rhapsodize in his prep-school magazine about the glorious future of a new art form. A year afterward, silent films began to give way to talkies. Agee's prediction came true, but the cinema he described was nearing its death; it survives only as a "legacy" form and an important part of artistic history, worthy of preservation and occasional imitation.

The third epigraph, from a 1979 Whitney Museum lecture by Hollis Frampton first published in a 2004 issue of *October*, has the benefit of a broader historical perspective. The topic is early cinema, but Frampton spends much of his time speculating on the future of the medium, which was confronting the rise of videotape and computers. Frampton argues that the invention of cinema needs to be seen in the context of an ongoing process of industrial revolution, and that cinema's traditions and monuments are constantly evolving and being reshaped, not only by individual talent but also by changes in technology. The cinema persists, he suggests, but not always in its original form.

At the time of Frampton's lecture, the silver nitrate used for early photographic prints was in short supply, and "what was once seen as a copious popular art" had become "paradoxically fragile, rare and bounded in time" (72). Scarcity enabled certain movies to return to what Walter Benjamin had termed the ritual basis of older arts, especially in museum retrospectives of rare films, which, Frampton observes, acquired their aura because "film and its allied arts of illusion are at once limitlessly plentiful and painfully fugitive" (72). A certain kind of movie was in fact dead or dying, but in his lecture Frampton confesses that he's puzzled by the so-called Lumière statement, for which he offers two possible explanations, neither having to do with the end of cinema. The first he dubs the "Person from Porlock" explanation, which takes its name from Samuel Taylor Coleridge's story about the composition of the fragmentary "Kubla Kahn." Coleridge had been inspired by a drug-induced dream, but when he began writing the poem a man from the nearby town of Porlock knocked at his door and caused him to forget how the dream ended. The cinema, Frampton proposes, might be regarded as an incomplete dream vision (perhaps not unlike Charles Foster Kane's Xanadu, named for Kubla Kahn's pleasure palace) that has yet to realize its full potential. His second possible explanation, which doesn't contradict the first, is quoted in the epigraph above: the cinema didn't have a future in Lumière's day because it didn't yet have a past. Whatever the cinema is, and whenever it began, it can be "invented" only by its ongoing history—or *historie(s)*, as Godard might say.

One of Frampton's most admired films, the thirty-eight-minute *Nostalgia* (1971), can be related to some aspects of this argument. The film is structured by Frampton's recollections of a group of still photographs he made before turning to cinema, plus one found photograph. We hear what seems to be his voice (actually the voice of Michael Snow reading Frampton's words) commenting on the history of the photographs, which an offscreen hand holds up one by one and then drops onto the hot element of an electric stove. As each photograph incinerates, it leaves behind a unique pattern of carbon residue, a fragile ash that looks as if it would dissolve at the touch of a breath. Meanwhile, the offscreen voice grows increasingly out of synch with the images and we begin hearing descriptions of pictures that haven't yet appeared.

Nostalgia can be viewed as an experiment involving personal memory, real duration, and cinematic time, but it's also a film about perishability and remediation. Unattractive as this last word might be, it's the best way I know to describe such things as a live symphony hall concert broadcast on the radio, a novel transformed into an audio book, a classic-era movie shown on television, and so forth. (For a broad discussion of remediation in today's world, see Grusin and Bolter.) Frampton's still photographs are fragile mementos preserved in a motion picture, but if he kept the negatives the photographs could be reproduced; if he didn't, we could attempt to restore them by making still photographs from individual frames of the film—a process at one remove from the source and inferior in resolution. Hence the film shows the destruction of photographs, but it also partly saves them. A further irony is that with the passage of time *Nostalgia*, too, has been "saved" by remediation. Good 16mm celluloid prints of the film are somewhat rare, and the most convenient ways to view it today are on the Internet or on a DVD produced by the National Film Registry of the Library of Congress, *Treasures IV: American Avant-Garde Film, 1947–1986*. (A similar irony can be found in the 2013 Blu-ray release of Bill Morrison's "Decasia" [2002], an avant-garde film composed of decayed footage from old movies.)

Frampton is correct that the history of cinema, understood as the history of moving images, transcends a particular technology (an argument similar to the one made by D. N. Rodowick in *The Virtual Life of Film*). There's no way of saying when this history began: some trace it as far back as the twenty-six-thousand-year-old "animated" cave paintings in Altimira, Spain, and others say cinema's oldest ancestor is the camera obscura, which was known to the ancient Chinese and Greeks as a means of studying light and was used in fifteenth-century Europe as an instrument for tracing images in perspective. It nevertheless seems safe to argue that the modern cinema's so-called pre- and posthistory extends at least from the industrial revolution of the eighteenth century to the digital revolution of the present.

The motion pictures of the Lumières and their contemporaries were the most spectacular invention of what is sometimes called the second industrial revolution at the end of the nineteenth century. This was the beginning of "modern times," characterized by the advent of the electric light, the typewriter, the linotype, the transoceanic cable, the telephone, the phonograph, and so forth. The same period was the beginning of large-scale advertising and leisure activities that would ultimately constitute the modern consumer society and a new kind of mass culture. Whoever the masses were, the products and modes of production associated with them seemed American rather than European in origin, and the emergence of a critical discourse about them had something to do with the intertwined forces of industrialization and capitalism. These forces are still with us; in a sense, they have a need for cinema, which repeatedly adapts to new technical forms.

All this will seem cold comfort to those who love projected film on big screens. As I write, theatrical exhibition throughout the world is undergoing profound change, the ultimate consequences of which are unclear. The major Hollywood distributors have banded together and signed the Digital Cinema Initiatives, which, by the time this book appears, will make film prints unavailable for commercial theaters; projection will instead take the form of the Digital Cinema Package (DCP). Meanwhile, video notepads and computers are streaming motion pictures on demand, and people are watching movies on cell phones or the backs of airline seats.

The digital era, like modernity in general, is both catastrophe and progress. As a university teacher of film history who spent many years threading 16mm prints into projectors and who once thought that showing film on video in the classroom was a sin, I've become acutely aware that projected DVD and Blu-ray not only make instruction easier but in most cases give superior resolution and life to old movies. I also have the good fortune to live in Bloomington, Indiana, where the state-of-the-art Indiana University Cinema and its remarkable director-programmer, Jon Vickers, enable me to compare a wide range of motion picture technologies projected according to the highest standards (most commercial movie theaters project badly, no matter whether you are watching 35mm or digital). In that facility I've seen fifty-year-old home movies in 8mm, silent masterpieces with a live orchestra, rare 16mm prints, archival 35mm prints, widescreen spectaculars, low-tech digital features by visiting directors Pedro Costa and Joe Swanberg, and 2k and 4k digital "restorations." My experience convinces me that cinema today has a variety of technical formats offering rich artistic possibilities, none of which is inherently superior to the others. It also demonstrates that remediation isn't evil. On a visit to Bloomington in 2012, Werner Herzog, who had several of his features converted to DCPs by Indiana University Cinema, announced with evident pleasure that the new process had made *Aguirre, Wrath of God* (1972) look to him as if it had been made anew. It was no longer quite like a film of the 1970s; it lacked the grain and haptic markings of a celluloid print, but in some ways it was more vivid and exciting than the original.

Unfortunately, few of us have access to the kind of theater I've just described, and we're entering a brave new world in which *all* movies, even when shot on film, will be viewed in the form of digital files. This change is more radical than any other in motion-picture history—quite different from the shift from silent pictures to sound, because in that case the photographic basis of the medium remained the same. Somebody once asked Mel Brooks what the most difficult aspect of making a film was, and Brooks said it was putting in all the little sprocket holes. The digital eliminates that problem; it's a more convenient technology, and convenience trumps quality in the mass marketplace. The question then becomes whether celluloid (or Mylar) will survive at all; and if so, whether film projectors will have even as much future as vinyl record players and typewriters. I have no confident answer, but I recommend David Bordwell's *Pandora's Digital Box* (2012), available for digital download at www.davidbordwell.net, which offers a discussion of the changes we're experiencing. As Bordwell points out, the DCP initiative consolidates the power of major distributors and threatens the survival of small theaters. It results in fired projectionists and junked projection equipment, and it will inevitably affect scholarship and formal analysis, making it nearly impossible, for example, to count frames on a film strip or choose an individual frame for reproduction.

For me, the biggest problem isn't the loss of the film strip but the degree to which predigital cinema can be saved by remediation—which, since the 1950s, has been the chief way of making older films widely available. I can recall the period of Cinemascope and 3-D, when theaters were trying to compete with television; as a kid in those days, I saw many good films in the new formats, but I was even more fascinated by old movies from the 1930s and '40s that were becoming available at home on the late show. A good deal of my cinema education came from product that was dumped onto TV and interspersed with commercials. Today we have Turner Classic Movies on cable TV and DVD or Blu-ray offerings that greatly enlarge the common viewer's knowledge of film history. But it remains unclear whether the business model for such things will survive in a world of streaming. As Dave Kehr noted in his *New York Times* video review column of December 2, 2012, "The major studios . . . have cut their full-scale releases of library titles to a minimum," and "Any time a pre-2000 title makes it out of the vault is a cause for rejoicing."

It is difficult to be positive about the changing mediascape without also being concerned about it. A wider range of movies is shown theatrically in the United States than ever before, but most independent and foreign films are seen in only a few big-city venues. Low-end digital technology has been used to superb effect by Pedro Costa, David Lynch, and Jean-Luc Godard, but the new cameras and digital editing equipment have also spawned hoards of lazily shot, slapped-together movies. Cinephilia is as alive as ever, but it no longer produces the kind of impassioned intellectual debate that went on in big-circulation newspapers and little magazines during the 1960s and '70s. Old films originally thought to have a short commercial lifespan are still reasonably valuable commodities; intelligent critical commentary on movies can be found in several places on the Internet; "orphan" movies and nontheatrical 16mm pictures are being digitally preserved; and, thanks to remediation, today's students of cinema have much greater access to cinema. Nevertheless, more films have been lost than preserved, more films continue to be lost, and the potential death of the flexible film strip is leading to what Manohla Dargis has called "deep ontological and phenomenological shifts that are transforming a medium" (*New York Times*, September 9, 2012).

To my mind, just how transformative these shifts will turn out to be remains to be seen. Several critics and theorists, among them J. Hoberman, have argued that the death of traditional photography marks the end of André Bazin's ideas about cinematic realism. The digital, this argument maintains, so greatly increases the tendency toward animation and so vividly creates virtual reality that it destroys our faith in the possibility of an indexical relationship between image and world and our faith in the difference between truth and fiction. But digital special effects aren't always as invisible as they try to be, and truth and fiction have long been intertwined. From the time of Georges Méliès the cinema has been associated with optical illusions. *Citizen Kane* (one of Bazin's touchstones of realism) is so filled with optical printing, lens distortions, black-art settings, painted backgrounds, and other visual tricks that it looks as if it aspired to the condition of an animated cartoon. A more neorealist film such as Powell and Pressburger's *A Canterbury Tale* (1944), now available as a Criterion DVD, gains charm and emotional power from nonprofessionals in minor roles and subtly romantic location photography by Erwin Hiller of the bombed-out town center of Canterbury, which the Nazis had nearly destroyed in 1942; it's fascinating as documentary record, but it also contains visual tricks that most viewers probably haven't noticed, including art director Alfred Junge's remarkably convincing re-creation of the interiors of Canterbury Cathedral.

Photography is neither inherently deceitful nor inherently indexical, and the same can be said of digital video. One of the infinitely precious attributes of photography is its ability to preserve traces of history or moments of long-ago time: the early motion pictures of Queen Victoria in a parade and of ordinary workers exiting the Lumière factory transcend art and are arguably more significant than art. But there's no reason why some of the amateur videos on YouTube won't someday have a roughly similar effect. Motion pictures that tell stories have always depended upon a dialectical tension between visual realism and visual magic. Digital technology has vastly increased animation in big-budget Hollywood movies, but it has also made it easier for contemporary directors to create documentaries and neo-neorealist cinema.

The loss of the film strip nevertheless raises a problem for preservationists, because DVDs and Blu-ray Discs are said to be more unstable than film. If we want to save the past, the preferred way of storing it is on celluloid. (Ironically, there is now also a need to preserve VHS, because many movies in library archives can't be seen in other forms.) For this and other reasons, I doubt that the old media will go away completely; indeed, many young filmmakers today are experimenting with 8mm and 16mm. We should keep in mind Raymond Williams's argument that any given historical moment is compounded of dominant, residual, and emergent forms of culture—an argument that applies not only to technology but also to ideas. Around 1960, for example, the idea of the postmodern (with which the following book is sometimes concerned) was emergent in Western industrial society; it soon became a dominant idea in the world of art and architecture, but now it is becoming a residual or period term like any other. Modernism (equally important to this book), which is associated with formally innovative, relatively difficult art in conflicted dialogue with industrial modernity, has a much longer residual life-span. With some qualification, we can speak of post–World-War II neorealism and the 1960s European art cinema of directors like Bergman, Antonioni, and Resnais as a recrudescence of the modernist impulse often associated with earlier directors like Eisenstein and Welles. As I try to suggest toward the end of this volume, a modernist spirit also animates what is nowadays called "world cinema," a phenomenon connecting Asian, Latin American, African, and Iranian films by such directors as Jia Zhangke, Apichatpong Weerasethakul, Abderrahmane Sissako, Abbas Kiarostami, and the late Raúl Ruiz. No matter what technology these artists use—usually it's digital—they've established continuities with the past and made this a remarkable time for cinema.

In contrast, most of the films I discuss in this book belong to a dead cinema—dead not only because it was produced by an old technology but also because the institutional, economic, and cultural conditions that determined it are things of the past. But as long as we can still see older films in a good form of remediation, the past isn't dead. Classic Hollywood films may not have the same significance or meanings for us as when they were originally shown (no matter how glamorized and studio-bound they are, they give us intriguing documentary evidence of a different America). Nevertheless, they're important achievements in the history of a still-living art and are worthy of ongoing criticism and theory.

Somewhat like film, my career as a writer about cinema is entering a late, perhaps last, phase, and the essays assembled here are chosen to reflect my chief interests over the span of that career. Most of them were published originally in academic journals or anthologies, but I have also written several new pieces especially for this volume. All the previously published essays have been rewritten, some in minor ways and others substantially, to correct errors, take note of subsequent research, and reflect changes in my thinking. I've avoided reprinting material from the books I've authored, although the piece on *Cabin in the Sky*, to which I've added a few things, closely resembles what became a chapter in *The Films of Vincente Minnelli* (1993), and occasional paragraphs or pages elsewhere are derived from arguments in my books on other film topics.

The collection has three parts. The first consists of essays on general or theoretical issues and the second of case studies. An overriding concern with value judgment should be apparent throughout, and certain topics recur: authorship; adaptation; acting; modernism and postmodernism; observations on the relation between style and politics; and commentary on such figures as Hitchcock, Hawks, Minnelli, Welles, Huston, Kubrick, and other figures associated with classic Hollywood. The third and final section, consisting of mostly new material, is a defense of criticism and film reviewing in an era when print journalism is facing a death similar to film, and when the academy seems to be losing interest in questions of aesthetics, taste, or evaluation. It contains essays on four American journalistic critics who quickened my early interest in film and expanded my knowledge of film history. Appended to these is a sample of my work as a critic/reviewer between 2009 and 2011, when I wrote an annual "Films of the Year" roundup in *Film Quarterly*. During those years I was particularly interested in the aforementioned "world cinema" and in what some people have called "slow cinema," which I would argue accounts for some of the most significant motion pictures in the past decade.

It remains for me to say a bit about my intellectual history and how it determines my approach to cinema. I've always been passionately interested in movies but never studied them in school. I majored in English and French at Louisiana State University, which was still under the influence of the New Criticism, and in English at the University of Wisconsin, where the department was organized by a "Beowulf to Virginia Woolf" version of literary history. Much of my writing about film tends to be inflected by literary training and an early interest in literary modernism. Equally important, my university years coincided with the civil rights and anti–Vietnam War movements. I became thoroughly politicized and was faced with the problem of how to reconcile my aestheticism with my politics. As a result, there's a sometimes subdued, sometimes explicit political quality to most of my writing, expressed in two ways: an overarching concern with the relationship between politics and culture, and a belief that formal analysis isn't enough; to slightly revise a remark by Lionel Trilling, I'm always asking what the text and perhaps the maker of the text *wants*, whether or not it is aware of it.

While in graduate school I was drawn to Madison's vibrant, mostly off-campus or ad hoc film culture, and from the moment I began a professional career I felt an urge to write about movies rather than literature. Discussion of cinema was spreading among public intellectuals and academics, and the cinema itself seemed to be undergoing a kind of revolution. I had already read Andrew Sarris's *The American Cinema* and everything I could find by Raymond Durgnat and Robin Wood. And, like every academic cinephile, I was affected by waves of ideas about film from a variety of theoretical or politically activist sources, including feminism, structuralism, semiotics, and everything associated with European High Theory (which, despite its radicalism, drew mostly from a French tradition critical and philosophical aesthetics). But I didn't jump from one paradigm to another. The ideas that shape my work tend to coexist, sometimes conflicting, sometimes interacting, overlaying one another like a palimpsest. The latest of these ideas grew out of academic cultural studies, which freed me from the sometimes puritanical doctrines of High Theory and fed my interest in the relations between "high," "popular," and "mass" art (terms I regard as discursive constructions rather than hard-and-fast categories). Even so, I've resisted what I see as a tendency in cultural studies toward populism, presentism, and relativism. Most of my work has been about classic Hollywood, and I've been more interested in films and critics than in audiences. I also have an ambivalent attitude toward the movie industry, a feeling of both fascination and anxiety.

Visual images have long been capable of provoking fascination and anxiety because of their power to shape beliefs and mass opinion: the Old Testament God forbade graven images, Protestant iconoclasts denounced the elaborate paintings and statuary in Catholic churches, and Marx and Engels compared bourgeois ideology to an upside-down picture at the back of a camera obscura. In the twentieth century, the "magic" of movies created both a sense of wonder and concomitant fears that dark forces are influencing the ignorant, complacent masses. Literacy rates actually rose during the first great age of cinema, at the moment when reformers and censors were condemning the medium's evils; but another concern emerged because moving imagery was increasingly controlled by big business and government. Among intellectuals, this issue became especially evident during the U.S. economic boom of the 1950s, when I was still a child and when television began to displace the already powerful forces of classic Hollywood. Much of what was produced in those years by movies, radio, television, and Henry Luce's slick magazines filled with photography was created by a factory system whose product was designed to appeal to as many social classes or class fractions as possible. Capital intensive and organized by complex divisions of labor, it was rationalized as entertainment and/or instruction rather than as art; by its nature, it tended to devalue originality and individuality, and it was usually supervised by committees and boards of executives.

The high modernists and the avant-garde constituted an aesthetic modernity in conflict with these developments. Of course, high modernism and the avant-garde sometimes blended with what Miriam Hansen has called "vernacular modernism": see Busby Berkeley's "Lullaby of Broadway" number in *Gold Diggers of 1935*, which is a breathtaking fusion of modern art, show-biz glamour, and pure cinema. There was nevertheless an inevitable tension between the movie industry and individual modern artists, nicely expressed by Orson Welles: "I love the movies, but don't get me wrong. I hate Hollywood."

I believe that the United States has by far the richest film history in the world, but from the end of World War II until the 1970s the most significant artistic movements in cinema—Italian neorealism, the French New Wave, the German New Cinema, the Brazilian cinema of poverty, the Los Angeles school of black filmmakers, and the various "third world" cinemas—were developed more or less in reaction against dominant forms of U.S. mass culture. Despite the familiar argument that postmodernism has ended the tension between high and low or resistant pop, this tension remains. Andy Warhol may have become a fashion celebrity, but his films were never commercial rivals of Hollywood, and his art shared with the old avant-garde a use of mechanical reproduction to shock and unsettle the values of established museums. Late-twentieth-century novelists such as Thomas Pynchon, David Foster Wallace, and Roberto Bolaño will never be adapted into movies, at least not in ways that closely resemble their fiction.

For these reasons, there's a paradox in my writing, which originates in a longstanding and deep love of both classic Hollywood and high modernism. Exciting movies continue to appear today, sometimes even as blockbusters, but in my view and that of many others, the most consistently good mainstream cinematic entertainment produced in the United States is found in long-form or series cable TV. The contemporary marketplace is fragmented, under the control of corporations yet more niche oriented, less "massified" than it once was. Hollywood's money-making hits have bloated budgets, saturation booking, and inescapable ad campaigns aimed at a young, mostly male demographic; and Hollywood's Academy Award contenders, aimed at an older audience and scheduled for December release, are seldom of great consequence. Nevertheless, in the year and a half in which I was completing this book, I saw a number of fine English-language pictures, among them Wes Anderson's *Moonrise Kingdom,* Shane Carruth's *Upstream Color,* Terence Davies's *The Deep Blue Sea,* Richard Linklater's *Bernie* and *Before Midnight,* Sarah Polley's *Stories We Tell,* and Robert Zemeckis's *Flight.* The pictures I saw from other parts of the world were even better: Leos Carax's *Holy Motors,* Jean-Pierre and Luc Dardenne's *The Kid with a Bike,* Kléber Mendonça Filho's *Neighboring Sounds,* Miguel Gomes's *Tabu,* Jafar Panahi's *This Is Not a Film,* Nuri Bilge Ceylan's *Once Upon a Time in Anatolia,* and Béla Tarr's *The Turin Horse.* I would conclude from this exactly what could have been said at several points in the history of the art form: A certain kind of cinema is dead. Long live cinema.

PART I

Issues

Authorship, Auteurism, and Cultural Politics

> The periods of human history prepare their prospective representatives; they seek them out, shape them, bring them to light, and through them make themselves known.
> ERICH AUERBACH, *Scenes from the Drama of European Literature*

Motion pictures and television are often described as collaborative media, but their modes of production are nearly always hierarchical, involving a mixture of industrialized, theatrical, and artisanal practices that give some people authority over others. Depending upon the circumstances under which particular films are made, anyone who functions in a creative job might, at least potentially, be viewed as an author. We obviously don't need to know who the author or authors were in order to enjoy a movie, but the term could be applied with more or less justification and qualification to certain writers (Anita Loos, Raymond Chandler), photographers (John Alton, Gordon Willis), composers (Max Steiner, Bernard Herrmann), choreographers (Busby Berkeley, Michael Kidd), stars (the Marx Brothers, Bette Davis), and producers (David Selznick, Darryl Zanuck). For the most part, however, film authorship is associated with directors. Names such as D.W. Griffith and F.W. Murnau have been fundamental to the establishment of movies as "respectable" art, and some histories of film are organized around them, just as literary history is organized around the names of poets or novelists. As a result, "Sergei Eisenstein," "Robert Flaherty," and "Alfred Hitchcock" have come to signify not only persons but also traditions, theories, and genres.

Despite the term "auteur theory," the practice of writing about movie directors has never been a true theory; it simply assumes the importance of directors and takes the form of practical criticism that can be done well or badly. But the discourse on the director-as-author has always been problematic, in part because of the industrial basis of the medium, but also because film directors began to be called "auteurs" in the 1950s and '60s, at the moment when the rise of theory in the academy was about to make authorship in general an embattled concept. During those years, the French *politique des auteurs*, or "policy" of canonizing favored directors, served as background for debates surrounding authorship in cinema. To make sense of the debates, we first need to make a distinction between writing about movie directors as authors—a practice as old as the feature film—and the more historically situated phenomenon called "auteurism."

AUTEURISM

As its suffix implies, auteurism was a kind of aesthetic ideology or movement. Like other movements in art history, it was generated by what Raymond Williams terms a "cultural formation"—a loose confederation of critics and artists (in this case made up almost entirely of white males) who had roughly similar objectives and who developed a body of polemical writing to justify their opinions. Such formations are especially important to modernity. As Williams notes, they're typically centered in a metropolis, at points of "transition and intersection" within a complex social history; and the individuals who both compose and are composed by them always have a "range of diverse positions, interests and influences, some of which are resolved ... , others of which remain as internal differences" (*Culture*, 85–86). Formations also tend to be ephemeral, spinning off into individual careers or breakaway movements but disseminating their ideas widely, leaving more or less permanent traces on the general culture.

Auteurism fits the profile of a modern cultural formation almost perfectly. It originated in Paris during the 1950s, at a moment when enthusiasm for American cinema was being voiced by several groups, including the left critics at *Positif* and the right critics at the "MacMahonist" *Présence du cinéma*. The most influential collective in those years, and the one most identified with auteurism, was at *Cahiers du cinéma*, but this group was more heterogeneous than it seemed; several members were Catholic, and their politics ranged from conservative to socialist. To some extent they resembled the historical avant-garde of the 1910s and '20s: they possessed a "left bank" aura; they made iconoclastic and at least mildly shocking value judgments; their ideas were articulated in a specialized magazine; they embraced certain elements of pop culture and used them to attack bourgeois values; they published manifestos, such as François Truffaut's "A Certain Tendency of the French Cinema"; and their group label served as a kind of banner to help publicize their early work.

The last point is important because many of the auteurists, including Truffaut, Jean-Luc Godard, Claude Chabrol, Eric Rohmer, and Jacques Rivette, were fledgling directors. Their call for "personal" cinema had been inspired to some extent by Alexandre Astruc's 1948 essay "The Birth of a New Avant-Garde: *La Camera-Stylo*," published in the socialist journal

L'Écran français, which spoke metaphorically of the camera as a pen, the screen as a piece of paper, and the director as an author. Astruc, who was both a novelist and a director, emphasized the inscribable or *lisable* properties of mise-en-scène, locating them in the gestures of actors, the performance of dialogue, the movement or framings of the camera, and the interaction or relationship between objects and persons. The auteurists strongly supported such ideas and gave them apparent practical application by moving from critical writing into filmmaking. Meanwhile, their reviews and essays were filled with flamboyant descriptions of directors as existentialist authors. Godard remarked apropos of Ingmar Bergman, "The cinema is not a craft. It is an art. It does not mean teamwork. One is always alone on the set as before the blank page" (*Godard on Godard*, 76). Truffaut, speaking of Robert Aldrich's *Kiss Me Deadly*, declared, "It is easy to picture its author as a man overflowing with vitality, as much at ease behind a camera as Henry Miller facing a blank page" (*The Films of My Life*, 94).

As Godard amusingly observed, "Nothing could be more classically romantic" (76). But neither Godard nor auteurism can be so easily pigeonholed. To appreciate why, we need only look at a couple of paragraphs from Godard's *Cahiers* review of the 1958 Douglas Sirk film *A Time to Love and a Time to Die*, starring John Gavin and Liselotte Pulver:

> I am going to write a madly enthusiastic review of Douglas Sirk's latest film, simply because it sets my cheeks afire. . . . In the first place I shall refer . . . to Griffith's *True-Heart Susie*, because I think one should mention Griffith in all articles about the cinema: everyone agrees, but everyone forgets none the less. Griffith, therefore, and André Bazin, too, for the same reasons; and now that is done, I can get back to . . . *A Time to Love and a Time to Die*. . . . But here I pause for a moment to say that, next to *Le Plaisir*, this is the greatest title in all cinema, sound or silent, and also to say that I heartily congratulate Universal-International on having changed the title of Erich Maria Remarque's novel, which was called *A Time to Live and a Time to Die*. . . . By replacing the word "live" by "love," they implicitly posed the director the question—an admirable starting-point for the script—"Should one live to love, or love to live?" And now, having finished my detour and comparisons: a time to love and a time to die—no, I shall never tire of writing these new, still imperturbably new, words, *A Time to Love and a Time to Die:* you know very well that I am going to talk about this film as I do about friend Fritz or Nicholas Ray, about *You Only Live Once* or *They Live by Night*, as though, in other words, John Gavin and Liselotte Pulver were Aucassin and Nicolette in 1959.
>
> This, anyhow, is what enchants me about Sirk: this delirious mixture of medieval and modern, sentimentality and subtlety, tame compositions

and frenzied Cinemascope. Obviously one must talk about all this as Aragon talks about Elsa's eyes, raving a little, a lot, passionately, no matter, the only logic which concerns Sirk is delirium. (135–36)

This is a far cry from academic criticism and belies some of the assertions often made about auteurism. It's customary (and not incorrect) to say that the young *Cahiers* critics were romantics—as when Thomas Schatz, in his valuable book *The Genius of the System*, tells us that auteurism "would not be worth bothering with if it hadn't been so influential, effectively stalling film history in a prolonged stage of adolescent romanticism" (5). Many contemporary writers would agree; but if we're going to call Godard a romantic, we should recognize that he's a strange variant of the type. His review reads more like a wild, calculated mime of the "delirium" he finds in Sirk's film; it's a parody or pastiche of romantic gestures, a "madly enthusiastic" account of "Aucassin and Nicolette in 1959."

One quality of parody is that we can't always tell when it's a full-out mockery. When Joyce opens the "Nausicaa" episode of *Ulysses* by writing, "The summer evening had begun to fold the world in its mysterious embrace," is he joking about the conventions of popular romance or acknowledging the seductive power of a certain kind of language? Is he engaging in a ventriloquist's act or taking pleasure in "bad writing," allowing his novel to become the thing it mimics? Godard's review has exactly this sort of ambiguity, and if I were to quote it at length in the original French we would discover that it contains Joycean puns. (At one point, he derides *"tous ces René qui n'ont pas les idées claires."*) He therefore resembles the modernists as much as the romantics. But he also has something in common with the historical avant-garde, which tended to welcome machine-made culture and its utopian possibilities. Like many of the auteurists, he's in love with Cinemascope; at a later point in his review he disputes what he calls the "fashionable" idea that "the wide screen is all window dressing" and remarks that Sirk's camera movements "give the impression of having been done by hand instead of with a crane, rather as if the mercurial brushwork of a Fragonard were the work of a complex machine." Throughout, he employs a familiar avant-garde strategy: he appropriates a high-culture style and turns it on its head; he half-comically apes the conventions of "serious" criticism ("I think one should mention Griffith in all articles about the cinema . . . and André Bazin, too") in order to challenge complacent assumptions about authorship and art.

The particular avant-garde with which Godard's review has affinities is surrealism. Although *Positif* had direct connections with the surrealists and sometimes attacked the critics at *Cahiers*, the two groups were in many ways similar. Both were fond of American films, particularly of B movies and film noir, and both sometimes used a lyrical, almost swooning language—as when

Godard tells us that *A Time to Love and a Time to Die* sets his cheeks afire. It's no accident that at one point in his review Godard alludes to the surrealist Louis Aragon, and it's almost predictable that he should proclaim *A Time to Love and a Time to Die* (next to *Le Plaisir*) as the "greatest title in all of cinema." At this point in his career he seems a dreamer of mass culture, looking for what André Breton had called "moments of priceless giddiness" (quoted in Hammond, 20). His review seems also to have a quasi-surrealistic conception of authorship, as when he tells us that the power of *A Time to Love and a Time to Die* rises out of Universal-International's mercenary decision to change the title of Erich Maria Remarque's novel. By this means, Godard suggests, the studio unleashed a ghost in the machine, giving the director an opportunity to set beauty and delirium in motion.

I don't want to overstate the connection with the surrealists; my point is simply that Godard's writing is made up of a mixture of familiar attitudes and can't be identified completely with any of them. It blends the voice of high culture with movie reviewing and blurs the boundaries between romantic aestheticism, modernism, and the historical avant-garde. It reminds us of things we've heard before but also sounds different and new. In some respects, Godard in 1959 resembles what we would nowadays call a postmodern critic.

"Postmodern" needs to be used guardedly because it suggests a quite un-Godard-like disavowal of a philosophical "center." Even so, it helps to indicate an important fact about the auteurists' place in film history. The classic cinema's technology and modes of production had grown out of the period when oil replaced steam and coal as a primary fuel, when "Fordism" became the chief means of industrial organization and when mechanical inventions proliferated at a dizzy rate. (One of the Lumières' first movies showed a train arriving at a station, as if the most important machine of the new era were paying tribute to its predecessors.) Auteurism, by contrast, emerged in the declining years of the studio system, at the dawn of the television age. Although the auteurists and their earliest followers in Britain and America nourished their cult enthusiasms at revival theaters and museums, they belonged to a generation that would begin to use TV like a cinematheque, viewing films in no historical order and regarding the classic cinema as something distant or dying. Over the next decade, widespread academic study of film was prompted partly by auteurism and partly by the easy accessibility of old movies on TV—a phenomenon that enabled everyone to participate in an investigation of Hollywood's past. As a result, whereas the movies were an invention of modernity, all film culture and all writing on film since the late 1950s has had something of a postmodern character. One irony of this situation is that while cinephiles today often call themselves students of film, most of them are students of teletheory, living in a world of recycled images.

Godard's review also has qualities in common with the account of postmodernism by Andreas Huyssen in his influential book *After the Great Divide*, which argues that sometime around 1960 a new aesthetic began to appear in Western society, signaled by the Pop movement in American art, the literary criticism of Susan Sontag and Leslie Fiedler, and the later architectural writings of Robert Venturi. What all these events have in common is a "break with the austere canon of high modern[ism]" and an "espousal of the commercial vernacular of consumer culture" (187). They involve a sometimes baffling mixture of elitism and populism, and they adopt a critical strategy that was eventually adopted by the academy. As Huyssen puts it, "Pop in the broadest sense was the context in which a notion of the postmodern first took shape, and from the beginning until today, the most significant trends within postmodernism have challenged modernism's relentless hostility to mass culture" (188).

Huyssen doesn't mention Godard or Truffaut, but the New Wave belongs on his list of postmodern developments. Godard's early work is roughly contemporary with Pop and clearly draws inspiration from the American commercial scene. To be sure, there was nothing special about a French intellectual who praised American movies. There was also a quality of old-fashioned enthusiasm in Godard and the auteurists, who were never as coolly detached as Andy Warhol and never so condescending to movies as Leslie Fiedler. Nevertheless, Godard used the language of high art to praise certain "pulpy" Hollywood auteurs, and as a filmmaker he borrowed imagery from such films as *Some Came Running* (1958), which Vincente Minnelli had designed to resemble what he described as "the inside of a juke box" (*I Remember It Well*, 325). Several passages of Godard's criticism could almost be used to define the Pop (or camp) sensibility—for instance, his description of a couple of his favorite scenes from Samuel Fuller's *Forty Guns* (1957):

> Barbara Stanwyck's brother grabs her to use her as a shield. "Go on, shoot, you dirty coward," he shouts to Barry Sullivan, who is covering them with his gun. And without hesitation Barry Sullivan calmly shoots Barbara Stanwyck, who crumples up, and then the brother, who falls mortally wounded in his turn. "Stop shooting, you dirty coward," cries the dying man—Bang! Bang! —"For pity's sake, stop shooting"—Bang! Bang!—"Stop shooting, can't you see I'm dying"—Bang! Bang! Bang!
>
> In another scene, Gene Barry is courting ravishing young Eve Brent, making her charming debut before the cameras in an eye-shade borrowed from Samuel. Eve sells guns. Jokingly, Gene aims at her. The camera takes his place and we see Eve through the barrel of the gun. Track forward until she is framed in close-up by the mouth of the barrel. Next shot: they are in a kiss. (62)

Godard is implicitly attacking not only the bourgeois tradition of quality but also certain features of modernism and the avant-garde. As Huyssen points out, "Modernism's running feud with mass society [and] the avant-garde's attack on high art as a support system of cultural hegemony always took place on the pedestal of high art itself." Godard and many of the other auteurists were different. They were opening the possibility for artists to engage in what Huyssen calls an "experimental mixing and meshing" of the old cultural domains (189). There was, moreover, an irony in the French fascination with American cinema: the auteurists' rise to success as filmmakers was facilitated by the decline of the Hollywood studios, which had dominated the marketplace in the years between the two world wars. In the United States, the major production companies were no longer in control of exhibition, censorship regulations were becoming liberalized, and European art films were making significant inroads in urban art theaters. The French New Wave was particularly well suited to the period because it managed to fuse certain elements of Italian neorealism with a fond, insouciant, distinctively Gallic attitude toward old-fashioned Hollywood genres and directors. In certain American contexts, its name became useful as a marketing strategy.

This doesn't mean that either the New Wave or auteurism can be reduced to a device for self-promotion. The latter began as a critical undertaking and marked an important change in the history of taste. One of the best sources for an understanding of what the French movement achieved is Jim Hillier's *"Cahiers du Cinéma": The 1950s*, which illustrates the diversity of opinion among the writers of the period and places French debates over American cinema in the context of larger concerns about neorealism, modernism, and the French film industry. As Hillier indicates, auteurism was never simply about American-based directors such as Samuel Fuller, Alfred Hitchcock, and Nicholas Ray. The Parisian cinephiles were interested in American auteurs, but French writing about Hollywood was tempered by an even stronger admiration for Roberto Rossellini, Michelangelo Antonioni, and Alain Resnais. Nor were the auteurists exclusively concerned with authorship. Particularly at *Cahiers*, their practice usually implied a contradictory set of theories about the phenomenology and techniques of cinema, and it produced excellent essays on stars and genres. Above all, it generated a relentlessly evaluative kind of criticism, involving a policy of liking some directors and films more than others. Thus if you wrote for *Cahiers*, you tended to favor Jean Renoir, Howard Hawks, and Kenji Mizoguchi over Sergei Eisenstein, John Huston, and Akira Kurosawa; you disliked well-made literary adaptations of Great Books, especially when they suggested a slick, middle-brow attitude toward Art; you had a late romantic, somewhat surrealistic passion for *amour fou* in pictures like *Gun Crazy* (1949) and

Vertigo (1958); you preferred low-budget films noirs such as *Kiss Me Deadly* (1955) over Big Productions with Important Themes such as *The Bridge on the River Kwai* (1957); and you praised wide-screen, color-coded melodramas like *Some Came Running* instead of Academy Award–winning "little" movies like *Marty* (1955).

Much of the philosophical underpinnings of 1950s criticism at *Cahiers* derived from Bazin, the editor of the journal; but Bazin himself, who famously praised the "genius of the system" in Hollywood, was never an auteurist. Although he produced seminal writings on a number of directors (Jean Renoir, Robert Bresson, William Wyler, Orson Welles, and the Italian neorealists), he chastised his younger colleagues for their habit of falling into uncritical hero worship and was explicitly disapproving of the "Hitchcocko-Hawksian" tendency in Truffaut's work. His influence on the younger generation lay not so much in the authors he favored as in his broad historical knowledge of cinema and the arts generally, his ability to take Hollywood genres and technical developments seriously, and his keen understanding of the way style gives rise to meaning. Above all, Bazin imbued the early New Wave with a spirit of existential humanism, which placed great emphasis on the cinema's ability to view the world from an objective standpoint. (The very word for the photographic lens in French is *objectif*.) He and the auteurists repeatedly favored "realistic," "democratic," or untendentious uses of the camera; as a result, *Cahiers* in the 1950s was preoccupied with wide screens, the "ethics" of mise-en-scène, and with directors who used invisible editing, long takes, or sequence shots rather than dialectical montage. Sometimes this aesthetic ideology was joined with a belief that the best American auteurs were existentialists *avant la lettre*. In his 1960 review of Fuller's *Verboten!* (1959), for example, Truffaut describes the director of the film as if he were an action painter making instinctive or primal decisions about what should be put on the screen: "This is direct cinema, uncriticizable, irreproachable, 'given' cinema, rather than assimilated, digested, or reflected upon. Fuller doesn't take time to think; it is clear that he is in his glory when he is shooting" (*The Films of My Life*, 108).

There was nevertheless a tension between Truffaut's existentialist ideas, which made him sympathetic to an "open" cinema of the kind practiced by Renoir and Rossellini, and his equally strong love of genre directors like Fuller and flamboyant stylists like Welles. One of the things that attracted Truffaut to the Americans was their sense of fairy tales or pure artifice. As Leo Braudy has pointed out, Truffaut and Godard were part of a movie-obsessed generation who were hyperaware of the conventions of the medium and who "showed their involvement with the special aesthetics of film most clearly when they considered genre films—the westerns, the detective films, the musicals—in which realistic materials were used unrealistically in a structure dictated less by story than by myth." Even when Truffaut discussed *Citizen Kane*, Braudy notes, "he implicitly contradicted Bazin's assumption of realist teleology in film history by celebrating the virtues of self-conscious stylization" (*Native Informant*, 47).

Where the auteurists chiefly differed from Bazin was in the delirious style of their cinephilia and their tendency to place directors of pop genres or assembly-line films alongside the work of more highly respected artists. One of their favorite devices for achieving these effects was the ten-best list, which could be used as a weapon against prevailing opinion. Godard announced not only the ten best films of each year but also such things as the "Ten Best American Sound Films" and the "Six Best French Films since the Liberation." The typical list in *Cahiers* contained several key works of the New Wave together with such unexpected choices as *Hatari!* (1962) and *A Time to Love and a Time to Die*. Both here and in their more discursive writings, the auteurists loved to elevate the lowbrow over the middlebrow. Godard was perhaps better than anyone at the technique, as when he remarked that "an alert Frank Tashlin is worth two Billy Wilders" (35). His reviews repeatedly took on a populist quality and balanced sophistication with idealism about certain Hollywood films. In most cases, he employed a language of puns, epigrams, and breathtakingly old-fashioned pronouncements. In 1952, writing under the name "Hans Lucas," he answered Bazin's question "What is Cinema?" with a single phrase, basing his response on auteurs like Griffith, Flaherty, Renoir, and Hitchcock: "the expression of lofty sentiments" (31).

Was he kidding? Yes and no. Godard's Olympian statement illustrates one of the fundamental paradoxes of auteurism. Although the movement was youthful, impetuous, and romantic, it was often dedicated to antique virtues and to praising the work of directors who were entering their twilight years. Josef von Sternberg's *Jet Pilot* (1957), Fritz Lang's *The Thousand Eyes of Dr. Mabuse* (1960), and Howard Hawks's *Red Line 7000* (1965) were all made during roughly the same period as the early films of the New Wave; but they occupied a world apart from both the current Hollywood hits and the new European art cinema, as if they were still clinging to dated formulas or dead modes of production. Few mainstream critics in the Anglo-Saxon world took them seriously, but the auteurists passionately embraced them, sometimes ranking them above the same directors' more celebrated films of the 1930s and '40s. One of the most sweetly charming features of auteurism lay in its love for old pros or cinematic father figures who were still alive, making unpretentious genre movies or quiet, meditative films such as Ford's *The Sun Shines Bright* (1953). Truffaut, who could be devastatingly sarcastic in some contexts, was quite touching when he spoke of such films, or when he used them to rebuke current fashions.

The paradoxes or tensions I've been describing—between old and new, between pop and modernism, between a humanist philosophy of photographic realism and a nascent idea of cinematic *écriture*—are also apparent in the early films of the New Wave. Truffaut's directorial style, for example, rises out of two apparently incompatible approaches to cinema: Renoir's free-flowing tolerance, which breaks down generic conventions, and Hitchcock's "murderous gaze," which exploits generic conventions to the utmost. Godard's *Breathless* employs a similar dialectic, but the effect is much more conflicted or ambivalent. A highly personal movie (at least in the intellectual sense), it gives its auteur an opportunity to identify with both Michel (Jean-Paul Belmondo), a French wise guy who is infatuated with everything American, and Patricia (Jean Seberg), a sensitive, rather intellectual young woman from America who fears that she might be getting too deeply involved with the underworld. The two facets of the director's imaginary identity are represented in the form of a perversely romantic and failed relationship, much like the ones in Hollywood film noir; and the relationship is echoed in a dense pattern of allusions to two different kinds of text: genre movies, mostly associated with Michel, and high-cultural literature, music, or painting, mostly associated with Patricia. The film alludes not only to Aldrich, Fuller, Budd Boetticher, Otto Preminger, and Raoul Walsh, but also to William Faulkner, Rainer Maria Rilke, Louis Aragon, Guillaume Apollinaire, and William Shakespeare. Godard is the implicit source of these allusions and is therefore identified with both the man of action and the would-be artist, with both the rebel and the conformist—although it may be significant that he makes a cameo appearance (imitating Hitchcock) as a man on the street who points out Michel to the cops.

The New Wave was fostered by postmodernity, but it retained residual features of romanticism and critical modernism. However it might be described, the important point is that French success in the art theaters gave the auteurist writings of Godard, Truffaut, Rohmer, and Chabrol a special authority. By the early 1960s the movement had spread far beyond France. In England, it influenced the best critics of the period, including Robin Wood, Raymond Durgnat, Victor Perkins, Peter Wollen, David Thomson, and the group of writers associated with *Movie*. Over the next decade it had a similar influence in America, shaping the work of critic-filmmakers Paul Schrader and Peter Bogdanovich and eventually affecting "New American Cinema." During the 1960s, its presence was quite strong in New York, where the avant-garde filmmaker Jonas Mekas briefly provided a space for auteurist criticism in the pages of *Film Culture*, where select revival cinemas featured retrospectives of Hollywood auteurs, and where *Film Comment* became an auteurist journal.

Manny Farber, who anticipated many of these developments, praised Hollywood's "underground," male-action genre movies and attacked the middlebrow or "quality" tradition in America (meanwhile persuading us that Howard Hawks, one of the most successful producer-directors of the previous two decades, was an underground artist). The most influential American exponent of auteurism, however, was Andrew Sarris, whose columns for *The Village Voice* and writings on directors in *The American Cinema* (1968) helped to establish what have become canonical works of classic Hollywood. Sarris's book is filled with sharp but productive contradictions—a mixture of populism and elitism, of appeals to individual expression and vigorous praise for Hollywood. In his case, as in that of Godard, I'm reminded of a passage in Oscar Wilde's "The Critic as Artist" (1891), in which the wise aesthete Gilbert tells his friend Ernest that critical impressionism is a form of art. Gilbert confesses that the Mona Lisa never makes him contemplate Leonardo; on the contrary, he can never look at the painting without thinking of Walter Pater, who wrote a famous essay about it. For my part, I can never see *A Time to Love and a Time to Die* without thinking of Godard, and I can never see *The Searchers* without thinking of Sarris. Like the best critics, these two were not only what Wilde would call artists but also what Walter Benjamin would call producers. Writers on film, whether auteurists or not, can hardly expect to do more.

THE DEATH (AND SURVIVAL) OF THE AUTHOR

Auteurism profoundly affected Hollywood's view of its own past and in the process enhanced the reputation of directors like Hawks and Hitchcock, who were making their late films at the height of the movement. It influenced the spread of college film societies, inspired a generation to write about film, and contributed to the growth of film studies as an academic discipline. In the Anglo-American world especially, academic film study proliferated in literature departments rather than in drama or art history departments. Literary specialists found auteurism compatible not only because it emphasized authors but also because it offered a provisional canon and a program for research into a vast, largely unexplored area of twentieth-century narrative; in addition, it required a scholarly effort to see everything, not for the purpose of cataloging or building an archive, but for the purpose of informed value judgments. To British auteurists such as Robin Wood, this project had something in common with the severely evaluative, somewhat antimodernist literary criticism practiced by F. R. Leavis and his followers at *Scrutiny* in the 1930s and '40s. Wood's early writings also have something in common with the American literary critic Lionel Trilling's espousal of "moral realism"; thus Wood began his famous book on Hitchcock with a chapter entitled "Why We Should Take Hitchcock Seriously" and went on to stress the "complex moral implications" of certain Hitchcock films (4). In more qualified fashion, the first edition of Peter Wollen's *Signs and Meaning in the Cinema* (1969) concluded with the suggestion that film study might join forces with the dominant form of literary education: "Hitchcock is at least as important an artist as, say, Scott Fitzgerald, much more important than many other modern American novelists who have found their way on to the university curriculum. I do not think time is wasted in writing about these novelists, all things being equal, and I do not think it would be wasted if hundreds of post-graduates were writing research theses on Jean Renoir, Max Ophuls or John Ford" (160–61).

These arguments owed something to the culture-and-society debates of the previous century, but they also realigned or decentered the academic canon and encouraged a certain curiosity about how canons are formed in the first place. For that reason and others, auteurism *as a movement* began to self-destruct. Ultimately it fell victim to internal contradictions, to the splintering of its original French advocates into different filmmaking careers, to the professionalism of academia, and to theoretical challenges from both the right and the left.

The first of the theoretical challenges, barely noticed at the time, was already inherent in the literary methodology that some of the American auteurists had adopted. The very idea of modern poetics in the Anglo-Saxon world derives from an "objective" formalism of a type best exemplified by T.S. Eliot, who argued in "Tradition and the Individual Talent" (1919) that "honest criticism and sensitive appreciation is directed not upon the poet but upon the poetry." In the literary sphere, Eliot and the New Critics mounted a devastating attack on a dusty, genteel, academic historicism, in which the names of great writers figured prominently. In the process, they warned against the "intentional fallacy" and advocated trusting the tale, not the teller. New Criticism also had democratic effects: it called attention to the way language constructs the world, and, in the words of Jonathan Culler, it enabled "the meanest student who lacked the scholarly information of his betters" to make "valid comments on the language and structure of the text" (3–4). And even though New Criticism gradually died out, all subsequent developments in textual analysis—including structuralism, poststructuralism, and contemporary narratology—have resembled the New Critics in being formalist or "objective." The overwhelming majority of introductory classes on media "language" taught in universities are still based on methods of formal analysis not completely unlike the New Critical analysis of poetry; as a result, they're less concerned with who makes films than with how films are made and with how they generate meanings and artistic effects.

But even though the main current of instruction and analytic criticism tends to leave the question of the author to one side, the major achievements in modem poetics, as represented by such diverse figures as Erich Auerbach, Leo Spitzer, Roland Barthes, and Émile Benveniste, are derived from close analysis of the Western canon. There would appear to be an unstated link between formalism, aestheticism, and the tendency to favor certain artists or kinds of texts. We should recall that, for all its apparent objectivity of method, the New Criticism advanced implicit ideological agendas, creating both a canon of modernist authors and a kind of priesthood of interpretation. It achieved such ends despite (or perhaps because of) the fact that it bracketed the important issue of historical authors and readers, leaving them outside the field of study, as unexamined entities who were extraneous to the understanding of self-sufficient works of art. Auteurism was different, not only because it validated Hollywood, but also because it openly fostered a cult of authorship and an impulse toward historical research.

Auteurism faced much greater challenges from inside film culture, which was deeply affected by the radical politics of the Vietnam years and by new forms of modernist cinema, largely centered in Paris. The late 1960s and '70s were a period when the Langlois Affair led to student riots and a general strike, when the Situationists made collage films, when Godard joined the Dziga Vertov collective, and when the radicalized elements of the French film industry began to express dissatisfaction with any system that designated directors as "bosses of meaning." (For a useful survey of the period, see Sylvia Harvey.) At roughly the same time, Third Cinema developed in Latin America and in nations that had recently escaped colonization, which led to a militantly political filmmaking that, although it was indebted in certain ways to the Italian neorealists and the French New Wave, defined itself in opposition to both Hollywood entertainment and personalized European art.

Meanwhile, French antihumanist "theory" (a term that had barely existed in the Anglo-American world) began to change the priorities for academic film criticism. Outside France, the change became apparent in the British journal *Screen*, which published Cohn MacCabe's writings on Brecht, Stephen Heath's two-part analysis of *Touch of Evil*, Laura Mulvey's study of "visual pleasure," and many other seminal essays. *Screen* theory as a whole was indebted to the program outlined in "Cinema/Ideology/

Criticism," a 1968 *Cahiers du cinéma* manifesto by Pierre Narboni and Jean-Louis Comolli, which marked the turn away from auteurism. Like Narboni and Comolli, *Screen* was suspicious of Hollywood entertainment and tended to subsume individual practices under generalized formal categories, to which it attributed ideological effects; it closely examined the ways a hypostasized "subject" was positioned by narrative conventions and the technical apparatus, and it repeatedly argued on behalf of a modernist or avant-garde cinema that was both politically activist and critically self-reflexive. Theory in this period was Marxist (via Louis Althusser), but just as disdainful of social realism as the auteurists had been. It was Freudian (via Jacques Lacan), but not at all interested in the neuroses of individual artists; instead, it argued that the dominant tradition of cinematic language (described by Christian Metz as an "imaginary signifier") was structured by a patriarchal ideology. On every front, theory replaced the study of the author with the study of the sign systems through which author and ideology were represented. In contrast to traditional Marxism, the author became a kind of epiphenomenon or ideological construction, and the human subject seemed to have no individual agency. Two celebrated French essays strongly influenced this tendency: in "What Is an Author?" Michel Foucault deconstructed the authorial "function," showing its relationship to early Christian exegesis, to the rationalist episteme of bourgeois society, and to legal or property rights; and in "From Work to Text," Roland Barthes contrasted the authorized work of art—which, he suggested, was little more than a reified commodity—with the open-ended process of textuality, which seemed to belong to the reader, or to nobody in particular.

Where film study was concerned, the names of theorists became more important than the names of directors, although the new writing favored a wide range of filmmakers who could be interpreted in modernist and avant-garde terms: Soviet radicals (Eisenstein and Vertov), pre-Hollywood pioneers (Porter and the photographers who worked before Griffith), certain Japanese directors (Ozu and Oshima), and a group of contemporaries who practiced "countercinema" (Godard, Jean-Marie Straub and Danièle Huillet, and Peter Wollen and Laura Mulvey). The auteurist canon didn't disappear from the advanced film journals, but it was treated differently. The new editorial collective at *Cahiers du cinéma* undertook a political and Lacanian analysis of John Ford's *Young Mr. Lincoln* (1939), most of the French essays on cinema and psychoanalysis were centered on Hitchcock, and even Comolli and Narboni said a good word about Jerry Lewis's *The Bellboy* (1960). Several of the original British auteurists, including Wollen and Wood, who were associated with the New Left, made increasing use of post-structuralist theory but chose to write about pictures by Welles or

Hitchcock. In the pages of *Screen* and elsewhere, cutting-edge theoretical papers were often devoted to films by Hawks, Walsh, Sirk, and Ophüls. These papers didn't try to establish particular individuals as artists; in most cases they were designed to reveal that the classic Hollywood auteurs were ideological partners in an illusionistic system that needed to be dismantled. They nevertheless had the indirect effect of keeping artistic reputations and auteurist tastes alive.

The Vietnam era gave way to the Reagan-Thatcher years, Hollywood learned to profit from blockbusters, the media were increasingly consolidated and globalized, and social protest fragmented. The succeeding generation of academic writers on film became skeptical of authoritarian or top-down models of communication (in part because Barthes had already pointed to the importance of the reader), and the theoretical conjunction of Saussurean linguistics, Althusserian Marxism, and Lacanian psychoanalysis was gradually replaced by another paradigm, associated with such figures as Antonio Gramsci, Michel de Certeau, Pierre Bourdieu, and the British and Australian exponents of cultural studies. The critical emphasis shifted from the avant-garde to the popular and from the ideological effects of cinematic narrative to the techniques of "resistance" or "poaching" employed by audiences. As a result, we began to hear more about reception than production, and more about Jean-Luc Picard than about Jean-Luc Godard.

Today, after more than two decades of film theory, academic writing tends to oscillate between large-scale arguments about the Hollywood "apparatus" and studies of genres or audiences. The critical study of authors is no longer a central activity. A great deal of contemporary historiography continues to treat the author in the manner of Foucault, as little more than a discursive function, and this tendency is reinforced by a long tradition of cultural theory, ranging from radicals like Walter Benjamin to conservatives like Daniel Bell, who argue that technology and the mass media systematically undermine the bourgeois values of originality, autonomy, and aestheticism upon which the idea of authorship depends. Each new technical development since the beginning of the century has helped to confirm this theory. In the age of the computer, the media are able to generate "hypertexts," apparently authorless words, sounds, and images manipulated by the reader/viewer according to structural conventions and a repertoire of older styles. A great many postmodern artists have adopted this strategy; like bricoleurs or samplers, they make new texts out of borrowed or retro motifs, becoming ironic about their originality.

And yet, as anyone can see from the latest movies, individual style hasn't gone away and the star director is as visible as ever. Timothy Corrigan has argued that such figures are especially important to the contemporary marketplace because they serve as a "commercial strategy for organizing audience reception ... bound to distribution and marketing aims that identify and address the potential cult status of an auteur" (103). I agree, although Corrigan seems to me to understate the fact that directors are also artists, and to overstate the difference between the past and the present. Orson Welles was a vastly more important artist than Michael Bay, but he was just as deeply involved in vulgar show business, and the marketing of his early pictures depended heavily on RKO's ballyhoo about his "genius." In their own day, Cecil B. DeMille and Frank Capra were publicized no less than Steven Spielberg and James Cameron. What makes the contemporary situation relatively new is the split between Hollywood and an audience of people who read reviews and make discriminations on the basis of directorial names like David Lynch, Sally Potter, and Atom Egoyan. In 1997, *Cahiers du cinéma* speculated on the question, "What happened to the *politique des auteurs?*" The journal's answer: nothing. As proof of an ongoing *auteuromorphisme* (defined as a persistent desire to make the film resemble the body of its creator), the journal offered interviews with five directors—Pedro Almodóvar, Takeshi Kitano, Alain Resnais, Robert Guédiguian, and Abbas Kiarostami—whose work had just opened in Paris (Baecque, 22–25).

The academic deemphasis on authors is out of key with this situation, although it offers an important counterweight to the overwhelming emphasis on stars, celebrities, and biographies in the mainstream market. In universities, nothing should prevent author criticism from contributing to our understanding of media history and sociology. French auteurism as a historical movement may be dead (its greatest influence lasted roughly two decades), but so are the tedious debates about the death of the author. The residual "auteur theory" in its various manifestations still affects our view of film history, and it still has lessons to teach us—among them, the three I list below:

1. The author is just as real (or as illusory and fetishized) as the money and the mechanical apparatus behind the cinema. The classic auteurs such as Hitchcock and Hawks imposed a style upon their films, as do contemporary directors, and any "materialistic" criticism needs to take this fact into account. It's true that authors are "written by" a series of historical, social, and cultural determinants, and that no author creates a film ex nihilo; but the author doesn't become less real simply because she's socially constructed or because she uses the common language and tradition. Critics need to understand the phenomenon of the author dialectically, with an awareness of the complicated, dynamic relationship between movie history, institutions, and artists, and with an appreciation of the

aesthetic choices made by individual agents in particular circumstances.

2. The study of authors is useful because it sometimes enables us to differentiate films more precisely. One can make valid generalizations about Hollywood studios and genres, but every western and every film noir is not the same. As Robin Wood has pointed out, the name "Hitchcock" points to a different nexus of ideological and psychological concerns from the name "Capra." These two individuals were themselves situated differently in history, and a study of their careers can produce a fine-grained understanding of both film style and the general culture. Echoing a statement by F. R. Leavis, Wood argues that it is "only through the medium of the individual that ideological tensions come into particular focus" (*Hitchcock's Films Revisited*, 292).

3. Contrary to what Foucault suggests in his famous essay on the idea of the author, it can be very important for us to know who is speaking. A good deal is at stake, for example, when we view *Citizen Kane* as an RKO production rather than as a product of Orson Welles's career; one way of looking at the film makes it seem like a Hollywood classic and the other emphasizes its critical or subversive edge. Of course we can derive a political interpretation from purely internal evidence, avoiding the question of the source altogether. When we do, however, we fail to engage with what Andreas Huyssen calls "the ideology of the subject (as male, white, middle-class)," and we forsake the chance of "developing alternative and different notions of subjectivity" (213). There is no good reason why everyone needs to follow the example of Barthes and Foucault, who, as European male intellectuals, were deeply invested in the attempt to kill off "papa." Less powerful individuals or groups need authors to help shape their identities. Thus in a recent book on Italian director Elvira Notari, Giuliana Bruno poses a rhetorical question: "Can or should we consider as dead an author, such as the female author, who is yet to be fully established in the public sphere and theorized?" (234; see also Flitterman-Lewis).

In many cases the study of authors is a conservative activity, bound up with the perpetuation of traditions and the manufacture of commodities. But in certain contexts it can serve as an attack on convention and a form of resistance. The best of the early auteurist criticism had something of this last quality. It was romantic, but it challenged received wisdom; it was ironic, but it never used irony as a defense against popular pleasure; it was subjective, but it implicitly demonstrated that the personal is political. We can build on what it accomplished without sacrificing theoretical insights or cultural critique. The canon of Hollywood, largely established by the original French auteurists, has yet to be explored, expanded, and challenged. We have plenty of biographies on major directors, but surprisingly few good books of criticism on their films. The vast area of post-1980s cinema and made-for-TV movies is largely uncharted territory. We need discussions of such things by people who work outside the studio marketing departments. The result might be to restore to film criticism the sense of iconoclasm and aesthetic sensitivity it had in the days of the *politique des auteurs*.

The Reign of Adaptation

My title alludes to a relatively little-known essay by André Bazin, "Adaptation, or the Cinema as Digest," written in 1948 but not translated into English until 1998, when it appeared in Bert Cardullo's useful anthology *Bazin at Work*. I especially recommend this essay to readers who think of Bazin almost exclusively as an eloquent proponent of a certain kind of humanist realism in the cinema. Without denying the importance of Bazin's writings on the phenomenology of the photographic image and the realistic uses of the camera, we need to remember that an entire volume of the French edition of his posthumously collected criticism, published in four volumes under the title *What Is Cinema?*, was devoted to the relationship between film and other media. The essay on adaptation is one of his most intriguing statements on behalf of what he called "impure cinema," and it enables us to see him in a new light, as a writer who has something to contribute to what academics today call cultural studies.

I shall return to Bazin, but first I want to comment on some of the reasons why his essay may have been neglected and why the very subject of adaptation has until fairly recently constituted one of the most jejune areas of scholarly writing about the cinema. One of the major reasons, as Robert B. Ray has pointed out, is institutional: a great many film programs in the academy are attached to literature departments, where the theme of adaptation is often used as a way of teaching celebrated literature by another means (Ray, "The Field of 'Literature and Film,'" 44–47). Thus we immediately think of *Mrs Dalloway* (1998) or even of the more freely derivative *Orlando* (1993) as adaptations, but not of *The Set Up* (1949, based on a narrative poem), *Batman* (1989, based on a comic book), *His Girl Friday* (1940, based on a play), *Mission Impossible* (1996, based on a TV series), or *Twelve Monkeys* (1995, based on an art film). Even within the realm of the novelistic, the range of things usually discussed under the rubric of adaptation is quite narrow. Twentieth Century Fox's 1940 production of *The Grapes of Wrath* is nearly always seen in relation to John Steinbeck, but the same studio's 1944 production of *Laura* is rarely viewed as an adaptation of Vera Caspary (even though the film's main title reads "*Laura*, by Vera Caspary")—probably because Caspary's protofeminist thriller has long been out of print and has seldom been taught by English teachers.

Unfortunately, most discussions of novelistic adaptation in film can be summarized by a *New Yorker* cartoon that Alfred Hitchcock once described to François Truffaut: two goats are eating a pile of film cans and one goat says to the other, "Personally, I liked the book better." Even when writing on the topic isn't directly concerned with a given film's artistic adequacy or fidelity to a beloved source, it tends to be narrow in range and constitutive of a series of binary oppositions that poststructuralist theory has presumably taught us to reject: literature versus cinema, high culture versus mass culture, original versus copy. Such oppositions are the products of what was once the submerged common sense of the average English department, which was composed of a mixture of Kantian aesthetics and Arnoldian ideas about society.

When I use the term "Arnoldian," I'm referring chiefly to Matthew Arnold's *Culture and Anarchy* (1869), which argues that culture is synonymous with great works of art and that the inherited cultural tradition of the Judeo-Christian world, embodied in "the best that has been thought and said," can have a civilizing influence, transcending class tensions and leading to a more humane society. The study of English literature in American universities owes its very existence to this argument, which was more subtly elaborated by such later figures as T.S. Eliot and F.R. Leavis; and, until recent years, English professors have been especially suspicious of mass-produced narratives from Hollywood, which seem to threaten or debase the values of both "organic" popular culture and literary culture. When I use the term "Kantian," I'm speaking of a slightly older, more complex mode of idealist philosophy that emerged toward the end of the eighteenth century in Europe, and that we commonly associate not only with Immanuel Kant but also with Georg Hegel, Johann von Schiller, and Samuel Taylor Coleridge. Beginning in the mid-nineteenth century and continuing throughout the period of high literary modernism, all art in the European world was theorized under what might be roughly described as a Kantian set of assumptions; that is, both the making and the appreciation of art were conceived as specialized, autonomous, and transcendent activities having chiefly to do with media-specific form (see Eagleton, 17–53). A locus classicus of such theorizing (perhaps even a parody of it) is the fifth chapter of James Joyce's *Portrait of the Artist as a Young Man* (1914), in which

Stephen Dedalus tells us that art differs from pornography because it does not elicit desire, from propaganda because it does not teach or move to political action, and from market goods because it has no entertainment value or practical utility. The proper effect of art, Dedalus says, is the "luminous silent stasis of aesthetic pleasure," which can be achieved only through the contemplation of formal matters.

Never mind that Joyce's own novel problematizes such ideas, and that his next novel, *Ulysses*, pushes aestheticism beyond its sustainable limits; some variation of aesthetic formalism rightly underpins every modern discipline that claims to be dealing with art. Consider, for example, David Bordwell and Kristin Thompson's excellent college textbook *Film Art*, which has long been used in introductory film study courses throughout the United States. Bordwell and Thompson are quite different from the literary dandies and philosophical idealists of the late nineteenth or early twentieth centuries; their approach is practical and undogmatic, grounded in empirical evidence from an exceptionally wide range of films, and their chief theoretical influences are contemporary narratology and the Russian formalists. Even so, they devote themselves to teaching us how to recognize cinema-specific codes and how to appreciate part-whole relationships within individual movies.

I, too, am something of an aesthete, and I strongly believe that no proper criticism of art can ignore questions of form. I was also an English major, and I don't think we can dismiss Matthew Arnold or that we should stop reading Great Books and seeing films based on them. It's nevertheless important to understand that both Arnold's defense of high culture and the aesthetic movement of the late nineteenth century are historically situated ideologies, generated largely in response to industrial capitalism and mechanical reproduction. Their culminating or extreme instance, and in one sense their crisis, was the period immediately before and after World War II, when New Criticism was in the ascendency in American universities and modernist intellectuals, including otherwise quite different theorists Theodor Adorno and Clement Greenberg, enunciated an idea of "authentic" art in defense against the culture industries. Greenberg's famous essay "Avant-Garde and Kitsch," for example, describes the essential project of modernism as "Content is to be dissolved so completely into form that the work of art or literature cannot be reduced in whole or in part to anything not itself" (25).

Greenberg's essay was written in 1939, when Fascism had overtaken Europe, when modern art, which had already been assimilated into bourgeois culture, was being assailed from both the left and the right for its decadence and elitism, and when aestheticism seemed caught in a struggle to survive capitalism and Stalinism. For Greenberg, the only refuge for "authentic" art lay in the realm of the "merely artistic," or in the radically formal exploration of artistic media. The artistic imitation of the natural or social world, he argued, needed to be replaced by the study of "the disciplines and processes of art and literature themselves" (23). Unfortunately, as Juan A. Suarez has observed, the result of this policy was "an exacerbation of formalism and a sort of art in exile from the values of audiences; that is, an art which seeks to remain untainted by reigning mercantilism and instrumental rationality" (6–7).

The capitalist movie industry, especially in Hollywood, operated by a dialectically opposite logic. It recognized from the beginning that it could gain a sort of legitimacy among middle-class viewers by reproducing facsimiles of more respectable art or by adapting literature to another medium. Film scholars William Uricchio and Roberta E. Pearson have demonstrated that as early as 1908, at the height of the nickelodeon boom and partly in response to the Reform movement in American politics, the Vitagraph film company in New York engaged in an aggressive, concentrated effort to appeal to the middle class by making one-reel adaptions of Shakespeare and Dante. At virtually the same moment, Parisian financiers established the Société Film d'Art, which made quite profitable feature-length films based on the dramas of Rostand and Sardou, as well as silent versions of Dickens's *Oliver Twist* and Goethe's *The Sorrows of Young Werther*. Historian David Cook remarks, "For a while it seemed as if everything written, sung, or danced (for photographed ballet and opera formed a large part of the film d'art corpus) in Western Europe between 1900 and the Renaissance, and Greek tragedy as well, found its way into one of these stage-bound and pretentious productions" (53). But uncinematic as the early adaptations may seem today, they were among the first feature films, and their drive for respectability pointed toward the development of the star system, the picture palace, and in one sense Hollywood itself. Equally important were the hugely successful Italian historical pictures of the same period, especially Enrico Guazzoni's *Quo Vadis?* (1912), a nine-reel spectacular based on a novel by Nobel laureate Henryk Sienkiewicz, which established the market for "blockbuster" movies such as *Birth of a Nation* (1915), also an adaptation.

The advent of the talkies and the Fordist organization of the major film studios produced a great appetite for literature among Hollywood moguls, who provided a source of major income, if not artistic satisfaction, for every important playwright and author in the United States, including Eugene O'Neill, F. Scott Fitzgerald, John Dos Passos, and William Faulkner. But here we encounter an important historical irony. At the same time that modernity and capitalism were bringing the movies, the legitimate theater, and the book publishing industry closer together, sophisticated literary artists in general were in active rebellion against bourgeois culture and were intentionally producing work that could not be easily assimilated into mainstream adaptations. Modernism was not only willfully difficult and formally "experimental," it was also sexually scandalous, critical of progress, and offensive to the Babbitts and the Bovarys who supposedly made up the viewing audience. Thus, at the height of the classic studio system, when Hollywood was absorbing every kind of artistic talent and establishing itself as the very emblem of modernity, the Production Code Administration (PCA) began to engage in what Richard Maltby calls "a conscious ideological project" aimed at preventing what one of its leaders described as "the prevalent type of book and play" from becoming "the prevalent type of movie" (Maltby, "To Prevent the Prevalent Type of Book," 81). This did not mean that modern literature was no longer adapted. Classic Hollywood wanted to acquire every sort of cultural capital, but it was especially interested in source material that could easily be recuperated into an aesthetically and morally conservative form of entertainment. Even after the qualified relaxation of censorship restrictions in the 1950s, the most adaptable sources for movies were the "readerly" texts of the nineteenth century rather than the "writerly" texts of high modernism, which were explicitly designed to resist being reduced" to anything not themselves.

Meanwhile, in still another historical irony, film was being regarded in some quarters as the quintessential medium for modernist and avant-garde art. Some of the most talented movie directors in the first half of the century approached the problem of literary adaptation in the spirit of intense aestheticism, as in Erich von Stroheim's version of *Greed* (1924) or Eisenstein's abortive attempt to film *An American Tragedy*. Modern experimental fiction was sometimes directly influenced by cinema, as when John Dos Passos began his *USA* trilogy shortly after meeting Eisenstein and reading the Soviet theories of montage. Eventually, the cinema was theorized as the dominant "way of seeing" in the modern world and as a condition toward which most of the visual and literary arts aspired. Cultural critic Arnold Hauser placed the whole of twentieth-century art, including such things as Cubist paintings and poems like *The Waste Land*, under the evocative rubric of "the film age." French critic Claude-Edmonde Magny proposed that the period between the two world wars should be called "the age of the American novel" and that the leading American writers, especially Hemingway and Faulkner, were guided by a "film aesthetic." American critics Alan Spiegel and Keith Cohen each wrote books arguing that modern Anglo/European literature, including Flaubert, Proust, James, Conrad, Joyce, and Woolf, was fundamentally "cinematic" in form.

It was not until 1957 that the movies seemed to have matured enough to produce the first full-scale academic analysis of film adaptation in America: George Bluestone's *Novels into Film: The Metamorphosis of Fiction into*

Cinema. In this book Bluestone argues that certain movies (his examples are all from Hollywood, including *The Informer, Wuthering Heights,* and *The Grapes of Wrath*) do not debase their literary sources; instead, they "metamorphose" novels into another medium that has its own formal or narratological possibilities. Such an argument seems unlikely to provoke controversy; one of its difficulties, at least insofar as Bluestone's general aim of giving movies artistic respectability is concerned, is that it takes place entirely on the grounds of modernist aestheticism. Given Bluestone's thesis, film can't acquire true cultural capital unless it first theorizes its own media-specific form. Hence Bluestone argues that "the end products of novel and film represent different aesthetic genera, as different from each other as ballet is from architecture" (5). At the same time, however, he tends to confirm the artistic priority and superiority of canonical novels, if only because they provide the films he discusses with their sources and artistic standards.

When we start from Bluestone's position, the only way to avoid making film seem belated, middlebrow, or culturally inferior is to devalue adaptation altogether. That's more or less what happened in Europe at almost the same moment when Bluestone's book was published. The central importance of the French New Wave in the history of worldwide taste and opinion was that it was able to break with traditional movie criticism and establish a truly modernist (as well as somewhat Arnoldian) film criticism by launching an attack on what Truffaut called a "tradition of quality" made up of respectable literary adaptations. One of the best-kept secrets of the New Wave was that many of their own films were based on books; the sources they chose, however, were often lowbrow, and when they closely adapted "serious" works or wrote essays about film adaptations (such as Bazin's essay on Bresson's *Diary of a Country Priest*), they made sure that the auteur would seem at least as important as the author. Along similar lines, they gave legitimacy to art-film directors who were less interested in adapting literature than in interrogating or "reading" it. One of the many who followed in their wake was Rainer Werner Fassbinder, an explosively antibourgeois filmmaker who once argued that cinematic transformation of a literary work should never assume its purpose is to realize the images that literature evokes in the minds of its readers. Such a goal is preposterous, Fassbinder wrote, because there are so many different readers with different fantasies. His own aim, as he described it in relation to *Berlin Alexanderplatz* (1980) and *Querelle* (1982), was to avoid a "composite" fantasy and to engage in what he called "an unequivocal and single-minded questioning of the piece of literature and its language" (Fassbinder, 168).

The French auteurists never treated movies as a "seventh art" or a separate but equal member of the cultural pantheon. Instead, adopting

Alexandre Astruc's idea of the *camera stylo*, they spoke of film as a language and the director as a kind of writer, wielding a lens instead of a pen. They elevated the cinematic mise-en-scène to a greater importance than the scenario, and partly as a result it's now commonplace for film historians to speak of directorial masterpieces or canonical works of cinema that revise and far surpass their sources. (My list includes Eisenstein's *October* [1928], Murnau's *Sunrise* [1927], Welles's *The Magnificent Ambersons* [1942], Ophüls's *Letter from an Unknown Woman* [1948], Hitchcock's *Psycho* [1960], and Godard's *Contempt* [1963].) They also made it a critical commonplace to observe that some of the best movie directors avoid adaptation of respected literature or radically deviate from their literary sources. The practice is enshrined during Hitchcock's interview with Truffaut, in which Hitchcock claims that the approach he usually takes to sources is to "read a story only once, and if I like the basic idea, I just forget about the book and start to create cinema" (71). He would never adapt *Crime and Punishment*, he says, in part because he thinks that feature films are more like short stories than like novels and in part because "in Dostoyevsky's novel there are many, many words and all of them have a function" (72). Truffaut quickly agrees, voicing one of the axioms of modernist aesthetics and pure cinema: "That's right. Theoretically, a masterpiece is something that has already found its perfection of form, its definitive form" (72). And indeed, Hitchcock's films lend support to these conclusions, although it should also be noted that there are exceptions to the rule: *The 39 Steps* (based on a novel by John Buchan), *Sabotage* (based on a novel by Joseph Conrad), and *The Birds* (based on a short story by Daphne du Maurier) are quite free adaptations, but the half-hour TV film "Lamb to the Slaughter," one of Hitchcock's minor but most perfect achievements, is a quite literal approach to a Roald Dahl short story, scripted by Dahl himself.

Since the 1980s, academic writing has become more aware that the relationship between film and literature is complex, involving a good deal more than the art of adapting books into films—see, for instance, Timothy Corrigan's useful textbook *Film and Literature: An Introduction and Reader* (1999), which explores a number of important sociological and historical issues. Where formal analysis is concerned, the study of adaptations has gained sophistication by making use of the structuralist and poststructuralist poetics of Roland Barthes, the narratology of Gérard Genette, and the neo-formalism of Bordwell and Thompson. For the most part, however, adaptation study has remained literary in nature and continues to waver back and forth between the two approaches exemplified by Bluestone and the auteurists. The Bluestone approach relies on an implicit metaphor of translation, which governs all investigations of how codes move across sign systems. Writing in this category usually deals with the concept of literary versus cinematic form and pays close attention to the problem of textual fidelity in order to identify the specific formal capabilities of the media. By contrast, the auteurist approach relies on an implicit metaphor of performance. It, too, involves questions of fidelity, but it subordinates media specificity and formal systems to an analysis of individual style.

The problem with most writing about adaptation as translation is that it tends to valorize the literary canon and essentialize the nature of cinema. One example is Seymour Chatman's "What Novels Can Do That Film Can't (and Vice Versa)," first published in *Critical Inquiry* in 1981. A theoretically informed, highly intelligent discussion of Jean Renoir's 1936 adaptation of Guy de Maupassant's "Une Partie de campagne," it shows how the same narrative is represented in different media. Chatman is unconcerned with questions of value, but his argument is based on respected literary and cinematic examples. He makes important observations about the ways description and point of view are treated respectively in realist fiction and narrative cinema, but he also makes dubious generalizations about the film medium. In the last analysis, cinema is an audiovisual recording and projection technology tied to a system of production, distribution, and exhibition. At the purely technical level, whether based on photography or digital imaging, it's capable of representing the whole range of signifying practices, including the printed pages of books. It obviously makes sense to ask what conventional novels can do that conventional narrative films can't (and vice versa), but the qualifying adjective "conventional" needs to be stressed, and we might learn somewhat more by broadening the textual milieu. Charles Willeford's relatively little known *Pick-Up*, a pulp-fiction masterpiece of the 1950s, would present more difficulty for a filmmaker than Joyce's *Finnegans Wake* (which has, in fact, been turned into a movie) for the simple reason that a crucially important word describing the central character doesn't appear until the final sentence. I refrain from a spoiler quotation of the word and simply recommend the book.

Another problem with most writing on adaptation as translation is that it deals of necessity with sexually charged materials and can't avoid gendered language associated with the notion of "fidelity." George Bluestone tries to defend certain movies against the accusation that they "violate" their sources; Seymour Chatman spends almost half of his essay analyzing the way Renoir adapts a description of a flirtatious young woman on a swing; and in a *New York Times* essay that is far less systematic and far more judgmental than Chatman's, "What Only Words, Not Film, Can Portray," novelist and critic Cynthia Ozick derides Jane Campion's 1997 adaptation of *A Portrait of a Lady* because it "perverts" Henry James, replacing his "gossamer vibrations of the interior life" and "philosophy of the soul" with "crudity," "self-oriented eroticism," and "voluptuous gazing" (January 5, 1997). Ozick reverses the standard imagery of high-cultural disdain, making the movies seem less like an ignorant shopgirl and more like a crude, lascivious male bent on despoiling a loved object. I'm reminded of the first sentence of Fredric Jameson's *Signatures of the Visible* (1990), a book about film by the most distinguished contemporary proponent of the modernist tradition: "The visual is essentially pornographic," Jameson declares, as if the very act of translating words into photographic images involves a move toward something bodily and nasty.

Brian McFarlane's extremely useful and well-informed study of adaptation as translation, *Novel to Film* (1996), is aware of some of the problems I've been describing. It begins with an attack on "fidelity criticism" and contains analysis of an interesting variety of adaptations, including MGM's *Random Harvest* (1942), which is based on a best seller, and Martin Scorsese's *Cape Fear* (1991), which is a remake of a film based on a pulp novel. And yet McFarlane himself is obsessively concerned with problems of fidelity—necessarily so, because his major purpose is to settle the issue of just how faithful an adaptation can be. He gives us a scrupulous demonstration of the degree to which the "cardinal" features of narrative, most of them exemplified by canonical nineteenth-century novels from British and American authors, can be transposed intact to movies. As he puts it, he sets up a distinction between "those novelistic elements which can be *transferred* and those which require *adaptation proper*, the former essentially concerned with *narrative*, which functions irrespective of medium, and the latter with *enunciation*, which calls for a consideration of two different signifying systems" (195).

Here as in most other places, the study of adaptation stops at the water's edge, as if hesitant to move beyond important formalist concerns and ask other, equally interesting questions. Writing about adaptation should be a flexible, animating discourse because it can address such a wide variety of things. As Dudley Andrew pointed out in 1984 in a seminal essay, every representational film (and every representational artifact) could be regarded as an adaptation—hence the very word "representation" (Andrew, "Adaptation," 96–106). Andrew estimates that more than half of all commercial movies have derived from novels, a figure that may be high but isn't wildly exaggerated. In 1985 the *New York Times* reported that one in fifty novels published in this country were optioned by Hollywood (July 14, 1985), and if we extend the idea of adaptation beyond novels, the number of "derivative" films is quite large. In 1998, *Variety* published statistics indicating that 20 percent of the movies produced that year had their sources in books of one kind or another (authors included John Grisham, Stephen King, Michael Crichton, Howard Stern, James Ellroy, and Leo Tolstoy), and another 20 percent was based upon plays, sequels, remakes, TV shows, and magazine or newspaper articles—meaning that only about half of the pictures that year were "originals" (February 2–8, 1998). Academics have limited the issues at stake, not only by focusing largely on novels but also by insisting on what Andrew calls the "cultural status" of a prior model. "In the case of those texts explicitly termed 'adaptations,'" Andrew writes, "the cultural model which the cinema represents is already treasured as a representation in another sign system" (97). Precisely; one could hardly expect to find a better definition of what adaptation means to most critics and historians. But the definition reveals that adaptation study in the limited sense is only partly about enunciative techniques or the "cardinal" features of narrative; it's also about the interpretation of canonical literature in more or less traditional fashion, a system of critical writing that tends to reproduce cultural orthodoxies.

To his credit, Andrew argues that "It is time for adaptation stud[y] to take a sociological turn" (104), although the things he recommends for investigation, while valid, are conventionally literary—for example, the changing history of naturalism in Zola, Gorky, and Renoir. What we need is a broader definition of adaptation and a sociology that takes into account the commercial apparatus, the audience, and the academic wing of the culture industry. Academics need to move the discussion of adaptation slightly away from the great-novels-into-great-films theme and give more attention to economic, political, and broadly cultural issues. For example, we need more analysis of the relation between TV and theatrical film. Postmodern Hollywood has created a virtual genre out of big-screen adaptations of old TV shows *(The Fugitive, The Mod Squad, Charlie's Angels)*, while, in an ironic reversal, TV has become increasingly interested in the literary canon. Until quite recently, *Masterpiece Theater* was the major producer of filmed adaptations of "respectable" literature in America, reaching audiences as large as Hollywood in its heyday and probably helping to identify a niche market for the successful Merchant Ivory adaptations of E. M. Forster that played in theaters. By the end of the twentieth century, cable TV was producing a good deal of similar material. In the United States in 1999, the A&E network aired a miniseries based on C. S. Forester's *Horatio Hornblower*, the USA network produced *Moby Dick*, and Bravo broadcast a new version of the much-adapted *The Count of Monte Cristo*. During the 1999–2000 season, TNT produced adaptations of *Animal Farm, A Christmas Carol, David Copperfield*, and *Don Quixote*. As this list suggests, Edwardian and nineteenth-century classics are the favored sources for "prestige" TV movies, just as they were for classic Hollywood, in part because they have a presold audience and are comparatively easy to adapt. Along similar lines, the literature most frequently adapted for twenty-first-century prestige TV is the popular mystery or melodrama, as in 2011, when *Masterpiece Mystery* adapted Michael Dibdin's novels about police detective Aurelio Zen and HBO produced Todd Haynes's adaptation of James M. Cain's *Mildred Pierce*.

The current economic environment, which is characterized by enormous mergers in the communications industry and the growth of home theater systems, makes it especially important for us to understand the purely commercial relations between publishing, cinematic, and broadcast media. We need to ask why certain books (or comic books) become of interest to Hollywood in specific periods, and we need more investigations into the historical relation between movies and book publishing. We also need to ask what conditions of the marketplace govern the desire for fidelity. As one example, an audience survey conducted by David O. Selznick in the 1940s determined that relatively few people had read *Jane Eyre* and that a movie based on the novel did not need to be especially faithful; on the other hand, Selznick had been a fanatic about maintaining fidelity in *Gone with the Wind* (1939) and *Rebecca* (1940) because he knew that a substantial part of the audience had read Margaret Mitchell's and Daphne du Maurier's bestselling books (Sconce, 140–62).

In addition to expanding the questions we ask, we need to augment the metaphors of translation and performance with the metaphor of intertextuality, or with what Mikhail Bakhtin called dialogics. This approach to adaptation is best demonstrated by Robert Stam, who emphasizes "the infinite and open-ended possibilities generated by all the discursive practices of a culture" and the "entire matrix of communicative utterances within which the artistic text is situated" (Stam, "Beyond Fidelity," 64). Stam takes us beyond simple attempts to compare "originals" with "transformations." If we followed his advice, adaptation study would be brought more into line with both contemporary theory and contemporary filmmaking. We now live in a media-saturated environment dense with cross-references and filled with borrowings from movies, books, video games, and every other form of representation. High modernism resisted adaptation and emphasized media-specific form, but postmodernism and the entertainment industry are bent on a busy crossbreeding between the media (thus satisfying the aims of late capitalism). Books can become movies, but movies themselves can also become novels, published screenplays, Broadway musicals, television shows, or remakes.

A minor but charmingly clever example of a film that reflects this protean, highly allusive environment is Richard Kwietniowski's *Love and Death on*

Long Island (1998), which tells the story of a sheltered British novelist who goes to see an E.M. Forster adaptation at the local Cineplex and wanders by mistake into *Hot Pants College II*. The novelist develops a crush on a young actor he sees on the screen, who reminds him of a Pre-Raphaelite painting of the death of Chatterton that he has seen in the Tate Gallery. I won't describe the plot any further, except to note that it's based on a novel by Gilbert Adair, which offers a rewriting of Mann's *Death in Venice* and Nabokov's *Lolita*. The film complicates things still more by introducing full-scale parodies of Hollywood B movies and TV sitcoms; it brings high culture and low culture, the literary and the cinematic, into ludic juxtaposition. Notice also that *Hot Pants College II*, the film that stimulates the lonely novelist's desire, is a sequel. On a theoretical level, sequels, remakes, parodies, and pastiches are quite similar to adaptations; they seldom if ever involve questions of media-specific form, but all are derivative or imitative, in danger of eliciting critical opprobrium because in one sense or another they copy "culturally treasured" originals. We need only compare the critical discourse surrounding Hitchcock's *Psycho*, a film adaptation that some American critics once regarded as a tasteless horror movie but that nearly everyone now acknowledges as a masterpiece, with the discourse surrounding both its sequels/prequel and its 1998 remake, which encountered nearly universal derision.

Viewed from the larger perspective of the engines of modernity, every movie tends to problematize originality and autonomy, if only because its photographs or digital images of the living world are taken out of their initial contexts. Walter Benjamin was aware of this phenomenon in his famous essay on mechanical reproduction, where he quotes Abel Gance's enthusiastic 1927 pronouncement, "Shakespeare, Rembrandt, Beethoven will make films." "Presumably without intending it," Benjamin remarks, Gance was issuing "a far-reaching liquidation" (151). André Bazin was aware of much the same issues in his 1948 essay on adaptation, to which I alluded at the beginning. In this remarkable essay, Bazin discusses adaptation mostly in terms of remediation (one of his examples is a concert orchestra broadcast over a radio) and asks us to think of film adaptations as similar to engravings that make the so-called original "readily accessible to all." Most discussion of such films, he notes, has been conducted on the level of formalist aesthetics, which is preoccupied with the nature of the "cinematic." But "one must first know," he writes, "to what end the adaptation is designed: for the cinema or its audience. One must also realize that most adaptors care far more about the latter than about the former" (Bazin, "Adaptation, or the Cinema as Digest," 44).

Bazin attacks the "clichéd bias according to which culture is inseparable from intellectual effort," and the "classical modes of cultural communication, which are at once a defense of culture and a secreting of it behind high walls" (45). He notes that adaptation has a number of important social functions, one of which, not always involving remediation, is directly pedagogical, taking the form of "digests" such as the "abridged" editions of classic literature used in classrooms. (Most film adaptations of novels are in fact digests or condensations of their sources, but one could add such things as *Classics Illustrated* comics, *Reader's Digest* condensed books, and plot summaries in *Cliff Notes*. Where the pedagogical uses of the digest are concerned, an interesting study could be written about the long and complex relationship between educational institutions and Hollywood. As one instance, Guerric DeBona has pointed out that David O. Selznick's 1935 adaptation of *David Copperfield* was marketed to high school English teachers by means of a free illustrated monograph on the art of cinematic adaptation, complete with study questions for students.) Still another function of adaptation, Bazin suggests, is in the creation of national imaginaries. How many of us have actually read *Moby Dick*, and how many of us have seen one of the comic-book, theatrical, TV, or film adaptations that give it a kind of mythic or folkloric significance for U.S. culture? Some of the most highly adaptable authors—Twain and Shakespeare are preeminent examples in the Anglo-American world—have been especially important to the formation of national identity, and for this reason it would be interesting to have more analysis of the ways books, plays, movies, and TV shows have been subject not only to remediation and remaking but also to cross-cultural or cross-national adaptation. Such uses are sometimes overlooked because of what Bazin refers to as "a rather modern notion for which the critics are in large part responsible: that of the untouchability of the work of art." The nineteenth century, he says, "firmly established an idolatry of form, mainly literary, that is still with us" (45). And the idolatry of form blinds us to the fact that all great novels—even the ones by Flaubert or Joyce—create characters that can be appropriated for many uses.

At this juncture and many others in his essay, Bazin sounds like a populist and a postmodernist. "The ferocious defense of literary works," he says, "is to a certain extent aesthetically justified; but we must also be aware that it rests on a rather recent, individualistic conception of the 'author' and the 'work,' a conception that was far from being ethically rigorous in the seventeenth century and that started to become legally defined only at the end of the eighteenth.... All things considered, it is possible to imagine that we are moving toward a reign of adaptation in which the notion of the unity of the work of art, if not the very notion of the author himself, will be destroyed" (49). Some people today believe we have already arrived at that point. I hope not, but it's time that writers on adaptation recognize what

Bazin saw in 1948. The study of adaptation needs to be joined with the study of recycling, remaking, and every other form of retelling in the age of mechanical reproduction and electronic communication. By this means, adaptation will become part of a general theory of repetition and will move from the margins to the center of media studies.

POSTSCRIPT

The argument above is a revised version of an introduction I wrote for *Film Adaptation*, published in 2000. Several books on adaptation were published in the wake of that volume, and I should mention a few particularly good ones here.

Robert Stam's *Literature through Film: Realism, Magic, and the Art of Adaptation* (2005) elaborates further on the theme of dialogism and intertextuality, in the process making significant contributions to the poetics of cinema and prose fiction. With Alessandra Raengo, Stam has also edited two large anthologies, *Literature and Film: A Guide to the Theory and Practice of Adaptation* (2005) and *A Companion to Literature and Film* (2005), both of which treat adaptation as what one of the writers, Dudley Andrew, calls "the life principle" of cultural production. Guerric DeBona's *Film Adaptation in the Hollywood Studio Era* (2010) is an incisive, well-researched account of "prestige" adaptations in classic Hollywood and is especially good at showing how the films in question were shaped not simply by their sources but by industrial and sociopolitical factors. Colin McCabe, Kathleen Murray, and Rick Warner are the editors of *True to the Spirit: Film Adaptation and the Question of Fidelity* (2011), which ends with an afterword by Fredric Jameson. In modernist fashion, and in contrast with most contemporary writers, Jameson argues that at some level all the individual media and their artists "seek each other's death, in the sense in which they brook no other gods besides themselves." The most productive course to follow in thinking about adaptation, he concludes, is to emphasize the "antagonism and incompatibility" between the media, at the same time insisting on the formal pleasures, ideological differences, and "psychoanalytic analysis or class receptivity" that become "most visible in the process of comparison" (231).

David Boyd and R. Barton Palmer have edited an intriguing anthology of essays on Hitchcock's adaptations, *Hitchcock at the Source: The Auteur as Adapter* (2011). A refreshingly wide-ranging discussion of literary and other kinds of cinematic adaptation is Thomas Leitch's *Film Adaptation and Its Discontents: From* Gone with the Wind *to* The Passion of the Christ (2007), which also offers a convincing argument about how the study of adaptation can help students write and think clearly. In addition to *Literature/Film Quarterly*, which has published scholarly articles on the subject since 1973, we now have *Adaptation*, which since 2008 has published articles on a variety of topics involving film and TV. But the recent theorist who most emphasizes the ubiquity of adaptation, covering everything from literature to Barbie dolls, is Linda Hutcheon in *A Theory of Adaptation* (2006). Hutcheon's concluding chapter poses the question "What is *not* an adaptation?" She defines the key term as "an extended, deliberate, announced revisitation of a particular work of art" (170); hence, for her, not all adaptations involve remediation (as examples, she cites J. M. Coetzee's *Foe* [1986], which revisits Daniel Defoe's *Robinson Crusoe* [1719], and Vincente Minnelli's *Four Horsemen of the Apocalypse* [1962], which remakes Rex Ingram's 1921 film of the same name). On the production side of adaptation, she points out, texts or works of art can be adjusted or altered by revision, editing, publication, display, and performance; on the reception side, they can be destabilized by translation, bowdlerization, censorship, and "cultural revision," in which receivers begin to refashion the initial works by remaking or remediating them. This "continuum model" offers several ways of thinking about adaptation—as retelling, rewriting, remediation, reinterpretation, and re-creation (172). Hutcheon also poses the question "What is the appeal of adaptations?" One of her answers, which requires that audiences know the source (often they do not), is that successful adaptations involve pleasures similar to theme and variation in music: "We find a story we like and then do variations on it.... It is not a copy in any mode of reproduction, mechanical or otherwise. It is repetition but without replication, bringing together the comfort of ritual and recognition with the delight of surprise and novelty" (173).

Finally, I should call attention to another of André Bazin's essays, "For an Impure Cinema: In Defense of Adaptation," which has been given a new translation by Timothy Barnard for *What Is Cinema* (2009), his English-language edition of *Qu'est-ce que le cinéma?* Although this essay is already well known, it deserves rereading, especially with Barnard's helpful editorial notes. Bazin gives us a salutary reminder that adaptation has a very old cultural history: like André Malraux, he describes Renaissance painting in its initial phase as an adaptation of Gothic sculpture, and he points out that Byzantine miniatures were enlarged in stone to the size of cathedral tympana. (He doesn't mention an equally early and perhaps even more striking example: *Le jeu d'Adam*, one of the oldest medieval mystery plays of the twelfth century, which dramatizes the Old Testament story of Adam and Eve.) His essay is filled with fine critical discrimination of individual film adaptations and also has interesting things to say about the relation between modernist literature and film. Unlike Claude-Edmonde Magny and most other critics, Bazin argues that cinema learned more from modern literature than modern literature learned from cinema: "It is impossible to tell whether *Manhattan Transfer* and *La Condition Humaine* (*Man's Fate*) would be very different without film, but I am certain that *The Power and the Glory* and *Citizen Kane* would never have been conceived without James Joyce and John Dos Passos" (120).

Notes on Acting in Cinema

Even a moment's observation should make it obvious that the art of acting is extremely important to most films, and yet critical literature on the subject is relatively sparse. There are excellent sociological studies of the star system and of individual stars, but not much close analysis of what actors do in specific films. In one sense, of course, movie actors are merely agents of narrative who are assisted by machinery; Lev Kuleshov famously attempted to prove that their performances can be constructed in the editing room, and Alfred Hitchcock once described them as experts in the art of "doing nothing extremely well." Nevertheless, the vast majority of films depend on a form of communication whereby meanings are acted out. The experience of watching them involves not only a pleasure in storytelling but also a delight in bodies, expressive movements, and familiar performing skills. Perhaps we also derive pleasure from the fact that films enable us to recognize and adapt to the fundamentally acted quality of everyday life: they place us safely outside dramatic events, a position from which we can observe people lying, concealing emotions, or staging performances for one another.

"Performance" is a much broader category than acting: we're all performers, and anyone who appears in a film, even an unwitting passerby on the street who is caught by the camera, becomes a sort of cinematic performer. Films also make use of acrobats, dancers, and concert musicians who perform much as they would on a stage and act in only a qualified sense. A person becomes a theatrical or cinematic actor of the sort discussed here when she or he functions as a developed character in a dramatic narrative. As with any other art form, there are no hard-and-fast rules for what constitutes the best film acting of this type. Certain players of the classic Hollywood era—I would name Peter Lorre, Agnes Moorehead, and Mickey Rooney—create such vivid characters that they make every film they are in, no matter how good or bad, slightly better; but the dogs who played Rin Tin Tin, Asta, and

Lassie were also fine actors in the context of their particular films, and nonprofessionals have given impressive performances in fiction pictures.

All good movie actors understand the characters they play, move to the marks that have been placed for them on the floor of the set, and have the ability to use props and costumes in expressive ways. Only occasionally do they abandon their normal mannerisms and impersonate recognizable historical figures: Helen Mirren's portrayal of Queen Elizabeth II in *The Queen* (2006) is a fine example of movie impersonation because it only suggests Elizabeth without slavishly imitating her. Awards are often given for this or any other kind of performance that makes the work of the actor clearly visible, as when the actor gains or loses weight, speaks with an accent, or pretends drunkenness or deformity. Acting is also made visible by dual roles or by performances within the performance. In *Mulholland Drive* (2001), for example, Naomi Watts plays two different personalities, one of whom is a perky young aspirant to Hollywood fame who auditions for a role in a movie at Paramount. When she prepares for the audition she interprets her lines literally and speaks in a big, angry voice; when she arrives at the studio, she whispers the same lines in a steamy voice and gives them erotic implication. We view the first performance-within-a-performance as "bad" acting and the second as "good" acting, but both are important to the film and Watts performs them equally well.

Film stars are actors (sometimes very good ones), but they are also iconic, extracinematic characters; their names circulate through all the media, their mannerisms become as familiar as those of the people we know intimately, and the screenplays of their films are often written to conform to the personality-images they've established. Their appearances on screen always create a double impression: it's John Wayne getting on a horse in *The Searchers*, not simply Ethan Edwards (Wayne is "played" by a man whose real name was Marion Morrison). Because of this effect, the star can show off acting skill by occasionally changing the sort of character she or he plays. Many of the best actor-stars—Marilyn Monroe, for example—create a single character type that they play brilliantly and definitively over and over, sometimes becoming prisoners of their creation. At an opposite extreme is a figure such as Johnny Depp, a "postmodern" performer who has managed to become a chameleon and a star at the same time. There would seem to be no recipe for what makes a star, beyond a certain level of charisma. In most cases the performer needs the requisite glamour and sex appeal to play leading roles in heterosexual romances and action-adventure pictures, but there are many exceptions: Shirley Temple, Marie Dressler, Will Rogers, and Bob Hope were all leading players and major box-office attractions in their day.

It has often been argued that the most cinema-specific form of acting is much less ostentatious and gestural than acting on the stage—more like Naomi Watts's studio audition in *Mulholland Drive*. V.I. Pudovkin, who wrote an early treatise on the subject, contended that films were ideal vehicles for what the celebrated theatrical director Konstantin Stanislavsky had described as "gestureless moments"—scenes involving "extreme paucity of gesture, often literal immobility," as in the cinematic close-up, when "the body of the actor is simply not seen" (334–35). One can think of many examples of film stars who seem to be merely *thinking* for the camera, or of performers who achieve an emotional subtext through minimal gestures. Yet the exhibitionistic Fred Astaire is as important a screen actor as the supposedly introspective Marlon Brando, and Astaire's work is entirely dependent upon graceful, highly stylized movements of his body—not only in dance scenes, but also when he merely lights a cigarette, sits in a chair, or crosses from point A to point B.

Realistic films favor restraint, as one can see in Heath Ledger's performance in *Brokeback Mountain* (2005), in which the character's tumultuous emotions are as tightly controlled as a closed fist; but comedies, musicals, and costume pictures often encourage a "stagy" style, as in the case of Steve Martin's wild abandon in *The Jerk* (1979). In fact, most movies contain a heterogeneous mix of performing styles and skills. Hollywood in the studio period usually required that supporting players, ethnic minorities, and women act in more vividly expressive fashion than white male leads, and the range of expressive behavior can be quite broad even in Method-influenced pictures: in *On the Waterfront* (1954), Marlon Brando is recessive but Lee J. Cobb chews the scenery. Notice also that certain directors impose differing styles on ensembles. By most accounts Fritz Lang was a sadistic personality who moved actors like puppets and Robert Altman was a sweetheart who gave them a great deal of freedom; this may explain the geometric rigidity of the blocking in a Lang film versus the roaming, freewheeling movements in an Altman film. Orson Welles wanted his players to execute actions quickly and overlap dialogue in a carefully planned fashion; Stanley Kubrick, who resembles Welles in some respects, favored an unusually slow, measured pace and actors who displayed over-the-top mugging (George C. Scott in *Dr. Strangelove* [1963]) or deadpan minimalism (Keir Dullea in *2001: A Space Odyssey* [1968]).

These qualifications and variations aside, the history of both stage and film acting since the late nineteenth century can be said to involve a movement from a semiotic to a psychological conception of performance, or from what Roberta Pearson terms a "histrionic code" to a "verisimilar code"—a phenomenon determined by changes in dramatic literature and the culture as a whole. The shift appears to have begun in the theater of the 1850s, with the rise of the "well-made" drawing-room drama, but it became most apparent in the period between 1880 and 1920 in the work of Stanislavsky and his followers. For at least two thousand years previously, acting was closely related to dance and oratorical rhetoric (the very word *actor* originally suggested the *actions* of oratory), and the major form of actor training was instruction in elocution and pantomime, in which the actor learned "proper" diction and a vocabulary of bodily and facial expressions. One of the most important representatives of this pantomime school in the nineteenth century was François Delsarte, a Parisian elocutionist who made one of the earliest attempts to codify expressive gestures and who exerted an indirect influence on the whole of silent cinema. The Delsarte system was adapted to American theater by Steele MacKaye, the immediate predecessor of David Belasco, and it resulted in numerous "cookbook" manuals of acting, such as Edmund Shaftesbury's *Lessons in the Art of Acting* (1889) and Charles Aubert's *The Art of Pantomime* (translated into English in 1921). The system often reinforced social stereotypes or genteel mannerisms, but it was well suited to silent cinema and at its best produced remarkable performances: Lillian Gish's eloquently expressive close-ups, Charlie Chaplin's balletic comedy, Lon Chaney's grotesque movement in horror films, and so forth. Its last flowering was in German expressionism, which arrived at an approximately Delsarte-like technique via a different, modernist aesthetic; examples include *The Cabinet of Dr. Caligari* (1920), in which Conrad Veidt moves with the languorous rhythms of a trained dancer, and *Metropolis* (1927), in which the entire cast gestures in the boldest, most elemental fashion.

Relatively few actors in talking films worked along such lines (Greta Garbo and Marlene Dietrich are qualified examples), but the pantomimic or histrionic style was sometimes adopted for ironic or thematic purposes, as in Gloria Swanson's flamboyant behavior in *Sunset Blvd.* (1950) or Robert Mitchum's frightening performance in *Night of the Hunter* (1955), which is a particularly clever fusion of old-fashioned melodrama and Germanic expressionism. These, however, are distinct exceptions to the rule. In general, a certain tendency toward verisimilar or naturalistic acting—a movement from "presentational" to "representational" performance—was at work from the origins of the classic narrative cinema. Like Stanislavsky, D.W. Griffith was interested in making blocking less artificial and acting more intimate and emotionally charged, and at each stage of cinema's technical history these general aims were increasingly facilitated. The earliest, so-called "primitive," films were devoted to straightforward action sequences, paying little or no attention to psychological motivation; the camera was usually situated at least twelve feet from the players, who moved parallel to the camera, stood in three-quarter profile when they addressed one another, and gesticulated broadly. After 1909, the camera began to move closer; the subsequent development of continuity editing, and especially of shot/reverse shot, enabled directors to reduce the amount of visibly rhetorical blocking and track the psychological nuances on the actor's faces in a pattern of action and reaction. When sound was introduced, an elocutionary style of speech was favored, but the invention of sensitive directional microphones eventually transformed the "grain" of the voice and the subtler levels of timbre into important expressive instruments. A wide range of rural or working-class accents became acceptable, and multitrack sound editing, looping, and sound mixing were used to record ordinary, low-key behavior in ways that would have dazzled Stanislavsky.

Films continued to use wide shots, and directors such as Howard Hawks and John Ford were especially good at bringing the actors' bodies into play. In a Hawks film, as has often been observed, characterizations usually arise from the way characters walk, sit, or perform small actions such as tossing a coin or striking a match; and in Ford there are many family rituals and communal dance scenes in which sharply individuated characters interact in the same shot. By the end of the twentieth century, however, the conjunction of digital editing systems with television-style shooting techniques, in which scenes are photographed with multiple cameras and long lenses, led to what David Bordwell calls "intensified" continuity editing, especially in large-budget Hollywood features. "Continuity cutting," Bordwell observes, "has been rescaled and amped up, and the drama has been squeezed down to faces—particularly eyes and mouths" (*Figures Traced in Light*, 27). Big-budget movie directors usually strive for close-up "coverage" of each line of dialogue and facial reaction, using multiple cameras and small wireless microphones attached to the bodies of the actors. As a result close-ups dominate, space is flattened, backgrounds are blurred, and the average shot length is shortened (most images are held on the screen for somewhere between two and eight seconds). In this environment movie stars such as Tom Cruise are valued for the intensity they bring to the smallest twitch of an eyebrow.

The apotheosis of what might be called the inner-directed, Stanislavskian approach to acting, which can be a useful training for the kind of movies that center on microscopic facial expression, was the American "Method," particularly as taught by Lee Strasberg at the Actors Studio in New York in the late 1940s and 1950s. Much was written in the popular press in those years about the "mumbling" and "shambling" of Actors Studio–trained actors, but such behavior was more advertised than practiced. Brando's clever performances as an inarticulate, sexy proletarian in *On the Waterfront*, *A Streetcar Named Desire* (1951), and *The Wild One* (1953) inspired the popular conception of the Method, but his greater importance was as a rebel celebrity who indicated a seismic shift in U.S. popular culture; he represented a new personality that was related not only to the emerging postwar bohemia and the fashion for existential *Angst*, but also to the rise of rock-and-roll figures such as Elvis Presley. Where Brando's acting style is concerned, Richard Dyer is correct to say that "the formal differences between the Method and, say, the repertory/Broadway style are less clear than the known differences between how the performances were arrived at" (*Stars*, 154). Shelley Winters, for example, was much more closely connected to Strasberg and the Actors Studio than Brando ever was, and yet Winters is seldom described as a Method actor.

Method training undoubtedly contributed to "lifelike" performances and enabled actors to fine-tune their delicate psychological instruments. It inspired a large number of extremely talented players over the next two generations (see virtually the entire cast of *The Godfather* [1972] and *The Godfather: Part II* [1974], in which Strasberg makes an effective appearance), but it also fostered a neglect of the physical training associated with the older pantomime tradition. In Strasberg's hands, it was narrowed down to a quasi-Freudian or therapeutic preoccupation with "emotional memory," and most of its jargon—"private moment," "freedom," "naturalness," "organic"—had a familiar ring, as they were the keywords of romantic individualism. There was, however, another form of acting, developed by the twentieth-century avant-garde and inspired by such popular institutions as the music hall, the circus, and vaudeville, which represented a counterapproach to Stanislavsky. In the period of the Russian Revolution, for instance, Vsevolod Meyerhold tried to create gymnastic actors who represented a proletarian ideal, and in the same period the Soviet and Italian futurists advocated styles of performance drawn from the variety theater, the early "cinema of attractions," and the American comedy films of Mack Sennett. The Stanislavskian actor and the Meyerholdian actor worked from different physical assumptions (Stanislavsky stressed relaxation and Meyerhold stressed dynamic, machinelike action), and in practice they could look as different from one another as Brando and Buster Keaton. In subsequent years Sergei Eisenstein and Bertolt Brecht, who were both influenced by futurist theater, became interested in the stylized acting of ancient Asia. Brecht was an especially important theorist of an antinaturalistic, antibourgeois form of performance in which ideology was never concealed by realistic illusion.

Although Brecht recognized that some degree of realism was essential to a committed drama and to popular taste, he emphasized that actors should produce *signs* (the most important of these he termed the *gestus*), and he wanted his players to feel an emotional estrangement from their roles, an "alienation effect" that made their performances presentational and didactic. Perhaps the best-known exponent of Brechtian acting in cinema is Jean-Luc Godard, especially in films such as *Two or Three Things I Know about Her* (1966), in which Marina Vlady and the other actors step in and out of their roles and frequently address the camera directly. A different but equally radical style can be seen in some of the films of Robert Bresson, who often worked with amateur players and who advocated a form of "automatism," in which the actor was instructed to think less about emotion than about gesture. (Alfred Hitchcock, who worked with Hollywood stars, resembled Bresson in the sense that he was impatient with Method-trained performers and was chiefly interested in actors who could produce elemental looks and gestures suitable for carefully edited sequences.)

Nearly all comic actors in film, especially "crazy" comics such as the Marx brothers and Jerry Lewis, employ a style that is entirely different from specialists in Stanislavskian drama. By its very nature comedy tends to be physically exaggerated, presentational, aimed at the head rather than the heart, and deconstructive of realistic conventions. Realistic acting strives for absolute expressive coherence between one shot and the next, or for a type of performance-within-performance in which the character's "act" for other characters is plausible and convincing: see, for example, the poker-faced calm of Walter Neff (Fred MacMurray) in *Double Indemnity* (1944), when a man who might identify him as a killer is brought to his office for questioning. By contrast, broadly comic films often depend on exaggerated forms of expressive incoherence, as when Peter Sellers, in the role of Dr. Strangelove, has to keep beating one of his arms down to keep it from springing up into a Nazi salute.

Since the late 1960s, there has been something of a return to movement-based, physical training of actors, a tendency prompted by such diverse figures from theater as Rudolf Laban, Jacques Lecoq, Joan Littlewood, and Julie Taymor. By the same token, several developments in digital technology—in particular CGI (computer-generated imagery), green-screen techniques, and motion-capture devices—have contributed to an increased interest in pantomime. Some writers have reacted to these developments by suggesting that the new technology is a threat to the very profession of acting. In support of their argument they point out that crowd scenes larger than Cecil B. DeMille could achieve are now composed of nothing but computerized figures, and that the face of the dead Oliver Reed has been pasted onto the moving body of a stand-in. Industrial society has entered an increasingly "robotic" stage of development, and digital animators the world over have spoken of their desire to achieve the holy grail of "synthespians" who seamlessly interact with human players. Whether or not CGI is qualitatively new and will lead to such a future, it certainly increases the amount of animation in movies. We should recall, however, that animators have often worked in collaboration with actors: in 1938, for example, the Walt Disney animators copied the photographed movement of dancer Marge Champion in order to create the "lifelike" figure of Snow White. (For an important discussion of acting and animation, see Donald Crafton's *Shadow of a Mouse* [2012].) CGI belongs squarely within this tradition, and even though it's often used to show morphing androids and missing body parts, it probably won't involve the elimination of human players. Most digital effects are recognizable, and from the time of *The Golem* (1920) and *Metropolis* to the time of *Blade Runner* (1982) and *Bicentennial Man* (1999), robots and simulacra have been acted by professional thespians. CGI has not so much replaced actors as required them to behave like animated figures or machines.

An obvious case in point is the *Terminator* series, in which Arnold Schwarzenegger's visibly "manufactured" physique and stiff acting fit perfectly with the computer-generated effects. An even better example is the Steven Spielberg / Stanley Kubrick production of *A.I. Artificial Intelligence* (2001). Spielberg, who inherited the project after Kubrick's death, knew that computer animation has yet to prove that it can create believable human figures in speaking roles. (One of the most elaborate attempts to do so is *Final Fantasy: The Spirits Within* [2001], a sci-fi adventure based on video games, which uses the voices of several well-known players but looks animated.) As a result, the robot is played by Haley Joel Osment, whose performance is especially interesting for the way it starts with a slightly digitalized, pantomimic style, very similar to what the Russian futurists called "bio-mechanics," and then shifts, at the moment when the robot's circuits are imprinted with Oedipal desire, into an analog, Stanislavskian style that supposedly reveals his inner life or soul. (Even in the final stage of his development, he never blinks his eyes.)

A similar reversion to uncanny forms of pantomime can be seen in Peter Jackson's *The Two Towers* (2002), for which Andy Serkis invented both a voice and a set of body movements to structure the computer animation for his character, Gollum. (New Line Cinema aggressively but unsuccessfully campaigned to have Serkis nominated for an Academy Award.) Ultimately, Gollum was created from a mixture of sculpture, puppetry, and digital effects, with Serkis donning a motion-capture suit and interacting with the other players on the set. Serkis also provided the "psychological" expressions that signify his character's split personality. To further elaborate these expressions, the animators consulted Gary Faigin's *The Artist's Complete Guide to Facial Expression* and Paul Ekman's *Darwin and Facial Expression*, two modern books that attempt to codify the semiotics of the face in much the same fashion as François Delsarte attempted to codify actors' gestures for the nineteenth-century stage. In other words, the digital era, coupled with the rise of fantasy and comic-strip films of various kinds, seems to involve a qualified return to a style that predates Stanislavsky. In some cases it causes human actors to behave like clockwork instruments, but it also expands the range of performance styles. Comic-book spectaculars, for instance, can give players an opportunity to show off their skills in dual roles or to behave expressionistically. (In *RoboCop* [1987] Peter Weller imitates Nikolai Cherkasov in Eisenstein's *Ivan the Terrible* [1943].)

Richard Linklater's *Waking Life* (2001) uses mini–digital cameras to record a series of actors speaking improvised monologues or dialogues, which it then transforms through digital rotoscoping techniques into colorful, animated imagery; this film contains a monologue about André Bazin, and everywhere it demonstrates how advanced technology can reveal the sign-making activity behind realist acting. Eric Rohmer's *The Lady and the Duke* (2001) is a costume drama set during the French Revolution, and, like most of Rohmer's work, it involves actors seated in rooms holding long, realistic conversations; but it also uses digital video and computerized imaging to create a visibly artificial, painterly mise-en-scène around the actors. Robert Rodriguez and Frank Miller's *Sin City* (2005) is even more radical in its transformation of actors into cartoon-like characters who inhabit a world of boldly graphic designs. Where more avant-garde experiments are concerned, Michael Snow's **Corpus Callosum* (2002) serves as a compendium of things that can be done with computer technology to bend, reshape, and manipulate human bodies. If these four examples are an indication, acting is crucial to the digital age. It would of course be possible to make digital films without actors, but that was true of motion picture photography. In any case, at the historical moment when analog human players seem about to be replaced by digital images, the players are with us as much as ever.

Imitation, Eccentricity, and Impersonation in Movie Acting

From the eighteenth until the early twentieth century, the Aristotelian concept of mimesis governed most aesthetic theory, and stage acting was often described as an "imitative art." Denis Diderot's "Paradoxe sur le comédien" (1758), for example, argued that the best theater actors played not from personal emotions or "sensibility," but from "imitation" (Cole and Chinoy, 162). According to Diderot, actors who depended too much upon their emotions were prone to lose control, couldn't summon the same feelings repeatedly, and were likely to alternate between sublime and flat performances in the same play; properly imitative actors, on the other hand, were rational observers of both human nature and social conventions who developed imaginary models of dramatic characters and, by imitating those models, reproduced the same nuances of behavior and colors of emotion every evening.

For centuries actors on the stage were taught to imitate a vocabulary of gestures and poses, and certain variations on the theory of acting as imitation persisted into modern times, as in the essays on aesthetics in the 1880 and 1911 editions of *The Encyclopedia Britannica*, which try to distinguish between the mimetic arts and the "symbolic" or abstract arts; in both editions, acting is described as an "imitative art" dependent upon and subordinate to the higher art of poetry. At a still later date, Brecht went so far as to argue that not only fictional characters but also everyday personalities and emotions are developed through a process of imitation: "The human being copies gesture, miming, tones of voice. And weeping arises from sorrow, but sorrow also arises from weeping" (152). For the past seventy or eighty years, however, the dominant forms of actor training in the United States have minimized or even denied the importance of imitation and the related arts of mimicry, mime, and impersonation. "The actor does not need to imitate a human being," Lee Strasberg famously declared. "The actor is himself a human being and can create out of himself" (Cole and Chinoy,

623). More recently, the website of a San Francisco acting school specializing in the Sanford Meisner technique (named for a legendary New York teacher of stage and screen performers) announced that its students would be taught to "live truthfully under imaginary circumstances" and to "express oneself while 'playing' imaginary circumstances" (www.themeisnertechniquestudio.com).

The change of emphasis from imitation to expression is due in part to motion pictures. Filmed performances are identical at every showing, making Diderot's paradox appear irrelevant, and movie close-ups of actors reveal the subtlest emotions, giving weight to the idiosyncrasies of personal expression. But the shift toward personally expressive acting precedes the movies. The first manifestations of the change appeared in the second half of the nineteenth century, with new forms of stage lighting, Henrik Ibsen's psychological dramas, William Archer's call for actors to "live the part," and Konstantin Stanislavsky's introspective naturalism. By the late 1930s, when variants of Stanislavsky's ideas were fully absorbed into U.S. theater and Hollywood achieved hegemony over the world's talking pictures, dramatic acting was nearly always evaluated in terms of naturalness, sincerity, and emotional truth of expression. A kind of artistic revolution had occurred, which, in some of its manifestations, was akin to the victory of romanticism over classicism at the beginning of the nineteenth century. As M.H. Abrams explains in a famous study of that earlier revolution, the metaphor of art as a mirror reflecting the world was replaced by the metaphor of art as a lamp projecting individual emotions into the world. "Imitation" became associated with such words as "copy," "substitute," "fake," and even "counterfeit." (Notice also that in some contexts the related term "impersonation" now signifies an illegal act.) The new forms of psychological realism, on the other hand, were associated with such words as "genuine," "truthful," "organic," "authentic," and "real." Thus V.I. Pudovkin's early book on film acting championed Stanislavsky's idea that "an actor striving toward truth should be able to avoid the element of *portraying* his feelings to the audience" (334), and in the theater the Actors Studio advocated the development of "private moments" and "organic naturalness."

The romantic revolution was concurrent with the democratic and scientific revolutions, which also changed attitudes toward "innovation," a term that had been reviled in the writings of Francis Bacon, Thomas Hobbes, and even Shakespeare, but which in the nineteenth century became a signifier of artistic achievement. As René Girard points out, however, where art is concerned, innovation depends upon an imitative or mimetic relationship between new work and prior models: "The main prerequisite for real innovation [in art] is a minimal respect for the past and a mastery of its achievements, that is, *mimesis*" (244). The postmodern spread of pastiche and quotation might be said to involve a return to just this sort of mastery, but postmodernism relies upon a quality of irony or knowingness quite different from the classical arts.

The irony of the situation is that classicism and romanticism have always been two sides of the same coin. As Raymond Williams convincingly argues in *Culture and Society* (1958), the eighteenth-century doctrine of imitation was never intended as slavish adherence to a set of rules or to previous works of art; at its best, it was a set of precepts that were supposed to help artists achieve what Aristotle called "universals." But romanticism also claimed to be dealing with universals; the imitative tradition and the cult of personal expression were therefore equally idealistic and equally committed to a representation of what they regarded as essential reality. Where the history of acting is concerned, the major difference between these two schools is that the former claims to be Plato's "second nature," achieved by mimesis, and the latter claims to be original nature, achieved by playing "oneself."

Both approaches to performance are capable of producing good acting, and in practice most modern actors are pragmatic rather than doctrinaire, willing to use whatever technique works in particular circumstances. In fact, a great many films require a mixture of naturalistic and imitative techniques. Consider Barbara Loden's raw, disturbing, utterly natural-looking performance in the title role of *Wanda* (1971), a film Loden also wrote and directed: she probably makes use of Method-style "sensory memory" to help create states of fatigue and hunger (as in the scene in which she sops up spaghetti sauce with bread and chews with gusto while also smoking a cigarette), but her performance also involves mimicry of a regional, working-class accent.

Although the technique of imitation and the technique of personal feeling are often opposed to one another by theorists, they aren't mutually exclusive; it's quite possible for pantomime artists or actors who use conventional gestures to "live the part" and emotionally project "themselves" into their roles. A remarkable testimony to this phenomenon has been given to us by Martin LaSalle, the leading "model" in Robert Bresson's *Pickpocket* (1959). LaSalle wasn't a professional actor when the picture was made and he found himself serving as a kind of puppet, executing whatever movements and poses Bresson asked of him. His performance is minimalist, seldom changing its expressive quality; at one point he sheds tears, but most of the time his off-screen narration, spoken quite calmly, serves to inform us of the intense emotions his character feels but doesn't obviously show on his face or in his voice. And yet LaSalle creates a memorably soulful effect, reminiscent in some ways of the young Montgomery Clift. In 1990, when documentary filmmaker Babette Mangolte tracked down

LaSalle in Mexico, where he has worked for many years as a film and theater actor, he described how the experience of *Pickpocket* had marked his entire life. He recalled that Bresson told his "models" to repeat actions over and over, never explaining why; at one point he shot forty takes of LaSalle doing nothing more than walking up a stairway. The technique nevertheless had emotional consequences for the actor. LaSalle believed that Bresson was trying to provoke "an inner tension that would be seen in the hands and eyes," as if he wanted to "weaken the ego of the 'model,'" thereby inducing "doubt," "anxiety," and "anguish tinged with pleasure." Although the performance was achieved through a sort of pantomime or rote repetition of prescribed gestures and looks, it was by no means unfeeling. "I felt the tension of the pickpocket," LaSalle told Mangolte. "I think, even if we are only models, as [Bresson] says, we still take part in and internalize the activity. I felt as if I were living the situation, not externally but in a sensory way." The astonishing result was that after *Pickpocket* LaSalle moved to New York and studied for four years at The Actors Studio with Lee Strasberg, who became the second great influence on his career.

As important as deeply felt emotion may be to a performer, there's something disingenuous about the modern pedagogical tendency to devalue imitation, for we can find many instances in which movie actors, even naturalistic ones, are required to perform imitative tasks: depending on the situation, they can be called upon to mimic accents and physical signifiers of age, social class, gender, and sexuality; to deliberately emphasize conventional poses and gestures; to "act" for other characters in visibly artificial ways; to imitate models of "themselves" by repeating personal eccentricities from role to role; and to impersonate historical figures or other actors.

We need only think of film comedy, which often involves the foregrounding of stereotypical behavior and the mechanics of performance. Alec Guinness, a distinguished stage actor whose work in dramatic films depended upon minimalism and British reserve, was one of the most natural-looking performers in screen history, yet he performed in a manifestly imitative way when he played comedy rather than drama. As George Smiley, the leading character in the British television adaptation of John le Carré's *Tinker, Tailor, Soldier, Spy* (1989), Guinness is so quiet, so natural, so lacking in energetic movement and obvious emotion, that he makes the actors around him look like Dickensian caricatures; he reveals a repressed emotional intensity only when he makes slight adjustments of his eyeglasses and bowler hat. Contrast his performance in Alexander Mackendrick's dark comedy *The Ladykillers* (1955): as the leader of a group of crooks who rent a room from a harmless little old lady, he wears comic buck teeth and sinister eye makeup, and his interactions with the landlady overflow with fake sincerity and oily sweetness. As Pudovkin might say, he *portrays* feelings so that the audience, if not the naïve old lady, can see his absurdly unconvincing act.

The burlesque comic Ed Wynn once distinguished between joke-telling clowns and comic actors. The first type, Wynn explained, says and does funny things, and the second type says and does things *funnily.* The distinction doesn't quite hold, because comic actors sometimes also say or do funny things; even so, light-comic genres often depend upon performers who can execute ordinary movements and expressions in amusing ways, as if "quoting" conventions. Ernst Lubitsch's Paramount musicals of the early 1930s are clear examples, requiring the actors to behave in a chic but visibly imitative style. In *The Love Parade* (1930), which employs a good deal of silent pantomime, Maurice Chevalier is cast as a Parisian playboy and military attaché to the unmarried and sexually yearning Queen of Sylvania, played by Jeanette MacDonald. When the two characters meet, their comically stiff formality soon dissolves into flirtation and then into a duet entitled "Anything to Please the Queen." Throughout, their every intonation and expression is so heightened and intensified that there's barely any difference between talking and singing. In the slightly later *One Hour with You* (1932), everyone poses, speaks, sings, and exchanges glances in this imitative fashion, heightened by moments of rhymed dialogue and direct address to the audience. Chevalier and MacDonald play a happily married couple whose relationship is threatened when the wife's sexually promiscuous best friend (Genevieve Tobin) secretly decides to seduce the husband. In the first scene involving the three, Lubitsch creates a gallery of conventionally expressive close-ups and obvious displays of body language. MacDonald stands with her arm around Tobin and smiles in delight as she shows off Chevalier. "Look at him!" she says proudly, "Isn't he darling?" In close-up, Chevalier looks down at the floor and gives an exaggeratedly modest, shy smile. Cut to Tobin, who slyly smiles and remarks, "I think he's cute." Cut to Chevalier, who becomes uncomfortable, squirming and frowning. MacDonald whispers something in Tobin's ear while Tobin stares at Chevalier, clearly impressed. "Oh!" she says, eyes widening in surprise. Another close-up shows Chevalier, still frowning but looking more puzzled and concerned. MacDonald whispers again. "He can?" Tobin asks, looking Chevalier up and down in frank wonder and admiration. "Yes, he can!" says MacDonald proudly. In his next close-up, Chevalier is baffled and open-mouthed. "Let's see him do it!" Tobin cries in delight. MacDonald crosses to Chevalier and sweetly pleads, "Darling, look like an owl!"

Lubitsch's nonmusical comedy *Trouble in Paradise* (1932) might seem different because it's filled with Samson Raphaelson's witty dialogue, but it, too, involves imitation. In an opening scene, Herbert Marshall stands in the moonlight on the balcony of a hotel in Venice, looking down at the Grand Canal as an obsequious waiter hovers behind his shoulder, addresses him as "Baron," and offers to serve him:

WAITER: Yes, Baron, what shall we start with, Baron?

BARON: Hmm? Oh, yes. That's not so easy. Beginnings are always difficult.

WAITER: Yes, Baron.

BARON: If Casanova suddenly turned out to be Romeo, having supper with Juliet, who might become Cleopatra, how would you start?

WAITER: I would start with cocktails.

BARON: Excellent. It must be the most marvelous supper. We may not eat it, but it must be marvelous.

WAITER: Yes, Baron.

BARON: And waiter?

WAITER: Yes, Baron?

BARON: You see that moon?

WAITER: Yes, Baron.

BARON: I want to see that moon in the champagne.

WAITER: Yes, Baron. (Writes.) Moon in champagne.

BARON: I want to see, umm.

WAITER: Yes, Baron?

BARON: And as for you, waiter . . .

WAITER: Yes, Baron?

BARON: I don't want to see you at all.

WAITER: No, Baron.

Amusing as the words are, the charm of the scene has as much to do with Marshall's performance, which epitomizes the popular 1930s idea of ultra-cosmopolitan masculinity. His well-cut tuxedo, his slicked-back hair, and his elegant pose, with one hand holding a cigarette and the other in a jacket pocket, all create an air of sophistication befitting an advertisement in a luxury magazine. Marshall also speaks amusing*ly*, in a plummy English accent, almost singing his lines in a tone of worldly, romantic melancholy. In keeping with the dialogue, he's too good to be real. Indeed, we soon learn that he's not a baron but a jewel thief, perfectly suited to a film in which almost all the characters are pretending or wearing social masks.

Another form of imitation can be seen when actors play characters that try to hide their true feelings from one another or that put on a comic or ironic act—something that inevitably occurs in films that have theater or playacting as a subject. Such films often make it difficult to distinguish truth from pretense. In *All about Eve* (1950), for example, Bette Davis plays an aging theatrical star threatened by the offstage machinations of an apparently naïve and worshipful young understudy, played by Anne Baxter. Baxter's performance is cleverly balanced between innocence and gimlet-eyed guile, so that we glimpse just a hint of her deception even when it fools others. Discovered as a waif standing in the rain outside a theater, she's invited into Davis's dressing room, where the star's director-husband and a famous playwright have gathered after the show. Humble and shy, she passionately praises Davis and flatters everyone else in the room, converting them into a hushed audience curious to hear the story of her life. Just as her story begins, Thelma Ritter, in the role of Davis's dresser and maid, suddenly enters and briefly disturbs the expectant mood. After a pause, Baxter proceeds: she's a poor farmer's daughter from Wisconsin who has always loved theater but took a job as a secretary in a brewery to help support her family; there she met and married her husband, Eddie, who also loved theater. But World War II intervened, and Eddie was killed in the South Pacific. Since then, she's been finding work wherever she can and attending Davis's performances at every opportunity. She tells all this with an absence of self-pity and an idealistic, worshipful attitude toward the stage, where "the unreal seemed more real to me." There are several clues that she's giving a performance: she's a bit too pretty and nicely made up, her voice is a bit too cultivated and melodic, and her story contains a few too many sentimental clichés. Even so, she causes Bette Davis, whose face is covered with cold cream, to pluck a tissue from a box and wipe a tear from her eye. Thelma Ritter, a woman who has seen many actors come and go, is also impressed. "What a story!" she sighs. "Everything but the bloodhounds snapping at her rear end!"

If *All about Eve* concerns an actor who feigns emotion, *Being Julia* (2004), adapted from Somerset Maugham's novel *Theatre*, concerns an actor whose excess of real emotion threatens to undermine her performances. Annette Bening plays a middle-aged British stage star of the 1930s, a larger-than-life character endowed with innate theatricality and acute emotional sensitivity. The realistic performance requires Bening to imitate certain conventional models; she must adopt a British accent, and her every gesture and expression, both onstage and off, must suggest the fragile histrionics of an aging diva. When we first see her, she makes a grand entrance into her husband-impresario's office, complaining with intense bravura that she's exhausted and in need of a rest. That evening she goes to an elegant restaurant and makes another grand entrance, smiling and nodding to acknowledge her admiring public; but when her homosexual dinner companion tells her that to avoid gossip they shouldn't keep seeing one another, she breaks into copious tears.

The ensuing plot concerns her affair with an American fan, barely older than her adolescent son, who seduces her and then turns her into a miserable, sexually dependent slave. When the affair begins, she's lifted out of a mild depression and becomes giddy and girlish; but when her lover withdraws and treats her coldly, she becomes a haggard, weeping neurotic, alternately angry and groveling. What helps her conquer the roller coaster of emotion is her memory of a long-dead director and mentor (Michael Gambon), who magically appears as a sort of ghost in moments of crisis, criticizing her everyday performance and dispensing advice. Gambon is a projection of her own critical self-consciousness, an internal monitor or coach, created through her professional ability to mentally observe her performances as they happen, both onstage and in real life. In Denis Diderot's words, Julia has within herself, like all the best actors, "an unmoved and disinterested onlooker" (Cole and Chinoy, 162). At her most anguished point, when she's weeping hysterically, Gambon appears and mocks her ability to "turn on the waterworks." He advises her to become a more imitative actor, exactly the sort of player Diderot might have admired: "You've got to learn to *seem* to do it—that's the art of acting! Hold the mirror up to nature, ducky. Otherwise you become a nervous wreck." In the film's concluding moments, this advice enables her to emerge victorious not only in her private life but also on the stage, where her lover's new girlfriend has been cast alongside her.

The stage acting in *Being Julia*, shown in close-ups, is manifestly artificial and full of tricks: we see heavy makeup on the actors' faces, we hear the actors' loud voices projected toward the theater auditorium, and we glimpse Bening struggling with a misplaced prop during a tearful scene. In the offstage sequences, however, the acting looks realistic and the emotions are sometimes expressed in nakedly exposed style. In the scene in which Bening has her tearful breakdown, she wears no apparent makeup and her pale skin becomes red and blotchy as she weeps. We can never know (without asking her) how this scene was achieved—she may have been feigning emotion, she may have been playing "herself" in imaginary circumstances, and she may have been doing both. No matter how she accomplished her task, her performance looks spontaneous, as if she were *being* Julia rather than imitating her.

At the same time, the audience recognizes Julia as Annette Bening, whose body and expressive attributes can be seen in other films. Her apparent authenticity of feeling, which earned her an Academy Award nomination for *Being Julia*, is essential to the cinema of sentiment or high emotion and is valued in all of today's popular genres; but the doubling or tandem effect of recognizing Bening alongside the character has a longer history, essential to the development of the star system and to the pleasures of theater itself. It achieved great prominence in the eighteenth century, at the time of Diderot, when leading actors such as David Garrick not only imitated Hamlet but also brought individual style or personality to the role. Thus, as time went on, it became possible to speak of "David Garrick's Hamlet," "John Barrymore's Hamlet," "John Gielgud's Hamlet," "Laurence Olivier's Hamlet," and even "Mel Gibson's Hamlet."

In motion pictures this phenomenon was intensified, with the result that stars often gained ascendency over roles, repeatedly playing the same character types and bringing the same personal attributes and mannerisms to every appearance. Consider again Maurice Chevalier, who at Paramount in the 1930s was cast as a military officer, a medical doctor, and a tailor, but who always played essentially the same character. Chevalier had been a hugely popular cabaret singer and star of the Folies Bergère in Paris during the 1920s, and Hollywood wanted him to display many of the performing traits associated with his success; at the same time, Lubitsch and Mamoulian modified those traits, making him less uninhibited and bawdy, more suitable to a general American audience. In his Paramount musicals of the pre-Code era, he's always the boulevardier in a straw hat, the stereotypical representative of what American audiences at the time thought of as "gay Paree"—sophisticated, exuberant, grinning, amusingly adept at sexual innuendo, eager to charm and seduce beautiful women. Hence in *The Love Parade* and *One Hour with You*, the films I've described above, he not only imitates certain conventional gestures and expressions for the sake of comedy, but he also reproduces the broad smile, the jaunty posture, the suggestive leer, the rolling eyes, and the distinctive French accent that were associated with "Maurice Chevalier." His public personality was in a sense unique, but it was nonetheless a carefully crafted "model" in Diderot's sense of the term, a model so idiosyncratic that Chevalier became a popular subject for generations of comic impersonators to imitate onstage and in film.

Chevalier's performances were stylized and extroverted, indebted to the musical revues of Paris, and for that reason he could be viewed as what the early futurists and the Soviet avant-garde called an "eccentric" actor; in fact, Sergei Eisenstein's doctrine of "eccentrism," which is most clearly evident in the grotesque caricatures of *Strike* (1924), was developed in part by analogy with music-hall performers. Relatively few of the leading players in classic Hollywood had this extreme kind of eccentricity, although comics like the Marx Brothers and W.C. Fields and unusual personalities like Wallace Beery, Marie Dressler, and Mickey Rooney certainly qualify. Many character actors of the period were also eccentrics; indeed the very term "character actor," which in Shakespeare's day referred to a performer who played a single vivid type, was often used by the film industry to describe supporting players with cartoonish personalities: we need only think of the lively crowd of eccentrics in Preston Sturges's comedies, including William Demarest, Eugene Pallette, Franklin Pangborn, Akim Tamiroff, and Raymond Walburn. Comedic females such as Marjorie Main and Thelma Ritter belong in the same category, as do many of the noncomic supporting players, such as Sydney Greenstreet, Elisha Cook Jr., and Peter Lorre in John Huston's *The Maltese Falcon* (1941).

Leading players, on the other hand, tended to have symmetrical faces and usually behaved in almost invisible fashion; their close-ups conveyed what Richard Dyer has called their "interiority," and the smallest movements of their bodies helped create a sense of their personalities. But the classic-era stars were no less carefully constructed performers than the character actors; their identities were created not only by their roles but also by their physical characteristics and idiosyncrasies or peculiarities of expression. In her intriguing essay on Humphrey Bogart, Louise Brooks makes precisely this point. "All actors know that truly natural acting is rejected by the audience," Brooks writes. "Though people are better equipped to judge acting than any other art, the hypocrisy of 'sincerity' prevents them from admitting that they, too, are always acting some role of their own invention. To be a successful actor, then, it is necessary to add eccentricities and mystery to naturalness, so that the audience can admire and puzzle over something different than itself" (64–65).

Bogart was certainly a natural-looking performer who seemed to have a reflective, mysteriously experienced inner life, an actor who appeared to be *thinking* in a way quite different from Garbo's blank-faced close-up at the end of *Queen Christina* (1933). But Bogart's "naturalness" was expressed through distinctive physical attributes and carefully crafted displays of personal eccentricities. To express thoughtfulness, for example, he often tugged at his earlobe, and to create an air of relaxed confidence or bravado he repeatedly hooked his thumbs into the waist of his pants. At one level Bogart was simply reacting as he naturally would, but the gestures were practiced and perfected until they became part of an expressive rhetoric, a repertory of performance signs. At the height of his fame he played many roles, among them a private eye, a gangster, a neurotic sea captain, a disturbingly violent Hollywood screenwriter, and an aging Cockney sailor; but his eccentricity persisted through variations of character. You can see the business with the thumbs in such different pictures as *The Big Sleep* (1946) and *The Barefoot Contessa* (1954). You can see it in a wartime short subject, "Hollywood Victory Caravan" (1945), where Bogart appears as "himself" and where, as Gary Giddins has observed, he stands with "thumbs under belt as though he were doing a Bogart impression" (43). You can also see it in a well-known news photo of 1947, when Bogart, Lauren Bacall, Paul Henreid, Richard

Conte, John Huston, and other Hollywood notables went to the U.S. capitol to protest the HUAC hearings on supposed communists in the movie industry: Bogart stands front and center of the group, his jacket spread and thumbs under his belt. He's imitating or copying a model of Humphrey Bogart.

Like Chevalier, Bogart was a star that comic entertainers liked to impersonate. Others have included Marlon Brando, Bette Davis, James Cagney, Kirk Douglas, Clark Gable, Cary Grant, Katharine Hepburn, Burt Lancaster, Marilyn Monroe, Edgar G. Robinson, James Stewart, and John Wayne. (One of the most popular subjects of comic impersonation as I write this essay is probably Christopher Walken, an eccentric if ever there was one.) Usually the stars are subject to impersonation because of a peculiar voice or accent, an oddity of facial expression, or a distinctive walk. Some have had all three. John Wayne had a deep voice with a drawling California accent, a habit of raising his eyebrows and wrinkling his forehead to express surprise or consternation, and an oddly rolling, almost mincing gait. Marilyn Monroe had a breathy voice, a parted mouth with a quivering upper lip (a quiver that, as Richard Dyer has observed, was designed not only to express yielding sexuality but also to hide an upper gum line), and an undulating, provocative walk that emphasized her hips and breasts. Some of the legendary stars, especially the stoic males like Dana Andrews or the flawless females like Ava Gardner, were difficult to mimic except perhaps in caricatured drawings. But even the less eccentric actors had performing quirks or tricks, such as Andrews's tendency to cock his elbow out to his side when he drinks from a glass. There are so many famous names one could mention in this context that eccentricity would seem the norm rather than the exception. Sometimes the eccentricity is sui generis, and sometimes it has an influence on the culture. Marlon Brando and Marilyn Monroe's mannerisms have been imitated by many other actors in more or less subtle ways; and James Cagney spawned a generation of teenaged performers, beginning with the Dead End Kids, who copied the early Cagney's ghetto-style toughness and swagger.

In the history of cinema there have been occasions when famous actors have not simply imitated but impersonated other famous actors. One of the best-known examples is Tony Curtis's impersonation of Cary Grant in *Some Like It Hot* (1959). (Curtis's equally amusing impersonation of a woman in that same film is based partly on Eve Arden.) A more recent instance is Cate Blanchett's remarkable impersonation of Bob Dylan in Todd Haynes's *I'm Not There* (2007), a film in which Dylan is also played by Christian Bale, Marcus Carl Franklin, Richard Gere, and Heath Ledger. Blanchett is the only actor in the group who tries to look and behave like Dylan, and her performance is a tour de force, achieving uncanny likeness to the androgynous pop star in the most drugged phase of his career. But impersonation in fiction film, especially when performed by a star, has a paradoxical effect; the more perfect it is, the more conscious we are of the performer who accomplishes it. Successful impersonation in real life is a form of identity theft, but in theater or film our pleasure as an audience derives from our awareness that it's Curtis pretending to be Grant or Blanchett pretending to be Dylan, never a complete illusion.

The example of Blanchett serves to remind us that the film genre most likely to involve overt imitation or impersonation of one actor by another is the biopic, especially the biographical film that tells the life story of a celebrity in the modern media. Film biographies of remote historical figures or real-life personalities from outside the media seldom if ever require true impersonation; we have no recordings or films of Napoleon or Lincoln, and the many actors who have played them on the screen needed only conform in general ways to certain painted portraits or still photographs. The audience seems inclined to accept fictional representations of historical characters and some types of modern celebrities as long as the performance is consistent and reasonably plausible: Willem Dafoe has played Jesus Christ, Max Shreck, and T. S. Eliot without radically changing his physiognomy, and Sean Penn is quite convincing as gay activist Harvey Milk in *Milk* (2008), even though he doesn't physically resemble Milk. When a conventionally realistic biopic concerns a popular star of film or television, however, the situation is a bit more complex. The actor needs to give a fairly accurate and convincing impersonation of a known model while also serving the larger ends of the story. No matter how accurate the impersonation might be, the audience will inevitably be aware that an actor is imitating a famous personage; but if it becomes too much a display of virtuosity, it can upset the balance of illusion and artifice.

Larry Parks's portrayal of Al Jolson in a quintessential Hollywood biopic, *The Jolson Story* (1946), deals with these problems by almost avoiding impersonation during the dramatic episodes of the film. Parks behaves with an ebullience appropriate to an old-time showman, occasionally speaking with a brash New York accent, but he makes little attempt to mimic the famous entertainer's distinctive looks or vocal tone; far more handsome than the real Jolson, who was alive and a star on the radio when the film was made, he simply adds his attractiveness, youthful vigor, and charm to the generally flattering, glamourizing aims of the project. When he breaks into song, however, he creates a different effect. We hear the actual Jolson's voice on the soundtrack—a voice that gives the film an aura of authenticity and convinces us of Jolson's talent—and Parks convincingly re-creates the singer's eccentric trademark mannerisms, most of which were derived from years of performing in provincial vaudeville and blackface minstrel shows. All the signature Jolson moves are on display: the rhythmic rocking from side to side, the strut across the stage, the broad grin, the widely rolling eyes, the clasped hands, the dropping to the floor on one knee with arms open wide, and so forth. These gestures and expressions had become so much associated with Jolson that he was relatively easy to impersonate; but they were also dated, as were songs like "Mammy," so that he was in danger of becoming a cliché or quaint caricature. (At one moment, the film seems to acknowledge this possibility: Evelyn Keyes, who plays Jolson's wife, does an enthusiastic but joking impersonation of Jolson singing "California, Here I Come." Only a few moments before, we've seen Larry Parks as Jolson singing that same number.) Parks's charisma and energy nevertheless manage to overcome these dangers, enlivening the film and even enhancing Jolson's image as a singer. Parks never jokes with the all-too-predictable Jolson persona and in the end becomes exactly what Hollywood wants him to be: an idealized version of Jolson as played by the star Larry Parks. (As Leo Braudy has observed in *The World in a Frame*, the sequel to this film, *Jolson Signs Again* [1949], creates a double impersonation and adds to the "Byzantine" relation between actor and character [238]. Parks plays the older Jolson, who makes a comeback when he records songs for the actor Larry Parks to lip-synch in *The Jolson Story*. In a scene in a screening room, we see Parks shaking hands with Parks while the real Jolson, seated in the background, makes an unacknowledged cameo appearance.)

Beyond the Sea (2004), a somewhat Felliniesque biopic about the short life of singer-actor Bobby Darin, is an interesting contrast with *The Jolson Story*. Kevin Spacey, who not only stars in the film but also produced, directed, and coauthored the screenplay, is an unusually gifted mimic and a sincere admirer of Darin. He sings all the musical numbers in the film himself, and he is such a skillful impersonator that when the film was released he went on tour performing a live re-creation of Darin's nightclub act. Ironically, however, the closer he comes to reproducing Darin's voice and mannerisms, the more he reveals a disparity between himself and the man he is imitating. A chameleon performer, Bobby Darin was the equal of Sinatra as a singer of ballads and swing arrangements and just as good at rock and roll, country, and social protest songs. His nightclub and television appearances were filled with sexy energy and exciting dance moves, and his few films demonstrate that he had fine acting abilities in both light comedy and Method-style psychological realism. Spacey, however, is a less dynamic and charismatic personality, and to make matters worse, he's slightly too old for the part. The whole purpose of the film is to celebrate Darin's talent, which was doomed from the start because of a childhood illness; unfortunately, though, it feels more like a vanity project in celebration of Spacey's talent for mimicry.

Biopics in general are crucially dependent upon a dialectical interaction between mimicry and realistic acting, an interaction that can become threatened when a major star undertakes an impersonation. In *White Hunter Black Heart* (1990), one of Clint Eastwood's most underrated films, Eastwood plays a character based on John Huston and in the process accurately imitates Huston's slow, courtly manner of speaking. Good as the imitation is, it has a slightly disconcerting or comic effect, if only because it's performed by an iconic star in the classic mold; any basic change in such an actor's voice and persona seems bizarre, almost as if he had donned a strange wig or a false nose. Probably for this reason, some of the most effective impersonations in recent films have been accomplished by actors who are not stars in the classic sense. Meryl Streep, for example, has performed a variety of characters and accents, so that when she impersonates the celebrity chef Julia Child in *Julie and Julia* (2009) there is no great dissonance caused by a difference between star persona and role.

Like Streep, Philip Seymour Hoffman possesses a particular kind of stardom that is based on his work as an actor, not on his sex appeal or public personality. One of the high points of his career is his impersonation of Truman Capote in *Capote* (2005), which won several awards and was widely praised by people who had known Capote intimately. We can see the actor behind the mask of Capote, but the actor doesn't have a consistent behavioral image that generates conflict with the mask. The impersonation, moreover, is never slavish, so nuanced and emotionally convincing that the display of imitative skill never causes a rift in the suspension of disbelief. Hoffman's achievement is all the more impressive because Capote was an ostentatiously eccentric figure, the kind of personality that might seem comically grotesque. An effective self-publicist who relished celebrity and society gossip, he was far better known than most writers in America; people who never read his books saw him often on television, especially as a guest on Johnny Carson's *Tonight Show*, but it was difficult to say whether the mass audience viewed him more as a witty TV conversationalist or as a freak. Short and chubby, with a round face resembling a dissipated child, he spoke in a high-pitched, nasal, quite effeminate voice that was marked by a whining Southern drawl, and he gestured with broad, limp-wristed movements. In the period when he became famous, few if any media personalities were so obviously and theatrically gay.

Very soon after *Capote* was released, the actor Toby Jones played Capote in *Infamous* (2006), which, like the Hoffman film, deals with the events surrounding the writing of Capote's *In Cold Blood*, a so-called "nonfiction novel" about the murder of a Kansas farm family and the capture and execution of the two killers. Even though Jones seems to have the advantage of a greater natural resemblance to the diminutive Capote, his performance is much less interesting than Hoffman's. In contrast to Jones, Hoffman's neck and chin are relatively strong and his physique sturdy; he's also a bit too tall for the role, although the film compensates for this problem by the way it frames and photographs him in relation to the other actors. At the technical level of impersonation, he adopts Capote's hairstyle and effeminate gestures, together with appropriate costumes such as the luxurious scarf and floor-length topcoat we see him wearing in the Kansas scenes. He stands as Capote did, with back slightly arched and belly thrust forward, and is especially good at duplicating the Capote voice and accent, which he masters to such a degree that he uses it effectively even in the softly spoken, intimate moments. (His costar Catherine Keener, who plays Harper Lee, the author of *To Kill a Mockingbird*, has far less need to impersonate because Lee was notoriously shy and reclusive, and thus lacked a celebrity image.) Beyond all this mimicry, however, Hoffman's portrayal is noteworthy for its naturalness and psychological nuance, which are worthy of the best Stanislavskian acting. In fact, his impersonation is wedded to a subtle psychological idea about the character. Largely through silent reaction shots, he enables us to see Capote's mingled voyeuristic curiosity and fear over the murders; his growing attraction to one of the killers; and his cunning manipulation of the Kansas community, the two condemned men, and the publishers of his book. As Robert Sklar has pointed out in his review of *Capote*, the contradictions and complexities of the character are also shaped and shaded by Hoffman's appropriation of typical Capote mannerisms: "In an early scene, Hoffman/Capote points his chin in the air, a movement signaling at once vanity and vulnerability. The actor conveys Capote's conviction that his inner demons can be controlled by regarding the 'self' as a constant performance. It's a life strategy that the film *Capote* puts to the test, and finds ruinously wanting" (57).

Capote and *Infamous* are examples of a subgenre that Thomas Doherty terms the "textual biopic," in which "a foregrounded artwork becomes background to a portrait of the artist during the process of creation" (4). The textual biopic isn't new (see Charlton Heston as Michelangelo painting the Sistine Chapel in *The Agony and the Ecstasy* [1965]), but recent years have produced a cycle of such films, all dealing with celebrities of the modern media. A signal characteristic of the pictures in the cycle is that the audience's knowledge of and in most cases admiration for the "background" artwork functions as ironic counterpoint to a more or less antiheroic depiction of the artist's psychological and professional conflicts. Cases in point are two films about Alfred Hitchcock that appeared in 2013: HBO's *The Girl*, directed by Julian Jarrold, which concerns the making of *The Birds* and

Marnie; and Fox Searchlight's *Hitchcock,* directed by Sacha Gervasi, which tells the story of the making of *Psycho.* Doherty observes that the filmmakers "traffic not only in reenactments [i.e., imitations] of scenes from their host films," but also "play an audiovisual mind game" involving intertextual references. The danger of this strategy is that Hitchcock fans might reject the reenactments as weak imitations; but even when the films succeed at the level of imitation, Doherty remarks, they "can only be pilot fish swimming in the wake of their great white sharks, a lesser order of Hitchcockian entertainment" (4).

The Girl and *Hitchcock* have a somewhat distracting effect because knowledgeable viewers are constantly in the position of judging how well the actors imitate their models. *The Girl,* derived from Donald Spoto's gossipy book *Spellbound by Beauty: Alfred Hitchcock and His Leading Ladies* (2009), centers on Hitchcock and Tippi Hedren, played by Toby Jones and Sienna Miller. Although Miller is an emotionally subtle and talented actor, for that very reason she lacks Hedren's brittle, almost affectless quality, which Hitchcock used so well to convey repression in both *The Birds* and *Marnie.* Jones does an excellent job of mimicking the Master of Suspense's accent, but he plays the character as nothing more than a sour, sadistic user and abuser of women, lacking even a trace of the on-screen charm and humor that made Hitchcock a popular personality. The situation is different in *Hitchcock,* based in part on Stephen Rebello's *The Making of Psycho,* which gives us a likable Hitchcock. Unfortunately, Anthony Hopkins, who plays the famous director, sounds too much like Anthony Hopkins and is smothered by an all-too-visible rubber face. Ageless beauty Helen Mirren doesn't remotely resemble Alma Reville (a woman unknown to the general public). Scarlett Johansson is appropriately bosomy as Janet Leigh but too voluptuously soft and rounded, lacking the somewhat birdlike figure and the mixed attitude of toughness and vulnerability we see in Leigh's Marion Crane. James D'Arcy, who plays Anthony Perkins, is the most effective mimic in the cast but has the thankless job of walking in the footsteps of one of the iconic performances in screen history.

To my mind, a more effective example of impersonation in a textual biopic is Simon Curtis's *My Week with Marilyn* (2011), which concerns the making of Laurence Olivier's *The Prince and the Showgirl* (1957), starring Olivier and Marilyn Monroe. Marilyn has been impersonated on stage, film, and TV more than any other movie star, and nearly as much as any historical personage. A partial list of women who have played her (omitting celebrities such as Lindsay Lohan and Madonna, who have posed as her in magazine photos or music videos) includes Melody Anderson, Susan Griffiths, Catherine Hicks, Ashley Judd, Blake Lively, Barbara Loden,

Sophie Monk, Poppy Montgomery, Barbara Niven, Misty Rowe, Mira Sorvino, Charlotte Sullivan, and Sunny Thompson. To this list we can add the more recent performances of Megan Hilty, Katharine McPhee, and Uma Thurman, who've played actresses competing for the role of Marilyn in a fictitious Broadway musical on NBC-TV's *Smash*. But Michelle Williams, who stars in *My Week with Marilyn* (aided by a bit of padding and what I suspect is a rear view of a nude body double), is especially good.

Neither Williams nor Kenneth Branagh, who plays Olivier, looks quite like their model, and their problems are exacerbated by the fact that they not only impersonate film stars but also perform very precise reenactments of scenes from *The Prince and the Showgirl*. Williams overcomes potential reservations by virtue of her luminous beauty and exemplary rendition of Marilyn's patented little-girl voice. Her performance of one of Marilyn's singing and dancing numbers, which uses the same costuming and camera angle as the original movie, looks almost as if a double exposure of her and Marilyn would perfectly match. At the more subtle and realistic level, Williams gives complexity to the character, suggesting Marilyn's insecurity and guile, curiosity and intelligence, and mixture of fear and pleasure over the power of her stardom. The film also gives her a chance to reveal that Marilyn's show-business image was the product of imitation: at one point, faced with a group of admirers, she asks her companion, "Shall I be her?" and breaks into an openmouthed display of voluptuousness. For his part, Branagh gives an amusing impersonation of the actor who has often been regarded as his predecessor. He's especially good at capturing Olivier's theatrical and narcissistic eccentricities: the tendency to raise his hand to his brow like a gentleman lifting a teacup; the rising, singsong inflection of his voice; the melancholic postures and sudden gusts of witchy, almost girlish business. He even accurately reproduces the comic "Carpathian" accent Olivier used in *The Prince and the Showgirl*.

One phenomenon peculiar to celebrity impersonation in the biopic is that, because of the realist nature of the genre, it always takes a few scenes for the audience to accept the mimicry and settle into a willing suspension of disbelief. This is especially true when an established movie star performs the impersonation. Near the beginning of Steven Soderbergh's *Behind the Candelabra* (2013), for example, Michael Douglas performs a reenactment of Liberace's Las Vegas nightclub act, and throughout the scene I feel a kind of amused wonder, thinking to myself, "It's Michael Douglas!" The thought never goes away but it gradually becomes less intrusive, in part because the film moves from a huge public spectacle to increasingly intimate scenes, and in part because, as the story develops, Douglas gives a good deal of complexity to the character.

When a relatively unknown actor performs an impersonation, the effect of the split between actor and role is slightly different because the audience doesn't know the actor's normal "self." An impressive instance is Christian McKay as Orson Welles in Richard Linklater's textual biopic *Me and Orson Welles* (2009). This film imagines a single week in New York in 1937, when, through a combination of boyish self-confidence and amazing good luck, an entirely fictional teenage acting hopeful played by Zac Efron finds himself swept up into the whirlwind staging of Welles's modern-dress *Julius Caesar*. The reenactment of events surrounding the rehearsal and staging of the play is flawed, giving virtually no sense of the politics of the Mercury Theater and too little evidence of why *Caesar* made such a powerful impression on those who saw it. And, when we witness snippets of the show on opening night, they lack the disturbing patterns of light and darkness and aura of violence that stunned the original audience. Instead, everything is subordinated to a comic portrayal of behind-the-scenes sexual shenanigans and to demonstrations of Welles's supposed will to power.

Like most movies about Welles, *Me and Orson Welles* seems to take more relish in depicting his character flaws (at least one of which, womanizing, he no doubt possessed) than in his artistic accomplishments. In this case we're shown a quarrel between technician Samuel Leve, who wants credit on the show's playbill, and Welles, who thunderously declares that *Julius Caesar* is "my vision." (Where this quarrel is concerned, I recommend that readers consult producer John Houseman's *Run-Through: A Memoir*, pages 296–98, where we're told that Leve's job, under the direction of Jean Rosenthal, was simply to convert Welles's design sketches into blueprints.) The film nevertheless gives a fine sense of how a romantic, idealistic theater company on the verge of great things can become an ambitious young man's family of choice, albeit a family with as many rivalries and disillusionments as any other. As its title indicates, it depicts not just Welles but nearly everyone in the Mercury Theater as amusingly self-preoccupied; even Efron, the star of Walt Disney's *High School Musical* franchise and the heartthrob of millions of teenage girls, cleverly reveals the calculation lurking behind innocence. Chief among the virtues of the film, however, is McKay. Welles has been played by many actors, including Paul Shenar, Eric Purcell, Jean Guérin, Vincent D'Onofrio (aided by the voice of Maurice LaMarche), Liev Schreiber, and Angus Macfadyen—but none have come this close to his looks, voice, and slightest movements. In contrast, the actors around McKay do little to imitate the real-life figures they represent: James Tupper looks a bit like Joseph Cotten, but Eddie Marsan, Leo Bill, and Ben Chaplin have no resemblance at all to John Houseman, Norman Lloyd, and George Coulouris. Almost the entire responsibility of creating a persuasive historical representation falls on McKay, who, before appearing in the film, had performed successfully in a one-man stage show about Welles and apparently come to know his model intimately. He captures the booming voice, the vaguely mid-Atlantic accent, the twinkle in the eye, the forbidding glance, and the heavy yet somehow buoyant walk. He's slightly too old (Welles was twenty-two at the time of *Caesar*) and never displays Welles's infectious laugh, but he merges with the character more completely than a star could have done and is just as convincing when he tries to seduce a young woman as when he proclaims ideas about theater. To hear him read aloud a passage from Booth Tarkington's *The Magnificent Ambersons* is to feel as if one were in the presence of Welles. Even so, the actor McKay is always present to us alongside the impersonation, taking obvious pleasure in the magic trick he performs, enabling us to see that Welles was not simply a flamboyant personality but an actor and director of seriousness and importance who could bring audiences to their feet.

Whenever we encounter an overt, creative impersonation such as the ones performed by Michelle Williams, Kenneth Branagh, Michael Douglas, and Christian McKay in the films I've mentioned, we can easily appreciate the singular skill of the performers. But imitation in all its manifestations has always been an important, even crucial, feature of the art of movie acting. The various forms of imitation discussed here—the copying of conventional gestures and accents, the rote repetition of predetermined gestures and movements, the development of model character types, the repeated performance of personal eccentricities, and the impersonation of historical characters—may not be the most valued aspect of what actors do, but they are sources of pleasure for the audience. They contribute to the system of genres and styles (as in the distinction between comedy and drama or between conventional movie realism and a director like Bresson), and more generally to the rhetoric of characterization and the formation of personality on the screen. In a more subtle and general sense, they complicate our ideas of personal autonomy and individuality; they make us at least potentially aware of the imitative aspects of our lives in the real world, as both personalities and social beings.

The Death and Rebirth of Rhetoric

> We make out of the quarrel with others rhetoric, but of the quarrel with ourselves, poetry.
> WILLIAM BUTLER YEATS, *Per Amica Silentia Lunae*, 1917

Most commentaries on film and rhetoric are indebted to the neo-Aristotelian school of literary criticism once practiced at the University of Chicago, and particularly to Wayne Booth's highly influential *The Rhetoric of Fiction* (1961), which is less preoccupied with overt argument or eloquence than with problems of ethical clarity and "the art of communicating" (i). Again and again, Booth emphasizes the artist's effort, through techniques of narration and characterization, to help readers grasp the full implications of the work and to impose a fictional or illusory world upon an audience. In a similar though more overtly ideological fashion, writing on the rhetoric of film has tended to deal with issues of point of view, focalization, and enunciation, and especially with debates over what Avrom Fleishman describes as the "narrator-effect" of fiction cinema. (Besides Fleishman's *Narrated Films: Storytelling Situations in Cinema History*, see Nick Browne, *The Rhetoric of Filmic Narration;* Seymour Chatman, *Coming to Terms: The Rhetoric of Narrative in Fiction and Film;* Sarah Kozloff, *Invisible Storytellers: Voice-Over Narration in American Fiction Film;* and George M. Wilson, *Narration in Light: Studies of Cinematic Point of View*.)

Granting the importance of such matters, I plan to say relatively little about them. I want to define rhetoric more broadly and theatrically, as an art of suasion and seduction that secures our belief in claims of truth and our pleasure in representation. The rhetorical event in this sense is only secondarily concerned with the clarity or veracity of its evidence (as in the "realism" of documentary photographs); before anything, it's intended to *move* us by means of verbal skill, bodily eloquence, spectacle, color, performance, and all the well-known elements of cosmetics, stagecraft, and mise-en-scène. Explicitly aimed at arousing the passions, it proves its worth or lack of worth through the emotional effects it creates on auditors or spectators at specific occasions.

As Jacqueline Lichtenstein has shown in her important book *The Eloquence of Color* (1993), this broad conception of rhetoric, which is quite old, has long been connected to acting, painting, and the visual arts in general. In ancient Greece, it was a *techne* that controlled the entire empire of communication, and at a later, more specialized, moment in its history, it became one of the three crucial disciplines of the Roman trivium, which eventually shaped the curriculum in European schools. Even so, as John Bender and David Wellbery have pointed out in their anthology *The Ends of Rhetoric* (1990), rhetorical art was never without critics, who usually accused it of fostering luxurious excess, irrational power, and demagogic manipulation. Plato, in his quarrel with the sophists, distinguished between the language of rhetoric, which deals in mere adornment and emotional affect, and the language of philosophy, which deals in truth. Francis Bacon and every major scientist from the Renaissance to the Enlightenment denigrated rhetoric in contrast to the neutral, transparent discourse of scientific discovery. Immanuel Kant described the major part of rhetoric as "the art of deceiving by a beautiful show" and attacked its use in both the law court and the pulpit on the grounds that it was designed "to win minds to the side of the orator before they have formed a judgment and to deprive them of their freedom" (*Critique of Judgment*, 171). Not long afterward, the romantic poets forsook what M. H. Abrams calls the "mirror" of neoclassical art with the "lamp" of individual expression, thus asserting the primacy of the literary artist's imagination over the need to communicate with an audience.

From the time of Plato and Aristotle until the nineteenth century, rhetoric was usually subordinated to philosophy and devoted to the study of *inventio, dispositio,* and *elecutio* in verbal language. By the mid-nineteenth century, it had narrowed to a typology of figures of speech, all of them labeled with Latin names, and to a genteel, highly controlled application of these figures and their appropriate gestures to the arts of acting and public address. The printed word had long since gained ascendency over oral communication, and verbal and visual rhetoric of the more flamboyant kind began to take on negative connotations associated with bourgeois pretentiousness, populist politics, and the newly emerging mass-communication and advertising industries. At this point, artistic modernism attempted to administer a deathblow to rhetoric. In the first two decades of the twentieth century, and particularly in the years immediately after World War I, there was a wholesale artistic revolt against the very term, which was seen as a discredited technique of an imperial establishment whose representatives usually spoke in the elevated tones of moral preachment.

What was at stake during these years was not so much an abandonment of suasion, which would have been virtually impossible, as a new and heterodox contempt for certain audiences—an antirhetorical rhetoric that almost defined the modernist ethos. The keynote of modernist architecture was the rejection of classical ornament in favor of less decorative forms derived from industry or landscape; modernist painting divested itself of the sentimental, representational imagery of the nineteenth century, becoming increasingly abstract; art photography favored the austere, intellectual qualities of *disegno* over the emotional qualities of *colore;* and modern dance was predicated on a rejection of the rhetorical hierarchies in ballet in favor of what was sometimes called "task performance." This suspicion of elevated tone and direct appeals to emotion was particularly apparent in modernist poetry, whose readers, according to T. S. Eliot, were never to be addressed "as if [they] were at a public meeting" (quoted in Stead, 169). Eliot himself went further, stripping poetry even of the social conventions of communication. *The Waste Land* (1922) was an ironic, deliberately antirhetorical poem addressed to a *hypocrite lecteur* and based on an art of verbal collage, or on what Hugh Kenner called "juxtaposition without copula" (quoted in Stead, 169). Despite the many academic commentators who tried to make it seem coherent, *The Waste Land* steered very close to surrealism, providing eloquence, rhetorical flourish, and a sense of luxury only through quotations.

Something roughly similar was happening in the novel, and this development, particularly in the hands of writers such as Joyce and Nabokov, later provoked Wayne Booth's criticism in *The Rhetoric of Fiction* on the grounds that it left readers with no moral and ethical guideposts. Whether or not one agrees with Booth, it's certainly true that the whole tendency of twentieth-century fiction was to become more ambiguous and in one sense "cinematic," less explicitly "rhetorical." In the English language, modernist fiction began in the first decade of the century with the attempts by Henry James, Joseph Conrad, and Ford Madox Ford to elevate showing over telling, and it culminated with James Joyce's "invisible" narration and pastiche of literary convention in *Ulysses* (1922). Significantly, the seventh or "Aeolus" chapter of that book is devoted to the art of rhetoric, which it treats satirically. It shows us a group of Dublin windbags, most of them journalists and small-time politicians, lolling about a newspaper office, quoting speeches and news reports from the good old days. The conversation of this group contains almost a hundred examples of Latinate rhetorical forms (*chiasmus, diasyrm, asyndeton, enthymeme, apostrophie, epigram,* etc.), but the two most sympathetic characters in the chapter, the adman Leopold Bloom and the poet Stephen Dedalus, are markedly plain, sometimes even cryptic in their speech. In different ways, both are estranged from Dublin's charmingly seductive but ultimately empty world of masculine palaver and antiquated eloquence.

An analogous development occurred in the theater. The word *actor* in English was originally meant to suggest the "action" of orators, and early textbooks on acting were designed to teach the artful employment of gestures and tones of voice to move, persuade, and embody traits of character. The connection between acting and speechmaking began to disappear around 1890, with the debates surrounding William Archer's *Masks or Faces?* (1888), which prepared the way for what I've elsewhere described as a "shift from a semiotic to a psychological conception of performance" (Naremore, *Acting in the Cinema*, 52). On the stage, actors sometimes stood in corners or turned their backs to the audience, and the writings of Konstantin Stanislavsky led to a complete rejection of a centuries-old tradition of codified pantomime. The Stanislavskian revolution didn't completely eliminate rhetoric, any more than novels or poems eliminated communication, but, like most forms of modern art, it was less openly solicitous or directly aimed toward the audience; it often relied on indirection, requiring viewers or readers to work at the discovery of meaning.

What, you may ask, has all this to do with movies? The answer is that Hollywood has a paradoxical or mixed relation to the modernist movements, at once participating in the general reaction against flamboyant rhetoric and fostering a full-scale return to bodily eloquence and visual suasion. D. W. Griffith is especially interesting in this regard because he's both a modern aesthete and a Victorian ideologue. *The Birth of a Nation* (1915) helps to create a new form of intimate, vernacular acting and an "invisible" style of continuity editing, but at the same time it's a definitive example of the cinema as argument—an emotionally charged, propagandistic melodrama, filled with spectacle and preachment, punctuated with title cards that aspire to old-fashioned oratory. When Griffith said that he was trying to make us "see," he was declaring his affinity not with Joseph Conrad but with the ancient orators—who, as Jacqueline Lichtenstein demonstrates, were trained to paint pictures with words, and who sometimes unveiled paintings before their audiences as a way of achieving emotional assent to their arguments. Lichtenstein points out that ancient philosophy usually tried to control the powers of this visual rhetoric because of its dangerous emotional effects. Plato and Aristotle were alike, she notes, "in their determination to grant the spectacle only a secondary function.... They suggest that the greatest danger for the poet's and the orator's arts resides in the performances of acting and staging ... and that a constant threat to the [priority of philosophy over] poetics and rhetoric lurks in the conditions of a spectacle whose presentation is, however, necessary" (71). If we follow this reasoning, Griffith can be seen as the philosopher's worst nightmare, as a powerful rhetorician who never eliminates language or undervalues plot, but who foregrounds the emotional power of the actor's body, the eloquence of camera placement, and the mute spectacle of staged conflict.

Gilberto Perez has described motion picture direction as an art of "dramatized showing," a phrase that nicely captures the fundamentally rhetorical nature of decoupage and mise-en-scène and that enables us to see point-of-view shots and other camera positions as rhetorical and theatrical, not merely narrational (62). But in the history of American cinema, directors have approached this art differently, and they can be categorized in terms of the degree to which they employ grandiloquent images in the service of an overt rhetoric. John Ford, for example, was a disciple of Griffith who claimed to have played a Klansman in *The Birth of a Nation* and whose films overflow with populist sentiment, patriotic symbols, and painterly images of military horsemen seen against spectacular landscapes. Ford's particular sort of masculine nationalism was memorably embodied by Will Rogers and Henry Fonda, plainspoken, folksy heroes who were quite unlike the grandiose orators of the nineteenth-century Eastern establishment, but were visualized in monumental style and posed in a way that invited us to see them as emblems of American history. Ford was also the director who propounded the notion that when the facts become legend, we should print the legend—the idea that rhetoric can be more important than truth. Thus in pictures such as *My Darling Clementine* (1946), the emotions seem authentic and the vistas breathtaking, even when the history is a lie.

At an apparently opposite extreme is a director such as Vincente Minnelli, whose musicals and melodramas create a luxurious excess of movement, light, fabric, and decor. Seen in relation to the ancient debates about rhetoric, Minnelli was a Sophist rather than a Platonist, because his pictures are so unabashedly about the flattery of the senses, the pleasures of dance, costume design, cosmetics, and above all color. Even in a small-town domestic melodrama such as *Some Came Running* (1959), he indulges in sentimental emotion, swirling action, and gaudy hues. To quote Lichtenstein again, "Flattery, cosmetics, artifice, appearance . . . all the terms of this metaphorical chain . . . qualify the effects of color as effects of seduction; they are the effects of illusion and pleasure. Essentially sophistic, color is also rhetorical, from the point of view of its effects: it is the figure of ornamentation and the ornament of figures" (53). Thus Ford and Minnelli, for all their differences, are opposite sides of the same coin: if the potential critique of Ford rests on a relatively recent notion of rhetoric as an instrument of phallic, masculine hierarchy, then the potential critique of Minnelli rests on an even older notion of rhetoric as a "feminine" and perverse practice of deception, an art of surfaces rather than essences.

In a different category altogether are the modernist directors, who employ an ironic rhetoric that questions its own validity. Luis Buñuel, Robert Bresson, and Carl Dreyer, for example, exhibit varying degrees of detachment from their audiences—as in Buñuel's *Land without Bread* (1932), which uses Mozart's music and a travelogue-style narration to create a bottomless, Swiftian irony. Orson Welles is another obvious example, particularly in *Citizen Kane* (1941), a film that sets out to expose the manipulative bombast of a media tycoon and that treats every instance of public address, such as *News on the March* or Kane's stem-winding campaign speech, as a hollow deception. The film's claims to truth reside in the whispered "Rosebud" and the spectacular but ambiguous conclusion, which places the audience in the position of trespassers and tells them that a word can't sum up a man's life. Consider also *The Magnificent Ambersons* (1942), which superbly adapts the rhetorical conventions of Booth Tarkington's old-fashioned, omniscient novel while at the same time evoking pathos in relatively unorthodox ways. What seems unusual here, as in *Kane* and several of Welles's other films, is the way in which the audience is invited to sympathize with characters that are also treated critically. "I believe it is necessary to give all the characters their best arguments," Welles once told a group of Spanish interviewers, "including those I disagree with.... I do not want to resemble the majority of Americans, who are demagogues and rhetoricians" (Cobos and Pruneda, 16).

Welles has something in common with Jean Renoir, whose characters all have reasons for what they do. But Renoir's camera style, with its remarkable openness to the world beyond the frame, is perhaps more consistent with a liberal or democratically socialist disposition. A similar uneasiness about rhetoric can be seen in some of the Italian neorealists, particularly as they were viewed by *Cahiers du cinéma* in the 1950s. Again and again, French writers in the period of the cold war argued on behalf of an antirhetorical cinema based on what one of their company, the Catholic priest Amédée Ayfre, called "phenomenological realism." The greatest danger, even for a religious director, according to Ayfre, would be "to want to take greater care of God's interests than he does himself by trying to direct events by force and constrain the audience to read in them a meaning which is only accessible to those who discover it freely" (Hiller, "*Cahiers du Cinéma*": *The 1950s*, 190). With this argument, which was articulated in more secular terms by André Bazin, we reach the extreme end of an idealism that doesn't foreclose the possibility of rhetoric, but that resembles Plato in its keen suspicion of manipulated imagery.

By contrast, Jean-Luc Godard in his Maoist phase is an openly rhetorical director, but one who, like Brecht, disavows rhetoric's love of illusion. For sheer illusionism, we usually go to Hollywood, which, despite its ostensible distaste for "messages," has always been a fundamentally rhetorical cinema, devoted to melodramatic emotion. Even so, the celebration of old-fashioned verbal eloquence is comparatively rare in latter-day Hollywood movies, and the depiction of rhetorical events is usually ironic. See, for example, *Patton* (1970), in which George C. Scott, dressed in full military regalia and standing before a gigantic American flag, delivers a profane battle speech; despite the color, the theatrical costume, and the grain of Scott's voice, the effect is ambiguous. See also Robert Duvall's performance in *The Apostle* (1997), which allows us to experience a charismatic preacher while also viewing his flawed private life.

We might ask if there is any point at which film can move beyond the domain of rhetoric. I'd answer with a qualified yes, at least on the theoretical level, but only if we think of rhetoric purely in terms of communication. Bazin and some of his contemporaries came close to advocating a cinema of pure automatism, based on a principle of *photogénie* that operates outside human control. Roland Barthes's essay on the "third meaning" of photographic images seems to be describing something of this sort; and in one of his last interviews, Gilles Deleuze followed suit by claiming that true forms of art lie outside the world of communication, which is controlled by politics and power ("Qu'est-ce que l'acte de création," 141). Certainly filmmakers such as Michael Snow, Ernie Gehr, and the "structural materialists" have little concern for communication in the everyday sense of that term. For example, it isn't clear that Gehr is trying to communicate anything in his fourteen-minute "History" (1970), a film created by nothing more than a lighted black fabric suspended in front of a movie camera without a lens. Manohla Dargis aptly describes this film as "a sparkly black-and-grey blob that brings to mind a hallucination of a night sky, like van Gogh on acid." The result, she says, is "film itself: those clouds of dye in color film and churning grains of black and white that make up the image you see" (*New York Times*, November 13, 2011). And yet this and other of Gehr's films and digital creations have a rhetorical aspect because they're capable of engendering emotions in a manner roughly analogous to Symbolist poetry or abstract expressionist painting.

In earlier times, the radical modernists and the historical avant-garde were interested in the purely aleatory effects of images and signs that would suggest an expressive, emotional realm beyond or beneath the protocols of the dominant society. Certain experiments of the surrealists were designed to tap into this realm, short-circuiting the normal communicative network and exposing a kind of social unconscious. But if, as Lacan argued, the unconscious is structured like a language, even it might be governed by a kind of rhetoric, in which case we are back where we began.

What seems clear is that the forces of modernity, which led to the disparagement and ostensible death of rhetoric in the intellectual and artistic sphere, have now swung in the opposite direction. Many intellectuals (with whom I don't fully agree) no longer believe in metaphysical truths, Enlightenment models of communication, romantic subjectivity, or scientific objectivity. Digital reproduction is replacing conventional print as the chief mode of receiving information, CGI techniques are turning the movies into a more painterly medium, and a couple of generations of poststructuralism and cultural studies in the academy have taught us to see language as politics and truth as situated. We've therefore entered an era not so much of rhetoric as of what Bender and Wellbury call "rhetoricality." An early sign of the times can be seen at the end of the influential 1983 volume *Literary Theory*, in which Terry Eagleton calls for a rebirth of rhetoric, to the point where it would become the center of the humanities curriculum:

> Rhetoric, which was the received form of critical analysis all the way from ancient society to the eighteenth century, examined the way discourses are constructed in order to achieve certain effects.... Its horizon was nothing less than the field of discursive practices in the society as a whole, and its particular interest lay in grasping such practices as forms of power and performance..... It saw speaking and writing not merely as textual objects, to be aesthetically contemplated or endlessly deconstructed, but as forms of *activity* inseparable from the wider social relations between writers and readers, orators and audiences, and as largely unintelligible outside the social conditions in which they were imbedded. (205)

Another sign of this paradigm shift could be seen at a Society for Cinema Studies conference in San Diego in 1998, where Bill Nichols presented a paper that aimed "to put rhetoric back on the agenda," particularly as it's performed in what he called the "middle voice" of engaged documentary filmmakers such as Marlon Riggs, Errol Morris, Deborah Hoffmann, Jill Godmilow, Isaac Julien, and Marlon Fuentes. In addition to studying rhetoric in relation to specific films, Nichols observed, we need to validate its worth, because philosophy alone "only possesses analytic concepts to represent what rhetoric, in all its eloquence of affect and voice, silence and gesture, figure and grain, can, in fact, achieve."

Whether or not philosophy and rhetoric can work in harmony, some kind of rhetoricality always underlies our words and representational arts; rhetoric could in fact be defined as any technique that transforms poetics and philosophy into ideology. We're therefore at a propitious moment for the development of a broader, more detailed theory of rhetoric in the cinema, one that would analyze not only "narrator effects" but also the sensual, spectacular, and emotional devices of the medium.

PART II

Authors, Actors, Adaptations

Hawks, Chandler, Bogart, Bacall
The Big Sleep

My subject is Howard Hawks's film adaptation of Raymond Chandler's 1939 novel *The Big Sleep*, but I'm not concerned with the problem of whether the film is adequate to, better than, or inferior to its source. The critical battles waged in the 1950s by the Hitchcocko-Hawksians have long been won, and few cinephiles today would argue that Hawks was a less important artist than Chandler—or maybe even than William Faulkner, who was Hawks's collaborator on this and other pictures. The film is certainly different from the novel, but no less entertaining or important. By exploring salient differences between novel and the film, however, we can learn more about Hawks, Chandler, and other key contributors to the project.

Hawks is rightly considered an auteur, and in his role as producer-director of *The Big Sleep* he had more creative control than any other individual who worked on the film; nevertheless, the film was designed to capitalize on the success of Chandler's novel and tries to bring Chandler's distinctive moods and sinister wit to the screen. Chandler provided an imaginative template and had several conversations with Hawks during the filming; he, too, was an author, albeit in absentia. *The Big Sleep* was also a production by Warner Brothers, a studio that gave the film much of its look and feel (Max Steiner's music, Sid Hickox's photography, Fred M. MacLean's sets, etc.), and, more crucially, its star player. Humphrey Bogart and the classic Hollywood star system can additionally be described as authors. To deal with the interaction of these elements, I've organized the discussion under three rubrics, each beginning with a quotation. And because writings about adaptation too seldom deal with the actors who incarnate the literary characters, I start with Bogart.

MARLOWE AND BOGART

In a letter to D.J. Ibberson in April 1951, Raymond Chandler wrote, "If I had ever had an opportunity of selecting the movie actor who could best represent [Marlowe] to my mind, I think it would have been Cary Grant" (*Selected Letters*, 270). The choice is surprising; it's difficult to imagine Grant as a hard-boiled detective, oiling his revolver and taking a swig of rye from the bottom drawer of a desk. His image as a star conveyed very little of the loneliness, self-pity, and angry pride we occasionally sense in Marlowe, although it would be interesting to know if Chandler saw Grant's performance as the romantically embittered flier in Hawks's *Only Angels Have Wings* (1939). In any case, Grant had what Chandler thought were the proper looks (in *The Little Sister*, Chandler's 1949 novel about Hollywood, a villain tells Marlowe that he should remove his sunglasses because "they don't make you look in the least like Cary Grant"), and Grant's mid-Atlantic, Cockney-inflected accent and urbane style were roughly analogous to the cultural oppositions in Marlowe's character.

In the letter I've just quoted, Chandler says that Marlowe was probably born in Santa Rosa, California (the town where Hitchcock shot *Shadow of a Doubt* [1943] and *The Birds* [1963]) and probably went to college for two years at the University of Oregon. But the Marlowe we meet in the novels is a more unusual and contradictory type, an American tough guy with an old-world code of honor, a private eye with an aesthetic sensibility and an aristocratic name ("sounds like a fag name," a cop says in Robert Altman's adaptation of *The Long Goodbye* [1973]). A similar mixture of traits can be found in Marlowe's stylish first-person narration, which is the product of Chandler's ear for the American vernacular and his classical education at Dulwich College in England. Chandler was born in Chicago but raised by the Anglo-Irish gentry; a literary intellectual, he migrated from London to California, took an executive job with an oil company, drank himself out of the job, and lived a semibohemian life in Los Angeles, where he began writing beautifully crafted crime fiction for the pulps. At the height of his fame he claimed that he had an American novelist's contempt for gentility and a French novelist's respect for form. His alter ego, Marlowe, was formed of dialectical interplay between California and Europe.

Cary Grant never acted a private eye, but when *The Big Sleep* was published in 1939, a glowing review in the *Los Angeles Times* proposed a movie version starring Humphrey Bogart. This was a remarkable idea at the time, because Bogart was the wrong physical type and the four pictures that were to make him a star—*High Sierra* (1941), *The Maltese Falcon* (1941), *Casablanca* (1942), and *To Have and Have Not* (1944)—were not yet on the horizon. The book reviewer may have been unduly impressed by Bogart's career as a Warner gangster, but nobody today would question the casting. In movies, radio, and television Marlowe has been played by thirteen actors, including such laudable performers as Dick Powell, James Garner, and the radio personality Gerald Mohr (who slightly resembled Bogart). But Bogart is culturally transcendent, an icon of 1940s noir, forever associated with both Marlowe and Sam Spade.

In a 1946 letter to his British publisher, Chandler was understandably impressed with Bogart's performance, which was "so much better than any other tough-guy actor that he makes bums of the Ladds and the Powells. As we say here, Bogart can be tough without a gun. Also he has a sense of humor that contains that grating undertone of contempt.... All he has to do to dominate a scene is to enter it" (*Selected Letters*, 75). Bogart seldom projected such authority in the 1930s, when he often played weak or neurotic characters, precursors of Fred C. Dobbs and Captain Queeg. But appearing in every scene and nearly every shot of this film, he moves in lithe, almost jaunty style, occasionally smiling with a knowing self-confidence and using his slightly lisping, cigarette-husky voice charismatically. He's a Hawksian man of action, and the film adds to his air of dominance in three ways: by placing him alongside shorter men such as Regis Toomey, Bob Steele, Elisha Cook Jr., and Tom Rafferty; by allowing him to play from a seated position in scenes with the much taller John Ridgely; and by acknowledging his relatively short stature at the outset. In the novel, Carmen Sternwood says to Marlowe, "Tall, aren't you?" and he replies, "I didn't mean to be." In the movie, Carmen says, "Not very tall, are you?" Bogart looks down at himself in fake innocence, probably remembering his experience playing alongside Ingrid Bergman, and replies, "I tried to be."

When Chandler's Marlowe pays his first visit to the Sternwoods, he wears a powder-blue suit with dark blue shirt, tie and display handkerchief, and socks with clocks on them. Bogart is austere by comparison—David Thomson says he looks like a cross between an urban priest and the angel of death—and yet he's equipped with ornaments that suggest an underlying dandyism and provide lures for the eye: the ring he shows off when he tugs thoughtfully at his earlobe; the classic wristwatch; the gold keychain that becomes noticeable when he opens or removes his coat; and the thin western-style belt with a shiny buckle that he displays when he repeatedly hooks his thumbs into the waist of his pants. Besides these accoutrements, he brings to the film a vestige of what Louise Brooks called the "Humphrey" as opposed to the "Bogie" side of his personality, hinting at the cultivated qualities in Marlowe. The son of a well-to-do surgeon and a suffragette who had studied painting with James McNeill Whistler, Bogart grew up on

New York's Upper West Side and briefly attended an elite prep school in Massachusetts, an experience in some ways like Chandler's years at Dulwich, except that Bogart was expelled. When he took up stage acting he was cast as an upper-class youth in tennis clothes, and late in his career he was quite convincing as an old-money New Yorker in Wilder's *Sabrina* (1954), a role that was originally intended for Cary Grant. He was one of the few virile male stars of his era who convincingly played literate characters, as in *In a Lonely Place* (1950) and *The Barefoot Contessa* (1954); in the role of Marlowe, who tells General Sternwood that he went to college "and can speak English if there's any demand for it," he's able to say "No one was more pleased than I" while still seeming tough, and he makes some of us doubt him when he claims he never heard of Proust.

Brooks tells us that at the beginning of Bogart's career racists made fun of what they called his "nigger" mouth, which had a small scar on the upper lip. He turned the supposed flaw to his advantage, practicing what Brooks describes as "lip gymnastics" alongside a battery of winces, fiendish grins, and eccentric movements. But as Brooks explains, to be a star in the classic studio period it was necessary to combine "eccentricity and mystery" with "naturalness" (64–65). By the 1940s Bogart was not only eccentric but also a performer who listened intently to other players and whose face seemed marked with a reflective, mysterious inwardness. André Bazin rightly contrasts him with the Method players, with their "anti-intellectual spontaneity" and "immediate impulses whose link to the inner life cannot be read directly." Bogart was expressively guarded but always visibly thinking, often conveying what Bazin describes as a mixture of "distrust and weariness, wisdom and skepticism" (in Hiller, *"Cahiers du Cinéma": The 1950s*, 100). This quality is valuable to *The Big Sleep*, in part because Marlowe is a detective, and in part because one of the film's chief departures from the novel is to dispense with Marlowe's first-person narration. Bogart's world-weary, skeptical thoughtfulness and history as a star—especially as the once-burned lover who makes a noble sacrifice in *Casablanca*—help to subtly counterbalance Hawks's easygoing, somewhat playful style, suggesting the inwardness and melancholy romanticism of Chandler's character.

Almost the only Hollywood leading man of his day who oscillated between heroic and villainous roles, Bogart had an ambiguous star image, which made him seem less obviously chivalric than the character Chandler had created and gave him a liminal quality appropriate to the legal position of a private eye. One of his special attributes as an actor was an ability to play attractively masculine figures who are subject to moments of emotional anguish and male hysteria: see the ruthless speech to Brigid O'Shaughnessy at the end of *The Maltese Falcon*, the "in all the gin joints in all the world" scene in *Casablanca*, and the fits of near psychotic violence in *In a Lonely Place*. This behavior surfaces only briefly in *The Big Sleep*, when Marlowe secretly witnesses the killing of Harry Jones (Elisha Cook Jr.), but in this film and all his later roles Bogart's face is visibly lined and dissipated, as if sculpted by a history of anguish. Production of *The Big Sleep* was repeatedly hampered by his drinking and absences as a result of his love affair with Lauren Bacall and collapsing marriage to Mayo Methot (see the studio memos of November 20 and December 26, 1944, in Behlmer, 244–45). Perhaps for that reason, one of the most intriguing aspects of his performance is the shadow of his age and mortality.

Viewing Bogart in hindsight shortly after he died in 1957, Bazin wrote that Bogart "epitomized the immanence of death" (in Hiller, "*Cahiers du Cinéma*": *The 1950s*, 98). In *The Big Sleep* he's ten years older than the character he plays and has already begun to show the effects of hard drinking and chain smoking. As in *To Have and Have Not* and *Key Largo* (1948), he's made to seem vigorous by virtue of scenes with the very young Lauren Bacall and older men who are lame or in wheelchairs. Occasionally, however, he looks haggard, and spittle forms around his lips when he draws on a Chesterfield. My wife tells me that in his automotive kissing scene with Bacall—a scene analyzed in a well-known essay by Raymond Bellour—she always feels that a bit of his saliva is visible on Bacall's chin, a detail almost as disconcerting as if his toupee had slipped. Elsewhere, a haunted frailty can be glimpsed beneath his tough exterior, a look appropriate to Chandler's title and the elegiac sentences near the end the novel: "What did it matter where you lay once you were dead? In a dirty sump or in a marble tower on top of a high hill? You were dead, you were sleeping the big sleep, you were not bothered by things like that."

WOMEN, HOMOSEXUALITY, ORIENTALISM

In a letter to Jean Bethel in April 1947, Chandler wrote, "The real distinction of the detective's personality is that, as a detective, he falls for nobody. He is the avenging justice, the bringer of order out of chaos.... But in Hollywood you cannot make a picture which is not essentially a love story, that is to say, a story in which sex is paramount" (*Selected Letters*, 93). Chandler was mostly correct about classic Hollywood, but the monastic solitude of Phillip Marlowe isn't a requirement of detective stories—see, for example, such tandem characterizations as Holmes and Watson or Nick and Nora. See also the credit sequence of Hawks's film, which features two silhouetted actors representing Bogart and Bacall, thus capitalizing on the recent marriage of the two stars and suggesting the possibility of a noir-like couple romantically involved in a detective adventure.

Marlowe's isolation in the novel may reflect Chandler's Edwardian or personal ambivalence toward sexuality, but it also has an American literary ancestry that can be traced as far back as Fenimore Cooper's Natty Bumppo. In his seminal *Studies in Classic American Literature*, D.H. Lawrence describes Natty as a "moralizer" who "lives by death" and is only "half tempted" by sex; he represents what Lawrence calls the "essential white American soul," which is "hard, isolate, stoic, and a killer" (329). Marlowe belongs in this tradition, and his "half tempted" attitude toward even casual sex is one of the major differences between the novel and the film of *The Big Sleep*. In Chandler's version, Vivian Regan covers up the killing of her husband, Rusty, by her wild, epileptic sister Carmen and then unsuccessfully tries to seduce Marlowe in order to block his investigation; in the film, Vivian isn't guilty of a crime and becomes Marlowe's sexual partner.

The difference is in part due to Hollywood convention, but also due to Lauren Bacall's stunning debut opposite Bogart in Hawks's previous film, *To Have and Have Not*, which made her the most successful incarnation of what critics have dubbed "the Hawks woman"—an independent, slightly androgynous, sexually forthright type, never coy or vampish, never angling for marriage, who becomes the hero's pal. An almost equally typical character in Hawks's films is the pretty young man who platonically loves the hero and becomes his symbolic son or partner: Montgomery Clift in *Red River* (1948), Ricky Nelson in *Rio Bravo* (1959), and Dewey Martin in several pictures. These female and male characters have long been of interest to feminist and queer studies and have been discussed by many fine writers, including Molly Haskell, Laura Mulvey, Naomi Wise, Peter Wollen, and Robin Wood. I won't rehearse the arguments about them, but I want to emphasize that Chandler's *The Big Sleep* is a problematic vehicle for Hawks's favored treatment of sexual relationships.

At the beginning of work on the adaptation, Hawks, who was not only the film's producer-director but also half owner with Warner Brothers of the movie rights to Chandler's novel, told screenwriters William Faulkner and Leigh Brackett to stay as close as possible to Chandler's plot, which indeed they did; but as the project developed, there was a growing need for the studio to capitalize on Bacall's success by making her resemble Slim, the provocative young saloon singer modeled on Hawks's wife, Nancy, who had entered into "no strings" companionship with Bogart in *To Have and Have Not*. The result, especially visible in the revised, 1946 release version of the film, was a grafting together of two different characters. Vivian in the novel is more like the conventional noir femme fatale: "She was worth a stare. She was trouble," Marlowe tells us when he first sees her. Marlowe's ethical and one might even say political integrity lies precisely in his ability to resist Vivian's and Carmen's sexual allure and wealth, just as he resists the violence and money of the gangster Eddie Mars. Hawks altered this situation to accommodate a romance plot, and in so doing made a film somewhat at odds with Chandler. Yet traces of the original conception remained. Vivian in the film, like Vivian in the novel, is a previously married woman of a higher social class than Marlowe, and she initially treats him with condescension and suspicion (when they first meet, he seems to her all the more like an underling because he has removed his coat and is covered with sweat). Even when she becomes Marlowe's lover and performs a musical number in a nightclub, she's a far cry from Slim, the sultry, sexually aggressive, adolescent-looking showgirl who wears revealing costumes and sings in a near baritone at a dive bar in Martinique.

When *The Big Sleep* was given an advance screening for U.S. servicemen in 1944, the audience reaction to Bacall as Vivian was predictably disappointing. Domestic release of the film was delayed for more than a year to make room for pictures with wartime themes, and in the meantime the publicity generated by Bacall's 1945 marriage to Bogart made the studio and Bacall's agent insist on revisions to boost her sex appeal. Scenes were reshot with Bacall in new costumes (one of them quite similar to a form-fitting checked dress she wore in *To Have and Have Not*), behaving more like a gutsy partner of the detective; and Hawks shot an entirely new scene by the uncredited Philip Epstein in which Bogart and Bacall meet in a bar and exchange bawdy double entendre. Chandler grumbled about this to his British publisher: "The girl who played the nymphy sister was so good she shattered Miss Bacall completely. So they cut the picture [and] made nonsense" (*Selected Letters*, 75). But even with the revisions, Bacall never quite achieves the likable, free-spirited sexiness she radiated in *To Have and Have Not*. The sexual relationships in Hawks's films usually have a friendly and sexy regressiveness, quite different from the threatening sexuality in Chandler. The revised version of *The Big Sleep* manages to include moments of Hawksian sexual byplay between the lead players—chiefly the scene in which Bogart and Bacall joke with a telephone caller to Marlowe's office—but it can't completely transform a Chandler woman into a Hawks heroine.

Hawks seems to have recognized this problem from the start, because he compensates for it at the level of supporting roles. Another of his major departures from the novel was to create a running joke by introducing a bevy of starlets who play working girls—a librarian, a taxi driver, a manager of a bookstore, a waitress in a diner, and so forth. They all behave like miniature versions of the Hawks woman, showing sexual interest in the private eye without being lascivious or coy like Carmen Sternwood. All are extremely young, between the ages of nineteen and twenty-two. (Bacall was twenty when she made the film, and Martha Vickers, who plays

Carmen, was nineteen.) One of their functions is to give the aging Bogart an air of youthful virility, and another was probably to give Hawks a potential harem. But in the original version of the film these young women had an additional value. Most of *The Big Sleep* was shot during wartime—hence the gasoline rationing stickers on Marlowe's car, the female cab driver, and the large picture of Franklin Roosevelt on the wall of the Acme bookstore. Hawks knew the film would be exhibited to overseas troops, so he chose women who had posed in pinups for military magazines, and perhaps he even arranged for them to appear in those magazines.

The most striking case in point is nineteen-year-old Dorothy Malone, who wore a two-piece swimsuit on the cover of *Yank* magazine. Unlike many of the women in supporting roles, she has a counterpart in Chandler's novel, but Chandler's handling of the scene is quite different:

> I flipped my wallet open on her desk and let her look at the buzzer pinned to the flap. She looked at it, took her glasses off and leaned back in her chair. I put the wallet away She had the fine-drawn face of an intelligent Jewess. She stared at me and said nothing. . . .
> "Would you have a *Ben Hur*, 1860, Third Edition, the one with the duplicated line on page 116?"
> She pushed her yellow law book to one side and reached a fat volume up on the desk, leafed through it, found her page, and studied it. "Nobody would," she said, without looking up. "There isn't one."
> "Right."
> "What in the world are you driving at?"
> "The girl in Geiger's store didn't know that."
> She looked up. "I see. You interest me. Rather vaguely."
> "I'm a private dick on a case. Perhaps I ask too much. It didn't seem much to me somehow."
> She blew a soft grey smoke ring and poked her finger through. It came to pieces in frail wisps. She spoke smoothly, indifferently. "In his early forties, I should judge. Medium height, fattish. Would weigh about a hundred and sixty pounds. Fat face, Charlie Chan moustache, thick soft neck. Soft all over. Well dressed, goes without a hat, affects a knowledge of antiques and hasn't any. Oh yes. His left eye is glass."
> "You'd make a good cop," I said.
> She put the reference book back on an open shelf at the end of her desk, and opened the law book in front of her again. "I hope not," she said. She put her glasses on.
> I thanked her and left.

The woman in Chandler is Jewish (at least she seems so to Marlowe), detached, preoccupied, supercilious. Hawks replaces her with a young actress from Texas (the jury is out on whether Chandler was anti-Semitic, but by several accounts Hawks was—Lauren Bacall said that she never told

Hawks she was Jewish). He also gives her warmth, humor, and seductiveness. She likes Marlowe and is flattered when he tells her she'd make a good cop. She's amused when he asks her to remove her glasses and let down her hair, and she enjoys having a shot of whiskey and a sexual interlude. As he puts it, she's a "pal," someone he can thank for the memory without her becoming too girlish and clingy.

For me, this is one of the most charming scenes in the movie. David Thomson sees it differently, describing the Malone character as "a placid whore, an available young bitch" who makes us wonder "just what the 'marriage' between Marlowe and Vivian is going to be like" (*The Big Sleep*, 62–63). In my view the Malone character is an intelligent, independent female and the best partner for Bogart in the film; even without her, I wonder how a marriage between Marlowe and Vivian could possibly happen. As I see it, her scene is a comic interlude, challenging the censors and allowing Bogart to make fun of his image. When he says, "I'm a private dick on a case," he reads the line with heavy innuendo and we hear a clap of thunder from the storm outside. When Malone tells him the man he's asking about is "fattish," he pulls in his stomach as she looks him up and down. It's an encounter between two intelligent people who are mutually attracted and who form a kind of sexual friendship. No doubt it's a Hollywood fantasy designed by and for men, but it allows the woman to make the first move without seeming like a vamp or slut.

An opposite character type, and one of the few females from the novel that the film doesn't change, is Carmen, who with some qualification might be called the Chandler woman. (I say "with some qualification" because Chandler's treatment of bad women is sometimes gallant, as in *Farewell, My Lovely*.) A depraved rich girl, Carmen has two nude scenes in the novel: Marlowe breaks into Geiger's bungalow and finds her posing for pictures in nothing but a pair of jade earrings; and, later, he returns home to find her naked in his bed. The first time he behaves like Galahad. The second time he throws her out, opens a window, takes a stiff drink, stares at the imprint on his sheets of her "small corrupt body," and "savagely" tears the bed to pieces. This latter scene has understandably tempted some critics to psychoanalyze the author. Where such matters are concerned, it may be significant that the underlying motive for half the novel's murders and the entire byzantine plot is Carmen's secret past, which is discovered at the end. It may also be significant that in a conversation with Hawks, Chandler proposed ending the film by having Carmen unintentionally machine-gunned by Eddie Mars's men. Hawks, in part because he was prodded by the studio and the censors, decided that the relatively guiltless Eddie Mars should be gunned down instead.

Hawks, of course, was also prevented by censors from showing nudity and from being explicit about other details surrounding Carmen's role in the novel. During the scene in Geiger's bungalow, for example, we see Bogart sniffing at a glass but never learn that it contains a mixture of ether and laudanum. More significantly, we're never told that Geiger is a pornographer and a homosexual. In the novel, Carol Lundgren, Geiger's male lover, arranges Geiger's body on a funeral bed and murders Joe Brody under the mistaken assumption that Brody was Geiger's killer. Chandler emphasizes the homosexual theme from the moment when Marlowe first enters Geiger's bookshop: "If you can weigh a hundred and ninety pounds and look like a fairy," he tells us, "I was doing my best." When Marlowe captures Carol Lundgren, whom he describes as a "very handsome boy indeed," he announces, "You shot the wrong guy, Carol. Joe Brody didn't kill your queen." He knocks the boy out, calls him a "pansy" and a "fag," and turns him over to the police.

The film is necessarily indirect about all this. It gives us Bogart's lisping impersonation of a gay book hunter, and in the role of Carol Lundgren it casts Tom Rafferty, who has the boyish good looks of a Montgomery Clift or a Dewey Martin. Its chief way of intimating Geiger's sexual propensities, however, is a prominent motif from the novel: Geiger has a "Charlie Chan moustache" and his bookstore and apartment are filled with chinoiserie and fake Asian art. The vaguely Chinese decor of the bookshop is enough to provoke Marlowe's gay act, and the Asian kitsch of the apartment, like Carmen's silken Chinese robe, connotes illicit sexuality.

Imagery of the exotic, enigmatic East, often associated with luxury, perversity and seductiveness, is quite old in American culture. In *The Scarlet Letter*, for example, Nathaniel Hawthorne tells us that the Puritan adulteress Hester Prynne "had in her nature a rich, voluptuous, oriental characteristic—a taste for the gorgeously beautiful." As I've previously noted in *More than Night: Film Noir in its Contexts*, this kind of Orientalism is pervasive in noir fiction and film, beginning with Dashiell Hammett's San Francisco crime stories and continuing through movies such as *The Shanghai Gesture* (1941), *The Lady from Shanghai* (1948), *Macao* (1952), *Chinatown* (1974) and many others. In Chandler's *Farewell, My Lovely*, the obviously gay Lindsay Mariott hires Marlowe to help him recover a jade necklace, and in *The High Window* Marlowe encounters a nightclub hat-check girl wearing "peach-bloom Chinese pajamas" who has "eyes like strange sins."

A more detailed analysis of the phenomenon in Chandler and elsewhere can be found in Homay King's *Lost in Translation: Orientalism, Projection, and the Enigmatic Signifier*, which makes the important point that Orientalism in noir is linked to the search into a mystery—a need to know that in some forms underwrites sexual desire. King argues that desire in general is often stimulated by enigmatic but fetishized signifiers, much like the tantalizing clues in a detective story. Feminist film theory has analyzed the noir femme fatale and the cinematic gaze in roughly similar fashion; and in purely historical and empirical terms, there can be no question that the Western notion of the "inscrutable East" has repeatedly been used in the service of noir's eroticized women and serpentine, mysterious plots. Moreover, the same cultural construction has often been associated with queerness in mystery films—see, as only one example, the statuary adorning Waldo Lydecker's apartment in *Laura*. Asia, like the femme fatale and male homosexuality, tends to represent what Richard Dyer has identified as a threatening excess of femininity. The homosexual aesthete and the promiscuous woman are equally Oriental, equally devious or bent, and equally prone to secrets and ciphers—and in Chandler's *The Big Sleep* they must be expunged or brought under control.

FUN, MORALITY, POLITICS

One of the shortest and most unintentionally amusing Hollywood studio memos on record is from Jack Warner to Howard Hawks during the filming of *The Big Sleep* in 1944: "Word has reached me that you are having fun on the set. This must stop" (quoted by McCarthy, 387). No doubt Hawks *was* having fun. He was a gifted director of screwball comedy, and very few of his dramatic films are without comic elements. On the other hand, some of his screwball pictures have deeply shadowed moments; the nocturnal scenes in *Bringing Up Baby* are both carnivalesque and threatening, almost in the vein of *A Midsummer Night's Dream*, and the night in *His Girl Friday* is filled with civic corruption and danger.

Hawks was nevertheless an unlikely director of film noir. He disliked making pictures about what he called "losers," and he rarely employed the fancy camera angles, POV shots, choker close-ups, and ostentatious tracking or craning that have, perhaps incorrectly, been associated with the noir form. Instead, he favored eye-level, middle-distance compositions and exhibited a good deal of skill in handling the marginal actions and minor characters that occupy what Manny Farber called "negative space." The acting and speech in his films is fast-paced (Hawks was one of the early proponents of overlapping dialogue), and yet it has a softly delivered, amusing, laid-back quality.

Hawks told Raymond Chandler that his method of directing was "to shoot from the cuff more or less . . . merely using a rough script to try out his scenes and then rewriting them on the set" (*Selected Letters*, 30). This was true of *The Big Sleep* in only minor ways; studio memos indicate that Hawks rewrote a few scenes on the set because of production delays and the need to revise Bacall's role (Behlmer, 244–45). Otherwise, the film is reasonably faithful to the Faulkner-Brackett-Furthman screenplay and retains a good deal of language from the novel. But Hawks did indeed encourage what he called "kicking around" scenes in rehearsal, a practice that no doubt contributed to the looseness and sense of improvised fun in his pictures.

In contrast, Chandler thought of his stories as carefully wrought popular entertainment for an audience that didn't necessarily recognize his talent. He wanted to be taken seriously as an artist, but he praised Dashiell Hammett for making the murder mystery "fun" (*Raymond Chandler: Later Novels*, 990) and resisted highbrow attempts to find deep meaning in his work. "Here I am halfway through a Marlowe story and having fun," he complained to Frederick Lewis Allen, "when along comes this fellow [W.H.] Auden and tells me I am interested in writing serious studies of a criminal milieu" (*Selected Letters*, 114–15). Philip Marlowe does indeed serve as a mordant commentator on American modernity, but his commentary is offset by wit and a ceaseless flow of dark, adventurous action. Chandler gives us melodrama and nuggets of social criticism in a romantic, quasi-poetic, wryly amusing, immanently quotable style. Most of the clever lines of dialogue in the film version of *The Big Sleep* come straight from his novel, as does most of the action.

Where plot was concerned, Chandler's advice to aspiring writers of tough thrillers was "When in doubt, have a man come through the door with a gun in his hand" (*Raymond Chandler: Later Novels*, 1017). In the novel versus the film of *The Big Sleep*, some of the differences between Hawks's and Chandler's ways of having fun can be seen when characters come through the door bearing guns. At one point in the novel, Eddie Mars calls in a pair of thugs to search Marlowe, and they enter reaching for their pistols. Marlowe describes one as "a good-looking pale-faced boy with a bad nose and one ear like a club steak," and the other as "slim, blond, deadpan, with close-set eyes and no color in them." Together they do an efficient if inconsequential job of frisking Marlowe. In the film, the scene is played more for broad comedy, as if by two of the Three Stooges, one of them short, chubby, and bald, the other tall, thin, and silly looking. Marlowe almost hits the thin fellow in the face with a lighted cigarette as he's being searched. He asks Mars if this fellow is any good, and Mars says he's just around to keep the other one company.

A richer example of the intermingling of comedy and danger is the longest episode in the film, when Marlowe visits Joe Brody's apartment and several guns are on display. In the novel, this scene involves four people, but Hawks adds a fifth, Vivian Routledge. As David Thomson observes, there are so many entrances and exits that the action verges on French farce. The players are arranged tableaux-style, framed from the knees up, and the copious dialogue is spoken swiftly, occasionally departing from Chandler's text to create amusing moments of overlapping lines. When Vivian enters, she and Marlowe bicker like a married couple while Joe Brody points a gun and tries to get a word in. The three step on one another's lines and repeat themselves: "Look at him, he's all curious and bothered." "Sure I'm all curious and bothered!" "Stop waving that gun around. I didn't have anything to do with him!" "Then how did he ... " "Can't you talk without pointing that gun?" "Don't argue with the man. Do as he says, sit down!" "You're ruining everything!" "I'm not ruining anything!" Soon Carmen comes through the door pointing a gun and a scuffle ensues, after which Marlowe has captured three guns and Carmen is crawling on the floor "like a Pekinese."

When Carmen and Vivian exit, Marlowe is left with Brody and Agnes. There follows a single three-and-a-half-minute shot in which Marlowe questions Brody about the deaths of Geiger and the Routledge family chauffeur. Brody is beautifully played by Louis Jean Heydt, who usually has his back to the camera and twists back and forth in a chair while Bogart paces around and gazes at him. Heydt nervously puffs a cigarette, speaking swiftly but gently, half smiling in apologetic fashion; a small-time and not very tough crook, he has trouble asserting authority and making up stories under pressure. Equally impressive is Sonia Darrin, who plays Agnes, and who for some reason wasn't credited in the film (some of her scenes were cut when the film was revised). Darrin gives a splendid demonstration of what Manny Farber has described as "termite art." Holding a single pose, she sits in the background, her lanky legs crossed, looking on in contempt at both men. In a weary monotone, she glances at Brody and says, "He gives me a pain in ... " "That goes for me, too," Brody interrupts. "Where's he give you a pain?" Marlowe asks. "Right in my ... ," she says, but Brody cuts her off again. Mournfully, she describes Brody as "a half smart guy. That's what I always draw, never once a guy who's smart all the way around the course." "Did I hurt you much, sugar?" Marlowe asks. The only woman in the film who isn't impressed by him, she rubs her wrist, which Marlowe has twisted to take away her gun, and answers in her usual monotone, "You and every other man I met."

Another source of fun is the involuntary surrealism in the novel and the film, both of which abandon the rational form of classic detective stories in favor of bewildering action spiked with alcohol, violence, and corpses. The most famous story about the making of the film involves the fact that Chandler's novel never explains who killed Owen Taylor, the chauffeur found underwater near the Lido pier. When Hawks and William Faulkner asked Chandler who did it, Chandler said he couldn't recall and joked that it might have been the butler. (According to Hawks's biographer, Todd McCarthy, when Sonia Darrin heard of the problem she declared that Howard Hawks did it.) For the 1944 version of the film, Faulkner and Brackett provided a scene in which Marlowe explains to the district attorney that Joe Brody is the killer; this scene was cut when the film was revised, but nobody seems to have missed it. David Thomson and Todd McCarthy argue that the revised version was a turning point in Hawks's career, convincing him that good scenes were more important than coherent narrative. Indeed, Hawks repeatedly said exactly this in interviews, turning it into a kind of mantra. Thomson goes so far as to call the revised version of *The Big Sleep* "radical" and "postmodern" in its wayward approach to storytelling (*The Big Sleep*, 67).

The problem with such arguments is that many of Hawks's later pictures have quite lucid narratives, and the incoherence of *The Big Sleep* was already there in the novel upon which the film is based. Chandler, who was never much interested in the puzzle aspect of mystery fiction, stitched his plot together from separate stories he had written for the pulps; as a result, the action of the novel tends to veer off in unexpected directions, making the goal of Marlowe's investigation unclear and the mystery as murky as in the film. In his letters and essays, Chandler repeatedly stressed that he preferred atmospheric scenes over action and plot. He told Frederick Lewis Allen that from the moment he started writing for the pulps, he set out to prove that people "just *thought* they cared about nothing but the action. . . . The things they cared about, and that I cared about, were the creation of emotion through dialogue and description" (*Selected Letters*, 115). To critic James Sandoe, he complained that at the end of writing *The Little Sister* he was "faced with the choice between a clear but boring explanation of who shot who, why and where etc., and more or less letting it hang in the air on the theory that who cared anyway" (ibid., 175). In another of his letters, he observed that "after working in Hollywood, where the analysis of plot and motivation is carried on with utter ruthlessness," he realized all the more that plot was an impediment to his aims as a novelist: "I'd write something I liked and then would have a hell of a time making it fit in to the structure. This resulted in some rather startling oddities of construction, about which I care nothing, being fundamentally rather uninterested in plot" (ibid., 87). And in the introduction to the stories he published in *The Simple Art of Murder*, he wrote, "The technical basis of the *Black Mask* type of story . . . was that the scene outranked the plot, in the sense that a good plot was one which made good scenes. The ideal mystery was one you would read if the end was missing" (*Raymond Chandler: Later Novels*, 1017). It seems likely that Hawks's vaunted discovery of the importance of scene over plot was something he actually learned from talking with Chandler. Although Chandler was unhappy with the revisions for the 1946 version of *The Big Sleep*, those revisions offer proof positive of his repeated contention that style or mood can trump narrative.

The postwar French critics who invented the idea of American film noir, many of whom were writing under the influence of surrealism, were equally unconcerned with the niceties of plot, and for them Hawks's convoluted narrative, half-hidden sadism, and dark humor were sources of subversive pleasure. Georges Sadoul praised *The Big Sleep* for being "opaque, like a nightmare, or the ramblings of a drunk" (quoted in Borde and Chaumeton, 11). Raymond Borde and Etienne Chaumeton, authors of the first book on film noir, especially admired the sense of disequilibrium in *The Big Sleep:* "There is, in this incoherent brutality, something dreamlike," they wrote (11). The film's oneiric quality, together with "the sordid settings and their bizarre details, the brief but merciless fistfights, the sudden reversal of roles, the 'objects' in the Surrealist sense of the word, . . . and the eroticism of blood and pain," resulted in what Borde and Chaumeton called "a major event in the history of American cinema" (57).

This was a moment in cinema's reception history when, for some critics, a kind of fun was linked to a surrealist-inflected, politicized aestheticism. Of course, where Hawks and Hollywood were concerned, *The Big Sleep* had no intended politics. Beyond the obligatory patriotism of his war pictures and the cynically libertarian satire of *His Girl Friday*, Hawks's work is notable for its avoidance of social themes and its preoccupation with male individuals or tight-knit, virtually all-male groups. Chandler, whose most famous essay, "The Simple Art of Murder," ends with a call for a "realist" detective fiction dealing with "a world in which gangsters can rule nations" (*Later Novels and Other Writings*, 991), is a somewhat different story. Moderately liberal but hardly an engaged writer, Chandler could defend himself against the vulgarity of modern America and the corrupt oligarchy that ruled Los Angeles only through pride in his work and an old-fashioned belief in a code of personal honor. If Dashiell Hammett was a proto-Marxist who depicted an ambiguous private eye in an ethically groundless world, Chandler was a romantic realist whose detective is a cross between what Mike Davis has called a "small businessman locked in struggle with gangsters, corrupt police and the parasitic rich" (38) and a knight in shining armor from an English public school.

But Marlowe is also a discriminating observer and explicit critic of Los Angeles. Another difference between Chandler's *The Big Sleep* and Hawks's adaptation is that the film is shot in a wonderfully atmospheric but studio-constructed city and therefore lacks the novel's accurately documented climate, flora, and architecture. The film also eliminates Chandler's overt social criticism, partly because Hawks wasn't interested in such things and partly because the Breen-office censors wouldn't permit them. Early in the novel, for example, Marlowe stands on the Sternwoods' front steps and looks down the hill at a row of oil derricks. The Sternwoods, he tells himself, are too far up the hill to smell the oil and stale sump water; if they wanted, they could still see the industry that made them rich, but "I don't suppose they would want to." (The oily sump water returns at the climax of the book and reappears in the elegiac closing paragraph.) In conversation with a Los Angeles county sheriff, Marlowe points out that the cops in every big city engage in cover-ups "to oblige their friends or anybody with a little pull." In another conversation with Vivian Regan, he remarks that during Prohibition there were two uniformed policemen in Eddie Mars's club every night "to see that the guests didn't bring their own liquor instead of buying it from the house." Later, a half-honest policeman tells Marlowe that he would like to see Eddie Mars in prison alongside "the poor little slum-bred hard guys that got knocked over on their first caper and never got a break since." But he's sure that won't happen, "not in a town half this size, in any part of this wide, green and beautiful U.S.A. We just don't run our country that way."

Despite these comments, Chandler's fiction was limited in its depth of social criticism and seriousness of purpose. Philip Marlowe is a different kind of hero from Jake Gittes, the devastated private eye in Roman Polanski's *Chinatown* (1974); he comes to admire General Sternwood, the novel's only representative of truly big money and power in Los Angeles; and for all the beatings he suffers and corruption he sees, he remains an outside observer, an agent of justice who looks into the heart of darkness but is never truly shaken or changed. Chandler was writing melodrama, not tragedy. He was nevertheless insistent that his novels had a social and moral purpose. In 1949, producer John Houseman, who had worked with Chandler on *The Blue Dahlia* (1947) and who many years later in his memoirs would tell a misleading story about the making of that film, wrote a slick-paper magazine article in which he decried *The Big Sleep* and other "tough" movies for depicting "a land of enervated, frightened people with a low moral sense, ... groping their way through a twilight of insecurity and corruption" (quoted in Maltby, "Politics," 41). Chandler responded in a personal letter to Houseman, describing the article as "artistically patronizing, intellectually dishonest and logically unsound ... the last whisper of the Little Theater mind in you." He was annoyed that Houseman hadn't noticed that, unlike the film version of *The Big Sleep*, "the book had a high moral content." Marlowe's struggle, he wrote, "is the struggle of all fundamentally honest men to make a decent living in a corrupt society. It is an impossible struggle ... because the bitter fact is that outside of two or three technical professions which require long years of preparation, there is absolutely no way for a man of this age to acquire a decent affluence of life without in some degree corrupting himself, without accepting the cold, clear fact that success is always and everywhere a racket" (*Selected Letters*, 197).

Whatever reservations he may have had about the film adaptation of his novel, Chandler clearly admired Hawks, whom he described as "a very wise hombre" (*Selected Letters*, 132). He may have been charmed by Hawks's pseudo–Ivy League manners and silver-haired elegance, which contrasted with most of the people he met in Hollywood. He probably also believed some of Hawks's tall stories. In *The Little Sister* he alludes to Hawks and even suggests that Philip Marlowe has met him. The scene is Marlowe's office, where a couple of villains enter and frighten him by pulling the trigger of an unloaded gun in his face. He responds by indirectly referring to an incident from *To Have and Have Not*:

> I said, slowly and thickly: "A friend of mine told me about a fellow that had something like this pulled on him. He was at a desk the way I am. He had a gun, just the way I have. There were two men on the other side of the desk, like you and Alfred. The man on my side began to get mad. He couldn't help himself. He began to shake. He couldn't speak a word. He just had this gun in his hand. So without a word he shot twice through the desk, right where your belly is."
> The big man turned a sallow green color and started to get up. But he changed his mind. . . . "You seen that in a picture," he said.
> "That's right," I said. "But the man who made the picture told me where he got the idea. *That* wasn't in any picture."

Nevertheless, Hawks was friendly with a class of studio chiefs that Chandler regarded as little better than gangsters. The politico-ideological distance between the two men, and perhaps between some aspects of the publishing industry and Hollywood, can be seen in the different ways the book and the film resolve the story. In Chandler's version, Eddie Mars and the corrupt police keep their power and Marlowe remains a lonely observer of a fallen world. In Hawks's, Mars is killed by his own men and the armed Marlowe, alongside his partner Vivian, gazes out a window at the untarnished officers of the law as they round up the villains.

One can argue that the film is relatively conventional and compromised; on the other hand, one can argue that the film is less misogynistic than the novel and that the ostensibly conventional Hawks is subtler than Chandler. It can at least be said that the last shot of the film achieves a nice balance between two different artists and remains true to a certain noir-like logic: darkness is gathering, the police lights are vaguely threatening, and we fade out on a pair of unlikely lovers whose embrace is endlessly deferred; they're a durable image of Hollywood romance, but not necessarily a permanent couple.

Uptown Folk

Blackness and Entertainment in *Cabin in the Sky*

Between 1927 and 1954, the major Hollywood studios produced only six feature films that took place in an all-black milieu: *Hallelujah!* (MGM, 1929), *Hearts in Dixie* (Fox, 1929), *The Green Pastures* (Warner Brothers, 1936), *Cabin in the Sky* (MGM, 1943), *Stormy Weather* (Twentieth Century-Fox, 1944), and *Carmen Jones* (Twentieth Century-Fox, 1954). Two other pictures represented blackness in a less substantial way: *Tales of Manhattan* (Paramount, 1942), which is an anthology film with one episode devoted to black characters, and *Song of the South* (Disney, 1946), which is a blend of animation and live action.

The period in question was the heyday of classic cinema, bounded at one end by the introduction of sound and at the other by a shift toward a decentered, "package unit" mode of production (see Bordwell, Staiger, and Thompson, 330–38). More importantly, 1954 was also the year when the Supreme Court ordered public schools desegregated, paving the way for a civil rights movement that would have a lasting effect on all the media. Until then, any studio film purporting to deal exclusively with black experience was truly exceptional and controversial. The films listed above are therefore among the most unusual products of American show business, and no proper history of the movies should ignore them.

Viewed from today's perspective, one of the most interesting of the "all Negro" productions was MGM's *Cabin in the Sky*, starring Ethel Waters, Eddie Anderson, Lena Horne, and a host of well-known black performers—interesting not only because of its entertainment value but also because it appeared at a crucial historical juncture, when African Americans were increasing their demands for better treatment from the movie industry, when black musical performers were achieving a degree of celebrity they had not enjoyed before, and when the federal government was engaged in a semiofficial drive to encourage more pictures with black casts. Although

Cabin was manufactured at a conservative studio, it was designed to appeal to a variety of audiences, binding them together in the name of wartime solidarity; in certain ways it can be described as a liberal or historically transitional work, telling us important things about the complex, sometimes troubled relations between ethnicity and modernity.

In general terms, *Cabin* was no different from the other five studio-produced films about blacks. All were symptoms of a segregated society; all were written, produced, and directed by whites; and all were musicals or melodramatic narratives that made extensive use of song and dance, thus reinforcing the white culture's perception of African Americans as a fun-loving, "rhythmic" people. As a group, the six films also depended upon a vivid opposition between city and country that structured both classic Hollywood and many aspects of the culture at large. This opposition was always crucial to any art or entertainment that involved blackness; notice, for example, how the country-city polarity functioned in early uses of "jazz," a term that had been appropriated by white songwriters from Tin Pan Alley and turned into an ambiguous, highly flexible signifier. Was jazz a primitive music, a people's music, or an entertainment music? All three possibilities were suggested by critics, and the term seemed to oscillate between diametrically opposed meanings: on the one hand, jazz was associated with flappers, skyscrapers, and the entire panoply of interwar modernity; on the other hand, because it originated with African Americans who migrated to the northern cities, it connoted agrarian or precapitalist social relations and could be linked to a pastoral myth. Kern and Hammerstein's *Show Boat* (1927) and Gershwin's *Porgy and Bess* (1935)—two celebrated "modern" stage musicals—were grounded in folkloric treatments of blacks. Even Warner Brothers' *The Jazz Singer* (1927) evoked both city and country: jazz represents a force of modernization that disrupts a conservative Jewish household, but when the protagonist enters show business he reasserts old-fashioned values by donning blackface and singing "Mammy."

The same oppositions can be observed everywhere in *Cabin in the Sky*, which uses black-influenced popular music to tell a story about a rural community threatened by gamblers and nightclubs. But *Cabin* creates a slightly different effect from earlier pictures of its type. Whatever its artistic merits (and these are far from negligible), its treatment of the country/city motif is ironic or insincere, signaling a modest change in mainstream cinema's negotiation of racial issues. Even though the film is never free of reactionary impulses, it's an entirely modern work, a musical that generates what Richard Dyer has described as a "utopian" feeling of energy, abundance, intensity, transparency, and community—a vision of "something we want deeply that our day-to-day lives don't provide" ("Entertainment and

Utopia," 177). Dyer qualifies his observation when he lists *Cabin* among a group of musicals that were "bought off by the nostalgia or primitivism which provides them with a point of departure" (188), but *Cabin*'s nostalgia is on one level quite superficial and its primitivism is transformed into a paradoxical sophistication. I would argue that the film is the product of a kind of capitalist progress, contributing to the breakdown of a pastoral, the death of a bogus authenticity, and the growing urbanization of black images in Hollywood. There's a sense in which *Cabin* was "saved" or made progressive by the very forces of mass-cultural aestheticism and commodification that leftist critics often condemn.

To fully appreciate such ironies, we should first examine *Cabin*'s historical context, bearing in mind Mikhail Bakhtin's observation that all art operates in a "dialogically agitated and tension-filled environment" (276). For obvious reasons, the environment surrounding this particular film was especially agitated and requires careful scrutiny. In what follows, I propose that *Cabin* was situated uneasily among at least four conflicting discourses about blackness and entertainment in America during World War II. I use "discourse" heuristically, to describe several conflicting voices. (For additional discussion of how films can become the sites of conflicting discourse, see Stam, Marchetti, and Shohat in *Unspeakable Images*. Where the response of actual historical spectators is concerned, I'll have less to say; for an important analysis of spectatorship and race, see Diawara.) The four discourses that interest me were composed of a variety of texts, including speeches, newspaper items, critical and theoretical writings, and artistic representations; for the most part they were generated outside Hollywood, and they tended to cut across the usual political divisions between right and left, affecting both the production and the reception of the film. By examining each in turn, we can begin to recover *Cabin*'s historical specificity, showing how several artists at MGM responded to the racial dialogue of their day.

FOUR DISCOURSES

Cabin was shaped first of all by a vestigial tradition of "folkloric" narratives having to do with poor blacks in rural southern communities. I should emphasize that nothing in the film was actually generated by an indigenous, agrarian culture, and that the idea of folklore itself is a suspiciously modern phenomenon, born of late-eighteenth-century attempts to distinguish between the learned and the popular. We should remember, moreover, that the discourse on the folk can have different uses. For the most part, the childlike mammies and pappies who once populated our songs, stories, and movies were figments of a reactionary white imagination, embodiments of what Peter Burke describes as everything "natural, simple, instinctive, irrational, and rooted in the local soil" (216). But another kind of folklore has been important to the historical consciousness of African Americans, and during the 1930s folkloric images of black people were frequently used by the WPA and the Popular Front on behalf of a progressive social agenda. The entire artistic culture of the Depression was somewhat "folksy" in tone, ranging from public murals to Lead Belly recordings, from the American Communist Party's folk-song movement to John Steinbeck's *The Grapes of Wrath*, and from off-Broadway theatrical productions like *Mule Bone* to Pulitzer Prize–winning hits like *The Green Pastures*.

Cabin in the Sky has an ancestry in this mostly liberal, 1930s-style folklorism. The film was based on a 1940 Broadway musical by Lynn Root concerning an impoverished Georgia laborer named Little Joe who is wounded by gunfire during a dice game. Joe's devout wife, Petunia, prays for his recovery, and black emissaries of God and the Devil are sent to earth to do battle for his soul. Joe is given a short reprieve so that he can mend his ways, but the Devil complicates matters, first by allowing Joe to win the Irish sweepstakes, and then by sending a temptress to lure him away from home. In the end, Petunia's faith wins out, and she and Joe ascend into heaven. Root's quasi-allegorical plot was rendered in the form of a colorful, mainstream spectacular, but many of the black performers, including such figures as Rex Ingram and Katherine Dunham, were associated in the public mind with a kind of folkloric art; indeed, the show's lyricist, John Latouche, had worked with the WPA and had written a famous Depression-era cantata entitled "Ballad for Americans." Not surprisingly, when MGM purchased the property it conceived the forthcoming film as a substitute for *Porgy and Bess* (which was unavailable for purchase), and it hired Marc Connelly, the author of *The Green Pastures*, to work on the screenplay (Minnelli, 21; Stephen Harvey, 41).

By the time *Cabin* went into production, however, African Americans had enlisted to fight in a war against fascism, and a second discourse about race was emerging, foreshadowing the civil rights movement of the next decade. Immediately before the war, Walter White, the executive secretary of the NAACP, had met with a group of Hollywood executives and stars—including Walter Wanger, David Selznick, Darryl Zanuck, and James Cagney—to discuss "the limitation of the Negro to comic or menial roles" (quoted in "The Papers of the NAACP," December, 1940). In 1942, the NAACP held its national convention in Los Angeles, where White called for an end to racial stereotyping and greater participation by black workers in Hollywood craft unions. Later that same year, at the invitation of Wendell Willkie, White made a similar speech to the East Coast Committee on

Public Relations of the Motion Picture Producers Association, which promised him it would "effect as rapid a change as possible in the treatment of Negroes in moving pictures" ("The Papers of the NAACP," April 1942).

Not coincidentally, *Casablanca* and *In This Our Life* were released by Warner Brothers in 1942, and several of the subsequent wartime pictures, including *Sahara* (1943) and *Bataan* (1943), showed urban blacks pitted against Nazi or Japanese antagonists. Equally important, the Office of War Information financed a handful of documentaries about black participation in combat, among them Carleton Moss and Stuart Heisler's *The Negro Soldier* (1944). During the same period, black musical performers, some of them bearing flamboyantly aristocratic names, were featured in movies about contemporary show business: Count Basie, Duke Ellington, and Nat King Cole worked at Republic Pictures in 1942–43, as did Louis Armstrong and Dorothy Dandridge; and in 1944, Fox produced *Stormy Weather*, starring Lena Horne and a virtual pantheon of jazz entertainers. Meanwhile, as Thomas Cripps has pointed out, the sentimental, folkloric depictions of plantation life in Julien Duvivier's *Tales of Manhattan* and Walt Disney's *Song of the South* were denounced by black organizations—this despite the fact that both films "might have been lauded for efforts in social progress" only a few years earlier (44).

When *Cabin in the Sky* and *Stormy Weather* went into production, the *New York Times* reported that both pictures had been given the explicit encouragement of the Roosevelt administration: "Two major studios, Metro-Goldwyn Mayer and Twentieth Century Fox, in producing pictures with all-Negro casts, are following the desires of Washington in making such films at this time. Decisions to produce the pictures, it is stated, followed official expression that the Administration felt that its program for increased employment of Negro citizens in certain heretofore restricted fields of industry would be helped by a general distribution of important pictures in which Negroes played a major part" (quoted in Bogle, 136–37). But even though Hollywood seemed to be collaborating with Washington in an effort to employ minorities, many black leaders were dismayed by the idea of MGM's musical about rural colored folk. *Cabin* had never been the sort of picture to appeal to most white southerners, but it also threatened to offend its more liberal audience in the predominantly urban centers where Lowe's owned theaters. One sign of the trouble the film might encounter was a letter from Hall Johnson, the conductor of a black choral group hired to perform in *Cabin*, to associate producer Albert Lewis. Johnson, who had also worked on the 1935 adaptation of *The Green Pastures*, warned that "Negroes have never forgiven the slanderous misrepresentations of [Connelly's play], and when after five successful years on the stage it was finally made into a picture, they did not hesitate to express their opinion" (quoted in Fordin, 74).

Almost concurrently, an influential group of white intellectuals was voicing a quite different complaint, growing out of what might be termed the discourse of critical modernism Some participants in this third discursive activity believed in an indigenous folk culture that could be captured on film, but they argued that the black folk and jazz music in particular had been commodified, controlled, and transformed by the media and the WPA; as a result, important local differences were being erased and America was moving ineluctably toward a one-dimensional society. A key instance of such reasoning was James Agee's "Pseudo-Folk," published in *The Partisan Review* less than a year after *Cabin in the Sky* was released. Agee was especially disturbed by the "decadence" of swing music and worried that the latest fashion in pop tunes would have a bad influence "among Negroes, our richest contemporary source of folk art, and our best people en bloc" (*Agee on Film*, Vol. 1, 407). To his ear, swing was a corruption of true jazz, which had been produced "where the deep country and the town have first fertilized each other" (405). As examples of the fake, mass-cultural populism that was destroying jazz and overtaking America like a "galloping cancer" (404), he cited the declining quality of Louis Armstrong's most recent work; the sleek big-band arrangements of Duke Ellington; the "pseudo-savage, pseudo-'cultured' dancing" (408) of Katherine Dunham and her troupe; and Paul Robeson's performances of John Latouche's "inconceivably snobbish, esthetically execrable 'Ballad for Americans'" (406–8). Although he never mentioned *Cabin in the Sky*, he could hardly have come closer to describing it. Both Armstrong and Ellington were featured in the movie, and, as we've seen, both Dunham and Latouche had contributed to the original Broadway show.

Max Horkheimer and Theodor W. Adorno's *Dialectic of Enlightenment* was roughly contemporary with Agee's essay. (The book was first published in 1947 but was written during the war, largely in California, and its early edition carries a 1944 copyright.) In making this connection I'm not suggesting an influence or equivalence. Unlike Agee, Horkheimer and Adorno came from a European Marxist tradition; they were never preoccupied by the folk (understandably so, since in Germany *völkish* theory had long been appropriated by the Fascists), and for the most part they regarded jazz as a pernicious outgrowth of the culture industry. Nevertheless, like many intellectuals of the left, right, and center, they believed that industrialized capitalism and big government of the interwar years was standardizing and reifying social relations, and they shared Agee's distaste for tendentious, fake, or "inauthentic" art. Adorno had described the "utopian" element in American life as a "desperate attempt to escape the abstract sameness of things by a kind of self-made and futile *promesse du bonheur*" (quoted in Calinescu, 228). In "On the Fetish-Character in Music and the Regression of Listening" (1938), he charges that "music for entertainment" serves only to assure that people are "confirmed in their neurotic stupidity" (286); and in his postwar essay "Perennial Fashion—Jazz," he describes jazz as a "slave" music in which it is difficult "to isolate the authentic Negro elements" (122). Agee's attitude was less stern; he remained a humanist and a lover of movies, but he was also a fierce critic of "sameness." When he claimed that a valuable "folk tradition" was being "thoroughly bourgeoizified" by the media (404), he was responding to the same rationalization and commodification that had given rise to the Frankfurt School's pessimistic, somewhat Weberian analysis of "late capitalism."

Arthur Freed, the producer of *Cabin*, was oblivious to such critiques; as a leading executive in America's most prosperous movie studio, however, he was sensitive to charges of racism. In an attempt to avoid controversy, he gave interviews to the black press in which he addressed "the Negro problem," committing himself to a "dignified presentation of a peace-loving and loyal people" and promising to "spare nothing" on the production (quoted in Fordin, 73). The last of these pronouncements was disingenuous, since *Cabin* was the lowest-budgeted musical in the history of the Freed unit; photographed in a sepia-tinted black and white, it borrowed its most spectacular visual effect—a tornado that destroys a nightclub—from old footage from *The Wizard of Oz*. Even so, the studio made a considerable investment in the picture: it hired Elmer Rice and Joseph Schrank to assist Connelly with the adaptation (Schrank wrote the first draft and received the sole credit); it commissioned Harold Arlen and E. Y. Harburg to supplement the original John Latouche–Vernon Duke score; and it selected the popular radio personality Eddie Anderson to replace Dooley Wilson.

MGM's production resources, the cast of star performers, and Freed's efforts at public relations all helped the film to earn a modest profit at the box office. According to Donald Bogle, *Cabin* was received enthusiastically by black audiences in the South and was widely shown at U.S. Army camps, where Lena Horne was a special favorite of black troops (132). But tensions were evident during the shooting (until a studio executive ordered the MGM commissary integrated, most of the players had lunch in Louis B. Mayer's private dining room; see Mordden, 163), and arguments over *Cabin*'s racial subject matter persisted throughout its distribution. Upon its release, certain reviewers were highly critical of the results. Although *Cabin* received good notices from the *New York Times* and the *New York Daily News* (the last of which had a substantial black readership), David Lardner of the *New Yorker* scoffed at MGM for trying to produce a "lovable ol' folk fantasy" (May 29, 1943), and the anonymous reviewer for *Time*—none other than James Agee—charged that the studio had treated its fine cast as "picturesque, Sambo-style entertainers" (April 12, 1943). *PM* remarked that the film was an example of "how not to fulfill a pledge such as Hollywood made to Wendell Willkie last year, to treat the Negro as a first-class citizen in films" (June 1, 1943). At least one review in the African American press was even more scathing. Writing in the *New York Amsterdam News* two weeks after *Cabin* had opened a successful run at the Criterion Theatre on Broadway, Ramona Lewis described the film as "an insult masking behind the label of folklore.... It pictures Negroes, heads tied up, with crap shooting inclinations and prayer meeting propensities at a time when [they] are daily proving their heroic mettle in battle and defense plant.... Since box office returns convince Hollywood more than anything else that it is in the right, it's too bad the actors didn't have the courage to refuse to make the film in the first place" (June 12, 1943).

In different ways, each of the negative reactions was appropriate. *Cabin* is a Hollywoodish depiction of black folklore saturated with inferential forms of racism—a carefully managed style of mass entertainment designed to serve the interests of a white corporation. Nevertheless, the film has a paradoxical effect, as if it wanted to dissolve oppositions between town and country, thereby unsettling the strategy of containment that usually operated in Hollywood's folkloric narratives. Placed alongside earlier pictures in the same vein, such as King Vidor's sincere but no less racist *Hallelujah!* or the Warner Brothers adaptation of *The Green Pastures*, it seems distinctly urban in spirit, keyed to the talents of Ethel Waters, Duke Ellington, and Lena Horne. This was in fact the period of what Donald Bogle describes as the "Negro Entertainment Syndrome," in which the nightclub was a recurrent setting for black performers (118–19). Ethel Waters had become a major star on American radio, and when the film was released Duke Ellington was presenting a series of forty-seven weekly hour-long broadcasts sponsored by the U.S. Treasury Department. Thus in true Hollywood fashion, the performers in *Cabin* are treated as celebrities, so that they take on a glamorous aura and sometimes appear in cameo roles as "themselves." And because these performers have a spacious, handsomely mounted vehicle staged on the visibly artificial, "utopian" sets that were a hallmark of the Freed unit during the 1940s, they're able to behave like something other than minstrel-show caricatures.

This is not to excuse MGM's racism. In certain ways the studio was responding to potential criticism from its black audience, but it was also attempting to preserve the imagery of cheerful, plantation-style darkies.

My point is simply that the film's folkloric project was vitiated, partly by the black critique of Hollywood, partly by the Roosevelt administration's desire to integrate certain aspects of the wartime economy, and chiefly by the growing commodification and modernization of American life. In this last regard, I would also argue that *Cabin*'s strong feeling of urbanity and sophistication derives in great measure from a fourth discourse about blackness: a chic, upscale "Africanism," redolent of cafe society, Broadway theater, and the European avant-garde.

I use the term "Africanism" in a limited manner to suggest a cosmopolitan artistic sensibility that pointed away from the American provinces, usually toward Harlem, Paris, French colonial Africa, and the Caribbean. This sensibility was prompted indirectly by developments within black culture itself, especially by the black internationalism described in a founding document of the Harlem renaissance, Alain Locke's "The New Negro" (1925). In this influential essay, Locke claimed that American blacks of the twentieth century were involved in a "deliberate flight not only from the country to the city, but from medieval America to modern" (515): "The pulse of the Negro world has begun to beat in Harlem. A Negro newspaper carrying news material in English, French, and Spanish, gathered from all quarters of America, the West Indies and Africa has maintained itself in Harlem for over five years.... Under American auspices and backing, three pan-African congresses have been held abroad for the discussion of common interests, colonial questions and the future co-operative development of Africa.... As with the Jew, persecution is making the Negro international" (522). "Africanism" also has something in common with "négritude," a word first used in print by poet Aimé Césaire in 1939. But the particular attitude I'm trying to identify was chiefly a white mythology, with distant origins in the artistic and intellectual revolutions that had swept Europe during the early twentieth century. (For a full account of these developments, see Torgovnick, 75–140). Its progenitors would include Conrad's *Heart of Darkness* (1902), Picasso's *Les Demoiselles d'Avignon* (1907), Fry's exhibition of the postimpressionist painters (1910), Freud's *Totem and Taboo* (1913), and the Dadaist experiments with "Negro poems" or *Negergedichte* (1916).

Throughout the 1920s and '30s, as European high modernism became institutionalized, African motifs found their way into "classy" forms of decoration and entertainment, operating in almost dialectical relation with narratives about the pastoral southland. (Meanwhile, in Germany, the Nazis branded both modernist art and the newer types of black entertainment as "degenerate.") This chic, highly commodified style—raised to delirious excess by Josef von Sternberg in the "Hot Voodoo" number of *Blonde Venus*

(1932)—offered a "savage" urbanity in place of a "childlike" pastoralism. It was already present to some degree in the original Broadway production of *Cabin in the Sky*, where the two primitivisms seemed to combine. It could also be heard everywhere in the work of songwriters employed by the Freed unit; for instance, Cole Porter had written a series of Africanist numbers for Broadway shows like *Jubilee* (1935) and *Panama Hattie* (1940), both of which were purchased by MGM. One of the leading exponents of the style, however, was a young director Freed hired for the film: Vincente Minnelli, who had never before been placed in charge of a feature picture.

Minnelli had begun his career in the early 1920s, at the birth of "modern times," by taking a job as a window decorator in the Marshall Field department store in Chicago; and throughout his later tenure in Hollywood, he consistently drew on post-1870s Paris—the cradle of artistic and commercial modernity—as a source of inspiration. (See *An American in Paris* [1951], *Lust for Life* [1956], and *Gigi* [1958].) A devoted student of European painting and a great admirer of the surrealists, he was valuable to MGM precisely because, in Geoffrey Nowell-Smith's well-chosen phrase, he furthered the studio's policy of bringing "refinement to the popular" (75). He was undoubtedly offered the chance to supervise *Cabin* because during the mid-1930s he had become famous as a director-designer of sophisticated Broadway revues featuring black performers. Ethel Waters had starred in two of his most successful New York shows, including *At Home Abroad* (1934), where she was cast as the "Empress Jones," a potentate of the Belgian Congo who travels to Harlem and brings the latest styles back to her subjects. ("Cartier rings they're wearin' in their noses now," she sang.) Minnelli had also created settings for Duke Ellington's big band at Radio City and was responsible for the extravagant and erotic costumes Josephine Baker wore in *The Ziegfeld Follies of 1936*. Robert Benchley of the *New Yorker* snidely accused him of having a "Negroid" sense of color (quoted in Minnelli, 58), but in his authorial signature and personal style he continued to exploit what Stephen Harvey has called "the totems of Africa moderne" (34). In 1937, *Esquire* magazine praised his own dress as "a perfect marriage of Harlem and the Left Bank" (quoted in Harvey, 30).

An example of one of Minnelli's designs for the unproduced 1939 Broadway musical *Serena Blandish* (intended as a vehicle for Lena Horne and Ethel Waters) is shown in figure 1, illustrating his tendency to blend surrealist motifs with an au courant Africanism. It should be emphasized that this style is no less racist than high modernism itself, and no more progressive than much of the commercial folklore of the 1930s. Like the folkloric artists, Minnelli relied on a kind of primitivism, explicitly associating

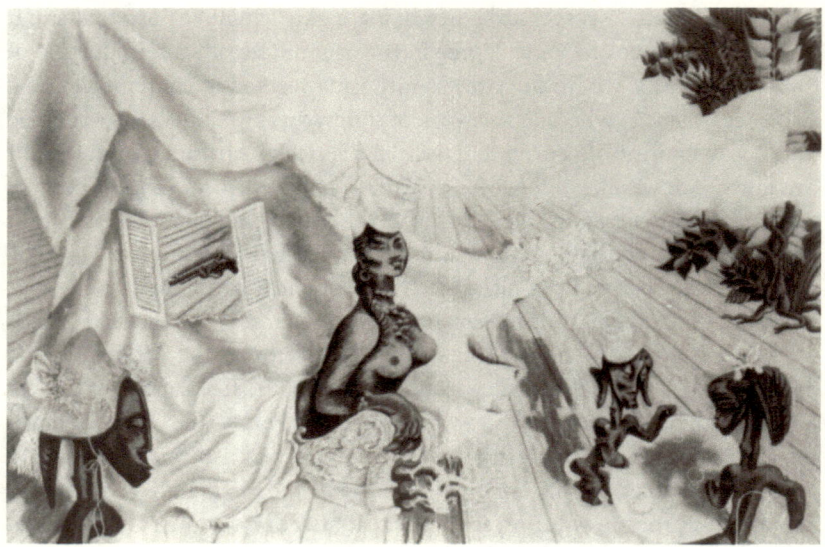

FIGURE 1. Minnelli's stage design for the unproduced S. N. Berhman stage show *Serena Blandish*, 1935. Photograph courtesy of Lee (Mrs. Vincente) Minnelli.

blackness with sexuality, instinctiveness, and the Freudian subconscious. At the same time, however, he promoted an uptown face of jazz, tied to contemporary fashion and big-time entertainment. In this context, blackness began to signify both wildness and sophistication. The African imagery was as stereotypical as any other cultural code, but it seemed attractive and denatured by parody or playful quotation; moreover, because it was regarded by audiences as in the vanguard, it tended to problematize the distinction between the savage and the cultivated.

However one might describe the political effect of such designs, the important point about Minnelli's work is that he was far more attuned to contemporary New York than to the Old South, and in a picture like *Cabin* his aestheticism tended to undermine the conservative implications of the original material. This is not to suggest that he was an artistic subversive. On the contrary, his elegance and exoticism were perfectly in keeping with the institutional needs of MGM in 1943, as we can see from the studio's promotion of the picture, which tried to deemphasize the story's rural atmosphere. Consider the lobby card from the original release showing Lena Horne, Eddie Anderson, and Ethel Waters gathered around a picket fence. The artwork and promotional copy are appropriate to a big-city nightclub, promising "entertainment galore" and "gorgeous girls" while depicting two richly costumed figures strutting off to a dance (fig. 2). Although the film is

FIGURE 2. MGM's promotion for *Cabin in the Sky*. © Turner Entertainment Co., 1943, all rights reserved.

less brazenly "citified" than this ad, MGM's publicity department was being reasonably faithful to the values Freed and Minnelli put on the screen.

CABIN IN RETROSPECT

The historical forces and discursive categories I've been describing—the vestigial folklore of the 1930s, the NAACP's mounting criticism of Hollywood, the increasing collaboration between mass entertainment and government, and the posh Africanism of high-toned Broadway musicals—have left their mark everywhere on the film, producing a kind of ideological schizophrenia. At the beginning of the credit sequence, for example, a title card announces "The Broadway Musical Play *Cabin in the Sky*," as if MGM wanted to legitimize the project by pointing to refined origins. When the credits end, however, a "crawl" moving across the screen informs us, "Throughout the ages, powerful thoughts have been handed down through the medium of the legend, the folk-tale, and the fantasy. . . . This story of faith and devotion springs from that source and seeks to capture those values." Here the film seems to be claiming a different lineage, even though the word "fantasy" mingles ambiguously with appeals to patriotism, folklore, and religion, opening the possibility for a more playful reading.

To be sure, *Cabin* continues to exhibit halfhearted concern with the religious beliefs of a "simple" couple who live outside the corrupting reach of modernity, together with a pervasive nostalgia for a lost home life. As Rick Altman has pointed out, the Hollywood "folk musical" is defined by these two qualities, especially by its preoccupation with "family groupings and the home" (273). Such films often involve both a desire for adventure and a recurrent homesickness, and they tend to be resolved by a *nostos* after a period of wandering. In *Cabin*, for example, Joe is torn between the artificial Club Paradise and the genuine paradise of a community church; between a sexy, brown-skinned mistress and a somewhat mammyfied wife; between a fast life of wine and easy money and a domestic life of lemonade and productive labor. He strays from home in order to find excitement and pleasure, but then he yearns for what he has left behind, and his return (or, more precisely, his recovery after a fevered, guilty dream) is essential to the happy ending.

As we've seen, *Cabin* is based on a paradigmatic tension between city and country, and it gives that tension a conservative resolution, making the town lead to Hell and the country lead to Heaven. Its racist implications become especially apparent when we realize how often the two opposed realms are depicted respectively in shades of blackness and whiteness. The nightclub is situated in a noirish street, whereas the cabin is often flooded with light; Joe wears a black tie and tails when he spends the Devil's money and a white robe when he ascends a stairway to paradise; the Devil's henchmen (costumed as big-city elevator operators) are dressed completely in black, in contrast with the soldiers of the Lord, who wear uniforms of glowing white.

But the town is nonetheless an attractive place, and the real story is elsewhere—largely in the photography, the art decoration, the costuming, the performances, and the musical numbers. In fact, in order to achieve a satisfying conclusion, *Cabin* finds ways to pull its two worlds into a kind of synthesis. The domestic woman moves briefly into the nightclub, wearing a shiny dress, performing a spectacular and amusing dance, and beating the siren at her own game. More importantly, the cabin becomes a performing space where tap dancing and lively pop tunes bring sexuality and entertainment under the benign influence of spirituality and married love. One of the best numbers in the picture, Ethel Waters's rendition of "Takin' a Chance on Love," is staged in the family kitchen and uses the metaphor of gambling (Joe's major vice) to speak about monogamous romance. Notice, too, *Cabin*'s portrayal of a gambler named Domino Johnson (John Bubbles Sublett, the original Sportin' Life in *Porgy and Bess*), whose privileged moment is a performance of Ford Dabney and Cecil Mack's "Shine." This song (also performed by Dooley Wilson in *Casablanca* and later recorded by Bing Crosby and Frankie Laine) is one of the more uncomfortably racist moments in the film, chiefly because of its title and references to "curly" hair, "pearly" teeth, and fancy clothes; from the point of view of the black actor, however, it functions self-reflexively and is the only occasion when a character is allowed to acknowledge racial difference. Moreover, while Johnson is supposed to be a villain, we're never invited to think of him as truly dangerous. Sublett's dancing makes him seem charming, and Minnelli's camera movements suggest a rapport with the figure of the black dandy.

Here as elsewhere, *Cabin* simply borrows a few stock images from a folkloric code, putting them in the service of a new form of musical theater. In the opening credits, it makes a patriotic appeal to folklore, but then it uses jazz and jitterbug to perform the function of hymns and work songs in earlier movies of the type. As a "folk musical," it therefore differs sharply from *Hallelujah!*, where, according to Rick Altman, "the tempered rhythms of the spiritual, sung in unison by the gathered community," are set off against "the syncopated rhythms of jazz and the chaotic sexual drive which they invoke" (292). Unlike King Vidor, Freed and Minnelli have utterly secular imaginations and their film contains no Manichean musical oppositions. In fact, the only religious song heard in *Cabin* is a snippet of "Old Ship of Zion," which is immediately preceded by "Little Black Sheep," an ersatz hymn written by E. Y. "Yip" Harburg.

Cabin might be properly described as suburban rather than folkloric, because it blends MGM's middle-class values with the Freed unit's relatively elite, Broadway ethos. To see just how much it tilts toward the city, however, one needs to step far outside the studio system, viewing it alongside Spencer Williams's *Blood of Jesus* (1941), an independent film directed by a black man and aimed at an audience of southern black churchgoers. Williams's film, which has none of the production values of MGM, was designed, in Thomas Cripps's words, "to mourn the passing of the great days when Afro-Americans were embraced by a familial certitude that would later be shattered by the great black diaspora from Southern farm to Yankee city" (92). It's more comic and satirical than this description suggests—it, too, is divided or ambivalent about conventional representations of the good country and the evil city—but it remains a kind of religious melodrama, portraying the devil in the style of *esthétique du cool* and making urban jitterbug seem a lurid music appropriate to a world of crime and prostitution. In *Cabin*, Freed and Minnelli used the same fundamentalist semantics, and yet their tone was different. For example, in one of the most exhilarating sequences of the

FIGURE 3. Duke Ellington and dancers in the Paradise Nightclub sequence of *Cabin in the Sky*. © Turner Entertainment Co., 1943, all rights reserved.

picture, a high-stepping couple, dressed in the latest fashion and moving to the beat of Duke Ellington's "Goin' Up," enter the swinging doors of the Club Paradise; the camera dollies backward as the couple glides onto the dance floor, and then, as a crowd of neatly dressed men in zoot suits and women in bobby socks gathers around, it cranes high above the room, drifting across the scene to close in on the bandstand (fig. 3). This is no smoky den of iniquity. It seems more like a showcase for a famous orchestra, and the lovely collaboration among Ellington's music, Busby Berkeley's choreography, and Minnelli's camera crane amounts to a kind of celebration.

It follows that if the nightclub is treated as relatively innocent fun, religion is depicted in perfunctory or comic ways. Unlike *The Blood of Jesus*, *Cabin* imagines the afterlife whimsically, in a style similar to Ernst Lubitsch's *Heaven Can Wait* (also released in 1943). It never mentions Jesus, it never shows a crucifix, and it barely alludes to scripture; instead, it offers a nonsectarian god who behaves rather like a cosmic cost accountant, and it proffers a few simple edicts against gambling and adultery. The Devil's henchmen do their work from the Hotel Hades, which resembles the office of an MGM producer during a story conference; and the entrance to Heaven—a vast, cloud-covered stairway flanked by black cherubim—seems to have been derived from a Ziegfeld production number.

By the same token, the quotidian, earthbound scenes in *Cabin* resemble a dream world. Most Hollywood movies about the folk at least claim to represent a specific place, but here the characters inhabit a poor but utopian black universe, structured by the absence of white people and decorated with an odd mixture of artifacts. One of the major differences between the Broadway show and the film is that in the film the battle between God and the Devil turns out to be something Joe *dreams*. This change gave the picture a happy ending and at the same time enabled Minnelli to invest the mise-en-scène with an Afro-Caribbean look that foreshadows his subsequent work on *Yolanda and the Thief* (1945) and *The Pirate* (1948). In his autobiography, he claims that he struggled with MGM's art department in order to keep the cabin from seeming "dirty" or "slovenly" (121), but his dreamy settings also motivated some condescending jokes. At one point, for example, Joe uses his earnings from a local feed mill to buy Petunia a washing machine; because there is no electricity in the cabin, however, he places the gleaming white appliance on his porch as a symbol of prosperity. The machine looks comically surrealistic, a bizarre objet trouvé that both satirizes and validates the society of consumption.

Not only the settings but also the manners and accents in the film are heterogeneous and fantastic. Hall Johnson had written to the producers advising them to use "an honest-to-goodness Negro dialect" (quoted in Fordin, 75), perhaps because the script was rendered in a series of excruciatingly condescending white versions of southern-black English. Here is the way Joseph Schrank and Marc Connelly imagined Petunia praying for Joe's recovery:

> If yuh lets him die de debbil gonna git him fo' sho'. An' he ain't wicked, Lawd—he jus' weak, dat's all. He ain't got no powah to resis' de debbil lest Ah watches him. (21)

And here is Joe when he discovers a pair of dice in his bedroom drawer:

> Right now I'm wrestlin' wid de devil. When I was lookin' for de necktie in de bureau drawer, I also found two clamity cubes. I ain't throwed 'em away yet. If I been redeemed, why don't I pitch 'em right in de stove? (9)

Fortunately, little of this language survives in the performances, an effect that becomes especially evident in the case of a minor player, Butterfly McQueen, who never uses the spacey singsong voice that audiences (even audiences of films produced by blacks) had come to expect of her. Petunia's prayer has been thoroughly revised for the completed film, and Eddie Anderson delivers the speech about "calamity cubes" in the same gravelly urban accent he used on the radio so that it hardly sounds like the same language. At one point

Ethel Waters sings a few lines of "Happiness Is a Thing Called Joe" in a fake dialect ("He gotta smile dat make de lilac wanna grow"), but everywhere else she sings in crisply enunciated standard English, using the slightly elocutionary vocal technique of her best-known recordings.

Where the design of the film is concerned, Minnelli seems to have taken pleasure in making a southern locale look like the big city. In one of the most revealing comments in his autobiography, he remarks that the set he liked best was "a southern ghetto, with a warm, golden look, created from a permanent version of a New York street" (122). He also tried to glamorize the featured players: whenever Ethel Waters is seen in a bandanna, she wears fashionable earrings reminiscent of the Cartier jewelry she had sung about in *At Home Abroad;* and when Lena Horne dresses up as a temptress, she exchanges her pill-box hat for a magnolia, pinning the blossom to her hair like Billie Holiday. In this context it might be noted that the most imposing and handsome males in *Cabin* are Kenneth Spencer and Rex Ingram, who play supernatural characters. Lena Horne is more obviously sexualized, playing a role similar to Nina Mae McKinney's in *Hallelujah! Cabin* is almost the only film in her career in which she functions as an agent of the narrative and moves provocatively around the set; even so, one of her singing numbers was cut because Minnelli staged it in a bubble bath.

Much the same thing could be said about the dressing of the sets. Minnelli painted his own "Africanist" murals on the walls of the Paradise nightclub and turned the cabin into a spacious interior, accented with reproductions of Victorian art. He gave Joe and Petunia an elaborate wrought iron bedstead, and in each of their rooms he placed white wicker chairs designed in lacy rococo filigree. (The same chairs show up again in 1944, helping to furnish Judy Garland's bedroom in *Meet Me in St. Louis;* in 1950, they reappear in MGM's *Two Weeks with Love,* a Jane Powell–Debbie Reynolds musical set in a fashionable Catskills resort.) To grasp the full implications of this style, we need only glance at the stills reproduced here. The first comes from Williams's *Blood of Jesus,* where a black household has been decorated with a single picture, a dime-store image of Jesus exhibiting his bleeding heart, visible at the upper left of the frame (fig. 4). The second is from *Cabin* and helps to indicate the comparative opulence of MGM. Notice especially the framed picture at the upper right of the frame, showing a white cherub kissing a sleeping boy (fig. 5).

Largely because of this elaborate, exquisite decoration, *Cabin* seems remote from anything we commonly associate with folkloric movies. A deliberate exercise in faux naïveté, it has more in common with what Rick Altman has called "fairy tale musicals" in the sense that it elicits identifica-

FIGURE 4.   Set decoration in Spencer Williams's *The Blood of Jesus*, 1941. Courtesy of the Black Film Center Archive, Indiana University.

tion "with fantasy, with the far away, with the imaginary" (153). Generally speaking, of course, all the classic Hollywood musicals were fairy tales; but *Cabin*'s oneiric quality has an odd relationship to its ostensible subject, making its folkloric setting seem a mere pretext. The deeper purpose of the film becomes evident when we consider two rhyming camera movements involving mirrors and typical of Minnelli, one near the beginning of the story and one near the end. In the first, Joe stands looking at a lottery ticket he has fastened to his bedroom mirror; as he leans forward in a trance, the camera cranes up and over his shoulder, moving toward the tilted surface of the glass as if to plunge him and us into an imaginary world. In the second, Petunia looks into a mirror that has survived the devastation of the Club Paradise; she notices something reflected there, and the camera cranes downward to share her viewpoint, revealing a stairway leading off through the clouds. These shots contrast Joe's dream of riches with Petunia's dream of Heaven, but they also serve as metaphors for two aspects of the Hollywood cinema. Like the movies, they appeal both to our desire for luxury and to our desire for a magical, nonmaterial existence. They invite the audience to form a subjective bond with a poor black couple, but in the process they make Joe

FIGURE 5. Set decoration in *Cabin in the Sky*. © Turner Entertainment Co., 1943, all rights reserved.

and Petunia seem like ideal consumers of entertainment, a pair of restless American dreamers caught up in a world of music, light, and dance.

Like virtually all the Freed unit musicals, *Cabin in the Sky* involves a good deal of what Jane Feuer has termed "conservative self-reflexivity"; it banishes every social contradiction, first by appealing to its own status as entertainment and then by presenting "a vision of human liberation which is profoundly aesthetic" (Feuer, 84). Notice also that the aesthetic sensibility is always expensive, dependent on signifiers of material abundance and rarified taste. Thus when Waters, Anderson, and Horne play the roles of folkloric characters, they don't look poor; and because they're treated as stars, they induce a feeling of playful masquerade. In a strange way, this transformation of blackness into a commodity on display has a salutary effect, even if the display has dubious purposes. We might say, echoing Richard Dyer's formulation, that the film gives us the feeling of "what utopia would feel like rather than how it would be organized" (177).

Clearly, the makers of *Cabin* were taking care to keep too much social reality from intruding on the attractive surroundings. Their strategy may seem offensive when so much of the actual experience of African Americans has been suppressed or driven into a political unconscious, but *Cabin* has a complex ideological potential. From the point of view of many social critics of the time, its Hollywood surrealism and freewheeling, commodified treatment of folklore were irredeemably decadent and false; and yet its design runs against the grain of a repressive and no more "true" set of conventions. After all, there's no such thing as an "authentic" folk movie, and *Cabin* may have been better off for its evident artificiality. Freed and Minnelli were hardly social activists, but by imbuing their film with a dreamy atmosphere and an urban Africanism, they and the performers turned it into what is arguably the most visually beautiful picture about black people ever produced at the classic studios. We might say that during the early 1940s, and within the context of a white entertainment industry, their aestheticism amounted to a modestly positive gesture.

Perhaps a better way of making the same point would be to repeat the familiar Marxist axiom that capitalism represents a progressive stage in history. Unfortunately, such progress always involves injustices and ironies. *Cabin* and every other studio film about blacks simply reinforced the hypocritical separate-but-equal policies of a segregated society. This injustice was compounded because whites were in charge of every behind-the-scenes aspect of the production, and because much of the debate over the film's merits was framed and conditioned by a white cultural establishment. It's ironic that *Cabin* can nonetheless be described as a step forward in the democratization of show business, and that a film containing so much nostalgia and synthetic folklore should have provided a showcase for some of the wittiest and most talented entertainers of the period. But the greatest irony of all is that the black performers, who were at last becoming full-fledged stars, were merely gaining membership in a conservative enterprise—a system devoted to praising the American way, and to promoting the values of glamour, charm, and illusion.

Hitchcock and Humor

One of my earliest boyhood memories from an Alfred Hitchcock movie is of a scene in the American version of *The Man Who Knew Too Much* (1956), in which James Stewart, searching for a gang of assassins who have kidnapped his son, visits a Camden Town taxidermist named Ambrose Chappell. The scene begins in typical Hitchcock fashion, with a slow tracking shot from Stewart's point of view as he approaches the taxidermist's shop at the end of a sinister alleyway. Inside, he encounters a shabby and benign-looking group of tradesmen, but the atmosphere is uneasy because we already know that people in this movie are not always what they seem, and because the stuffed animals arrayed about the room lend a menacing, eerie quality to the mise-en-scène. Stewart threatens the shop owner, accusing him of being a kidnapper, and when the taxidermists call the police, a scuffle breaks out. But then, in the midst of the fight, everything turns into a vaguely uncanny form of slapstick. Stewart realizes too late that the taxidermists are innocent, and the taxidermists alternately try to protect their stuffed animals and use them as weapons against Stewart, whom they regard as a madman. As Stewart struggles to escape, he catches his hand in the open mouth of a stuffed tiger, and at one point a fat little man threatens him with a dead sawfish. The sequence ends with a clever flourish of Bernard Herrmann's music and a huge close-up of a snarling lion, who gazes ferociously at the audience.

What impressed me as a boy about this scene was that it was frightening, perverse, and funny *at the same time*. On some inarticulate level I was aware that I had experienced a quick shift in dramatic tone, but the scene also involved an intertwining of my laughing and screaming impulses; it began with a menacing tension that led to fearful laughter, then achieved a sublation of fear, and then capped everything with a scary surprise in the form of a lion who seemed to be saying "boo." It did all of this, moreover, while making me pleasurably aware that the emotional machinery was being manipulated by a clever entertainer behind the scenes.

Today the struggle in the taxidermist's shop no longer strikes me as quite so clever, and I doubt that anyone would argue that it marks an especially important moment in Hitchcock's career. Although it remains an entertaining diversion, it probably doesn't have a strong emotional efficacy for contemporary audiences, who are likely to find the stuffed creatures in Ambrose Chappell's shop much less spooky and witty than the ones in Norman Bates's parlor. I suspect, however, that everyone would agree that the scene is characteristic of Hitchcock; indeed, the emotional effects I've been trying to describe are among the chief things that enable us to distinguish him from, say, a director like Fritz Lang, who was an equally great exponent of stories about crime and suspense. Lang also directed a Brechtian musical comedy, *You and Me* (1938), but his tone is more somber than Hitchcock's—perhaps because, as Tom Gunning has remarked, Lang is "less concerned with the psychological complexity of characters ... than with their interface with social systems, with technology and politics" (xi–xii).

In retrospect, it seems odd to me that Hitchcock's critics have never paid close attention to his habit of mingling of suspense and humor. As Gilberto Perez has pointed out, the analytic literature on Hitchcock is now so large that it threatens to outstrip his true importance; "for he would have to be incomparably the greatest of all filmmakers to merit the amount of critical and academic attention bestowed on him, well in excess of any other director's share and giving no sign of diminution" (9). Then again, one could argue that he *is* the greatest filmmaker for that very reason; and yet, while the literature says a great deal about how Hitchcock creates suspense, shock, and psychological unease, it says relatively little about how he also produces jokes and laughter. In the useful introduction to *Hitchcock on Hitchcock*, editor Sidney Gottlieb briefly surveys the many critical approaches that have been taken to the director and then remarks, "It surprises me that we still have not had a full treatment of the comic Hitchcock" (xxiii). We do, of course, have important commentaries by Lesley Brill and Stanley Cavell on Hitchcock's uses of pastoral or romantic comedy; and, as Gottlieb observes, we have Thomas Leitch's fine book on Hitchcock as trickster and game player. But there's an especially important aspect of Hitchcock's work, described by British director Bruce Robinson as an "ability to make anxiety amusing," that everyone recognizes and almost nobody analyzes (quoted in a Hitchcock supplement to *Sight and Sound*, 35). In what follows, I want to offer some thoughts about this kind of amusement, which is significant enough to justify adding a few more pages to the library of critical commentary.

Let me emphasize that my chief interest here is in the affective quality of "amusing anxiety," or in what I shall call "humor," as opposed to the broader and more generic notion of comic cinema. At the outset, however, a few words about comedy seem appropriate. A useful place to begin is with the fact that some of Hitchcock's favorite themes and narrative structures are equally well suited to tragic, melodramatic, or comic treatments. The mistaken identity plot, for example, can be found in both Sophocles and Plautus and in both *The Wrong Man* and *North by Northwest*. By the same token, the characteristic emotional effects of a Hitchcock movie—suspense and surprise—are typical of both the cliff-hanging thriller and the practical joke. American director Andrew Bergman, an exponent of classic Hollywood's screwball tradition, makes a similar point when he observes that "what [Hitchcock] did in this thrillers is very close to what one attempts in comedy—placing ordinary characters in extraordinary situations" (quoted in Hitchcock supplement to *Sight and Sound*, 36).

Actually, the ordinary/extraordinary formula can account for most films of the classic studio era, regardless of their ostensible genres. The standard Hollywood movie in the period is a modern variation on what classical scholars call "Greek New Comedy," a formula that Northrop Frye describes as follows: "What normally happens is that a young man wants a young woman, that his desire is resisted by some opposition, . . . and that near the end of the play some twist in the plot enables the hero to have his will" (163). In Hollywood's case, this formula produces a boy-meets-girl story about beautiful but "ordinary" people in unusual circumstances, which usually ends with a kiss and a fadeout—a resolution that can sometimes appear both chaste and coyly suggestive, balancing the conflicting demands of traditional marriage and sexually liberated capitalism. As Dana Polan has argued, the formula is so pervasive that "each and every genre (and each and every scene within the films) is easily rewritable, the tone of each work easily transformable into its opposite" (137). Hence a picture about a sheriff who defends a town from outlaws can be treated seriously, as in *High Noon*, or somewhat amusingly, as in *Rio Bravo*, and the difference is largely a matter of tone rather than plot.

Hitchcock was the sort of director who enjoyed playing variations of tone within a given film, and classic Hollywood's all-purpose plot conventions tended to facilitate his style, enabling him to shift easily from light comic banter to melodramatic danger, sometimes within a single scene. Even so, he directed only one Hollywood film that was not about murder or death, the screwball comedy *Mr. and Mrs. Smith* (1941), scripted by Norman Krasna and starring Carole Lombard and Robert Montgomery. This picture appeared late in the screwball cycle and was overshadowed by two other examples that have become legendary: Howard Hawks's *His Girl Friday* (1940) and Preston Sturges's *The Lady Eve* (1941). Perhaps for that reason, critics have usually regarded it as an oddity or a project unsuited to Hitchcock's particular talents. But in fact, he had already made two straightforward comedies in England, *Champagne* (1928), which Raymond Durgnat describes as "a kind of playgirl's *Sullivan's Travels*" (83), and *Rich and Strange* (1931), which is a fairly lighthearted treatment of suburban marriage.

In a recent essay, Lesley Brill has demonstrated that Hitchcock's American pictures, for all their atmosphere of anxiety and death, have a surprising number of important things in common with those of Preston Sturges; even a somber film like *Vertigo*, he notes, deals with many of the same themes as *The Lady Eve* ("Redemptive Comedy," 205–20). Dana Polan takes this argument further, showing how most of Hitchcock's pictures could be rewritten as generic screwball comedies, just as screwball comedy itself could be rewritten in a more troubling mood. For example, the funniest scene in *Mr. and Mrs. Smith* takes place in a nightclub where Robert Montgomery undergoes a series of public humiliations during a failed attempt to show his estranged wife that he has a date that is more impressive than hers. As Polan observes, the scene is replete with what we usually regard as anxious Hitchcockian themes: "sexuality as a battle of gazes; public space as an agonic site overrun by a crowd turned mob, mocking one's every project; the self as finally nothing but vulnerable materiality" (134). These same themes are not far beneath the surface in the most hilarious moments of Sturges's *The Lady Eve*, but they can also be found in the most agonizing noncomic scene in Hitchcock's *Rebecca* (1940), when Joan Fontaine discovers she has worn the wrong dress to a ball. Consider as well *The 39 Steps* (1935), which places Robert Donat in all kinds of public situations where he has to put on an act, and which keeps veering from screwball romance to melodramatic danger to perverse anxiety. An equally obvious case in point is *Rear Window* (1954), which derives much of its fascination from the way it interjects harrowing violence into a New Comic plot. Probably the most extreme example (though it doesn't quite succeed in its comic/romantic moments) is *The Birds* (1963), which was designed by Hitchcock and screenwriter Evan Hunter to start out as a screwball comedy (spoiled heiress Tippi Hedren meets small-town bachelor Rod Taylor) and then become an apocalyptic horror movie; notice, moreover, that the two different modes of the film are linked by sly jokes, such as the bird-in-a-cage imagery of the opening scene, which is echoed later when the heroine is trapped in a phone booth and attacked by seagulls.

If we accept Northrop Frye's theory of fictional modes in *Anatomy of Criticism*, the tale of murder itself has an inherently comic tendency. It begins in the era of Sherlock Holmes as what Frye calls a "low mimetic" sharpening of attention to detail, so that "the dullest and most neglected trivia of daily living leap into mysterious and fateful significance," and quickly merges with the thriller "as one of the forms of melodrama" (46–47). In its melodramatic form, it deals with the "triumph of moral virtue over villainy" and is always in danger of becoming "advance propaganda for the police state" (47). Nevertheless, Frye notes, the genre tends to be surrounded by "a protective wall of play," and the more serious and melodramatic it becomes, the more likely it is to be looked at ironically, with "its pity and fear seen as sentimental drivel and owlish solemnity." From this point, it easily develops toward the opposite pole of melodrama, which Frye describes as "comic irony or satire" or as the tendency to define "the enemy of society as a spirit within that society" (47).

The scene I've described from *The Man Who Knew Too Much* can be viewed as a condensed and rather apolitical illustration of the process Frye has charted. It begins in melodrama, with the search for an innocent child who is kipnapped by terrorists from Morocco or from somewhere in the Balkans and it quickly modulates into comedy, irony, and satire, with an American tourist wrestling a bunch of English shopkeepers. In Hitchcock's more darkly romantic or serious work, this same propensity toward dramatic irony creates a remarkable blend of melodrama and satire, so that it is often difficult to say where one feeling ends and the other begins. Isn't it vaguely amusing, in a detached and absurdist fashion, that the doctor in charge of an insane asylum should turn out to be psychotic? Or that a sailor from a sunken Nazi submarine should be rescued by a lifeboat filled with Americans and then turn out to be the most capable person aboard? Or that a beautiful woman should start out a film as an alcoholic and then almost die from drinking poisoned coffee? The list of these situations could be greatly lengthened; the ones I've mentioned are respectively from *Spellbound* (1945), *Lifeboat* (1944), and *Notorious* (1946), and they comprise what most people think of the Hitchcock "touch"—a feeling of iconoclastic laughter lurking behind classically wrought stories about romance, murder, and suspense.

The iconoclasm can be latent or overt. In nearly three decades of showing Hitchcock films to American college students, I've found that two scenes from his work are guaranteed to produce big laughs: the moment in *Strangers on a Train* (1951) when the villain, Bruno Anthony, uses his cigarette to explode a child's balloon, and the moment in *North by Northwest* (1959) when the hero Roger Thornhill finds himself standing over the dead body of a U.N. diplomat, holding a bloody knife and being photographed by newspaper reporters. In each case a suspenseful melodrama spins on its heels and becomes a comic satire, and in each case the audience's laughter derives in part from the feeling that melodramatic convention is being reversed, mocked, or amusingly exaggerated. One might say that the audience takes pleasure in a deliberately "inappropriate" laughter that exposes the solemnity and sentiment of the ordinary murder story.

This effect is all the more interesting when we consider that most of the laughter depicted inside Hitchcock's films, at the level of the diegesis, is also inappropriate, but in a more discordant and disconcerting way. Consider the laughter (or perhaps the grimace) on the face of the painted clown in *Blackmail* (1930); or the laughter of Bruno Anthony in *Strangers on a Train* when he looks at his mother's abstract painting and thinks it resembles his father; or the laughter of Roger Thornhill's mother and nearly everybody aboard a crowded elevator in *North by Northwest* ("You gentlemen aren't *really* trying to kill my son, are you?"); or—most troubling of all—the laughter of Rose Balestrero in *The Wrong Man* (1956) as she stands in a tenement hallway and descends from depression and anxiety into madness.

One of the subtlest uses of this sort of ironic laughter can be heard in a sound transition in *Sabotage* (1936), at the climax of the scene in which little Stevie Verloc is killed by a bomb. Viewers of *Sabotage* may remember that the story as a whole begins with a saboteur's failed attempt to blow up a power station. On the next day, newspaper headlines sneer at the bomber's ineptitude and proclaim "London Laughs." The agents who control the saboteur warn him that "London must not laugh again tonight," and indeed, at least on the surface, there is nothing amusing about the second attack. Hitchcock pulls out all the melodramatic stops, showing us a towheaded boy, a puppy, and a little old lady riding along in a bus while a time bomb ticks away in a package the boy is holding. Suspense is generated by crosscutting between the bus and the moving hands of the city's clocks, and the pace of the cutting steadily accelerates until the moment when, somewhat to our surprise, the bus and the boy are blown to smithereens. The sequence ends with a visual and sound dissolve that takes us from the exploded bus to Winnie Verloc's parlor, where the sound of the explosion melts into polite, rather strained laughter among her guests—a laughter that, in this context, resembles nothing so much as the sound of broken glass or shattered debris. (Whenever I've isolated the sequence in the classroom, my students have broken into uneasy laughter.)

With examples such as these, we've moved some distance from pure comedy and have entered the domain of a macabre form of amusement that has special names. In *Jokes and Their Relation to the Unconscious* (1905), Sigmund Freud calls it simply "humor," a term I am adopting for this essay, even though in the English language it usually needs a modifier such as "gallows humor."

Freud himself illustrates it with a joke about a condemned man being led off to the gallows on a Monday who is overheard to say, "What a way to start the week!" He also cites instances of humor from *Simplicissimus,* a famous comic weekly published in Munich, and from the frontier writings of Mark Twain. All such joking, he explains, functions as *"an economy in the expenditure of affect"* (228–29). Unlike the witty or "crazy" forms of comedy, humor arises only when "there is a situation in which, according to our usual habits, we should be tempted to release a distressing affect and if motives then operate upon us which suppress that affect *in statu nascendi"* (228). This ability to suppress the unpleasant feeling, Freud writes, is "one of the highest psychical achievements," enjoying "the particular favor of thinkers" (228). It involves "something like magnanimity" by virtue of the humorist's "tenacious hold upon his customary self and his disregard of what might overthrow that self and drive it to despair" (229).

In 1928, Freud returned to the same theme in a short paper entitled simply "Humor," in which he observes that "the essence of humor is that one spares oneself the affects to which the situation would naturally give rise and overrides with a jest the possibility of such an emotional display" (216). As with wit and the comic, Freud finds something "liberating" about humor; but the humorous attitude also contains what he calls a "fine and elevating" quality, resulting chiefly from a "triumph of narcissism" and "the ego's victorious assertion of its own invulnerability" (217). In every case of humor, he writes, the ego "refuses to be hurt by the arrows of reality or to be compelled to suffer." Instead, the narcissistic aspect of the psyche insists that "it is impervious to wounds dealt by the outside world, in fact, that these are merely occasions for affording it pleasure" (217). This attitude, Freud emphasizes, is quite different from emotional resignation; it is "rebellious," signifying "the triumph not only of the ego, but also of the pleasure principle," which is strong enough to assert itself in the face of "adverse real circumstances" (217).

At another juncture in the same essay, Freud elaborates on the psychic process that creates humor, showing how it involves "the subject's removing the accent [of emotion] from his ego and transferring it onto his [protective or parental] super-ego" (218–19). Humor can therefore be described as the dialectical opposite of wit, which "originates in the momentary abandoning of a conscious thought to unconscious elaboration." If wit is "the contribution of the unconscious to the comic," humor is "a contribution to the comic made through the agency of the super-ego" (220). Perhaps for that reason, Freud notes, humor does not always require an audience; it can be experienced purely subjectively, usually by social outsiders who "narcissistically" defend themselves against pain. It is also what Freud terms a "rare and precious gift," for "there are many people who have not even the capacity for deriving pleasure from humor when it is presented to them by others" (221).

Another, equally familiar, name for gallows humor is "black humor," which is the English translation of what the surrealist André Breton, a disciple of Freud and the major theorist of subversively dark literary comedy, called *humour noir*. The immediate ancestor of this term, Breton tells us, is *"umour,"* borrowed from the English "humor" and coined by Jacques Vaché, a veteran of trench warfare in World War I and an important contributor to the surrealist movement, whose *Lettres de guerre* (*Letters from the Front*, 1920) was published shortly after Vaché and one of his friends had taken part in a double suicide, or perhaps a murder-suicide. ("I object to being killed in wartime," Vaché had written. "I will die when I want to die. . . . But then I'll die with someone else. Dying alone is too boring.") Breton's *Anthologie de l'humour noir* (*Anthology of Black Humor*), compiled in the mid-1930s but not published until 1940, at a time when Breton claimed that the historical situation was appropriate, contains excerpts from Vaché's book along with samples from the work of more than forty other black humorists. In the introduction to the volume, Breton quotes Freud's account of gallows humor and also calls attention to Hegel's earlier notion of "objective humor," an extreme form of the Romantic or aesthetic sensibility, involving both a repudiation of external circumstance and a love of detachment or "external contemplation" (xvi). According to Breton, objective humor is closely related to *humour noir*, which constitutes *"a superior revolt of the mind"* against bourgeois convention (xvi).

For Breton, black humor is the "mortal enemy of sentimentality" (xix) and the essential element or keynote of every worthwhile modern art and philosophy. The purpose of his anthology is to define such humor and give a sense of its genealogy by using short examples drawn from a wide range of literary sources: Jonathan Swift ("the first black humorist"), the Marquis de Sade, Edgar Allan Poe, Charles Baudelaire, Friedrich Nietzsche, Arthur Rimbaud, André Gide, Alfred Jarry, Franz Kafka, and many others (given this list of names, black humor might appear to be solely the product of white males, but we can find examples by all races and genders; most contemporary African American comics employ it, and it has a long tradition in Jewish comedy, as Freud no doubt knew). Breton also notes in passing that black humor can be seen at the cinema—for example, in the early comedies of Mack Sennett, in certain of Chaplin's less sentimental pictures, and of course in Buñuel's *Un Chien Andalou* (1928) and *L'Age d'or* (1930).

I would argue that black humor is one of the hallmarks of modernist art, and that Alfred Hitchcock, who is not mentioned by Breton, was not only one of its great practitioners but also the artist most responsible for bringing a spirit of surrealist laughter into the vernacular modernism of Hollywood movies. Hitchcock was certainly not alone in producing such laughter, as one can see from almost any film directed by Billy Wilder; but more than any of his contemporaries, Hitchcock came to be identified with black humor, which he repeatedly packaged as mass entertainment. His propensity toward the effect is perhaps least evident during his first years in America, when he collaborated with David Selznick and was restrained from turning the opening scenes of *Rebecca* into a series of jokes; but the humorous feeling isn't entirely absent during that period, partly because Selznick's romanticism and taste for *amour fou* have a natural affinity with the surrealist sensibility. In *Rebecca*, for example, the title character is a woman who, even in death, seems to laugh mockingly at the earnestness and sentiment of Maxim de Winter and his new wife. Even in Hitchcock's overtly propagandistic wartime work, which includes *Lifeboat* and the two short films he made for the British Ministry of Information in 1944 (*Bon Voyage* and *Aventure Malgache*), the sense of detached irony and objective humor almost undercuts the patriotic messages. Ultimately, his career as a whole can be described in terms of different degrees or shadings of black humor, a quality that unifies such different pictures as *The Trouble with Harry* (1956) and *Psycho* (1960), which Thomas Leitch has claimed are "the two most disparate films in Hitchcock's entire *oeuvre* ("The Outer Circle," 60). In some of his most glamorous comedies, such as *To Catch a Thief* (1955), the dark jokes are slickly eroticized, most notably in the famous seduction scene when heiress Grace Kelly offers her jewelry to cat burglar Cary Grant. (When he was making this film, Hitchcock complained to André Bazin about "the necessity of renouncing adult, masculine humor in order to satisfy American producers" [Bazin, "Hitchcock vs. Hitchcock," 65]). In his noncomic pictures about romantic obsession, such as *Under Capricorn* (1949) and *Vertigo* (1958), which were among his least commercially successful productions, the fetishism is less conducive of laughter and the feeling of humor derives chiefly from the twists of the plots. In his spy thrillers such as *The 39 Steps*, dark humor mingles with sexual innuendo and utopian romance, and the movement between these modes is often treated like a dialectical montage.

One characteristic of black humor, as both Freud and Breton observed, is a somewhat elevated or "objective" tone. Hitchcock managed to convey this feeling through both his fastidious control of cinematic enunciation (as in his lofty bird's-eye shots) and his carefully constructed persona, which audiences found especially amusing. Then, too, his films sometimes steered close to the sardonic effects of high literary modernism. A passage from

T. S. Eliot's *The Waste Land* could serve as an ironic epigraph to a light entertainment like *Rear Window:* "Oh keep the dog far hence, that's friend to men,/Or with his nails he'll dig it up again." In other films, Hitchcock seems rather like a slick, slyly commercial practitioner of the kind of nightmarish wit we find in Kafka. (Whether or not he ever read Kafka, his celebrated thrillers of the 1930s were filmed at the very moment when *The Trial* and *The Castle* were first translated into English, and when the influence of Kafka was pervasive in British art.) And when he depicts the lowest fringes of the middle class, as in parts of *Sabotage* and in *The Wrong Man*, he has something in common with the spooky, quotidian humor of W. H. Auden, the leading poet of Britain's "Age of Anxiety." Consider Auden's "As I Walked Out One Evening" (1937), which uses a nursery-rhyme meter to create a sense of dread: "The glacier knocks in the cupboard,/The desert sighs in the bed,/And the crack in the teacup opens/A lane to the land of the dead."

Today black humor is ubiquitous, appearing in everything from museum exhibits to television commercials. No doubt it has always played some role in American popular and commercial art; in the 1930s, for example, at about the same time that Hitchcock became an international celebrity, Charles Addams began drawing cartoons for the *New Yorker*. But if I had to name the period when black humor fully entered the consciousness of the American public and reached a saturation point in the marketplace, I would say the 1950s—a supposedly complacent decade that nonetheless produced Vladimir Nabokov's best-selling *Lolita*, EC Comics, whose entire line was based on the grisliest forms of black humor, and the *Alfred Hitchcock Presents* television show, which might as well have been subtitled *Anthologie de l'humour noir*. (There are connections between these apparently different examples: Nabokov once discussed the possibility of writing a screenplay for Hitchcock, and EC Comics' horror comics used a ghoulishly comic narrator who made jokes somewhat in the manner of Hitchcock.) This was also the period when Hitchcock gave his name to *Alfred Hitchcock's Mystery Magazine*, a widely circulated "pulp" journal formed on the model of *Ellery Queen's Mystery Magazine*, which specialized in darkly comic or ironic stories about murder by such gifted writers as Henry Slesar, Roald Dahl, and Stanley Elkin. The television series drew material from many of the same writers, and in one instance Robert Stevenson directed an episode based on Evelyn Waugh's "The Man Who Liked Dickens," an ironic horror story that Waugh rewrote as the last chapter of one of the darkest comedies in modern literature, *A Handful of Dust*.

When *Alfred Hitchcock Presents* debuted in 1955, Hitchcock told the press that it would be "bringing murder into the American home, where it has always belonged" (quoted by McNeil in *Total Television*, 23–24). Over the next ten years he made good on his promise, at the same time becoming a paradoxical kind of star—a popular, even beloved, figure who took a dandified, darkly satiric approach to many of the things the nation was supposed to hold dear. The series was supervised by Joan Harrison and Norman Lloyd, and James Allardice wrote the commentaries that Hitchcock delivered so wittily; but to conclude that Hitchcock himself had little to do with its success, as some commentators have done, would be a bit like arguing that Bob Hope or Jack Benny was a mere figurehead on his own broadcast. Hitchcock directed some of his most characteristic films for the program, and he contributed a comic persona and a set of generic expectations that he had developed throughout the previous decade, not only in films but also on the radio, where he made frequent appearances as a guest star.

On July 22, 1940, shortly after coming to America, Hitchcock "directed" and played host for a radio adaptation of his British silent film *The Lodger*, which became the pilot episode for *Suspense*, a long-running CBS exercise in noir that was in many ways a precursor of *Alfred Hitchcock Presents*. (The subsequent host of *Suspense* was an anonymous and unfunny character called "The Man in Black.") Throughout the 1940s he made witty appearances on *Information Please*, a popular quiz show that featured celebrities and public intellectuals; and in 1951 he hosted a weekly half-hour broadcast entitled *Murder by Experts*, featuring "tales by the leading writers of mystery fiction." In these venues and others, he perfected the upper-crust manner and the propensity toward gallows humor that would ultimately find their greatest popular expression on television. By the end of the 1950s, he had become a brand name that signified a refined, black-comic sense of bloody murder, and a character who, in Thomas Leitch's words, was "ironic, aloof, anecdotal, manipulative and fond of witty reversals, even if they make nonsense of the stories that have led up to them" ("The Outer Circle," 65).

If *Alfred Hitchcock Presents* was closely attuned to Hitchcock's previously established star image, it was also, inevitably but no doubt unintentionally, very much in keeping with some of the writings that had been collected in André Breton's surrealist anthology of 1940. For example, Breton had published an excerpt from Thomas De Quincey's nineteenth-century memoir, *On Murder Considered as One of the Fine Arts* (1827 and 1839), which treats the theme of murder from an aesthetic rather than a moral point of view. A prototypical dandy, De Quincey insists that there is a properly artistic way to go about committing mayhem: "As to old women, and the mob of newspaper readers," he writes, his tone anticipating Nietzsche and a host of modernist intellectuals, "they are pleased with anything, provided it is bloody enough. But the mind of sensibility requires something more" (quoted in Breton, 56). This humorous, iconoclastic argument became the foundation of a literary tradition and was an acknowledged influence on Oscar Wilde's "Pen, Pencil and Poison" (1889), which tells the true story of Thomas Wainewright, an aesthete, "a forger of no mean or ordinary capabilities, and . . . a subtle and secret poisoner almost without rival in this or any age." (When a friend criticizes Wainewright for doing away with a young woman, he responds in distinctly Wildean fashion, "Yes, it was a dreadful thing to do, but she had very thick ankles" [1004]). Hitchcock probably knew the Wilde essay, and he certainly knew De Quincey, whom he once quoted in an address to the Film Society of Lincoln Center (see Peucker, 141–56). Indeed Peter Wollen has suggested that *On Murder Considered as One of the Fine Arts* was as important to Hitchcock's work as the short fiction of Edgar Allan Poe, laying the foundations for criminal connoisseurship and providing a direct inspiration for films like *Rope* (1948) ("*Rope:* Three Hypotheses," 75–85). Equally important, De Quincey also provided the inspiration for Hitchcock's public persona and the famous speeches he delivered on television.

Another influential name in the Breton anthology was the popular turn-of-the-century American author O. Henry, who wrote short tales with ironic or surprise endings. The structure (if not the tone) of the typical O. Henry story is in many ways similar to the half-hour broadcasts on *Alfred Hitchcock Presents*, and it reminds us as well of Hitchcock's earliest, perhaps most revealing, artistic creations—the short fictional pieces he wrote for the "house" magazine of W.T. Henley's Telegraph Works, in the days before he entered the movies. As Patrick McGilligan has shown, there were at least seven of these stories, and most of them were constructed like jokes, with a sudden revelation in the last lines that throws humorous light on everything that has gone before. The jokes tend to be playfully grim or frightening, involving fantasies of death or sexual humiliation that are banished by the surprise endings. As one instance of what McGilligan calls a narrative "turnaround," consider "The Woman's Part," a 1919 entry told from the point of view of a husband who seems to be passively, secretly watching his wife and her lover discuss a murder and then embrace one another. In the last line of the story, we discover that the husband is viewing the scene from the cheap seats in a theater, and that his wife is acting in a melodrama.

In his commentaries for the *Anthologie de l'humour noir*, Breton pointed out that both De Quincey and O. Henry deserved to be called black humorists because they shared an instinctive "benevolence and compassion" for the criminal classes (189). *Alfred Hitchcock Presents* had the same attribute; in fact, as my colleague Christopher Anderson has pointed out to me, it might be the only network television show in American history that consistently invited its audience to identify with the point of view of criminals. A more darkly funny and unorthodox project than Hitchcock's feature films, which depicted criminal psychology through the "wrong man" device and always ended by restoring the world to conventional order, the television show was virtually devoid of innocent characters. Its most memorable programs were based on morbidly satiric material that was quite rare in movie theaters, and sometimes its criminals went completely unpunished. Remarkably, only one episode was deemed too dark for the network. "The Sorcerer's Apprentice" featured Brandon deWilde as a mentally handicapped youth who, after watching a magician, accidentally saws someone in half. (This episode was never broadcast by CBS, but it can now be seen on TV nostalgia channels.)

Critics have often suggested that other episodes of the television show were "saved" only because Hitchcock's closing remarks lightened the atmosphere and provided a conservative resolution. Hitchcock himself told *TV Guide* that his commentary offered a necessary gesture to morality. But did audiences really believe it when he told them that the Barbara Bel Geddes character in "Lamb to the Slaughter" had been captured by police when she tried to kill her second husband with a prematurely defrosted leg of lamb? Obviously not, because the show's fun derived from the fact that people sometimes got away with murder. By the same token, Hitchcock got away with jokes about the sponsors. ("Crime does not pay—even on television," he remarked on the first episode. "You must have a sponsor.") This was an old device from network radio, practiced by Fred Allen, Phil Harris, and even Orson Welles. But Hitchcock was different because his tone was more contemptuous and because he never spoke the name of an advertiser or endorsed a product. Throughout the series he maintained the comic attitude of a British eccentric who was a victim of vulgar commerce, and his audience seems to have loved him for it.

Alfred Hitchcock Presents led directly to *Psycho*, Hitchcock's most brilliant and frightening exercise in black humor, which shaped his public identity in later years. This film invites audiences to identify first with a thief and then with a murderer, and its entire mechanism of suspense, surprise, and bloody horror is structured like a practical joke—although at times, especially in the performance of Anthony Perkins as Norman Bates, it also achieves an impressive blending of menace and pathos. In interviews, Hitchcock always emphasized the film's amusing qualities. At one point he told François Truffaut that an English newspaperwoman who lacked a sense of humor had described *Psycho* as the work of a "barbaric sophisticate." He seemed intrigued or even pleased by the description. "If *Psycho* had been intended as a serious picture," he remarked, "it would have been shown as a clinical case with no mystery or suspense.... The only question then is whether one should always have a sense of humor in dealing with a serious subject. It seems to me that some of my British films were too light and some of my American movies have been too heavy-handed, but it's the most difficult thing in the world to control that so as to get just the right dosage" (201–2).

The "right dosage" would soon become impossible for Hitchcock to calculate. He never fully entered the pure, unalloyed world of black comedy that we find in some of Jim Thompson's novels or Stanley Kubrick's movies, but he had moved so close to that world that he could no longer easily return to the polished entertainments of his earlier career. *Psycho* was a watershed film, marking a shift away from Hollywood's restrained New Comic formulas and foreshadowing the 1970s trend toward gross-out—a form that not only embraces bad taste but also, in William Paul's words, "transforms revulsion into a sought after goal" (10). There's no space in this essay to review the many determinants of the cultural change, so I shall merely refer interested readers to Paul's excellent *Laughing Screaming*, which explains the "striking inversion" whereby "low-class genres became high-class product" (33). As a result of the inversion, black humor lost some of its aura of sophistication; moreover, the supposedly "higher" forms of satire and irony were challenged by what Paul describes as a repressed, "Old-Comic" tradition of farce, ribaldry, and forthright vulgarity. In this environment, Hitchcock's work began to seem slightly antiquated.

Looked at today against the background of the gross-out slasher films it influenced, *Psycho* clearly belongs to a more repressed period. Until this point Hitchcock's art had usually depended upon a formally controlled, "classy" atmosphere that was inflected with rebellious black humor. In *Psycho* he experimented with what was regarded at the time as an exploitation genre, and he was more frank than ever about lower-body anxieties; but he also created an austere black-and-white example of "pure cinema" in which violence was indirect and "barbarity" was offset by irony and wit. Thus, even though *Psycho* was a carnivalistic experience for its original audiences, Robin Wood and Raymond Durgnat were able to give it cultural capital and art-movie status by comparing it with the writings of Swift and Conrad.

In subsequent years, as his reputation flourished and the movie industry changed, Hitchcock's films grew manifestly darker and perhaps more serious; but the disjunction between his grim jokes and his apparently light genres became starker and more difficult to manage. The bird attacks in *The Birds*, the rape scene in *Marnie* (1964), the protracted killing of an enemy agent in *Torn Curtain* (1966), and the rape-murder in *Frenzy* (1972) tend to overpower the respective conventions of the screwball comedy, the romantic melodrama, the spy story, and the "wrong-man" thriller. Hitchcock's aloof irony remains, but violence ruptures the glamorous surface to such a degree that the humor dies or grows sour. Paradoxically, just at the moment when black comedy dominated the culture at large (and just at the moment when Brian De Palma was refashioning many of Hitchcock's motifs for a younger audience), Hitchcock seemed no longer willing or able to sustain the complex atmosphere of his most admired films. The important point to emphasize, however, is that in a lifetime that spanned two world wars and the major social upheavals of the twentieth century, his artistry had always derived from his special ability to treat horror with humor. Few directors have been so entertaining or have enjoyed such serene and orderly careers, even though the serenity was achieved by virtue of a detached, aesthetic, willfully amused response to primal anxieties. At some level Hitchcock must have agreed with a remark by Thomas De Quincy, who seems almost to define the Freudian version of black comedy: "The reader will think I am laughing.... Nevertheless I have a very reprehensible way of jesting at times in the midst of my own misery" (quoted in Breton, 54).

Hitchcock at the Margins of Noir

The discourse on film noir belongs largely to postmodernist culture but is preoccupied with modernist values in a series of Hollywood thrillers or bloody melodramas from the 1940s and '50s. The pictures it names are a heterogeneous group, dealing with everything from hard-boiled detectives (*The Maltese Falcon*) to bourgeois women in distress (*Caught*), from love on the run (*Gun Crazy*) to foreign intrigue (*The Mask of Dimitrios*), from costume melodrama (*Reign of Terror*) to western adventure (*Pursued*), and from sleek eroticism (*Gilda*) to naturalistic social satire (*Sweet Smell of Success*). Even so, we can make a few generalizations about them. Considered generically, they involve what Jean-Paul Sartre called "extreme situations" and are usually located in a realistic realm somewhere between gothic horror and dystopian science fiction. Stylistically, they tend to be associated with angular photography, subjective modes of narration, and an approximately Freudian or deterministic view of character. Commercially, they blur the distinction between formula pictures and art movies.

Why, then, does the literature on film noir have so little to say about Alfred Hitchcock? Much of his work would at first glance seem to belong somewhere within the broad category I've just described, and yet Alain Silver and Elizabeth Ward's *Film Noir: An Encyclopedic Reference to the American Style* gives detailed treatment only to *Notorious, Shadow of a Doubt, Strangers on a Train,* and *The Wrong Man*. Patrick Brion's lavishly illustrated coffee-table reference, *Le film noir*, includes all of these plus *Rebecca, Suspicion, Vertigo,* and, in more qualified fashion, *North by Northwest*. (If the last, why not virtually everything else?) Critical studies of noir, with the notable exception of Seymour Hirsch's *Film Noir: The Dark Side of the Screen,* usually mention Hitchcock briefly or in passing, and writings on Hitchcock as an auteur seldom deploy the idea of noir. Slavoj Žižek even goes so far as to argue that "Hitchcock's universe is ultimately incompatible with that of the *film noir*" ("In His Bold Gaze My Ruin Is Writ Large," 258). Few critics would take such a radical position, but even when they acknowledge Hitchcock's importance to the so-called noir movement or genre, they often describe him as sui generis or a "strange case."

This tendency can be traced back to the very origins of critical writing on American film noir. The French cinephiles who created the category (which has less to do with a body of artifacts than with a discourse and a set of values that determine how certain films will be read) recognized from the beginning that Hitchcock was one of its practitioners, but they spoke about him in qualified or tangential ways. Consider Nino Frank, the critic often regarded as the first person to apply the term *noir* to American movies, whose well-known 1946 essay on noir in *L'Écran français* is chiefly concerned with a series of "criminal adventures" that had recently been released in Paris: *The Maltese Falcon, Double Indemnity, Laura*, and *Murder, My Sweet*. Frank observes in passing that Hitchcock's *Suspicion* belongs at least technically in the same group as the others; it, too, is a literary adaptation, inspired by an "admirable novel by Francis Iles," and it emphasizes criminal psychology rather than mystery or detection. In Frank's opinion, however, *Suspicion* is an "absolute failure" (14; translation mine). Apparently Frank was in agreement with Billy Wilder, who, just prior to the release of *Double Indemnity*, had publicly declared his intention to "out-Hitchcock Hitchcock."

Raymond Borde and Etienne Chaumeton's groundbreaking historical study, *A Panorama of American Film Noir, 1941–1953*, translated into English in 2002, makes a roughly similar argument, situating Hitchcock at the borders of "true" Hollywood noir, which Borde and Chaumeton regard as a quasi-surrealistic form determined by an American social and cultural context. Hitchcock's prewar British films (particularly *The 39 Steps, Sabotage*, and *Jamaica Inn*) strike Borde and Chaumeton as noir-like to a degree but only a "feeble" influence on the American style (22). In their view, *Rebecca* and *Suspicion* are formative pictures in an emerging noir series, but *Spellbound*, which takes a quasi-clinical approach to psychoanalysis, is closer in spirit to a social-problem picture like Anatole Litvak's *The Snake Pit. Shadow of a Doubt*, on the other hand, is a "major opus" (33), helping to shape a new, distinctively American style of dark movies about attractive killers and morally ambiguous protagonists. After the war, during what Borde and Chaumeton describe as the "grand epoch" of noir (1946–48), three of Hitchcock's productions—*Notorious, The Paradine Case*, and *Rope*—can be termed noir "in varying degrees" (72). The most noir-like of these pictures, Borde and Chaumeton argue, is *Notorious*, an oneiric and erotic melodrama (not unlike Charles Vidor's *Gilda*) that demonstrates an acute sense of the surreal quality in such ordinary objects as a wine bottle, a door key, and a coffee cup. Next in line is *The Paradine Case*, "an excellent documentary about English justice" (72), distinguished mainly by its ironic courtroom scenes, which in their view are worthy of comparison with Carl Dreyer's *Joan of Arc*, Mervyn LeRoy's *They Won't Forget*, and Orson Welles's *The Lady from Shanghai*. As for *Rope*, Borde and Chaumeton say it belongs in company with other dark films chiefly by virtue of its emphasis on gratuitous crime, criminal psychology, and "spellbinding sadism" (3). They also note that in the last, "decadent" phase of the noir cycle (1949–50), Hitchcock produced *Under Capricorn*, a darkly psychological costume picture blending the technical experiments of *Rope* with the gothic romanticism of his early films with Selznick. At the end of the period, however, he directed a "masterpiece," *Strangers on a Train*, based on a *roman noir* by Patricia Highsmith. According to Borde and Chaumeton, "the essential elements of the noir genre [oneiricism, gothicism, eroticism, ambiguity, and cruelty] are present here in an original cocktail that possesses its share of humor" (103).

Borde and Chauemeton's influential commentary may account for the fact that in subsequent writings about noir, *Shadow of a Doubt*, *Notorious*, and *Strangers on a Train* are the pictures by Hitchcock most frequently cited. Given the particular values that Borde and Chaumeton emphasize, however, there seems no good reason why we can't describe virtually every Hitchcock movie—or any reasonably "adult" picture about murder or criminal adventure produced in America from the late 1930s until the present day—as a film noir. In *A Panorama of American Film Noir* and most other places, "noir" is simply the name for modernist, European-influenced crime stories that convey some degree of skepticism toward established institutions and involve subjective narration, psychological views of character, and eroticized violence. Hitchcock was manifestly important to the history of such a form. His pre-Hollywood thrillers have something in common with German expressionist cinema of the 1920s and poetic-realist French films noirs of the 1930s; his American career begins at almost the same moment as the so-called classic or historical period of Hollywood noir; one of his close associates, Joan Harrison, was the producer of Robert Siodmak's *Phantom Lady* and other canonical films noirs of the 1940s; and several of the "original" American movies in the category, including *The Maltese Falcon* and *Double Indemnity*, were explicitly compared to his British work by contemporary reviewers. More importantly, we can find a great many of Hitchcock's signature themes or motifs in what we usually regard as "true" films noirs. The wrong-man plot, for example, is central to *The Blue Dahlia* and *The Big Clock*, and the rear-window motif can be seen in *Pushover* and *Killer's Kiss*. Notice also that several of Hitchcock's most memorable characters are anticipated by definitive examples of the film noir: Mark McPherson in Otto Preminger's *Laura*, like John "Scottie" Ferguson in *Vertigo*, is a hard-headed detective of Scottish ancestry who is haunted by the image of an upper-class woman; Ralph Hughes in Joseph H. Lewis's *My Name Is Julia Ross*, like Bruno Anthony in *Strangers on a Train*, is a psychopathic killer who is excessively attached to his dotty mother; and Al Roberts in Edgar G. Ulmer's *Detour*, like Marion Crane in *Psycho*, is an obsessed character who drives by night across an American wasteland, ultimately encountering violence and death in a cheap motel.

In my own view, the two most impressive Hollywood directors in the 1940s and '50s were Hitchcock and Orson Welles, who seemed equally attuned to a noirish repertory of situations and images. As many critics have observed, the inquisitive camera movements at the openings of *Rebecca* and *Citizen Kane* echo one another, as do the closing shots of the burning "R" and the burning "Rosebud." (Here we might remember that Welles adapted both *The Thirty-Nine Steps* and *Rebecca* on the radio in 1938, and that David Selznick wanted the movie version of the du Maurier novel to resemble the Welles broadcast.) Welles's production of *Journey into Fear* is influenced by Hitchcock's espionage movies of the 1930s, particularly in its clever blending of comedy and menace, and his production of *The Stranger* is influenced by *Shadow of a Doubt*. Welles experimented with the wrong-man or "exchange-of-guilt" story on several occasions, most notably in *The Trial* and *The Lady from Shanghai*, both of which also contain a good many absurdist jokes reminiscent of Hitchcock (as when Michael O'Hara escapes from his trial for murder by walking out of the courtroom among the jurors). Last but not least, *Touch of Evil* anticipates *Psycho* in many ways, especially in the motel scenes with Janet Leigh and Dennis Weaver.

If both Hitchcock and Welles are not totally subsumed under the rubric of film noir, that's partly because of the different questions we ask when we study individual films or artists as opposed to genres or signifying systems, and partly because of the way the name of the author functions in relation to the name of the genre. American film noir became important to international film criticism during the heyday of the French auteurist movement, when New Wave productions were often based on *série noire* thrillers and when the best writing about Hollywood movies attempted to reveal a surplus of personal meaning. In the case of Welles, whose reputation was founded on unorthodox projects such as *Citizen Kane* and *The Magnificent Ambersons*, it was quite easy to show that individual style transcended generic formulas. Hitchcock, however, was another matter. Despite the fact that he made a variety of films during his long career, few major directors have been so exclusively connected with a specific type of movie. (Cecil B. DeMille was known for biblical epics, John Ford for westerns, and Vincente Minnelli for musicals, but even these figures were not completely synonymous with a genre.) Thus Hitchcock became one of the great tests of the auteur theory and a kind of genre unto himself. A paradoxical figure, he was described as the "master of suspense" who used formulas as a mere pretext; as the Hollywood professional who, in the words of Gilles Deleuze, appeared "at the juncture of the two cinemas, the classic that he perfects and the modern that he prepares"; and as the noir director who was somehow an exception to the rule.

And yet Hitchcock's off-center position in the pantheon of noir can't be explained entirely on the basis of auteurist reception or the reluctance of certain critics to see him in relation to the cultural, industrial, and historical trends of his day. There are, I would suggest, intrinsic qualities of subject matter, tone, and style that make his films appear slightly alien to the noir universe, especially when we think of noir as a phenomenon produced by Hollywood in the 1940s and '50s. If we define noir in terms of a prototypical series of crime pictures from the rather narrow historical context of post–World War II Hollywood, we can use the concept as a kind of foil, bringing certain distinctive qualities of Hitchcock's "world" into bold relief. By way of illustration, let me consider four aspects of Hitchcock's work that constitute some of his most specific and least "noir-like" traits.

BRITISHNESS

The idea of film noir can be traced back to the French poetic-realist cinema of the 1930s and more particularly to French intellectual culture of the *avant-guerre*. In the years immediately after World War II, however, French critics strongly associated noir with the hard-boiled or tabloid-realist school of American literature. Most of the Hollywood pictures they admired featured tough-guy protagonists in business suits who moved fairly comfortably among the proletariat and the urban underworld. (This is true even of *Laura*, in which Dana Andrews's working-class policeman is vividly contrasted with Clifton Webb's Park Avenue aesthete.) Hitchcock never explored such materials, nor did he deal with the theme of existential angst that French critics sometimes extrapolated from Bogart thrillers. At one point he attempted to hire Dashiell Hammett as screenwriter for *Strangers on a Train*, and he eventually offered the job to Raymond Chandler, but he found Chandler's work so disappointing that he rewrote the entire film in collaboration with a woman screenwriter, Czenzi Ormonde. Although he sometimes used seamy, low-rent settings (as in parts of *Shadow of a Doubt, The Wrong Man,* and *Psycho*), most of his films took place in a prosperous, virtually all-white milieu that was characterized, at least outwardly, by a feeling of whimsy, sophistication, and good manners—in other words, by qualities that the typical American associated with upper-class Britishness.

Despite or perhaps because of his Cockney origins, Hitchcock's carefully constructed public image was almost a parody of British reserve. His first American work was done under contract with David Selznick, an Anglophile producer whose studio was modeled on the homes of the WASP aristocracy, and at the end of his career he became "Sir Alfred" when he was knighted by Queen Elizabeth. Hitchcock often satirized the gentry by placing comments about them in the mouths of charming rogues—nowhere more so than in *Rebecca,* in which Jack Favell (George Sanders), a suave scoundrel who makes his living as a "motor-car salesman," climbs into the back seat of Maxim de Winter's limousine, munches a chicken leg with one hand, smokes a cigarette with the other, and speculates on what it would be like to "live comfortably without working." (Later, Favell accuses de Winter and the other leaders of the community of behaving like a "trades union.") In both the Selznick period and afterward, however, Hitchcock's distinctive "world" looked polite and relatively well-to-do, if only because he repeatedly used actors who spoke with cultivated British or mid-Atlantic accents (Laurence Olivier, Cary Grant, Claude Rains, Louis Calhern, Charles Laughton, Ray Milland, Grace Kelly, Cedric Hardwicke, John Forsythe, Edmund Gwenn, James Mason, Leo G. Carroll, John Williams, etc.). By the same token, a great many of his Hollywood pictures were set in Britain, and in several cases he required American stars to imitate English characters: see, for example, Gregory Peck's awkward impersonation of a barrister in *The Paradine Case* (Hitchcock had wanted Olivier or Ronald Colman) and Jane Wyman's only slightly more convincing portrayal of a Royal Academy of Dramatic Art student who works as a lady's maid in *Stage Fright.*

The rather ersatz, postcard view of England we find in Hitchcock's American features is in one sense quite typical of Hollywood's A-budget productions in the classic period and is no doubt a symptom of both American fantasy and Beverly Hills snobbery. To some extent, it has less to do with Hitchcock himself than with the industry in which he worked and with the commercial value of promoting the director as an English eccentric. It must be emphasized, however, that "Britishness" had great dramatic advantages for Hitchcock, enabling him to intensify one of his most important effects: the feeling of repressed anxiety or violence breaking through a well-ordered surface. His rather mannered and artificial settings, which create what he liked to call a "counterpoint" between the civilized and the sordid, tend to reverse the priorities of hard-boiled film noir. In Chandler adaptations such as *The Big Sleep* or *Murder, My Sweet*, we always sense a fascination with "the dark side of town." The world in these films is *manifestly* corrupt, pervaded by Baudelairean decadence, expressionist gloom, and *nostalgie de la boue*. In Hitchcock, by contrast, the world is often calm and well lit, and when we glimpse the gutter it has terror but no romantic fascination.

All this may help to explain why, on the few occasions when Hitchcock uses the outward paraphernalia of the hard-boiled thriller, he works against our expectations of the genre. The early scenes of *Shadow of a Doubt* show a dreary rented room and an urban alleyway, but the film soon changes its locale, becoming the study of a patrician killer who visits a polite family in small-town America. The first half of *Psycho* offers a virtual survey of noir settings, including a cheap hotel, an insurance office, a used-car lot, a nocturnal drive, and a neon-lit motel; but the second half looks more like a cross between a provincial melodrama and a James Whale horror movie.

Even more remarkable is *The Wrong Man*, one of the most underrated and least "British" of Hitchcock's films. Like *Call Northside 777* and several other police procedurals from the 1940s and '50s, this picture is photographed at the actual scene of a "true crime" and contains many stylistic or iconographic features we associate with classical noir: black-and-white film stock; night-for-night exteriors; deep-focus perspectives; radical camera angles; cops and criminals who wear overcoats and snap-brim hats; a sleek Manhattan nightclub where people dance the rumba; a seedy police station; a courtroom; a dilapidated rooming house; and a psychiatrist's office. And yet Hitchcock subtly undermines or deflates all the hard-boiled conventions he employs. As Jean-Luc Godard remarks in his superb commentary on *The Wrong Man* (one of the longest critical essays Godard ever wrote), Manny Balestrero's lawyer only "play[s] at being the Perry Mason of Stanley Gardner's novels" (54), and Manny himself suffers from "semi-inertia and [a] taste for playing—like the bourgeois family in *Shadow of a Doubt*—the detective of thrillerdom" (48). The police and the frightened women at Manny's insurance company may think they inhabit a film noir, but they're obviously wrong. Even though Manny fits one of the stereotypical images of the Hollywood gangster (an Italian American musician who works in a nightclub), he's in fact an idealized yet curiously passive paterfamilias who has exceedingly regular habits. The terror of the film arises not from violence in the "naked city" but from an ever-present economic anxiety that helps determine the madness at the core of Manny's family life. One of the chief ironies of *The Wrong Man*, as Renata Salecl has observed, lies in the fact that the criminal atmosphere and the documentary treatment of justice are little more than catalysts for a deeper trauma—a depression that afflicts Rose Balestrero from the beginning of the film and that ultimately overtakes her completely. As Godard puts it, *The Wrong Man* differs from the usual Hitchcock suspense story in that "what one was afraid of happening does not finally happen" (51). What *does* happen, however, is terrible to contemplate. A title card at the end of the picture assures us that Rose has recovered, but we never see her restored to health. *The Wrong Man* is less about crime and punishment than about the breakdown of a fragile lower-middle-class marriage under the pressure of debt and patriarchy, and the slow descent of one of its members into an unglamorous darkness. One of the bleakest movies ever produced in Hollywood, it leaves us with a far more downbeat impression than the usual film noir.

SUSPENSE AND CLASSICAL FORM

Borde and Chaumeton define film noir on the basis of affective qualities that disorient the spectator and remove the psychological guideposts of classic narrative. Hitchcock deals in these qualities (eroticism, perverse violence, moral ambiguity, etc.), but, as everyone recognizes, the overriding aim of most of his pictures is to create suspense. As a result, he depends more upon clarity than upon disorientation. Compared to his work, films noirs such as *The Big Sleep, The Lady from Shanghai,* and *Kiss Me Deadly* seem murky, confusing, and not at all suspenseful; indeed, the film noir is usually admired by critics precisely because it dispenses with logical coherence, elevating "mood" or "tone" over plot. The very term *noir,* as David Bordwell has pointed out, functions to describe "patterns of nonconformity" within the classical system, chief among them a tendency to complicate the spatial, temporal, and moral coordinates of narrative (Bordwell, Staiger, and Thompson, 74). Hitchcock doesn't quite fit this model, or at least his nonconformity manifests itself in different ways. For all his interest in absurd or improbable situations, he never allows characterization, cultural detail, or atmosphere to predominate over suspense and the pursuit of a narrative goal. "I am against virtuosity for its own sake," he tells Truffaut during their interview. "The beauty of image and movement, the rhythm and the effects—everything must be subordinated to the purpose" (68). And the "purpose" is usually a feeling of anxious waiting created by a lucid, relentless logic of narrative exposition.

Hitchcock's images are composed with the directness and simplicity of a storyboard or a cartoon and their sequential organization is intended to lead the audience step-by-step through the action, providing exactly the information that will condition their response. For example, the American remake of *The Man Who Knew Too Much* goes to elaborate lengths to prepare viewers for the climactic Albert Hall sequence: at the end of the credits it shows a set of cymbals and announces that musical instruments are going to change a family's life; later it shows the villains listening *twice* to a recording in which a crucial passage of music is punctuated by a crash of cymbals; and finally, at the concert, it pans across a sheet of music and stops on the single note that will be played by the cymbalist. Recalling the film in his interview with Truffaut, Hitchcock comments, "Ideally, for that scene to have maximum effect, all of the viewers should be able to read a musical score." He also describes the great pains he took to establish key points: "In the audience," he remarks, "there are probably many people who don't even know what cymbals are, and so it was necessary not only to show them but even to spell the word. It was also important that the public be able not only to recognize the sound of the cymbals but to anticipate it in their minds. Knowing what to expect, they wait for it to happen" (63).

At every juncture, the audience in a Hitchcock film is made keenly aware of the various possibilities or logical paths of the narrative. "I've often found," he tells Truffaut, "that a suspense situation is weakened because the action is not sufficiently clear. For instance, if two actors should happen to be wearing similar suits, the viewer can't tell one from the other; if the location is not clearly established, the viewer may be wondering where the action is taking place.... So it's important to be explicit, to clarify constantly" (63). It follows from this concern that the "look" of a Hitchcock picture is less shadowy and prone to optical distortions than the prototypical examples of Hollywood noir. Significantly, Hitchcock was one of the first directors of murder stories to experiment with color, a medium that makes expressionist lighting less necessary; and in his black-and-white films he often stages horrific situations in broad daylight or in bright interiors, without dramatically cast shadows. Except for a few shots in *Strangers on a Train* and *The Wrong Man*, he avoids the extreme wide-angle, deep-focus perspectives or bizarrely out-of-kilter compositions that are typical of a director like Orson Welles or a photographer like John Alton. By the same token, he made relatively few films involving flashbacks (*Spellbound, I Confess, Stage Fright,* and *Marnie* are examples), and the emotional texture of his most popular work is more like a thrill ride or a slowly rising anxiety than a poetic-realist meditation on the dark past. Perhaps most importantly, his American work seldom bears the marks of poverty. Not until *Psycho* did he produce a film in the B-picture style often associated (accurately or not) with the noir sensibility. On the contrary, he made his reputation in

Hollywood as a director of high-end productions—glamorous, star-filled movies that were manufactured as solidly, cleanly, and expensively as a Rolls-Royce.

Because of his desire to play games of suspense, Hitchcock is concerned with symmetrical design, straightforward narrative logic, and classical editing. Even when he makes a supposedly authentic film noir such as *Strangers on a Train*, he remains committed to classical decoupage and the total effect is less a repudiation of the dominant Hollywood style than a triumphant illustration of its fundamental tenants. How appropriate that the chief formal device of *Strangers*, a film in which the motif of the "double" is so obvious, is parallel editing. The spectacular climax involves exactly the kind of suspenseful crosscutting that was first perfected by D.W. Griffith— although Hitchcock intensifies the power of the technique with an elaborate pattern of visual or graphic conflicts worthy of Eisenstein. First we see a close shot of Guy Haines, dressed in sporting whites and violently swinging a tennis racquet on a grassy, sunlit playing field; then we see a close shot of Bruno Anthony, dressed in a gray business suit and trying to retrieve a lost cigarette lighter from the shadowy recesses of a city storm drain. Each character is racing against the clock, but the motions of Guy's arm are large and sweeping, whereas the movements of Bruno's hand are small and measured. The most unorthodox element of this brilliant sequence lies not in its form, but in Hitchcock's sly willingness to reveal that everything is in one sense pointless, founded on a formal technique or a trick. At the end of each character's desperate effort to achieve a goal—after Guy has won the tennis match and Bruno has retrieved the lighter—the audience realizes that its anxiety has been slightly in excess of the real situation. Despite all the urgency of the scenes we've been watching, a great deal of time remains left on the clock. Bruno can't plant the incriminating evidence against Guy until the sun goes down, so he has to sit and wait for an hour or two at an empty carnival while Guy rushes to meet him.

WOMAN AND MASS CULTURE

The American film noir is for the most part a masculine form of entertainment built on ambivalence about sexual romance. To make this point clear, I need to elaborate somewhat, first by emphasizing that most of the films initially described as noir were shaped not only by male-oriented adventure fiction but also by a long-standing misogynist ideology that developed within high modernism and often expressed itself through cultural debates over Hollywood. In *After the Great Divide* (1986), Andreas Huyssen convincingly argues that one of the salient characteristics of modernist art during the first half of the twentieth century was a hostility toward a sleek, Americanized, and supposedly "feminine" mass culture. The male modernists who voiced this attitude were speaking not about proletarian literature or residual folk art but about lending libraries, best sellers, books-of-the-month, radio programs, Hollywood movies, and all the products of the capitalist culture industries, which they repeatedly portrayed as appealing to shallow female consumers. As Huyssen observes, intellectual attacks on mechanically reproduced kitsch inevitably mingled with a misogynist discourse "which time and again openly states its contempt for women and for the masses and which had Nietzsche as its most eloquent and influential representative" (49).

Huyssen's argument needs to be qualified on two counts. First, some of the high modernists were feminists; and second, "mass culture," which often functioned as modernism's debased "other," was increasingly inflected by modernist aesthetics. Nowhere was the modernist influence on mass-produced art more evident than in pulp writers such as Hammett and Chandler, who were immediately recognized as literary innovators working in a popular field. Significantly, the hard-boiled school of detective fiction appeared at virtually the same moment as Ernest Hemingway's early short stories and was sponsored and praised by vanguard literary intellectuals. *Black Mask* magazine was partly owned by H.L. Mencken, America's leading "man of letters" in the 1920s, who was an important commentator on Nietzsche and who published Hammett's and James M. Cain's early writings in *The Smart Set*. Edmund Wilson, the major American critic of the 1930s and the author of a famous book on high modernism *(Axel's Castle)*, was a great booster of Hammett, Cain, and what he called "the boys in the back room." The best of the pulp authors also saw themselves as proponents of an authentic culture, and for that reason they were explicitly critical of the feminine masses. Raymond Chandler's literary manifesto, "The Simple Art of Murder," was an attack on best-selling British novelists Agatha Christie and Dorothy Sayers, together with their supposedly female readers, who enjoyed a type of fiction that seemed to Chandler like "a cup of luke-warm consomme at a spinsterish tea room." Such gendered assaults on Main Street America and the women consumers of pop culture were fairly typical in "tough" fiction and were not greatly different from the assaults we find in an overtly high-modernist and distinctly noir-like novel such as Nathanael West's *Miss Lonelyhearts,* which symbolizes the voice of the public in the form of a vapid, sentimental, and totally imaginary woman author of a newspaper advice column.

Similar attitudes can be found in the 1940s and '50s cycle of films derived from the hard-boiled writers. These films are filled with techniques associated with modern art (expressionist lighting, dynamic camera angles, nonlinear narratives, dream sequences, etc.), and, in keeping with the ideological agenda I've been describing, they openly criticize certain aspects of industrial modernity. As Mike Davis has pointed out in *City of Quartz* (1990), many of the classic films noirs can be understood as a deliberate reaction by intellectuals and European émigrés against Hollywood itself—particularly against the movie moguls, Southern California power brokers, and real estate salesmen who promoted visions of a sunny utopia for the masses. In the classic film noir, however, the consumers and emblems of what Orson Welles's Mike O'Hara called the "bright, guilty world" often turn out to be females. One thinks of Phyllis Dietrichson, the black widow in *Double Indemnity*, who wears vulgar ankle bracelets and lacquered hair and who plans murder in a supermarket; or of Elsa Bannister, the femme fatale in *The Lady from Shanghai*, who looks like a synthetic Hollywood pinup and who lures men to death by singing a pop tune in a soft-focus close-up; or even of certain bit players, such as the silly but attractive hat-check girl in *In a Lonely Place*, who tells Bogart the story of a best-selling romance novel that he can't bear to read. Many of these women are threatening to the male hero, but not simply because they're sexually desirable. They also represent a somewhat tawdry capitalism—to love them or even to become romantically involved with them is to "sell out," compromising one's values at the level of both sex and money.

Hitchcock doesn't fully participate in this attitude. On the one hand, he has a rigorous, quasi-scientific temperament, and his films are strongly influenced by vanguard European art (especially by German expressionism, French surrealism, and Soviet montage). By the 1940s, he had fully attained his reputation as a "master," a term that connotes phallic power and control. But on the other hand, when he came to America the tone of his work changed, and he was accused by some critics of selling out, becoming slick and Hollywoodish. (This opinion was voiced by several British reviewers and by such distinguished American critics as James Agee and Stanley Kauffman; it's also a minor theme in Raymond Durgnat's 1977 book on Hitchcock.) His early pictures in California (except for *Shadow of a Doubt*) lacked a realistic social milieu, and to make matters worse he was a practitioner of the female gothic—a director who, in collaboration with Selznick, specialized in glossy, romantic "women's pictures."

Again and again, Hitchcock invited his audience to identify with the point of view of women, and in films such as *Rebecca*, as Tania Modleski has observed, his adaptation of a "feminine" best seller constitutes "a challenge to the male spectator's identity" (55). Even in *The Paradine Case* (scripted by Selznick, with assistance from Hitchcock's wife, Alma Reville), in which we encounter a true femme fatale, the emotional or psychological effect is different from a hard-boiled detective story. Mrs. Paradine is a remote beauty (Alida Valli) who coldly rejects the attentions of an infatuated investigator-barrister but suffers from her own *amour fou* in the form of a passionate attachment to a rather androgynous groom (Louis Jourdan) on the estate of her blind husband. The barrister's fascination with his treacherous client makes him seem ineffectual and masochistic, in vivid contrast to the sadistic old judge (Charles Laughton) who presides over the trial; nevertheless, both the judge and the barrister have bourgeois marriages in which their wives play utterly subordinate roles. Mrs. Paradine comes from a different world and is a different kind of wife; by openly voicing her sexual desire in a crowded courtroom, she not only humiliates the barrister but also threatens the social hierarchy of the film. "My only comfort," she says to her defender as she admits to a crime that will send her to the gallows, "is in the hatred and contempt I feel for you."

Perhaps because Hitchcock required his audience to identify with women, his complex manipulations of scopic and narrative pleasure have been crucial to the development of radical psychoanalytic theory, chiefly through Laura Mulvey's ground-breaking essays of the 1970s and '80s. Notice also that on the level of heterosexual romance, his work as a whole is open to quite un-noir-like interpretations—as in the first edition of Robin Wood's *Hitchcock's Films* (1965), which puts great emphasis on the moral or "therapeutic" quality of Hitchcock's love stories, and in some parts of Raymond Durgnat's *The Strange Case of Alfred Hitchcock*, which points out that all but one or two of Hitchcock's movies can be seen as "New Comedies." Durgnat's suggestion is greatly reinforced in the excellent studies of Hitchcock by Lesley Brill and Stanley Cavell, who view the director not in the context of dark thrillers but in the context of utopian romance.

Hitchcock celebrates the romantic union to a degree seldom found in film noir, where the threat of sexual relationships is palpable and in one sense deeply political. He nevertheless treats romance with an undercurrent of dark irony, and it's impossible to say how much his repeated use of the woman's point of view is due to his personal inclination and how much to his commercial calculations. Throughout his career he had a tendency to represent female subjectivity on the screen; but from Selznick he arrived at the conclusion that the audience for classic Hollywood entertainment was chiefly female, and that box-office success depended on satisfying women consumers. He says as much during his interview with Truffaut, at a point when the two men are engaged in a protracted debate over whether or not sex on the screen should be implicit (as in Hitchcock) or explicit (as in the film noir):

> FT: My guess is that this is one aspect of your pictures that's probably more satisfying to the feminine viewers than to the male audience.

AH: I'd like to point out that it's generally the woman who has the final say on which picture a couple is going to see. In fact, it's generally the woman who will decide, later on, whether it was a good or a bad picture. (Truffaut, *Hitchcock/Truffaut*, 168)

In an earlier encounter with André Bazin, Hitchcock seemed almost resentful of the female audience, who—according to him—lacked a taste for dark humor. Here is Bazin's summary of remarks by Hitchcock, mediated by an interpreter on the set of *To Catch a Thief:* "Hollywood films are made for women; it is toward their sentimental taste that scenarios are directed because it is they who account for the bulk of the box-office receipts. In England films are still made for men, but that is also why so many studios close down" ("Hitchcock versus Hitchcock," 65). Later in the same discussion, Hitchcock returned to the theme: "Hitchcock appeared to me to be somewhat conventionally concerned with correcting [the] criticism of being commercial by affirming that it was easy to make an 'artistic' film but the real difficulty lay in making a good commercial film.... Such as it was, the sense of his first self-criticism was unequivocal and the necessity of renouncing adult, masculine humor in order to satisfy American producers was presented as exquisite torture" (65–66).

Notice, too, that Hitchcock's films express comic contempt for certain females, especially for rich American matrons such as the ones played by Gladys Cooper in *Rebecca,* Constance Collier in *Rope,* and Marion Lorne in *Strangers on a Train.* (The charmingly witty exception is Jessie Royce Landis in *To Catch a Thief* and *North by Northwest.*) Moreover, the closer he comes to the prototypical atmosphere of American film noir, the more he treats women with derision. When Bruno Anthony almost strangles a society lady in *Strangers on a Train,* there's a distinct cruelty in the way Hitchcock lingers on a close-up of the woman's face, inviting us to laugh. Earlier in the film, we identify with Bruno as he reaches out to strangle Guy Haines's promiscuous wife, Miriam (Laura Elliott), who loves vulgar amusements and is almost a symbol of woman as mass culture. These two sorts of female—one rich and the other cheap—also have peripheral but significant roles to play in *Shadow of a Doubt,* Hitchcock's most "American" project of the 1940s, and a film in which the noir-like connection between women and capitalist mass culture is somewhat clearer. Homicidal maniac Charlie Oakley is not simply a momma's boy who murders out of an oedipal compulsion; he's also on some level a rebel against modernity, a Luciferian aesthete or dandy who is keenly aware that his sister has moved down in the world by marrying a bank clerk. Using his considerable charm and vaguely aristocratic manner, Oakley preys upon the rich widows of Santa Rosa, California, meanwhile forming a perverse bond with his niece and namesake, a vibrant young woman who lives a life of quiet desperation among "ordinary" folk. In a local restaurant, where a barmaid lingers over the table and comments that she would "kill" for an expensive ring, Uncle Charlie tells niece Charlie that the houses in her neighborhood are facades to conceal "swine." We're supposed to be horrified when the madman drops his mask, but the film also makes his critique of an idealized Norman Rockwell community seem at least partly valid. Throughout *Shadow of a Doubt*, Hitchcock depicts the American town as a petit-bourgeois matriarchy, filled with timid, emasculated males like Joe Newton and his next-door neighbor, Herbie Hawkins. He makes us admire and identify with niece Charlie, who represents the town, but also suggests that she's a spiritual double for the villain and that she has too little control over her destiny to become a true heroine. The ostensible happy ending leaves her shaken and depressed, standing outside a local church with her prospective bridegroom, about to be fully integrated into the community. Off screen, we hear a priest delivering a hypocritical eulogy for her murderous relative. The modern world, represented by women, has won, but the victory seems hollow.

NOSTALGIA

In *Shadow of a Doubt*, Charlie Oakley suffers from a delusional nostalgia for a nineteenth-century belle époque, signified by the elegant ballroom dancers and the "merry widow" waltz during the credit sequence. A similar memory of a bygone world can be found in other films we describe as noir; according to Paul Schrader, who wrote one of the most influential commentaries on the topic, the "overriding" themes of such films include "loss, nostalgia," and "fear of the future" (58). But the sense of past-ness in Hollywood's dark cinema of the 1940s and '50s usually has more to do with personal than with historical time. Noir protagonists such as Swede in *The Killers*, Jeff Bailey in *Out of the Past*, or Nancy Blair in *The Locket* don't feel the loss of an older society; they suffer from dark memories that are fully situated within what Vivian Sobchack calls the noir "chronotope." Charlie Oakley may resemble these characters in his compulsion to repeat his past, but his specific nostalgia has historical dimensions, pointing to a nineteenth-century hierarchical society. Hence the thematic structure of *Shadow of a Doubt* is somewhat less like a typical film noir and more like Welles's *The Magnificent Ambersons* (a quality intensified by the coincidence that Joseph Cotten stars in both pictures).

There are, to be sure, several examples of noir "costume" movies or nineteenth-century melodramas (*Gaslight, Dr. Jekyll and Mr. Hyde, The Spiral*

Staircase, etc.), but such films tend to be exceptions to the rule and they rarely mix images of the modern and the historical past. In Hitchcock, by contrast, the entire meaning or emotional effect often depends upon a strategic use of certain familiar cultural codes of the nineteenth century alongside images of the present day. Perhaps because of his European background, but more probably because he collaborated so often with Selznick, his early American films seem preoccupied with sharp contrasts between the old world and the new. The baronial mansions in *Rebecca, Suspicion,* and *The Paradine Case* become virtual characters, symbolizing a mixture of patriarchal oppression and passionate romance, and they strongly affect the modern-day people who inhabit them. This sense of the past also remains an important feature in some of Hitchcock's later work. In *Psycho,* for example, the surreal juxtaposition of a gothic mansion and a motel is central to the meaning of the narrative, and it tends to upset our usual expectations of noir iconography.

The Hitchcock film in which historical imagery figures most prominently is *Vertigo*, which resembles both a conventional private-eye melodrama and a surrealist ghost story on the order of Selznick's *Portrait of Jennie. Vertigo's* many imitations, including *Obsession, Body Double, Final Analysis,* and *Basic Instinct,* are closer in spirit to the classic film noir precisely because they omit the theme of the old world. Compared to these films, *Vertigo* seems more like a mixture of Dashiell Hammett and Edgar Allan Poe. It tells a story of a solitary urban investigator at the fringe of the middle class who is fascinated by a rich, duplicitous woman, but it soon becomes preoccupied with historical romance, necrophilia, and the uncanny return of an aristocratic past—a past belonging to what Eric Hobsbawm has called the "Age of Capital," when bourgeois patriarchy was in the ascendency, when Hollywood didn't exist, and when men had "the power and the freedom," as one character says, to cast their unwanted women aside. Ultimately, its images of contemporary San Francisco give way to a premodernist setting, and the spirit of Poe dominates the film. Madeleine Elster seems to echo Madeline Usher, the woman who rises from the grave at the end of Poe's *Fall of the House of Usher.* (The difference, and what most infuriates Scottie Ferguson, is that Madeleine is only pretending to be a ghost; much to his frustration, she also assumes the guise of a mass-cultural, American type named Judy Barton, who comes from Kansas.) The last lines of one of Poe's most famous poems, "Annabel Lee," might almost serve as an epigraph to *Vertigo:* "And so, all the night-tide, I lie down by the side / Of my darling, my darling, my life and my bride, / In her sepulcher there by the sea—/ In her tomb by the side of the sea." An equally good epigraph would be a line from Poe's essay "The Philosophy of Composition," which argues that the most "poetic" theme in art is "the death of a beautiful woman."

Vertigo is exemplary of Hitchcock in many ways, and its historical nostalgia seems to me to blend with most of the other qualities I've discussed in this essay, enabling me to draw my argument to a conclusion. Notice that even though *Vertigo* stars an icon of "Americanness" (James Stewart), it's chiefly about the central character's ironic, painful longing for an old, vaguely British world of refinement and power. (Gavin Elster, played by the British actor Tom Helmore, represents that world, and his rich, exceptionally masculine office is filled with nineteenth-century paintings of sailing ships.) The film is almost completely lacking suspense (and even Hitchcockian humor), but it remains pellucidly clear in execution, sharply aware that the classic Hollywood narrative requires the end of the story to answer the beginning—indeed, it gives us closure with a vengeance. It offers a photographic expressionism and a bizarre dream sequence but seldom looks noir-like, partly because it experiments with a color photography that dispenses with cast shadows, and partly because it's shot in the glamorous, big-budget, "Hollywood" manner. It deals with a private eye and a duplicitous woman, but at crucial junctures it shows the world from the woman's point of view, and it retains a feeling of old-fashioned, passionate romanticism even when it makes us sharply aware of the protagonist's neurosis and perversity.

Vertigo was based on a French novel, and it was the French who taught us to appreciate not only the American film noir but also Hitchcock and Edgar Allan Poe. If we consider Hitchcock's entire career in this light, we can see that he functions as a kind of transitional figure in a tradition that the French helped to create. He has an obvious affinity with the Hollywood directors of film noir but is also quite similar to Poe, who might be regarded as the progenitor of the *roman noir*. Like Poe, Hitchcock takes a quasi-scientific approach to his work; like Poe, he specializes in horror and the irrational; and like Poe, he's an aesthete who appeals to a popular audience. In fact, all the "Hitchcockian" qualities I've listed can be explained in terms of the director's middle position between the nineteenth and twentieth centuries—a position that reveals certain links between Europe and America, between Poe and Hollywood, and between aestheticism and modernism. Another way of making the same point would be to say that Hitchcock's work tends to show its roots in the ur-surrealist romantics and the early films of D. W. Griffith, even while it reveals the darker side of twentieth-century art. In the last analysis, one could argue that Hitchcock is central to the larger, more broadly cultural history of noir, or to the long tradition of what the Victorians called "sensation fiction." He seems marginal only in a somewhat parochial context, when we consider him in relation to the American film noir's Hollywood manifestations in the 1940s and '50s.

Spies and Lovers
North by Northwest

Although Alfred Hitchcock is identified with a certain type of thriller or murder story, he actually made a wide variety of films, including two costume pictures, a prize fight melodrama, an adaptation of a Seán O'Casey play, a screwball comedy, and (believe it or not) an operetta. His reputation as the "master of suspense" evolved slowly and was determined in large part by a series of critically and commercially successful spy movies he directed at Gaumont British and Gainsborough Pictures between 1934 and 1938. In Hollywood during the early 1940s, he filmed two patriotic adventures about espionage, and over the next twenty years he periodically returned to the theme, treating it in a somewhat more ambiguous style appropriate to the cold war. Of his dozen features in this vein, however, none was more popular, influential, or commonly associated with his authorial signature than the comic-romantic epic *North by Northwest* (1959).

Produced by Hitchcock under a special one-picture arrangement with Metro-Goldwyn-Mayer, this film drew on the talents of the director's most brilliant collaborators, including actor Cary Grant, cinematographer Robert Burks, composer Bernard Herrmann, production designer Robert Boyle, and graphic artist Saul Bass; it was released at the peak of Hitchcock's celebrity on American television, and in many ways it functioned as a capstone to or summary of his career. In the course of their book-length interview, François Truffaut told Hitchcock that "Just as *The [39] Steps* may be regarded as the compendium of your work in Britain, *North by Northwest* is the picture that epitomizes the whole of your work in America" (249).

Hitchcock neither supported nor denied Truffaut's claim, perhaps because many of his most characteristic films were less about political intrigue than about sexual guilt and anxieties in private settings. But screenwriter Ernest Lehman has confirmed that *North by Northwest* was intended as a kind of homage or retrospective. In 1957, Lehman was hired by Hitchcock to develop a script from Hammond Innes's novel *The Wreck of the Mary Deare;* he soon abandoned the job, feeling that neither he nor Hitchcock had any real interest in it. According to Lehman, the two men continued to converse until a better idea emerged: "One day I said, 'I want to do a Hitchcock picture to end all Hitchcock pictures.' And by that I meant a movie-movie—with glamour, wit, excitement, movement, big scenes, a large canvas, innocent bystander caught up in great derring-do, in the Hitchcock manner. And then one day he said, a little wistfully, 'I've always wanted to do a chase sequence across the faces of Mount Rushmore'" (quoted in Spoto, 343).

Hitchcock had been fond of staging melodramatic chases against the backdrop of imperial monuments ever since *Blackmail* (1929), which climaxes with the police scurrying across the roof of the British Museum. The mere idea of a cliff-hanging scene on Mount Rushmore was enough to start Lehman working on a new project, entitled *In a Northwesterly Direction*. (At later stages the film was called *Breathless* and *The Man on Lincoln's Nose;* MGM's story editor, Kenneth MacKenna, suggested the title that was eventually adopted.) Lehman's screenplay, developed after a series of story conferences in which Hitchcock described various surrealistic episodes that might be used, was an obvious attempt to draw together themes and situations from at least three of the director's previous films about international espionage, blending them into a spectacular and definitively "Hitchcockian" entertainment. As in *The 39 Steps* (1935), an ordinary man falls by accident into a bizarre adventure; falsely accused of a murder, he leads the police on a treacherous and amusing cross-country chase, in the course of which he meets a beautiful woman, exposes a group of foreign agents, and proves his innocence. As in *Saboteur* (1942), the protagonist finds himself locked in a climactic life-and-death struggle with a sadistic spy atop a national monument. And as in *Notorious* (1946), a coolly pragmatic American bureaucracy persuades an insecure woman to sleep with the enemy for "patriotic" reasons; when the woman complies, the hero and the villain become jealous rivals for her love, and neither side in the ideological struggle can lay claim to moral or ethical purity.

Most criticism of the film has concentrated on such issues, although Lehman's screenplay was equally predicated on Hitchcock's ability to "get a Cary Grant with the greatest of ease" (Lehman, quoted in Brady, 205). There is a sense in which Grant "coauthored" *North by Northwest:* he was as big a star as Hitchcock, he received a larger share of the film's profits, and he significantly influenced both the tone and the content of the narrative. He and Lehman sometimes argued passionately about the script: "Cary Grant and I had a few fierce battles in the back seat of a limousine on location at Bakersfield during the crop-duster sequence," Lehman has said. "He would sit there and go over some of his scenes with me. 'This is ridiculous,' he'd say. 'You think you are writing a Cary Grant picture? This is a David Niven picture'" (Brady, 226). But despite Grant's reservations, the completed film is obviously designed to exploit his acting skills and his star image. The famous crop-dusting sequence derives most of its wit from the mere sight of Grant running across a prairie, garbed in the same costume he had worn in countless movie drawing rooms. Throughout, Hitchcock and Lehman joke about the actor's unrumpled charm, and they sometimes allow him to peep through his role. ("I know," Grant says at one point, adjusting a pair of Hollywoodish sunglasses, "I look vaguely familiar.") Our constant awareness of his stardom is enhanced by Hitchcock's lifelong interest in the paradoxes of theatricality and identity, and by Lehman's story of a person who is created out of nothing. "George Kaplan," the fake spy manufactured by government agents, is similar in many ways to "Roger O. Thornhill," a stereotypical Madison Avenue executive whose middle initial stands for zero; by extension, both characters have something in common with "Cary Grant," who was created by Archie Leach and the entertainment industry out of a made-up proper name, a set of performing skills, and a series of narrative functions.

Elsewhere I've commented at length on Grant's performance, showing how he mixes the light-comic sophistication of an Alfred Lunt and the music hall clowning of a Charlie Chaplin with the glamour of a fashion model and the athleticism of a Hollywood action hero (*Acting in the Cinema*, 213–35). He sharpens the timing of the film's dialogue and gives literal pace to the sequences in which he strides across hotel lobbies or runs away from his pursuers. Equally important, the decision to cast him affected the very writing of the screenplay, which is not only a "wrong man" thriller but also a "comedy of remarriage," similar to the pictures that secured his reputation in the 1930s. Stanley Cavell has noted that *North by Northwest* shifts the emphasis of the remarriage plot from the "creation of a new woman" to the "revival" of a much-divorced man (249–61), but elements of the old formula are preserved and Grant's uniquely attractive romantic style remains intact. As Andrew Britton has remarked, one of the actor's important achievements was to embody an unorthodox male heterosexuality, arrived at through a relationship "in which the woman appears so often as the educator of the male, and of his pleasure" (17). Partly because of this quality, *North by Northwest* offers a greater sense of utopian playfulness than one usually expects from Hitchcock. As in *Suspicion* (1941) and *Notorious*, Hitchcock suggests that dark impulses lie beneath Grant's charm, but here the actor's cheerful and courteous attributes seem more evident; his beautifully judged comic reactions recall the antic grace of his screwball comedies, and he lends a polite, ironic reserve to his intimate moments. In fact, a close comparison of the continuity script with the published screenplay (issued by Viking Press in 1972, but now out of print) reveals that Grant rarely speaks his lines exactly as they were written. He invests his smallest phrases and gestures with an air of modest discretion, and in most ways the personality he creates is very different from the boozing playboy Lehman had envisioned.

Certainly other collaborators of Hitchcock had a significant effect on the film. Bernard Herrmann's score provides a feeling of expansive adventure and gothic tension, and Saul Bass's graphic designs may have influenced the grid-like, geometric minimalism of certain of the images. Suffice it to say that *North by Northwest* is both a collaborative effort and a "Hitchcock picture to end all Hitchcock pictures." At the level of generic conventions, it's also symptomatic of a transitional moment in the evolution of spy fiction: it draws many of its best effects from an extensive and mostly British tradition of narratives about international intrigue to which Hitchcock himself had been a major contributor. At the same time, it predicts certain features of the sleekly commodified James Bond movies that followed in its wake.

The full extent of the film's generic background is suggested by Michael Denning's useful study of British spy fiction, *Cover Stories*, which points out that all the major changes in narratives about espionage have been marked by shifts in the economics and cultural politics of book publication. The form emerged at the beginning of the twentieth century, when "the existence of rival imperialist states made it increasingly difficult to envision the totality of social relations" (13). Several of the most distinguished authors of the period—Rudyard Kipling, Henry James, Joseph Conrad, and Somerset Maugham—were interested in the activities of secret agents, but the spy story was also taken up by a series of popular craftsmen—John Buchan, William Le Queux, and "Sapper" (H. C. McNeile)—who borrowed effects from the American dime novel to praise the civilizing effects of the British empire. Perhaps the most reputable and recognizably modern practitioner of the genre is Maugham in *Ashenden*, a 1927 volume of stories about a World War I secret agent that established a model for the realistic, antiheroic narratives later perfected by John le Carré. In the late 1930s and '40s, spy fiction was also embraced by the cultural arm of the Popular Front, notably by Eric Ambler (*The Dark Frontier* [1936], *Epitaph for a Spy* [1938], and *Cause for Alarm* [1938]) and Graham Greene (*Confidential Agent* [1939] and *Ministry of Fear* [1943]), who brought a degree of realism to the old melodramatic plots, winning approval from literary reviewers and the growing middle-class membership of subscription book clubs.

Finally, during the cold war, with the rise of the paperback industry and *Playboy* magazine, the James Bond craze began; the realist tradition remained alive (as in Len Deighton's *The Ipcress File* [1962]), but the Bond novels reverted to the square-jawed heroics of the original popular stories, all the while providing luxurious and sexually explicit fantasies that were symptomatic of a burgeoning consumer economy.

Hitchcock's work needs to be understood in the context of these events. Even though his medium was the movies rather than literature, many of his characteristic themes and stylistic effects were developed in close relation to the British novel of espionage—a type of entertainment that sometimes lives a double life, supporting patriotic agendas even while it explores a Kafkaesque borderland between the individual subject and the authoritarian state. *North by Northwest* is a highly self-conscious example of such narrative duplicity, poised neatly between a heroic adventure story and a nightmarish scenario in which personal identity and the sense of "knowable community" are threatened with dissolution. And because it appeared at a relatively late stage of Hitchcock's career, it had an unusually pivotal effect: looked at today, it seems to encapsulate the entire history of a genre, gathering up familiar motifs from all of Hitchcock's sources and transforming them into a new style, perfectly keyed to a changing marketplace.

Among the major British novelists of the early twentieth century, Conrad and Maugham were especially adept at describing the social and psychological ironies of the borderland where spies operate. Hitchcock adapted their work for two of his best pictures of the 1930s: *Secret Agent* (1935), based on the Ashenden stories, and *Sabotage* (1936), based on Conrad's *The Secret Agent*. (Where the last of these is concerned, see R. Barton Palmer, "*Secret Agent*, Coming In from the Cold, Maugham Style," in Palmer and Boyd, eds., 89–101). But he had just as much in common with John Buchan, the virtual creator of mass-market spy fiction, who published *The Thirty-Nine Steps* in 1915 (Hitchcock's adaptation of the novel was entitled *The 39 Steps*, a distinction I've observed elsewhere in this book). A Scottish businessman and later the governor-general of Canada, Buchan was essentially a writer of boy's adventure stories designed to promote British national interests. The key to his success lay in the fact that his protagonists were amateurs rather than members of a high diplomatic service; as Graham Greene later observed, Buchan realized "the enormous dramatic value of adventure in familiar surroundings happening to unadventurous men, members of Parliament and members of the Athenaeum, lawyers and barristers, businessmen and minor peers: murder in 'the atmosphere of breeding and simplicity and stability'" (167). Thus Richard Hannay, the protagonist of *The Thirty-Nine Steps*, is a well-bred citizen, thoroughly at home in the modern city, who accidentally plunges through the orderly surface of British society into a primal underworld of national warfare. His discovery of a hidden network of power is dangerous but thrilling, allowing him to behave rather like a swashbuckling hero. Along with the therapeutic derring-do comes knowledge of a fundamental truth. In the words of one of Buchan's other protagonists, "Now I saw how thin is the protection of civilization. An accident . . . a false charge and a bogus arrest—there were a dozen ways of spiriting one out of this gay and bustling world" (quoted in Greene, 167).

Hitchcock acknowledged the importance of this theme during his interview with Truffaut, in which he noted, "Buchan was a strong influence on my work long before I undertook *The Thirty-Nine Steps,*" chiefly because of his "understatement of highly dramatic ideas" (65). A film like *North by Northwest* may seem anything but understated, but it depends on a vivid contrast between a breathtaking adventure and a cast of polished, reserved actors. Nearly all the comedy, suspense, and sexual unease derive from the threat of violence in an atmosphere of "breeding and simplicity and stability." Roger O. Thornhill, the complacent Madison Avenue executive who finds himself interpellated under the name George Kaplan, is a lineal descendant of Buchan's heroes, inhabiting a more thoroughly modernized and politically treacherous society. (In using the verb "interpellate," I refer to Louis Althusser's "Ideology and Ideological State Apparatuses," which argues that ideology "recruits" its subjects "by that very precise operation which I have called interpellation or hailing, and which can be imagined along the lines of the most commonplace everyday police (or other) hailing: 'Hey, you there!'" [174–76]. Seen in Althusserian terms, *North by Northwest* could be described as a comic allegory about interpellation, in which the name "George Kaplan" is revealed as an empty signifier.) Like Hannay, Thornhill is accused of murder (in this case, the victim is a kindly diplomat who is knifed in broad daylight in the crowded reception lounge of the United Nations); and like Hannay, he flees a menacing urban life, heading north and west, where he tracks an archvillain to his lair (Hannay ran to Scotland, whereas Thornhill heads for South Dakota).

It seems only natural that Buchan's novels should have provided an inspiration for Hitchcock, since mainstream cinema has always relied on the conventions of melodrama and romance. But the widespread critical recognition and artistic legitimacy Hitchcock achieved in the interwar years came at least in part from his ability to temper Buchan's romantic and rather dated plots, which were based in a polite ethos of gentlemanly games, with an opposite quality, sometimes called irony or realism. Hitchcock always regarded himself as a serious artist working in a popular medium; he was keenly aware of vanguard artistic movements such as expressionism and surrealism, and he seems to have recognized quite early on that the key to success lay in capturing the attention of reviewers and intellectuals. Hence his work in the 1930s shared certain traits with figures like Greene and Ambler, who were his approximate contemporaries. (He and Ambler had both professional and personal associations: In 1943 Hitchcock wrote an introduction to *Intrigue,* a collection of Ambler's fiction, and in 1958 Ambler married Joan Harrison, Hitchcock's former associate producer. And the script for *The Wreck of the Mary Deare,* which Hitchcock and Lehman had been working on before *North by Northwest,* was rewritten by Ambler and directed by Michael Anderson in 1959.) Together with several other writers and directors of the period, he took popular formulas and "crossed over" into a realm admired by critics, transforming melodramatic values and establishing what Michael Denning calls a full-fledged aesthetic ideology, which was "marked by the 'literary' as it was understood in the early twentieth century, perhaps crucially by the concern for the issue of point of view" (for a full discussion, see Denning, *Cover Stories,* 59–90). To understand properly what a later Hitchcock picture like *North by Northwest* inherits from this ideology, we need to view the film in light of four essential features of what I shall term the modernist or "artful" suspense story:

1. Skepticism toward established legal and political institutions
Hitchcock's British spy films were antifascist, and during the early 1940s he made occasional gestures on behalf of wartime propaganda. On the whole, however, he was a disengaged artist, and in this respect he was quite different from Ambler and Greene. His frequently discussed plot device, the "MacGuffin," when employed in the service of spy fiction, implies a satiric or cynical attitude toward politics, since it reduces the causes of espionage to a trivial absurdity. (In *North by Northwest,* the MacGuffin becomes a self-reflexive joke: a statuette containing government secrets breaks open to reveal what looks like a roll of 35mm motion-picture film.) Even so, Hitchcock was also in some ways an explicit critic of government orthodoxy: the agents or officers of the law in his pictures are nearly always depicted ironically and the narratives focus relentlessly on the psychic anxieties of middle-class characters in danger of being arrested, punished, or manipulated by an ideological apparatus.

Hitchcock's cynical, anxious attitude toward the state is everywhere apparent in *North by Northwest,* where he and Lehman satirize the cold war. The film was released in the final year of the Eisenhower presidency, at a time when the daily news was filled with conflicting stories about diplomacy and international conspiracy. In the same issue of *Time* magazine in which *North by Northwest* was reviewed, readers were informed of a "cold thaw," precipitated by a forthcoming visit to the United States by Nikita Khrushchev; the magazine also noted that Richard Nixon had just returned from the Soviet Union bringing a report on the poor condition of the Russian consumer economy, and that the United States was launching its ninth satellite into space, hoping to overcome the military advantage achieved by Sputnik in 1957. At almost the same moment, Allen Dulles, the director of the CIA, had emerged from a meeting with forty-five U.S. governors in San Juan, Puerto Rico, at which he announced that "the Soviets intend to use nuclear blackmail as a major weapon to promote their objectives—namely, to spread Communism throughout the world." In response to Dulles, New York's Nelson Rockefeller was proposing a nationwide system of private bomb shelters and a federally sponsored army of civil defense experts for every community in the country (*Time*, August 17, 1959, 17–22).

Given such an atmosphere, Hitchcock and Lehman poked fun at the CIA, subtly linking its activities to the "expedient exaggerations" and image-making techniques of Madison Avenue (a favorite target of Hitchcock's television programs during the same years). They gave the chief of their fictional U.S. spy agency (Leo G. Carroll) a vague resemblance to Dulles; they salted the film with joking allusions to real-life conspiracies, as when a pre-Columbian statuette containing microfilm is described as "the pumpkin" in reference to the Alger Hiss–Whittaker Chambers case; and they allowed Cary Grant to suggest that the United States "ought to start learning how to lose a few cold wars." Hitchcock's almost Wildean aestheticism added to the feeling of irreverence. "For me, art comes before democracy," he told *Cahiers du cinéma* when the film was released (Domarchi and Douchet, 19), and he reinforced the point in the chase atop Mount Rushmore, where he ironically juxtaposed two movie stars and a small, dark Native American sculpture against the massive chalky carvings of the presidents. When the U.S. Park Service refused him permission to depict characters suspended from the presidential faces (even on a set rather than the actual location), he reluctantly moved all the action to the rocks between them. In his *Cahiers* interview with Domarchi and Douchet, he claimed that the Department of Interior withdrew from credit on the film, chiefly due to the fact that he had shown Cary Grant punching a park ranger.

2. A morally ambiguous, quasi-psychoanalytic treatment of character

Unlike Buchan's novels, which preserved the firm moral categories of popular melodrama, the modernist spy stories were psychologically and ethically complex. The characters often suffered from an ontological insecurity and the familiar doppelgänger theme of gothic fiction was given a clinical twist, as if to suggest that the nominal hero was motivated by the same dark impulses as the villain. Most of Hitchcock's films were marked by these qualities, although *North by Northwest* treats its psychoanalytic subtext lightly. Vandamm (James Mason), the master spy, is in many ways an anachronistic figure, reminiscent of the evil Germans in Buchan's work or in countless Hollywood melodramas about World War II; nevertheless, he physically resembles Roger Thornhill and has a similar urbanity and self-confidence. The film suggests that he's bisexual, emphasizing his closeness to Leonard (Martin Landau), but it also suggests that Roger has a sublimated romantic attachment to his delightfully cynical mother (Jessie Royce Landis). Above all, the two men are alike in their desire for Eve Kendall (Eva Marie Saint), an affinity Hitchcock underlines in his clever staging of the auction house sequence, in which Roger and Vandamm stand face-to-face, with Eve sitting between them, looking impassively forward, like an objet d'art they're in competition to possess.

3. Systematic control of focalization or point of view

In its move toward psychological realism, modernist literature as a whole became increasingly subjective, exploring the tension between individual consciousness and a problematic, unknowable totality. Henry James and Joseph Conrad were early exponents of the technique, and their work had an important influence on the 1930s generation of British spy novelists: Greene's *Ministry of Fear* is centered in the mind of a protagonist who doubts his own sanity, and Ambler's *A Coffin for Dimitrios* (1939) borrows its plot from Conrad's *Heart of Darkness*, allowing the central character to take shape impressionistically, through the subjective accounts of various narrators.

Hitchcock's own interest in modernized narrative was stimulated by a number of vanguard developments in the style of late silent movies. He shares many qualities with Lev Kuleshov and the Soviet montage school of the 1920s, who were intensely concerned with Pavlovian mastery over the audience by means of graphic design and the skillful juxtaposition of images. (One of Hitchcock's associates, Ivor Montague, an associate producer at Gaumont British and a scriptwriter for the British version of *The Man Who Knew Too Much* [1934], was an avowed Communist and an early translator of Eisenstein.) Equally important was his apprenticeship during the 1920s at UFA, the German studio where F.W. Murnau and other filmmakers experimented with subjective narration for the camera. Perhaps because of his formative experiences in Germany (and his affinities with surrealism), Hitchcock became the cinema's most famous exponent of a kind of psychological editing, in which the meaning of a sequence derives from careful alternations between "inner" and "outer" points of view.

James Agee was aware of this fact in 1946, when he reviewed *Notorious*. "One would think," he wrote, "that the use of the camera subjectively—that is, as one of the characters—would for many years have been as basic a movie device as the closeup, but few people try it and Hitchcock is nearly the only living man I can think of who knows just when and how to" (*Agee on Film*, Vol. 1, 214).

Hitchcock's technique, which reminded Agee of that of "a good French novelist," depends upon a careful manipulation of two formal extremes: the purely subjective shot/reverse shot, focalized through a character; and the purely objective shot, often positioned from a bird's-eye vantage, looking down on a scene. Again and again, his films veer back and forth between an uncanny private perspective and a schematic, godlike omniscience (or between what Jacques Lacan would call the imaginary and symbolic registers). These interdependent formal effects can be seen everywhere in *North by Northwest*, and they make us especially aware of the director's control over the story. The bird's-eye view occurs at several important junctures, usually at the beginning or end of a sequence, as in the conclusion of the murder scene at the United Nations building. In the sequence in which Roger Thornhill speeds down a dark highway in a stolen Mercedes, Hitchcock keeps the camera inside the car, viewing all the near accidents from Roger's drunken point of view; then at the end, in the comic collision with the police, he cuts to an almost proscenium-style wide shot that declares his coolly detached presence. The best example of his method, however, is the crop-dusting episode, which opens with a lofty view of a straight highway running through a barren prairie, and then fragments the landscape into a series of ground-level shots. Lehman's original script had proposed crosscutting between the pilot of the biplane and Roger, but Hitchcock designed the episode in a rigorously subjective manner, showing virtually everything from Roger's perspective, until the moment when he sneaks offscreen and rides away in a stolen pickup truck.

Elsewhere, the film cleverly manipulates narrative information, controlling how much the audience knows in relation to the characters. During the first part of the story, we're placed almost completely in Roger's position, and like him we're baffled by the sinister goings-on; then the perspective shifts to an intelligence agency, where Hitchcock looks down on the action from a lofty angle, allowing us to learn important information that Roger doesn't possess. From this point onward, we alternate between two positions, sometimes sharing in Roger's surprise or anxiety, sometimes watching helplessly while he tries to cope with a dangerous situation that we fully comprehend. The technique is raised to the level of tour de force in the penultimate episode, when Roger attempts to rescue Eve from Vandamm's mountain retreat: at strategic moments, the camera substitutes for the eyes of Roger, Vandamm, Leonard, and Anna the housekeeper; all the while, the film plays a series of tricks, sometimes revealing information to create suspense (as when Leonard conceals a gun from Vandamm), and sometimes withholding information to create surprise (as when Vandamm discovers that the gun contains blanks).

4. The use of melodramatic violence to depict an eruption of the real into imaginary social relations

Of all the "artful" characteristics I've been describing, this is the most important, not only for Hitchcock's films but for all sorts of noirish narratives that portrayed civilized life as a protective veneer covering a "reality" of sordid violence. Thus in Fritz Lang's *Ministry of Fear* (1944, adapted from the Greene novel), a Bond Street tailor enters a plush dressing room and stabs himself to death with a pair of shears in order to avoid capture by government agents; and in Lang's *Cloak and Dagger* (1946), there's a scene rather like the one Hitchcock later staged in *Torn Curtain* (1966), in which a protracted and clumsy fight to the death takes place amid relatively placid surroundings. Popular melodrama at the turn of the century—in the hands of such different artists as David Belasco, D.W. Griffith, and John Buchan—had used violence cathartically, in the service of an overtly moral attitude: virtuous characters were crushed by brutes, but evil was usually punished by righteous force. In sharp contrast, Hitchcock and his contemporaries imagined a world where justice triumphed ironically, and where violence had deep-seated psychological motives. Hitchcock in particular was fond of giving a Freudian emphasis to Buchan's idea about the "thin" protection afforded by civilization, showing chaotic desires and acts of cruelty breaking through an orderly, middle-class propriety, as if the "real" forces of the id were attacking the imaginary or rationalized defenses of the superego.

Much of the violence experienced by Roger Thornhill in *North by Northwest* has this feeling, rather like a comic nightmare in which the political and sexual unconscious return, exploding the surface of a smug Madison Avenue lifestyle. Repeatedly, the film subjects Roger to threats, embarrassment, and exposure in public places; at the same time, however, it resembles a wish-fulfilling, Mittyesque dream, allowing him to become an old-fashioned adventurer who triumphs over evil and wins the hand of a fair lady. Hitchcock keeps the two implications in perfect balance, so that romance and irony intermingle. The daring chase across Mount Rushmore, for example, is hallucinatory (all the more so because of the artificial look of back projection and optical printing), and the brilliantly economical conclusion operates by free association, lifting Roger and Eve out of one kind of dream and into another. Especially in the second half of the film, suspense is generated less by the spy plot than by a fantastic network of male jealousies and fears of betrayal, extending from Roger to Vandamm to Leonard, with Eve always in danger of being savagely exterminated. Meanwhile, the love scenes have the same darkly suggestive logic as the action sequences. Eva Marie Saint plays a typical Hitchcock blonde (elegant, buttoned-up, and repressed on the surface but exuding a smoldering carnality), and when she and Grant embrace on the *20th Century Limited*, Hitchcock introduces a characteristically sadomasochistic note: "Maybe you're planning to murder me right here, tonight," she murmurs seductively. He raises his hands to her shimmering hair as if he would like to strangle her. "Shall I?" he asks. "Please do," she responds.

But if *North by Northwest* is everywhere shaped by these four defining features of modernist melodrama, it also represents something new. Significantly, the film was released at the very moment when American show business was about to enter a postmodern phase. In 1959 the classic studio system had been replaced by a variety of package-unit arrangements and Hollywood had become the chief purveyor of material for television. The artifacts left behind by the old industry were being recycled and mythologized, while the new industry worked toward a more thorough consolidation of the different media. Hitchcock was in an excellent position to take advantage of the changing conditions. Partly because of his special relationship with Lew Wasserman of the MCA talent agency, he had become the "editor" of *Alfred Hitchcock's Mystery Magazine* and the impresario of *Alfred Hitchcock Presents*, one of the most popular television shows in America; he was also in charge of his own unit for theatrical films, so that he could oscillate between sardonic, low-budget television programs and colorful, star-filled theatrical shows. In 1960, he synthesized the two forms in *Psycho*, his single most profitable undertaking. Meanwhile, in France, the critics of the New Wave were reevaluating classic Hollywood, elevating Hitchcock to canonical status.

Little wonder that *North by Northwest* should manifest so many of the attributes Fredric Jameson has attributed to the cultural logic of late capitalism. It isn't simply a film directed by Alfred Hitchcock and starring Cary Grant, but a film in the Hitchcock and Grant "manner," an ultraglamorous "movie-movie" involving pastiche of their previous work. Its tongue-in-cheek style and direct appeals to romantic fantasy seem to predict subsequent developments in the industry, affecting not only the James Bond cycle but also such pictures as Stanley Donen's *Charade* (1963), Arthur Hiller's *Silver Streak* (1976), Brian De Palma's *The Fury* (1978), and Jonathan Demme's *Something Wild* (1986). By the same token, its special effects and exhilarating spirit of high adventure are echoed in the blockbuster films of Steven Spielberg and George Lucas. Consider *Close Encounters of the Third Kind* (1977), in which a man and a woman clasp hands across a mountaintop and in which François Truffaut makes a speech about ordinary people caught up in extraordinary adventures. Consider, too, *Raiders of the Lost Ark* (1981), in which most of the chase sequences try to achieve a feeling of extreme peril in travelogue settings.

To be sure, *North by Northwest* is in many ways different from the films I've just mentioned; my point is simply that Hitchcock was a shrewd commercial artist, and that *North by Northwest* allowed him to develop new, more spectacular possibilities for a kind of entertainment narrative he had perfected many years earlier. By the late 1950s, he had become such a valuable commodity that his directorial signature could be foregrounded as never before: *North by Northwest* is therefore designed as a blatantly intertextual event, recapitulating his earlier triumphs and containing one of his most ostentatious appearances as an extra.

It should be remembered that, even though Hitchcock was a sophisticated ironist who could openly mock the pieties of Hollywood melodrama (as in *Vertigo* and *Psycho*, the films he made before and after *North by Northwest*), he was able to maintain his position in the industry only because he respected certain traditional standards of production. He frequently relied on the star system, and he combined a gift for sexual suspense with a highly developed taste for luxury and charm. Actually, he never strayed far from the values of Selznick, who had brought him to Hollywood in the 1940s. He merely arranged his career so that he could mix glamorous projects involving upper-class characters, such as the Cary Grant vehicles, with somber pictures like *Shadow of a Doubt* (1943), in which the psychotic Uncle Charlie tells his innocent, small-town niece that "the world is a foul sty."

Hitchcock's fastidious, suspenseful treatment of love and violence has often been related to his private obsessions, and to a more systemic pathology of masculine desire underlying the classic cinema. But these same qualities, reinforced by his polished commercialism, have equally important social implications. Interestingly, his spy movies seldom ventured into "Greeneland"—the term literary critics have given to the spiritually seedy, impoverished mise-en-scène of Graham Greene's novels. In British films like *Sabotage*, Hitchcock tried to achieve what he called a "real lower-middle-class atmosphere" (LaValley, ed., 34), but in general he took advantage of the genre's tendency to become a species of travel literature. He was fond of describing his method to interviewers, as when he told François Truffaut about the need to invest *Secret Agent* with entertainment values so that he could compensate for the lack of a happy ending: "The action takes place in

Switzerland. I said to myself, 'What do they have in Switzerland?' They have milk chocolate, they have the Alps, they have village dances, and they have lakes. All of these national ingredients were woven into the picture" (74).

The only critic to have commented at length on the social implications of Hitchcock's picture-postcard settings is Virginia Wexman, who has suggested that the director was a cultural imperialist and a cinematic "tour guide" (32–41). The full implications of Wexman's argument become clear if we note a remark Hitchcock makes during the *Cahiers* interview on *North by Northwest*: "[Cary Grant] succeeds in evading the police disguised as a porter in a red cap. Porters in red caps are one of the characteristic features of Chicago" (Domarchi and Douchet, 19). Perhaps so, but Hitchcock fails to mention that in 1959 Chicago's red-capped porters were black men. (We see blacks on several other occasions in the film, working as porters, as valets, and even in one early scene as a red cap.) The comic escape scene in LaSalle Street Station therefore depends on a temporary suspension of verisimilitude, a deliberate transformation of America into a tourist's fantasy land suitable for the adventures of a well-to-do, somewhat British set of characters. This tendency may explain why *North by Northwest* seems to anticipate Hollywood in the 1970s and 1980s. There's no scene in the picture like the one in *The 39 Steps* in which Richard Hannay spends an evening with a cruel old farmer and his young wife, and no intentionally grotesque Hitchcockian jokes that disturb the beautiful surroundings—no dowager putting out a cigarette in cold cream and no country gentleman holding up his hand to show an amputated finger. The working class and the peasants have been moved to the margins of the action and nothing occurs outside the boundaries of commercial travel aboard clearly advertised trains, planes, and buses.

Wexman contends that Hitchcock's glossy American thrillers—especially *Vertigo*—entailed not only a kind of tourism but also a "displacement of racial and class issues into the sphere of sexuality" (36). In this regard, she observes that no psychoanalytic critic has ever remarked upon the curious equation Hitchcock made, during a discussion of *Marnie* with Truffaut, between fetishism and miscegenation (Truffaut, 227). Notice that earlier in the same interview, Hitchcock recalled newspaper photos of people being taken to jail and seemed to misremember his use of an idea he took from the photos: "They showed the head of the New York Stock Exchange being jailed. He was handcuffed to a Negro. Later on I used that in *The [39] Steps*" (34).

I would put the case somewhat differently: a film like *Vertigo* clearly reveals Hitchcock's interest in the relationship between class and sex, even if his attitudes are perversely conservative or controlled by the demands of

Hollywood glamour. In similar fashion, the settings in some of his movies have a contradictory function: they seduce the audience into a romantic fantasy but often seem ironic or surrealistic, as if a bourgeois spectacle were being defaced by something grotesquely inappropriate. Just as Hitchcock used movie stars to implicate the audience in the characters' voyeurism, so he used what he called "national elements" to disturb the consumerist gaze. He remained firmly committed to his role as commercial entertainer but demonstrated a remarkable ability to have everything in two ways. On television in the late 1950s, he made fun of his sponsors, but at the same time he brought them high ratings. In *North by Northwest*, he joked about Madison Avenue and the presidential monuments, but he also produced a Technicolor, VistaVision daydream involving two beautiful, superbly dressed people having brook trout and sex on the *20th Century Limited*. Even the title of his film was double-edged: on the one hand it alluded to *Hamlet*, but on the other it provided an opportunity to stage a scene in an airport where a sign for Northwest Orient Airlines was prominently displayed.

Perhaps because Hitchcock was chiefly interested in sexual anxiety, he could retain his commercial instincts without forsaking the more unorthodox aspects of his "vision." He sometimes directed social-realist projects like *The Wrong Man* (1956), but even in dealing with quotidian subjects his imagery had an eerie, dreamlike effect. The fascination of his work derived in part from a conflict between his irony and his pellucid syntax, which gave each sequence a clean, orderly look. There was a vaguely pornographic impulse lurking at the edges of his films, inviting critics to speculate about the psychosexual mechanisms of popular cinema; but his carefully controlled imagery also hinted at a latent Orwellian fear of descending into the lower classes. In both respects, he was a director who specialized in repression. The anal-compulsive neatness he brought to the construction of his films was rather like an austere dandyism, reinforcing the psychic and social tensions he was trying to dramatize.

These tensions are never far away in *North by Northwest*, which is one of the most crowd-pleasing entertainments of Hitchcock's career. He seems to have been in a lighthearted mood when he produced the film, and yet he gave melodrama the feeling of a guilty dream and romantic comedy an air of danger. Throughout, he made satiric use of the American landscape, turning every colorful tourist stop and national icon into a slightly paranoid vision. He depicted spies as insensitive organization men and jealous lovers, and when he gave us the pleasure of watching Cary Grant and Eva Marie Saint, he tinged each moment with anxiety. Ultimately, he swept away all the troubling ambiguities, concluding the film with a normative, heterosexual marriage between Roger and Eve. The ending, however, was accomplished by a kind of directorial sleight of hand, in the form of a match cut; and if the release of tension works better here than in *Strangers on a Train* (1951), that is only because it is more swiftly and playfully executed. (Several commentators on the film, including Robin Wood, Stanley Cavell, and Lesley Brill, have treated the marriage plot as if it signified progress toward a mature and loving relationship, but Raymond Durgnat makes the important point that several problems remain unresolved—notably the fact that Roger Thornhill seems to be returning to his life as a Madison Avenue executive.) In the delightful concluding scene, Hitchcock shows Roger and Eve aboard a luxury sleeping car, speeding away into a night of sexual bliss. But the last shot—a bird's-eye view of the phallic train entering a tunnel—signals his derisive sense of humor, provoking ironic laughter and a chastened awareness that every fairy tale has hidden meanings.

Welles, Hollywood, and *Heart of Darkness*

As I've argued in an earlier book, there are several reasons why Joseph Conrad's *Heart of Darkness* (1899) could be regarded a distant ancestor of the film noir. Like Hollywood in the 1940s, Conrad employs a first-person narration that involves subjective focalization and a good deal of shifting back and forth in time; he calls attention to the narration by dramatizing it in a manner roughly analogous to the first-person openings and closings of movies like *Double Indemnity* (1944) and *Murder, My Sweet* (1944); and he gives a great deal of attention to a shadowy, somber mood, so that the meaning seems to lie on the atmospheric surface—in Marlow's famous words, on "the outside, enveloping the tale."

Although Conrad's plot has a family resemblance to a series of nineteenth-century adventure stories about British imperialism, his style is hallucinated, oneiric, greatly concerned with the psychology of the narrator, who says at one point, "It seems to me I am trying to tell you a dream." Hence, no less than any of the classic films noirs, *Heart of Darkness* has provoked psychoanalytic interpretation. Perhaps the novella's most general affinity with noir, however, is that although it belongs to the genre of bloody melodrama, it strives to seem relatively unmelodramatic. It does so through a familiar device of gothic fiction that can be seen in such movies as *Shadow of a Doubt* (1943), *Laura* (1944), *Strangers on a Train* (1951), *Blue Steel* (1990), and *Basic Instinct* (1992): everyone is a bit guilty and the ostensibly "good" character representing reason and ordinary decency is in some ways a double of the manifestly evil or guilty character. This "secret sharer" theme, combined with Conrad's foregrounding of style and pessimistic view of Western progress, gives *Heart of Darkness* a liminal position in modern culture: like most noirish fiction and film, it blends popular adventure with certain traits of modernism. As Fredric Jameson says, it belongs in a zone somewhere between Robert Louis Stevenson and Marcel

Proust, and it enables us to sense "the emergence of what will be contemporary modernism ... but also, still tangibly juxtaposed with it, what will variously be called popular culture or mass culture, the commercialized cultural discourse of what, in late capitalism, is often called media society" (*Political Unconscious,* 206).

Heart of Darkness became a sort of ur-text for Anglo-American modernism, influencing T. S. Eliot's "The Hollow Men," F. Scott Fitzgerald's *The Great Gatsby,* and the novels of William Faulkner. In the realm of popular fiction it had a similar influence, especially among sophisticated writers of thrillers. Raymond Chandler's first-person narrator is named Marlowe; Graham Greene's "entertainment" novels, all of which became films noirs, were inspired by his reading of Conrad's novella; and Greene's script for *The Third Man* (1949) not only borrows its narrative structure from *Heart of Darkness* but also contains a minor character named Kurtz. Where later movies are concerned, the novella also became an intertext for pictures about U.S. imperialism in Vietnam: Francis Coppola's *Apocalypse Now* (1979) is modeled on *Heart of Darkness,* and Stanley Kubrick's *Full Metal Jacket* (1987) has distant echoes of the same source. Surprisingly, however, few filmmakers have been interested in adapting the novella itself. A canonical work known by virtually every college student in the English-speaking world, *Heart of Darkness* constitutes a "presold" commodity, and by virtue of its brevity it might seem to present fewer problems for a screenwriter than the novels of Jane Austen or Charles Dickens, which have been adapted many times. Yet to my knowledge only one film is based directly on the story: Nicolas Roeg's adaptation for Turner Network Television, starring Tim Roth as Marlow and John Malkovich as Kurtz, which was filmed in Central America and broadcast in the United States in 1994. This picture was nominated for a Golden Globe by the international press, but it rarely achieves the haunted, dryly ironic quality of its source and in most other ways is a disappointment.

Perhaps *Heart of Darkness* hasn't been filmed more often because it has no heroic action, not much dialogue, and a great deal of what F. R. Leavis called "adjectival insistence" on horror (119). Leaving aside its racist and patriarchal implications, which create another set of problems, it holds our attention through a kind of spellbinding trickery, the literary equivalent of smoke and mirrors. But I suspect there's another reason. Any cinematic adaptation of the novella is likely to be overshadowed by a legendary film that was never made: Orson Welles's 1939 *Heart of Darkness,* which was developed at RKO, the most noir-like of the Hollywood studios, in the period immediately before Welles began work on *Citizen Kane.*

The very idea of such a project is enough to fascinate cinephiles and create an anxiety of influence in later directors. We can never know if Welles's adaptation would have succeeded; nevertheless, Robert Carringer's *The Making of Citizen Kane* provides tantalizing details about its production, and Jonathan Rosenbaum and Guerric DeBona have each written essays that provide further information. Welles's script and production-company records have survived, giving us a good sense of his plans. His *Heart of Darkness* would have been an intriguing picture by any measure, of interest not only for its political and aesthetic qualities but also, in secondary ways, for what it suggests about the tension between modern literature and Hollywood, and about the problem of fidelity in adaptation.

In 1938, when Welles was offered a three-picture contract at RKO, a Gallup poll conducted by the studio determined that audiences most wanted him to appear in a "man from Mars" film related to his *War of the Worlds* broadcast. Welles countered with an offer to film *Heart of Darkness* and a couple of Hitchcock-style thrillers on contemporary political themes. RKO agreed, and Welles brought most of his Mercury Theater organization to Hollywood to prepare for the Conrad production. He had already directed a moderately successful one-hour radio adaptation of the novella, starring Ray Collins as Marlow and Welles as Kurtz, which aired on CBS only a week after the Mars-invasion show, and he seemed enthusiastic about a film version. His associate, John Houseman, was paid fifteen thousand dollars to assist in developing a script but was frustrated by the job. "I never understood why Welles had chosen such a diffuse and difficult subject," Houseman wrote in his memoirs. "Joseph Conrad had used all sorts of subtle literary devices; the evil that destroyed [Kurtz] was suggested and implied but never shown. In the concrete medium of film no such evasion was possible" (435).

Under the circumstances, Houseman grew increasingly frustrated and withdrew from the job. Welles wrote the script alone, and despite Houseman's reservations *Heart of Darkness* was a logical choice for Welles's initial film. His theatrical reputation was based on spellbinding, somewhat gothic stagecraft; "The Mercury Theater of the Air" was initially subtitled "First Person Singular" and was devoted to experiments in subjective narration; and in the Conrad novella he saw a good opportunity to do something rather like his stage production of Shakespeare's *Julius Caesar*, which transformed the play into an antifascist parable. Furthermore, many of Welles's most important stage projects, including the Harlem *Macbeth* in 1936 and *Native Son* in 1941, were concerned with the theme of racial blackness; in fact, one of the actors he planned to use in the Conrad film was Jack Carter, who had played Macbeth in Harlem.

Besides all this, *Heart of Darkness* was well suited to what Michael Denning has identified as the "middlebrow" cultural project of the Mercury Theater—a project shared in slightly different ways in the 1930s by the

Book of the Month Club, the Modern Library, and NBC's radio symphonies, all of which attempted "to popularize and to market high culture" (*Cultural Front*, 392–94). Denning, somewhat like Pierre Bourdieu, mounts an effective defense of middlebrow art, at least where Welles's Popular Front activities are concerned, pointing out that under the right circumstances it can serve as a vehicle of class struggle and social progress. Thus, just at the moment when Horkheimer and Adorno were developing their critique of the culture industry, Welles tried to use the mass media as a democratic weapon, popularizing high culture on behalf of left interests, mixing Shakespeare with thrillers and science fiction, and blurring the boundaries between the classic and the vanguard.

Having caused a nationwide panic with a radio broadcast, Welles also saw the autobiographical resonance of stories about demagogues who manipulate the masses. *Citizen Kane* was designed to suggest certain ironic parallels between Welles and Charles Foster Kane, and the film version of *Heart of Darkness* would have contained similar parallels between Welles and Kurtz. Like Kurtz, Welles had a mesmerizing voice and had recently shown what Marlow calls "the power to frighten rudimentary souls." An idealist and a liberal, he was nevertheless regarded by the press as a Byronic type; perhaps for that reason, he was attracted to stories about the Faustian temptations of political power, and he sometimes used these stories as a form of indirect self-criticism. In his preliminary notes on the script for *Heart of Darkness*, he describes Kurtz as "the Byron of a totalitarian state, what Byron would be if he had become president of Greece." On a more covert level, according to John Houseman, he also considered modeling Kurtz's fiancée, "the Intended," on Chicago socialite Virginia Nicholson, to whom he was married. In his notes for the film he names this character Elsa Gruner and describes her as a woman with "a tremendously appealing and lovely kind of gravity.... She is not militantly honest, she is simply without guile. There is probably only one thing she doesn't know about Kurtz, who is her lover, and that is how little any woman must mean to such a man" (*Heart of Darkness* files, Orson Welles archive, Lilly Library; all subsequent quotes of the production materials and the screenplay dated November 30, 1939, are from this source).

Welles's method of writing the script was similar to the one he and his staff had used in adaptations for the Mercury Theater radio show: he found a copy of the novella in a pocket-sized anthology, cut out the pages, pasted them onto sheets of typing paper, and began deleting material, retaining a good deal of narration but changing a phrase here and there in marginal notes. On the first few pages he eliminated Marlow's listening audience—the unnamed narrator of the opening paragraph, the lawyer, the accountant, and the Director—and altered certain lines in Marlow's opening speech. An important passage in the original reads, "The conquest of the earth, which mostly means taking it away from those who have a different complexion or slightly flatter noses than ourselves, is not a pretty thing when you look into it too much. What redeems it is the idea only. An idea at the back of it; not a sentimental pretense but an idea; and an unselfish belief in the idea—something you can set up, and bow down before, and offer a sacrifice to." Welles changed "flatter noses" to "slightly different noses" to remind his audience of anti-Semitism and rewrote the last sentence to give it a more skeptical, less imperialistic tone: "What redeems it is the idea at the back of it; sometimes it's a sentimental pretense, something you can set up, and bow down before, and offer a sacrifice to."

In his book-length interview with Peter Bogdanovich, Welles says he believed his adaptation of *Heart of Darkness* might have been a success because it made considerable use of Conrad's language, mostly as offscreen narration. "I haven't got anything at all against a lot of words in movies," he explained. "I don't see how you can do Conrad without all the words" (31). Nevertheless, Welles always took liberties with his sources, and his adaptations were interesting precisely because they weren't slavishly faithful. *Chimes at Midnight* (1965), for example, is a "digest" of several Shakespeare plays, and *The Trial* (1962) conducts a sort of quarrel with Kafka. *Heart of Darkness* was no exception. Some of the changes Welles made were motivated by his political aims, some by his desire to make the novel more "cinematic," and others by the need to make a popular Hollywood entertainment. One of his most significant decisions was to set the film in the present day and to make Marlow an American, thereby translating the novella into what he described in notes to the studio as an "attack on the Nazi system" and a "psychological thriller" about a representative man thrown into the midst of "every variety of Fascist mentality and morality."

The screenplay opens in New York on the Hudson River, with Marlow's voice speaking of a "monstrous town marked ominously on the sky, a brooding gloom in the sunshine, a lurid glare under the stars," while a series of lap dissolves show lights being turned on across Manhattan at dusk—the bridges, the parkways, the boulevards, the skyscrapers. The camera tours the length of the island accompanied by a montage of sounds—snatches of jazz from the radios of moving taxis; dinner music from the big hotels; a "throb of tom-toms" foreshadowing the jungle music to come; the noodling of orchestras tuning up in the concert halls; and finally, near the Battery, the muted sounds of bell buoys and the hoots of shipping. Next we enter New York harbor, where we find Marlow leaning against the mast of a schooner, smoking a pipe and directly addressing the camera. "And this also," he says, "has been one of the dark places of the earth."

In the process of changing Marlow into an American, the script deletes Conrad's chauvinistic assertion that in the British colonies "some real work is done" and gives the story a more thoroughgoing anticolonial implication. Marlow's politically well-positioned aunt is also deleted. Aimless and romantic, he applies for a job in what the script describes as a "Central European seaport town," at a trading company that occupies a vast building "in the best Bismarck style." The company doctor examines his cranium in the interests of confirming the superiority of the Aryan race and sends him off to an unnamed, generic "Dark Continent," where the landscape and tribal customs derive from a mélange of African, Stone Age, and indigenous American cultures, all of which had been elaborately researched by Welles's staff at RKO. The exploitation and murder of the black population is carried out by obvious fascists. "This shouldn't surprise you," one of them says to Marlow. "You've seen this kind of thing on city streets." Kurtz, the most successful of the fascist types, has been installed in the jungle by his political opponents, who want him removed from Europe. As a result of his unlimited authority and will to power he has become a ruthless demagogue. "I have another world to conquer," he says when Marlow finally meets him. "Five more continents and then I'll die." When Marlow asks, "Is that all you want?" Kurtz replies, "I want everything."

A good deal of dialogue has been invented for the screenplay and its rhythms are carefully stipulated, to the point in many scenes of specifying the precise words on which the actors are supposed to interrupt or speak over one another. The result is a distinctive style of rapid, fevered, almost musical overlapping of voices, similar to what we hear in *Citizen Kane* and most of Welles's other films. In keeping with the political allegory, the array of characters Marlow meets on his journey along the river has also been altered and elaborated. Most of them join Marlow on the riverboat in search of Kurtz. At the outer station Marlow encounters Eddie (Robert Coote), an effete British citizen who has brought a piano and several cases of champagne to the jungle, where he acts as an ineffectual spy on the European interlopers. "They'd like to own the country, I guess," Eddie says to Marlow. "It's ours, you know ... England's. That's why I'm here. To keep my eyes open. Never can tell, you know, when they might take a plebiscite among the cannibals." At the next station Marlow comes across de Tirpitz (John Emery), a Germanic aristocrat with a clubfoot who harbors an intense hatred of Kurtz because, as Welles wrote in background notes for the production, "Kurtz is to him the perfect example of the ascendant lower-middle class which has stolen his inheritance" (Lilly Library). Aboard the riverboat, Marlow's steersman and assistant is called simply "the halfbreed" (Jack Carter) and is described as "an expatriate, tragic exile who can't remember the sound of his own language."

One of the major differences between the screenplay and Conrad is in the character of Elsa, "the Intended," who in the novella makes her only appearance in the climactic scene and is presented as a figure on a pedestal—guileless, naïve, and incapable of facing the stern truths known to men. Partly to give the film the suggestion of a romantic interest, Welles transforms her into a more active woman who goes to the jungle in search of her lover. Marlow meets her at the outer station of the Dark Continent, where she smiles and remarks on a striking physical resemblance between him and Kurtz. While Eddie plays his piano, she uses a pencil and a rough pine board to draw a crude map of the river journey Marlow is about to take, marking all the stations along the way, explaining what he can expect to find and creating a mood of suspenseful foreboding. Despite everyone's protestations, she insists on traveling down the river aboard Marlow's steamer. During the trip she and Marlow have a conversation in the pilothouse, and from Marlow's perspective we see his face and hers partly reflected in the front window, mingled with the changing patterns of the jungle. She explains that she waited in Europe for four months without letters from Kurtz: "I was afraid. He was almost too popular. There was no good reason for sending him to the Dark Country—except to get him out of Europe.... I didn't like him at first. I thought he was—I don't know *what*. Cruel—ruthless. First impressions. I wasn't very intelligent or grown up.... It's not easy to refuse him anything. He wanted to know me—I got to know him." She remains on the boat until it almost reaches its destination, but when scores of headless bodies are discovered in the jungle Marlow sends her back in a canoe manned by a couple of his crew members. She then reappears in a climactic scene like the one in Conrad's story, with Kurtz's ghostly image hovering behind her as Marlow tells her a lie.

In addition to using a great deal of offscreen narration, Welles wanted to create a cinematic analogue for Conrad's narrative technique, and to this end he planned a radical innovation: the story would be told almost entirely from Marlow's point of view, with a first-person camera. The device had been used intermittently in previous Hollywood pictures—the first ten minutes of Rouben Mamoulian's *Dr. Jekyll and Mr. Hyde* (1932) are told entirely through the eyes of Jekyll—but Welles appears to have been the first director to attempt it for an entire film. Given his unorthodox approach, he intended to begin *Heart of Darkness* with a brief prologue "designed to acquaint the audience as amusingly as possible with the [subjective camera]." This prologue has been discussed and completely reproduced in Jonathan Rosenbaum's

Discovering Orson Welles, so I'll describe it only briefly. It opens with Welles's voice heard over an entirely black screen. "Don't worry," he announces. "There's just nothing to look at for a while. You can close your eyes if you want to." He explains that he is about to "divide this audience into two parts—you and everybody else in the theater. Now then, open your eyes." Iris into the subjective viewpoint of a bird looking out of a cage at Welles's hugely magnified chin and mouth. "You play the part of a canary," Welles says. "I'm asking you to sing and you refuse. That's the plot." Welles's chin moves down until his fiercely glaring eyes become visible. "Here is a bird's eye view of me being enraged," he says. "I threaten you with a gun." He slides the muzzle of a pistol through the bars of the cage until it looks like Big Bertha. "That's the way a gun looks to a canary," he says. "I give you until the count of three to sing." He then goes on to create a series of other dramatic situations, some wish fulfilling, as when "you" are granted the ability to fly, others nightmarish, as when "you" are strapped to the electric chair. Finally, looking straight into the lens, he says, "Now, if you're doing this right, this is what you ought to look like to me." Dissolve to the interior of a theater seen from the point of view of the screen: the camera pans around the room and we discover that the audience is made up entirely of motion-picture cameras. "I hope you get the idea," Welles says. Fade to black. A human eye appears at the left of the screen, an equal sign appears next to the eye, and at the right appears the first-person pronoun. The eye winks and we dissolve to the beginning of the picture.

This witty and sadistically entertaining opening, which would have contained a few shots in color, such as a "blinding red stain" that flows over the lens in the electrocution scene, creates a very different effect from the script proper—more like the "cinema of attractions" than like the immersive, hypnotic experience of Conrad's story. Running beneath its playful tone is an implicit commentary on the potentially authoritarian nature of the film medium. By putting us in the position of passive subjects, Welles gives us a cinematic analog of the manipulation and demagogic deception practiced by Kurtz; but at the same time he occasionally gratifies our fantasies of power, subtly prefiguring a link the film will later establish between us and a fascist demagogue. As Rosenbaum puts it, "the multiple equations proposed by the introduction, whereby I = eye = camera = screen = spectator, are extended still further in the script proper, so that spectator = Marlow = Kurtz = Welles = dictator" (*Discovering Orson Welles*, 31).

The equations would have been reinforced by Welles's plan to play both Marlow and Kurtz. His voice, and by this time his face, were so well known to the public that when the camera came eye to eye with a homicidal dictator in the jungle, a mirror-image effect would have been created. Welles intended to stage the scene in darkly humorous, somewhat anticlimactic fashion: Kurtz is discovered at the shadowy end of a vast wooden temple filled with skulls; as the camera/Marlow/spectator moves in to a close-up of his face, he looks back and asks, "Have you got a cigarette?" Welles did makeup tests in costume as Kurtz, looking unusually gaunt and wearing a scraggly beard. He told Bogdanovich that just when the film was about to begin shooting he changed his mind and decided to have the character played by someone else, preferably an actor who was cast against type, thereby creating the kind of surprise and irony that the discovery of Kurtz generates in the novella; there is, however, no evidence that he followed through with this idea, and he confirmed to Jonathan Rosenbaum that, had the picture actually gone into production, he would have played the dual role as originally planned.

One of the most important questions posed by the unfilmed production is whether the subjective camera would have been dramatically effective. Historians often argue that Robert Montgomery's adaptation of Raymond Chandler's *Lady in the Lake* (1947), in which the camera becomes Philip Marlowe, offers proof positive that the first-person device inhibits identification, eliminating the suturing effect of ordinary continuity editing and making the audience excessively aware of the apparatus. But this argument doesn't take into account Montgomery's leaden direction or the fact that Chandler's private eye is a very different sort of character from Conrad's sailor. Unlike Marlowe, Marlow is largely an observer rather than a participant—at any rate, he is never punched in the face or kissed by a beautiful woman—and his narration creates the feeling of a waking dream. Welles's plan for the subjective camera was more technically and affectively complex than Montgomery's straightforward literalism. The technique, he explained to Bogdanovich, was ideal for Conrad's story, which consists largely of a man piloting a boat down a river; the film could minimize "that business of a hand-held camera mooching around pretending to walk like a man" (31). As Jonathan Rosenbaum has pointed out, the screenplay's more flamboyant or gimmicky uses of the subjective camera are reserved for the early scenes, such as the one in which Marlow has his skull measured by a doctor; elsewhere, the camera seems relatively unobtrusive. Equally important, and despite both Welles's and the Mercury publicists' repeated claim that "the *audience* plays a part in this film," Welles appears to have wanted to create a tension between identification and estrangement. His script is often moody and hypnotic in the manner of Conrad, but when it describes characters facing the camera, it feels as if Welles wanted to undermine the "keyhole" effect of conventional cinema; in strategic ways, it turns the audience into guilty participants rather than absorbed viewers.

Photographer Stanley Cortez later used a subjective camera for one of the long sequences in *The Magnificent Ambersons,* in which George Amberson Minafer walks through every room of the shuttered Amberson mansion and then kneels to pray at his dead mother's bedside; RKO cut everything but the concluding image from this sequence, but Welles told Bogdanovich that he wasn't troubled by the cut because he was unhappy with the results. He thought *Heart of Darkness* was a more suitable story for the technique, and before production he shot one experimental sequence (involving Robert Coote as Eddie) that convinced him he had made a correct decision. "It would have worked, I think," he said in the Bogdanovich interview. "I did a very elaborate preparation for *[Heart of Darkness],* such as I've never done again—never could. I shot my bolt on preproduction on that picture. We designed every camera setup and everything else" (31).

Welles's screenplay, composed with the technical assistance of RKO script supervisor Amalia Kent, is one of the most camera-specific ever written, containing a detailed plan of the decoupage and even indicating the arrangement of figures in the frame for several of the shots. Only one sequence, involving multiple characters and chaotic action, is left for the director to work out on the set. To photograph a few scenes, Welles proposed that studio engineers equip a camera with one viewfinder for the operator and another for himself, but for many shots he wanted a handheld Eyemo camera equipped with a gyroscope—a device he claimed had been employed during the silent era—which is rather like the present-day Steadicam. He planned to construct most of the film out of long takes, the longest of which he estimated would run twelve minutes. This would have required the kind of deep-focus photography later used in *Citizen Kane,* but with a great deal more tracking, craning, and panning. Temporal ellipses would be signaled with dissolves, which would occasionally shift us back to Marlow in New York harbor, but most of the subjective shots would be imperceptibly linked with what Welles described as a "feather wipe." In shot A, Marlow's "head" would turn and the camera would a pan across a wall or a stand of trees, ending at a precisely measured spot; in shot B, the camera would be repositioned at the same distance from the designated spot and the panning movement would resume. As Robert Carringer points out, one of the most elaborate and difficult series of these linkages occurs when Marlow arrives at the First Station: "Marlow as the camera was to proceed up the hill from the docks, pass the excavations, discover the dying natives, enter the settlement . . . , go to the British representative's quarters [where he meets Elsa], have a conversation, retrace his steps through the settlement to the manager's office, and have another conversation there—all continuously and without an apparent cut" (10).

Welles's experiments with duration and invisible editing might have delighted André Bazin because of their respect for the continuity of space and time, but Welles's camera would also have been highly expressive and self-reflexive. In the script it occasionally shows things from an omniscient perspective, such as brief shots of Marlow's boat moving downriver; and, like Conrad's prose, it shifts focalization within a scene, moving without a visible cut from a literal point-of-view shot to a poetic or symbolic image—as when it tracks backward with Marlow out of the manager's office at the First Station, tilts down to look at a sick man dying on the floor, passes through the front entrance, cranes over the roof to show the jungle beyond, and tilts up to a starry sky. In many sequences grotesque faces bob in and out of Marlow's view (one of the eeriest scenes involves a search for Kurtz across a marsh in heavy fog, with faces suddenly looming up out of a white limbo), and disorienting effects are created by offscreen sounds, especially when Marlow hears voices and turns to look at them or when he overhears scraps of heated conversation from another room.

Mild shocks are administered whenever any of the characters look at the lens, and, significantly, many of these characters are black. At the First Station Marlow walks past a "big, ridiculous hole in the face of a mud bank, filled with about thirty-five dying savages and a pile of broken drain pipes.... Into some of these pipes the natives have crawled, the better to expire.... As Marlow looks down, CAMERA PANS DOWN for a moment, registering a MED. CLOSEUP of a Negro face, the eyes staring up at the lens. The CAMERA PANS UP AND AWAY." Elsewhere, we and Marlow are confronted by the "half-breed" steersman, the dark woman who is Kurtz's lover at the Central Station, and the anonymous black man who announces, "Mister Kurtz, he dead." The film as a whole could in fact be described as a hallucinated white dream about blackness (Marlow suffers literal hallucinations toward the end, when he becomes ill with a fever), or as a symptom of how white anxiety about blackness is sublimated into artistic discourse. Whatever interpretation we might offer, Welles's *Heart of Darkness* would have been the first and only time in the history of classic Hollywood when a white gaze would have been troubled by a returning black gaze.

As plans for the film advanced, Welles had models constructed for the sets in order to determine camera angles, and he screened a number of films so that he could become familiar with technical matters. Studio records indicate that he watched John Ford's *Arrowsmith* (1931), which is set in the tropics and contains several wide-angle, deep-focus shots exactly like the ones Welles and Gregg Toland later used in *Citizen Kane*. Welles also viewed Ford's *Stagecoach* (1939), Jean Renoir's *Grand Illusion* (1937), useful for the study of long takes, and Julien Duvivier's *Pépé le Moko* (1937), filled with atmospheric North African exoticism and grotesquerie. Meanwhile, RKO designers and special effects technicians began preparatory work on the film. Marlow's journey was originally designed in six stages involving six different kinds of jungle atmosphere. Welles wanted to send a photographic crew to the Florida Everglades for background imagery, but eventually he decided to use stock footage from jungle movies, with which he planned to create a back-projected collage of increasingly strange scenery. Among the films from which he planned to appropriate images were *Chang* (1927), *Four Feathers* (1939), *Sanders of the River* (1935), *Suez* (1938), and a couple of low-budget shorts called *Congorilla* and *Baboona*. He also screened such oddities as *Jungle Madness, Crouching Beast,* and *Hold That Wild Boar*. This may seem risible, but there's every reason to believe he would have used the appropriated material brilliantly. The matte photography in *Citizen Kane* is consistently fascinating, as in the nocturnal party in a Florida swamp, which involves sinister prehistoric birds from *The Son of Kong* (1933), and Welles's other films are noteworthy for the way they employ the process screen as a poetic rather than a realistic device, as in the surreal exoticism of the San Francisco aquarium scene in *The Lady from Shanghai*.

The complex choreography of camera and players required what Welles described in a note to the studio as "absolute perfection of preparation before the camera turns" (Lilly Library). He brought composer Bernard Herrmann into the process quite early and wanted the Mercury players to record the entire script so that Herrmann would have a guide for the composition and placement of music. (Besides the actors already mentioned, other members of the cast included John Hoysradt, Vladimir Sokoloff, Gus Schilling, Everett Sloane, George Coulouris, and Erskine Sanford.) In a memo to RKO, he argued that careful preplanning would save time and money, but studio executives probably raised their collective eyebrows when he also noted that because of the camera technique, the completed film couldn't be shortened except by cutting whole sequences. As if in compensation, he offered a great deal of spectacle: a giant snake landing on the deck of the steamboat; cannibal natives firing metal arrows and pinning one character's hand to the boat rail; a severed head on a pole; hundreds of blacks bowing down to Kurtz and forming long serpentine lines to haul ivory out of the jungle; a temple erected on stilts in the midst of a jungle lake; a cloud of bats scurrying down from the ceiling of the temple; Kurtz's throne surrounded by a wall of human skulls similar to the bizarre wall of human faces in Welles's 1938 stage production of Georg Büchner's *Danton's Death*; Kurtz crawling on all fours into the jungle; Kurtz's frail body lifted from the ground by servants and silhouetted against a campfire as he murmurs, "I was on the verge of great things"; a tremendous conflagration in the jungle; and a climactic lightening and rain storm inspired by Conrad's *Typhoon*, during which Kurtz keeps repeating "The horror! The horror!"

One of the most amusing documents in the Mercury files on *Heart of Darkness* is a somewhat disingenuous list of spectacular elements and enticing "story angles," probably written by Mercury Theater publicist Herbert Drake, which was intended to be used in selling the film to RKO executives and ultimately in publicity by the studio marketing department:

> The story is of a man and a girl in love. . . . There is a hell of an adventure going up the river. There is an unhappy ending which we won't need to mention. . . . There are cannibals, shootings, native dances, a fascinating girl, gorgeous, but black, a real Negro type. She has an inferred, but not definitely stated, jungle love-life with our hero. There is a jungle in flames and heavy storms of a spectacular nature. . . . We don't know who [will play the white girl] but she is going to be a great beauty . . . sexy without waving her hips around. She is to have a calm, half-smiling face, perhaps over a full bosom, for instance. . . . Theory of the story is two moderns who have a hell of an adventure in the dark places of the earth. The idea is, more or less by implication, that this is the God-damnedest relation between a man and a woman ever put on the screen. . . . Everyone and everything is just a bit off normal, just a little oblique . . . in surroundings not healthy for a white man.

RKO probably had doubts about all this, but it kept faith until December 5, 1939, when a detailed budget and day-to-day production schedule was submitted. The picture would have taken thirty weeks to complete at a cost of approximately $1,058,000, which was considerably more than RKO intended to pay. After a week of intense work, the Mercury organization offered cost-cutting suggestions that reduced the budget to $985,000. This was not beyond the means of the studio (*Citizen Kane* cost approximately $750,000), but it was too much for a picture that, from their point of view, had other problems. It was still unclear who would play Elsa. (Welles tried to obtain Ingrid Bergman, who had yet to appear in a U.S. film; he eventually decided to cast Dita Parlo, whom he had seen in *Grand Illusion*, but she encountered difficulty getting out of France). There were few close-ups, no shot/reverse shots, and the director/star would appear only briefly on screen. An even bigger problem for RKO was that Welles wanted to photograph lots of black people. He resisted the studio's proposal that extras in blackface could be used in crowd scenes, and he planned to suggest a sexual relation between Kurtz and a black woman—this despite the fact that miscegenation was strictly forbidden by the Motion Picture Production Code. The end came on January 9, 1940, when *Variety* reported that *Heart of Darkness* had given the studio cold feet and that Welles's organization had been paid $160,000 to shelve it.

Conrad's novella nevertheless remained one of Welles's preoccupations for long afterward. In 1945 he produced a second adaptation for radio and announced during the broadcast that perhaps someday he would be able to make it into a motion picture. It seems to have influenced various aspects of his later work, including the narrative method of *Citizen Kane*, the Latin American scenes in *The Lady from Shanghai*, and the elaborate tracking camera in *The Trial*.

As important as Conrad was for Welles, however, his attempt to adapt *Heart of Darkness* for the movies had brought at least three irresolvable contradictions uncomfortably to the fore. First was the contradiction between modernism and mass culture, which became apparent when Welles added expensive spectacle and a love interest to an oblique narrative technique that subsumes adventure within an introspective monologue. Second was the potential contradiction between Welles's democratic idealism and his fascination with Byronic individualists such as Kurtz. Third, and most significant, was the contradiction between Welles's often courageous opposition to fascism and racism and his interest in a story that expresses what Chinua Achebe has identified as a conservative and racist ideology. Conrad's *Heart of Darkness* is an implicit attack on Rousseau; although it shows the cruelty of Belgian exploitation in the Congo, it approves of a "good" colonialism that represses Africa's putative savagery and controls the ancient bestiality in the human heart. As Patrick Brantlinger has observed, it offers "a powerful critique of at least certain manifestations of imperialism and racism, at the same time that it presents that critique in ways that can only be characterized as imperialist and racist" (364–65). Welles's adaptation completely rejects colonialism, places the action in a Dark Continent of the mind, and tries to become a commentary on fascism, but it doesn't avoid Conrad's primitivism. From the opening moments, when jazz drums in Manhattan foreshadow jungle drums in the "dark places of the earth," the politics of the film become confused. The effort to retain aspects of Conrad's rhetoric only adds to the problem. Welles was a liberal activist, but, like many white liberals of his era (and our own), he sometimes equated black culture with a kind of atavistic energy. His script seems to take melodramatic relish in Conrad's references to a "black and incomprehensible frenzy" and a "night of the first ages," and the film's treatment of women would have been fairly close in spirit to Conrad's misogyny.

We might recall that in the 1897 preface to *The Nigger of the "Narcissus,"* Conrad described art as "a single-minded attempt to render the highest kind of justice to the visible universe" and his own task as "before all, to make you *see*." D.W. Griffith adopted that last phrase as a motto, and Welles gave it a potentially subversive implication through his plans for a subjective camera. Welles's *Heart of Darkness* was in many ways a brilliant visual experiment, especially when it updated the action of the novella, introduced cinematic effects homologous with Conrad's prose, and suggested a link between European fascism and U.S. racism. But even had the film reached the screen, it would have been caught on the horns of a dilemma, forced to be either too faithful to Hollywood or too faithful to Conrad. There is of course no reason why fidelity should always be a primary concern in film adaptations, but in this case neither a mass-cultural nor a high-modernist rendition of the original text, no matter how revisionist, could have avoided the ideological contradictions of Conrad's novella. Any attempt to expurgate, condense, or modernize the narrative is faced with the choice of retaining these contradictions or of becoming some other kind of thing. Orson Welles embraced the contradictions, which were part of his own artistic history. To borrow a metaphor from Conrad's *Lord Jim*, we might say that he chose to immerse himself in the potentially destructive elements of both Hollywood and *Heart of Darkness*. The results on screen would likely have been problematic at the level of politics, but there's no doubt they would have been cinematically fascinating.

Orson Welles and Movie Acting

Orson Welles began his career as a stage actor, and his work as a film director was enabled and conditioned by the fact that he was a celebrity performer. He was best known to the general public in the 1930s and '40s as a radio personality but later became famous as the man who played Harry Lime in *The Third Man* (1949). Throughout his career he depended on his star image in order to acquire financing for his favored projects. He was, in fact, one of the few Hollywood auteurs of the sound era who performed in almost every film he directed. (*The Other Side of the Wind* was a rare exception; even in *The Magnificent Ambersons* [1942] he's present as the unseen narrator.) Perhaps he ought to be described as an amateur director and a professional actor, because he usually worked behind the camera for love and in front of it for money.

Welles can also be numbered among a relatively small group of filmmakers, including Bresson, Hawks, Kazin, and Kubrick, whose pictures are marked by a distinctive acting style. In 1939, after becoming the most influential U.S. director of conceptual theater and causing the infamous Mars panic on radio, he gave a lecture entitled "The Director in the Theatre Today" to the New York Theatre Education League, where he amusingly speculated on his ability to impose a style on an acting ensemble. (He had also recently signed a contract with RKO to begin directing films.) The director, he noted, was a relatively new character in theatrical history; Shakespeare would not have recognized such a person, and during much of the nineteenth century "stage managers" had watched over the action of plays, functioning rather like lowly traffic cops. Under the latter arrangement, Welles explained, it was chiefly the starring performers who determined the theatrical mise-en-scène and the behavior of the supporting players:

When Mr. Sullivan, for instance, arrived in a town like Galway to play *Macbeth* . . . he would arrive at the theater at seven o'clock for a consultation with [the] stage manager.

"I always come in at the center for 'They have tied me to the stake,'" Mr. Sullivan would declare. . . . "Please have Lady Macbeth when she takes the daggers away take them by the blades."

"All right. Is there anything else?"

"No. Just have everyone stand six feet away and do their damndest."

Then, Welles observed, in the period between the 1880s and the 1920s, concurrent with the rise of cinema, a new fashion emerged, typified by the carefully designed spectacles of David Belasco and Hardin Craig and the director-centered ensembles of Konstantin Stanislavsky and Vsevolod Meyerhold. The rise of the director, however, did not necessarily mean the death of the star actor's potential control over things: "We are so proud of the fact that we don't allow old-time stars on the stage today," Welles wrote, "we forget that their influence from the fifth row center [where the director is seated in rehearsal] can be much more insidious" (Orson Welles archive, Lilly Library, box 4, folder 26, 3).

As a man who admired and in one sense emulated the "old-time stars," Welles always managed theater and film in such a way as to keep his own conceptions and performing idiom at the center of our attention. This was true even in some of the films he didn't direct. Notice that the most striking close-up of his movie career, his initial appearance in Carol Reed's *The Third Man*, is uncharacteristic in that it depends very little on makeup and not at all on Welles's much-discussed voice; nevertheless, as Michael Anderegg has observed, it functions as a kind of signature, enabling the star to enter the film in spectacular and witty fashion, like a rabbit from a hat (Anderegg, "Orson Welles as Performer," 73). The camera tilts slightly to one side and looks down obliquely at the smiling Welles, who collaborates with the out-of-kilter effect by lowering his head, turning to a three-quarter profile, and looking up toward the camera from under his lashes in a sidelong manner. The shot represents what Joseph Cotten sees as he looks across a darkened street in Vienna, but it also allows Welles to engage in almost direct address to the audience. Shrouded in dramatic shadow, wearing a black hat and a topcoat that looks rather like a cape, he provokes a frisson of sinister unease mingled with a sense of amused recognition. Like Laurence Olivier as Richard III and Anthony Perkins as Norman Bates, he's a villain who threatens and charms the audience by acknowledging them. But, unlike Olivier and Perkins, he also projects a feeling of himself—"your obedient servant," as he often said on radio and TV, slyly taking a bow.

Most of Welles's performances had something of the ambiguity or doubleness of this close-up, and a double purpose carries over into nearly all the dramatic shows he directed for radio, film, and TV. One of his major accomplishments as both an actor and a director was to synthesize two apparently contradictory forms of theatricality: he was a brilliant practitioner of what John Houseman called "magical effect," and he was clearly indebted to a romantic or gothic tradition of Shakespearian drama, grand opera, and stage illusionism; but he was also a didactic, somewhat Brechtian storyteller whose cultural politics were shaped in the 1930s and whose acting technique was visibly rhetorical, dependent upon direct address. The tension between these extremes—in other words, the tension between Welles as conjurer and Welles as narrator—accounts for many of the special qualities of his work in general.

The dialectical relation between the two opposing tendencies can be seen most clearly in *F for Fake* (1974), where Welles appears in the role of narrator-magician and where he functions as both a pedagogue and a con man. At the beginning of the film he makes an ordinary door key appear and disappear; then, in his role as narrator guide, he informs us that the key "isn't symbolic of anything" because "this isn't that kind of movie." Later, he confesses to being a "charlatan" and quotes Robert-Houdin to the effect that "a magician is an actor playing the role of a magician." But after expounding at length on the philosophical implications of trickery and forgery, he easily slips back into his illusionist persona, fooling us with a cleverly edited shaggy-dog story about Picasso.

In a sense, Welles's entire career was predicated on an ability to dazzle audiences while lecturing to them—a complicated purpose that was both enhanced and threatened by the machinery of mechanical reproduction and often inhibited by the Hollywood industry's normal way of doing things. In 1940, at about the time he was beginning work on *Citizen Kane*, he assembled typescript notes for another unpublished lecture, "The New Actor," in which he theorized the need for an intense, sometimes overtly rhetorical performing style that would run counter to both Stanislavskian theater and classic Hollywood movies. He began by making a distinction between what he called "formal" and "informal" drama. The first type, he argued, belonged to rigidly hierarchical cultures and was ritualistic, rather like a church service or a bullfight; the second type grew out of modern, relatively democratic societies and produced idiosyncratic actors who have quasi-personal relationships with their audiences. In the informal drama, which for Welles included all European theater from Shakespeare to the present, "it is impossible to be a great actor unless you deal with your audience." The celebrated Russian actor Feodor Chaliapin, for example, "sneered at the big people and played for the gallery when he played Boris Goudonof." But in more recent times, things had changed: "Even before the movies," Welles observed, "actors stopped considering audiences. It was the constant effort of people like Stanislavsky in a very serious way and John Drew in a frivolous way to pretend there is a fourth wall. This is death to acting style. It is practically impossible to create a new acting style which excludes the direct address to the audience" (Orson Welles archive, Lilly Library, "The New Actor," typescript notes, box 4, folder 26).

Welles's argument was congruent with one of the chief effects he was trying to achieve as a director and it has something in common with Brecht, although the two men should be kept somewhat distinct because they had slightly different politics. Welles was for a time a politically committed artist who certainly knew of Brecht's theories of acting: the Federal Theater production of Marc Blitzstein's *The Cradle Will Rock* was dedicated to "Bert" Brecht; the Mercury Theater adaptation of Richard Wright's *Native Son* made use of Brechtian staging; and at one point Welles was under consideration as the director of the first production of Brecht's *Galileo*. According to Barbara Leaming's authorized biography, Welles even inserted a playful series of allusions to Brecht's essay on Chinese acting into *The Lady from Shanghai* (1947). Even so, he remained a political liberal and a star; unlike Brecht, he didn't encourage the public to talk back to the spectacle, and his idea of both theater and movies remained "magical" in a secular, quasi-Freudian sense. His work was usually dependent on structures of fascination and illusion and on his own implied presence as star-manipulator. Within the entertainment industry he was sometimes regarded as a "showman," albeit an uncooperative one with a social agenda.

Their differences aside, Welles shared with Brecht a hatred of fascism, a love of pedagogy, and a critical attitude toward bourgeois realism. Both men favored drama that used a good deal of narration, and both were aware that the cinema and the radio inhibited direct address by mediating between the performer and the audience. Welles enjoyed the trickery inherent in the film medium and belonged to a long line of cinematic magicians; but at the same time he was a critic of the mass media's potential for demagoguery— a theme particularly apparent in his abortive filming of *Heart of Darkness* and, of course, in *Citizen Kane*. As a result, his best work is both imaginative and cerebral, both oneiric and satiric, and his attack on what he once referred to as the "pallid" realism of mainstream Hollywood was twofold. On the one hand he experimented with certain kinds of alienation effects, especially involving narration; on the other, he drew upon a rather old-fashioned theatrical flamboyance and heightened intensity. He filled his own appearances on-screen with signifiers of impersonation, wearing false noses, brandishing cigars, dressing in black, or speaking in accents or Shakespearian tones, and he elicited unorthodox behavior from the people he directed. Stars like Rita Hayworth and Charlton Heston seemed to be participating in a masquerade when they worked for Welles, and everyone else became unusually animated or stylized.

Like John Ford, Welles enjoyed making films with a "stock company," but in his hands the actors look caricatured, grotesque, or theatrically exaggerated. George Coulouris, who played Thatcher in *Citizen Kane*, once told an interviewer, "The scene in which we argue back and forth in the newspaper office is not conventional movie acting. With other actors or another director, it would have been 'brought down' a lot and lost a good deal" (Gilling, 42). The technique Coulouris describes can be seen throughout *Kane* and would become increasingly important to Welles's later work: the players project their lines, ignoring the conventional idea that acting for the camera ought to be low-key. Agnes Moorehead, Ray Collins, and Dorothy Comingore are all a bit more wide-eyed and loud than they need to be; Collins, for example, underplays the villainy of Jim Gettys but handles the quieter lines of dialogue like a stage actor, creating an illusion of calm while speaking at a high volume. The early episodes contain many deliberate echoes of Victorian melodramatics, and the later scenes with Susan Alexander are particularly high-pitched, creating a sort of repressed hysteria.

In Welles's later pictures this style was pushed in more radical directions. Consider the many grotesque exaggerations in *Touch of Evil* (1958): Joe Grandi and his boys rush around the streets of Los Robles and squabble like the Three Stooges; Menzies expresses grief by dropping his head down on a table and speaking in operatic despair; the hot-rod gang twitches and snaps their fingers like the chorus in a Michael Kidd dance routine. Perhaps the most obvious example is Dennis Weaver's performance as the crazy Mirador Motel "night man." According to Weaver, Welles told him, "Never let anyone get in front of you" (quoted in the program booklet *Life Award to Orson Welles*, American Film Institute, 1975, p. 10); as a result, he plays most of his scenes on a diagonal with the other actors, repeatedly scurrying from one point to another and jerking his head in what Manny Farber once described as "spastic woodpecker" effects. When he finds a joint in Janet Leigh's room he literally screams, and outside the motel after the rape scene he embraces a windblown tree and babbles like one of Shakespeare's fools.

Welles was almost alone among American moviemakers of his day in striving for this kind of theatrical intensity—a "hot" form of acting that has more in common with Griffith or Eisenstein than with the realism of American talking pictures. He told Peter Bogdanovich that in his view there was no essential difference between stage acting and screen acting: "Stage actors are supposed to be too big [for movies]. Well, Cagney was a stage actor and nobody was ever bigger than that. He came on in the movies as though he were playing to the gallery in an opera house.... Sure, [film] acting can be too broad. Broad is wide—spread out. Cagney was focused... like a laser beam!" (*This is Orson Welles*, 143). At an earlier point in the interview with Bogdanovich he insisted even more strongly on this idea:

PB: How about radio acting, Orson—would you say that it's similar to the acting required for movies? I mean in the sense that—

OW: That you don't have to make yourself heard in the gallery? The famous difference between stage acting and acting for the camera? It's all nonsense, you know....

PB: You don't believe in playing down for the camera?

OW: You can play *up* for the camera. With enough energy behind it, you can't ever go too high....

PB: But surely there's a limit, Orson. The camera isn't a theatre.

OW: The camera is an eye. And an ear. It takes you where it's *put*. The theatre is where you *get* put.

PB: OK, but are you saying it's impossible to be too broad in front of the camera?

OW: Big [film] acting isn't wide. It's sharp, pointed, vertical.

(*This is Orson Welles*, 14)

Where Welles was concerned, the difference between theater and film acting wasn't a matter of intensity or energy but, as he explained in regard to Cagney, of *focus*. When he argues that film acting isn't broad or wide, he's referring to the stage actor's need to aim performance toward the full width of an auditorium. In film, the situation is reversed; instead of many eyes watching from different vantage points, there's a single camera eye, which "takes [the actor] where it's put." The actor can use full, undiminished energy narrowed to that one spot.

In film, Welles wanted "sharp, pointed, vertical" rather than broadly horizontal performances. An ideal actor for his purpose was Agnes Moorehead, whose portrayal of the spinster Aunt Fanny in *The Magnificent Ambersons* (1942) is so forceful and intense it threatens to burn a hole in the screen. Moorehead conveys Fanny's tormented neurosis in every birdlike gesture of her body, frequently drawing the spectator's eye into corners of the frame where she simply stands or sits, doing nothing yet generating a force field. She treats the spoiled George Amberson Minafer with overwrought maternal concern, but then she pursues him like a fury, goading him into jealousy over Eugene Morgan. ("George! What are you going to do, George?") Near the end of the film, impoverished and exhausted, she collapses on the floor of the Amberson kitchen in childlike despair, her back against a water heater. "It isn't even hot!" she shouts at George, combining rage, frustration, and a feeling of black comic absurdity. Moorehead was exhausted when this scene was shot, but she projects a shrill emotional pain seldom seen in movies; her energy is in one sense theatrical, yet nobody can deny that she's an impressive cinematic performer who registers heartfelt affect with an intensity that can be difficult to watch.

Welles seems to have relished the opportunity to work with other vivid character actors—Akim Tamiroff, Everett Sloane, Glenn Anders, and so forth—and he loved to people films with international types who sometimes scurried about making broad gestures and almost yelling their lines. He required not only "laser-beam" force but also speed, and because his early films made use of long takes or sequence shots, he needed performers who could skillfully interact with one another while executing complex movements in relation to the camera. The long takes in *Citizen Kane* usually involve precise forward or backward movements of the players, who arrange themselves in deep space (see, for example, the famous hoarding-house scene in which Mary Kane signs her son over to Thatcher); but in the later films movements become busier and more complex. *Touch of Evil*, for example, contains an elaborately choreographed sequence involving three long takes and seven actors who move through three rooms of an apartment while the camera dollies forward, backward, and side to side; the actors duck in and out of the frame, take up different positions in the background, and occasionally step forward into close-up, all the while speaking rapidly and overlapping their dialogue at specifically designated points. Even in such films as *Othello* (1952) and *Mr. Arkadin* (1955), which were shot on small budgets and under circumstances that made it difficult for Welles to stage long takes, the actors are required to execute crisp movements as they speak. Welles seldom resorts to ordinary shot/reverse shot editing, in which actors merely deliver lines back and forth to one another. Usually he sets the camera at a low level, showing a wide-angle view of two actors, the first of whom speaks, crosses the screen, and steps out of the frame while the second turns, looks offscreen, and replies; he then cuts to a reverse angle that shows the first actor pausing, turning to look back, and speaking again. The result is a dynamic, slightly vertiginous effect, enhanced by the odd camera angles and often by overlapping speeches.

In this last regard we should perhaps remember that there was nothing especially new about overlapping dialogue when Welles began making films; a fashionable technique in American theater during the 1920s, it had been given impetus by Ben Hecht and Charles MacArthur's hugely successful *The Front Page*, which was adapted by Hollywood at least four times beginning in the early 1930s. The Howard Hawks adaptation of the play, *His Girl Friday* (1940), which appeared a full year before *Citizen Kane*, was filled with overlapping speech. As François Thomas has observed, however, in Hawks's pictures the actors tend to overlap at the beginning and end of lines, so that only banal, unessential words and phrases are covered over. Welles placed the overlapping in the *middle* of speeches and therefore put greater demands on the actors. An innovative director of radio drama, he had an acute awareness of how voices could be orchestrated and interwoven to create quasi-musical, sometimes harmonious and sometimes dissonant sounds. His screenplay for *Heart of Darkness* is remarkable for the way it designates specific words that should overlap, and most of his subsequent films have scenes in which voices interrupt and clash with one another. See, for example, the nocturnal scene aboard a yacht in *The Lady from Shanghai*, in which the swimsuited Rita Hayworth reclines in the moonlight singing "Don't Take Your Love from Me" while Everett Sloane snarls bitterly and Glenn Anders drawls in a sarcastic, exaggeratedly effeminate tone.

From the moment he arrived in Hollywood, Welles was intrigued by the fact that movie soundtracks could be manipulated apart from the images. The advantage of the technique, at least in theory, was that it enabled him to separate two of his major tasks; he could achieve the line readings he wanted and then be free to give full attention to the visual imagery and the blocking of action. Several times he experimented with having actors prerecord their dialogue and mouth their lines to a playback, much like the singers in Hollywood musicals. When he began making low-budget pictures in Europe, he relied heavily on post-synchronization, often dubbing his own voice in place of such gifted character actors as Robert Coote, Mischa Auer, and Akim Tamiroff. He believed—not necessarily correctly—that this approach could save time and money, but he was also the kind of director who wanted to exert a good deal of control over every detail of the performances. We can glimpse some of his methods in a valuable series of outtakes from *Mr. Arkadin* that were discovered several years ago in the Luxembourg Cinémathèque and are now available in the United States as supplements on the Criterion DVD edition of the film. Welles's thunderous voice can be heard offscreen as he directs close-ups of Robert Arden and Paola Mori; he requires them to repeat lines over and over, supplying character motivation and often telling them exactly when they should move their heads, how slowly or rapidly they should speak, and what emphasis they should place on certain words. We can safely assume that he didn't manage the performances of more experienced actors in quite so authoritarian a fashion. Several of his actors have spoken of his ability to charm them, and he thought of himself as a director who didn't try to dominate the cast; it seems obvious from all his films, however, that he carefully mapped the actors' every movement in and out of shadow, their every advance or retreat from the camera, and their every pause at a particular spot on the screen.

Always conscious of his own acting range, Welles cleverly designed his own performances. A large, imposing presence, he's nevertheless somewhat flat-footed and graceless in movement (see the risible fight scene at the beginning of *The Lady from Shanghai*, in which he tries unsuccessfully to give the impression of a man of action), and most of his best performances are in the roles of old men who move stiffly. Perhaps because of his personal limitations, he gives us few moments when the camera simply stands by and allows the actors' bodies a natural freedom. His own strongest attribute is his resonant, declamatory voice, with which he speaks rapidly, almost throwing away whole phrases but then pausing to linger over a word, like a pastiche of ordinary excited speech. He appears to know that if he glances slightly away from the person to whom he is speaking he will capture our attention. His slightly distracted look gives his acting what François Truffaut called a "softly hallucinated" tone (*Life Award to Orson Welles*, 10) and a decentered rhetoric that calls attention to his status as enunciator, allowing him to engage in a kind of indirect address to the audience. There are precedents for such a technique in Shakespeare's theater, but as Michael Anderegg has pointed out, Welles's presentational style is also reminiscent of Brecht's idea that the actor should stand *between* the audience and the text. In Welles's portrayal of Franz Kindler in *The Stranger* (1945), for example, he repeatedly gives a sense of what Anderegg describes as "commentary in tandem with representation" (Anderegg, "Orson Welles as Performer," 76), as if his dialogue were meant to have the "quoted" feeling that Brecht favored.

This style became especially noticeable when Welles acted in movies directed by other people. Late in his career, when he often appeared in cameo roles, he almost always positioned himself in three-quarter profile, looking at a space somewhere between the camera and the other players. As he spoke he occasionally glanced sidelong at the person he was ostensibly addressing, acknowledging their presence but at the same time making his speech seem a bit like a soliloquy. He also assumed an unorthodox posture when he worked as a visible narrator in films. Most on-camera narrators look squarely into the lens, but Welles barely seemed to notice it, sometimes appearing lost in thought or behaving like a speaker confronting a group of people arrayed around the room. His alienated form of movie address is especially noticeable in *F for Fake* and the Welles-directed TV shows *Orson Welles' Sketchbook* (1955) and *The Fountain of Youth* (1958), in which he makes us continually aware of the motion-picture apparatus. At virtually every other level of his later appearances, Welles created a slight split between the performer/enunciator and the role. His makeup in *Mr. Arkadin* is so visible that we can't know whether the star or the character is in disguise. In *The Immortal Story* (1968) and the unfinished *The Merchant of Venice* his stage makeup sets him off from all the other players. In the 1960s, during one of his several guest appearances on TV on *The Dean Martin Show*, he brought a makeup kit onstage and began telling the story of *The Merchant of Venice* as he transformed himself into Shylock; when the beard, wig, and false nose were in place, he launched into the "Hath not a Jew eyes" speech.

Along similar lines, Welles's films hovered between showing and telling. (Brecht and Erwin Piscator had developed their concept of "epic" theater from Goethe, who used the word to describe *narrated* drama, and one could argue that nearly all of Welles's films have something of the "epic" quality Goethe described.) In *F for Fake*, he not only provides a running commentary but also appears with Oja Kodar in a dramatic episode in which both players are posed abstractly against a cyclorama, as if they were narrating their respective roles. In *The Fountain of Youth*, a seldom seen but immensely inventive pilot he directed for an unsold TV series, he recounts most of the story, often breaking into the dramatic action to speak the lines of both the male and female characters as their lips move. Elsewhere he had an obvious fondness for different forms of oral narrative and for *discours* alongside *histoire*: the series of narrators in *Kane*, the brilliant appropriation of Victorian omniscience in *Ambersons*, O'Hara's story about sharks in *The Lady from Shanghai*, Arkadin's parable of the scorpion and the frog, Kafka's parable of the law in *The Trial* (1962), and so forth. One of the most interesting examples of his experiments with "narrated drama" is the unfinished *Don Quixote*, in which he reads Cervantes to a child, dubs his voice in place of the actors in the dramatized scenes, and occasionally slips out of his non-diegetic narration in order to hold conversations with the characters.

Welles's interest in narration can be traced back to his radio shows of the 1930s, which, as Jonathan Rosenbaum has pointed out, have a "neo-Brechtian" quality (*Discovering Orson Welles*, 127). In fact, his chief contribution to the history of radio drama was his tendency to think of the medium as narrative rather than purely dramatic: "When a fellow leans back in his chair and begins 'Now this is how it happened,'" he wrote, "the listener feels that the narrator is taking him into his confidence; he begins to take a personal interest in the outcome" (*New York Times*, April 10, 1938). In films he often played storytellers or public speakers, no doubt because of his hypnotic voice: Charles Foster Kane giving an election speech, Father Mapple recounting the story of Jonah and the whale, Clarence Darrow summing up a case. In many of his movie appearances as an on-screen narrator, however, he adopted an air of self-deprecating irony or playful seriousness that prevented him from seeming authoritarian. Welles the pedagogue had something in common with Welles the magician: in both forms he was capable of fooling us, but he liked to reveal his trickery. Perhaps the most important thing to say about him is that he never lost his democratic instincts. He wanted to move or persuade us, but he never let us forget that he was an actor.

Welles and Kubrick
Two Forms of Exile

Orson Welles and Stanley Kubrick were child prodigies—Welles a theatrical wunderkind and Kubrick a teenage chess master and photographer for *Look* magazine—and both became iconic representatives of the cinema of the auteur. Both worked on the borderland between Hollywood and the art film, both made the same number of feature pictures, both directed two excellent films noirs, and both were virtuosos of depth of field photography and the long take. Both used radical distortions of the wide-angle lens to give the world a bizarre appearance, and both encouraged unorthodox acting styles—in Welles's case an overheated, theatrical technique combined with carefully orchestrated overlapping dialogue, and in Kubrick's a systematic oscillation between over-the-top mugging and almost Beckett-like minimalism. Both were attracted in subtle ways to nonrealist forms of narrative—Welles to the fable and Kubrick to the fairy tale. Both were caricaturists and satirists (Kubrick more consistently than Welles), and the emotional quality of much of their work derives from the same family of affects: the darkly humorous, the absurd, the surreal, and the grotesque. Both died at age seventy.

There are nevertheless significant differences between the two. Welles's grotesque, for example, is Shakespearean and festive, whereas Kubrick's is anxiety-ridden and laced with shock effects. Welles loved comedy and once boasted—stretching the truth—that he was the uncredited author of more than a third of the script for Howard Hawks's *I Was a Male War Bride* (1949). His magic act involved comic impersonation; many of his unfilmed scripts—*The Unthinking Lobster, Une Grosse Légume,* and *Operation Cinderella*—are comic and filled with amusing incidents; and even his most black-comic projects, such as *The Landru Story*, which became Chaplin's *Monsieur Verdoux* (1947), are different in tone from a movie like *Dr. Strangelove* (1964). Welles was a bon vivant and a gregarious personality, whereas Kubrick was a clever businessman and a steely perfectionist on the set. Welles made films about plutocrats or kings, and his comedy was often mingled with tragedy; Kubrick made films about scientists, soldiers, and the American nuclear family, only rarely dealing in tragic or sentimental emotions.

Despite these and other differences, the influence of Welles on the young Kubrick was palpable. When Kubrick's *The Killing* was released in 1956, *Time* magazine claimed that its twenty-seven-year-old director had "shown more audacity with dialogue and camera than Hollywood has seen since the obstreperous Orson Welles went riding out of town on an exhibitor's poll" (June 4, 1956). *The Killing* did, in fact, look very much like a Wellesian version of *The Asphalt Jungle* (1950)—it had bizarre camera angles, wide-angle distortions, mesmerizing long takes, a jigsaw-puzzle plot, a narrator who sounded as if he worked for *News on the March,* and even a screeching cockatoo. This may explain why Welles told a group of Spanish interviewers in the mid-1960s that of the directors he considered as belonging to "the younger generation," Kubrick seemed a "giant." "I believe that Kubrick can do everything," Welles said. "He is a great director who has not yet made his great film. What I see in him is a talent not possessed by the great directors of the generation immediately preceding his, I mean Ray, Aldrich, etc. Perhaps this is because his temperament comes closer to mine" (Cobos, Rubio, and Pruneda, 22).

Whatever their respective temperaments, Welles and Kubrick were arguably the most sophisticated American-born representatives of artistic modernism in Hollywood. Several writers, among them Fredric Jameson, have argued that Kubrick's late films are postmodern (*Signatures of the Visible,* 91–92), but if that term designates retro and recycled styles, waning of affect, lack of psychological "depth," loss of faith in the "real," and hypercommodification, then Kubrick was a modernist to the end. An avid reader of the Anglo-European and largely modernist literary and philosophical canon of dead white men (plus a great deal of pulp fiction and scientific literature), Kubrick maintained a lifelong interest in Nietzsche, Freud, and Jung. Most of his films are rather like "late modernist" manifestations of the aesthetic detachment we find in Kafka and Joyce, or of the "cold" authorial personality in Brecht and Pinter; and no matter how much his work might have derived from Hollywood genres, it remained very close in spirit to the Euro-intellectual cinema of the 1960s. Where Welles is concerned, the connection with modernism is even more obvious. Certain aspects of *Citizen Kane*'s symbolism and narrative structure are redolent of Kafka, its newsreel sequence and Hearst-like protagonist might have been inspired by Dos Passos, and its manipulations of time, memory, and point of view have evoked critical comparisons with Proust, Conrad, Faulkner, and Fitzgerald. *Kane* also synthesizes the major schools of European filmmaking before 1941—German expressionism, Soviet montage, and French surrealism—at the same time employing what André Bazin called a new filmic language based on the long take. Welles's subsequent Hollywood films, no matter how diverse their genres or subjects, have similar qualities; *The Magnificent Ambersons* (1942) transforms Booth Tarkington's genteel fiction into a darkly atmospheric Freudian drama, and *The Lady from Shanghai* (1948) uses a pulp novel as the basis for an exercise in surrealist eroticism and *Caligari*-like visual design.

Modernism was a distinctly international movement involving a kind of dialectic between American modernity and the European avant-gardes. Given its embattled relation with the economic, social, and political upheavals of the twentieth century, it also produced a great many exiles and émigrés. In this context a comparison between Welles and Kubrick becomes especially interesting, for one of the most significant things the two have in common is that they both found it difficult, or at least undesirable, to work in Hollywood. They became American exiles, although we need to apply that term loosely, and to understand their careers we need to examine the different reasons why they lived so much of their lives abroad.

Even though Welles and Kubrick belonged to different generations, they both became émigrés from the United States during the cold war. Welles enjoyed his most dazzling success in the Roosevelt years, and the seven pictures he produced and/or directed in Hollywood during the 1940s (one of them the incomplete *It's All True*) were an outgrowth of his Popular Front activities in the previous decade. The decline of his Hollywood fortunes was overdetermined but clearly related to his unorthodox film style, his so-called "highbrow" interests, his purported inability to attract a large popular audience, and, in no small measure, his tendency to provoke resentment and schadenfreude in some quarters of the movie colony. *Kane* made the Hearst press his enemy, and *Ambersons* was disastrously recut by RKO because it was a more mature, leisurely, unsensational film than the Hollywood industry would allow. Even in its recut version, *Ambersons* remains one of the few movies to display the characteristics that Georg Lukács and Fredric Jameson have associated with the most important forms of the classic historical novel: narratives that depict historically representative fictional characters whose lives are changed by large-scale social forces, and that tell of struggles between emerging and once-dominant forms of society without completely picking sides in the contest and thereby descending into costume melodrama. The supreme example of a film that fits the Lukács-Jameson model is arguably Luchino Visconti's *The Leopard*

(1963). In its original form *Ambersons* might have been the equal of that picture, and in any event the loss of that version is tragic.

Welles's problems were exacerbated by the death of Roosevelt and the postwar reemergence of the American right wing. Writing from the vantage point of California in the mid-1940s, cultural theorists Max Horkheimer and Theodor Adorno argued, "Orson Welles is forgiven all his offenses against the usages of the craft because, as calculated rudeness, they confirm the validity of the system all the more zealously" (102). In fact, however, beginning with *Citizen Kane* and continuing until 1956, Welles was not only disliked by the Hollywood studios but also closely observed by J. Edgar Hoover's FBI, which compiled roughly two hundred pages of reports about him. For nearly ten years FBI operatives tracked his political activities, personal finances, and love life, following up tips from industry insiders, the American Legion, isolated crackpots, and gossip columnist Hedda Hopper, who worked for the Hearst press. In 1945, near the beginning of a Red Scare that would influence Hollywood for the next decade, the FBI secretly designated Welles a Communist and a "threat to the internal security" of the nation. (A complete discussion of the FBI files, which I obtained through the Freedom of Information Act, may be found in Naremore, "The Trial," 22–27.)

Although Welles had been one of the most celebrated directors of Popular Front theater and radio in the 1930s, the FBI took no interest in him until April 1941, one month before the U.S. premiere of *Kane* and at just the moment when William Randolph Hearst's minions were mounting an attack on the film. At that juncture Hoover sent a memo to Assistant U.S. Attorney General Matthew McGuire listing Welles's membership in over a dozen organizations "said to be communistic in character" and registering particular concern over his recent involvement with the Free Company, a group of writers and actors who were producing radio dramas on civil liberties for CBS. Welles's contribution was a show called "His Honor, the Mayor," which dealt with racial prejudice. Hoover noted that an American Legion post in California had described the show as "encouraging racialism" and that "spokesmen" for the group had charged it and other shows in the series with being "subversive in nature and definitely communistic in aims although camouflaged by constant reference to democracy and free speech."

As a result, Hoover ordered the FBI to compose a biographical sketch of Welles based on *Who's Who* and journalistic sources. The resulting document noted his membership in Spanish relief committees, his support of Harry Bridges (the militant onetime Communist head of the International Longshoremen's Union), and his stage production of *The Cradle Will Rock*. Agent F. E. Foxworth, author of the sketch, reported that, according to an anonymous informant, "Welles has written stories which were apparently for the movies and . . . considered too far to the left." Soon afterward the bureau compiled reports on two "subversive" productions by Welles: the Mercury Theater's 1941 stage adaptation of Richard Wright's *Native Son*, and *Citizen Kane*. The file on *Native Son* contained a copy of Wright's novel and sixteen pages of clippings from newspapers such as the *Daily Worker* and the *New Masses*, all purporting to show "the communist teamwork involved in the production of this play." The much larger file on *Citizen Kane* contained thirty-two pages of clippings from left-wing journals, including an essay Welles had written three years earlier for the *Daily Worker* ("Theater and the People's Front," April 15, 1938). The report emphasized that William Randolph Hearst was often the victim of attacks by the Communist Party. "In fact," its author said, breaking into a blustering tone worthy of Walter Parks Thatcher, "the evidence before us leads inevitably to the conclusion that the film 'Citizen Kane' is nothing more than an extension of the Communist Party's campaign to smear one of its most effective and consistent opponents in the United States."

Six months later, as Welles was preparing to leave for South America and begin shooting *It's All True*, the FBI received a letter that set off a brief investigation. I quote parts of it below, with the errors in the original left intact:

Gentlemen:

Orson Wells whose activities and interests in Communistic circles and whose American sympathies are nil, one whose record you have in your files, has been cooking up some scheme having to do with Brazil in S. America. He is known to be pro-Russian. . . . He is associated in this scheme with [deleted] who lives in [deleted]. This man is a hothead, big word individual who is supposed to represent some newspaper [deleted] but hobnobs with *alien Italians* and is in reality a native of Portugal. . . .

These two plan to leave in a very few days for Brazil either by plane or ship.

They should be investigated at once and possibly prevented from going down there if you find cause for detention. . . . Its possible their intentions are legal but from reports, there is something screwy about this whole set up. . . . There is no time to waste on this tip.

> From one who with others is engaged in quiet investigation of subversive actions. Take it or leave it, that's up to you.

[Signature deleted]

The bureau decided to "take it," but soon they discovered that their informant had used a fake name. When they made "undisclosed identity" phone calls to people mentioned in the letter and checked voter registration lists in Los Angeles, they learned that one of Welles's sinister associates was a

Republican. When they were subsequently notified that Welles had been given State Department permission to make a film in South America, they temporarily called off their agents. No additional information was filed until the next year, when agent D.M. Ladd reported to Hoover's assistant Clyde Tolson that Welles was involved in the effort to defend seventeen Latino teenagers charged in the Sleepy Lagoon murder trial in Los Angeles. (In 1944, after numerous legal abuses and time in jail, these defendants were acquitted.) Later that year the FBI clandestinely searched the office of the Los Angeles County Communist Political Association but could find no record of Welles's membership. Undeterred, the Los Angeles office of the FBI recommended that Welles be given a Security Index Card listing him as a native-born subversive and a communist.

Three weeks later Hedda Hopper alarmed the bureau by informing them that Welles was engaged in "special work" on behalf of FDR. Shortly afterward, on February 22, 1945, Hoover sent an order for Welles to be placed on the FBI Security Index, which contained "only the names of those individuals who can be considered to be a threat to the internal security of this country." Regular reports on such individuals were required, Hoover added. Agent R.B. Hood, who was in charge of the Los Angeles office, began submitting the reports to Hoover, passing on more news from Hedda Hopper, such as the rumor that Welles would be going to Russia to film *Crime and Punishment*, and gathering the sort of information one might use for blackmail. According to Hood, Welles was spending "considerable evenings with [name deleted], former Main Street burlesque strip tease artist, who has recently promoted herself to a higher type of nightclub appearance. . . . Also some time ago, when WELLES appeared in San Diego in connection with a bond tour[,] he took some girl, other than his wife." His finances were being mishandled by an unnamed associate, Hood reported, "leaving him practically broke," and his marriage to Rita Hayworth appeared to be ending. To top things off, he was also having an affair with "a movie actress [name deleted] who has recently been receiving considerable publicity." At the conclusion of one of the reports, Hood appended a list of persons in Hollywood—their names deleted from the official document—who would be "glad to be of any possible assistance." "Proper coverage of the telephone conversations between WELLES and [name deleted] may reveal information of interest," he added.

The timing of these actions was significant. The war was coming to an end and a purge of American leftists was in the offing; Welles had campaigned vigorously for FDR's fourth term and for Henry Wallace; and over the next few years he would become involved in the newly formed United Nations and Louis Dolivet's Free World Association, meanwhile writing a syndicated political column for the *New York Post* and flirting with the idea of running for office. By 1948, however, his Hollywood career was virtually at an end: *The Lady from Shanghai*, which he was able to make only because of his marriage to Hayworth, was loathed by Columbia Pictures and mangled in the studio's reediting; and the extremely low-budget *Macbeth* was recut by Republic Pictures (in the process removing one of the first ten-minute takes in the history of movies) and its soundtrack completely redubbed. By the early 1950s, as the House Un-American Activities Committee hearings and the McCarthy era dawned, and at about the time when Jules Dassin and Joseph Losey became expatriate directors, Welles was in Europe and North Africa making *Othello*. An anonymous informant sent the FBI a photo of Welles dining with Palmiro Togliatti, the legendary head of the Italian Communist Party, along with a message in French saying that the photo ought to be brought to the attention of the State Department with the aim of having Welles "brought before a court in charge of prosecuting actors suspected of Un-American activities and perhaps even excluded from Hollywood definitely." But the investigating agent concluded that Welles was being "bled white" financially by communist sympathizers, had never actually been a member of the party, and was no longer any particular threat.

Welles did not return to America for any significant length of time for almost a decade. Most of his theatrical and cinematic activity in those years—during which he starred in *The Third Man* (1949), wrote several film scripts, and directed *Othello* (1952) and *Mr. Arkadin* (1955)—took place in Italy, North Africa, France, Germany, England, and Spain. This was also the period in which he began acting in bad pictures in order to raise money for the movies he wanted to direct. In 1953 he was briefly in New York to act in Peter Brooks's TV version of *King Lear*, and in the late 1950s he returned to the United States for a longer period, performing a magic act in Las Vegas, making numerous guest appearances on TV, and filming a brilliant TV pilot ("The Fountain of Youth") for the Lucille Ball–Desi Arnaz production company. In 1958, slightly more than a decade after *Macbeth*, he was given the opportunity to write, direct, and act in the Universal Pictures production of *Touch of Evil*. The resulting film was recut by the studio before its release and had no financial importance for its producers. Welles began filming *Don Quixote* in Mexico and then returned to England, Spain, France, and various other European locations for another decade, the period of *The Trial* (1962), *Chimes at Midnight* (1965), and *The Immortal Story* (1968). From approximately 1968 until his death in 1985 he divided his time between Hollywood and Europe, making frequent guest appearances on the Dean Martin television show and filming *F for Fake* (1974) and a number of incomplete pictures, including *The Deep* and *The Other Side of the Wind*.

Several of Welles's European producers gave him at least as many problems as the old Hollywood studios had done. Information on the costs and box office receipts of his post-Hollywood films is almost irrelevant because those films are so far afield of the budgets and marketing strategies that dominated the industry after midcentury. Late in his career he encountered major tax problems in the United States because of money he had earned in Europe, and he began to take on increasingly dubious backers, including, against all his progressive instincts, the Shah's government in Iran. He was revered by the French New Wave and frequently honored by American cinephiles, but in the nearly forty years after he filmed *Macbeth* (1948) he only once exercised his talents in a Hollywood film. His later work is less political and satiric than his work in Hollywood. The major part of his career was spent as a pioneering independent director/producer, an artist who created films almost as an avocation. Still a kind of celebrity from the 1950s until his death, his career made hash of highbrow, middlebrow, lowbrow distinctions. Michael Anderegg puts it nicely: most of Welles's post–*Citizen Kane* work in the movies was an attempt to "drive his gypsy wagon outside the great hall of the culture industry" (*Orson Welles*, 57).

Stanley Kubrick's first professional opportunity came just as Welles's American career was winding down. In 1945, at the age of seventeen, he sold *Look* magazine a photograph of a New York newspaper vendor grieving over the death of Franklin Roosevelt. This image enabled Kubrick to became a member of *Look*'s photographic staff, a job that sent him traveling around the United States and Europe and resulted in the publication of more than nine hundred of his pictures. Between 1945 and 1950 he was directly involved with the New York School of photographers, which included Lee Friedlander, Robert Frank, and Diane Arbus. Like Kubrick, many in this group were from Jewish immigrant families, and their livelihood was made possible by the burgeoning market for photojournalism in the slick picture magazines and the tabloid newspapers. Its senior members had lectured at the New York Photo League, a Popular Front organization that nurtured the careers of Weegee, Berenice Abbott, Morris Engel, and Lisette Model. Kubrick's early self-produced films, especially *Killer's Kiss* (1955), which was shot on the streets of New York, show a strong indebtedness to this cultural milieu; but his later films, made in the period of the Cuban missile crisis, the assassination of JFK, and the Vietnam War, convey a bewildering mixture of political attitudes.

Although most of Kubrick's career was spent abroad, he remained a star director, manufacturing dream images of space travel, the Vietnam War, and contemporary Manhattan all from within a few miles of his English residence. By the mid-1960s he had acquired the aura of an intellectual Mr. Cool who adopted silence, exile, and cunning as a way of dealing with his career. But while he was often portrayed as a maverick and an exile, the truth is more complicated. In the best account yet written of Kubrick's business relationship with Hollywood (from which I have taken economic statistics), Robert Sklar has pointed out that Kubrick never left the big studios behind:

> Stanley Kubrick's career as a filmmaker is deeply interconnected with the American motion picture industry. He has worked at one time or another with nearly all the so-called "majors": United Artists, Universal, Columbia, MGM, and Warner Bros. These companies have distributed his films and have participated in financing some of them. These connections have enmeshed Kubrick and his films in the structures of the American film business; despite his geographical self-exile from Hollywood, Kubrick continues to be regarded as an American filmmaker, while other expatriate directors, like Richard Lester and Joseph Losey, worked more closely with British and continental production and distribution companies and came to be seen as members of the Anglo-European film community. ("Stanley Kubrick and the American Film Industry," 114)

Sklar appropriately calls Kubrick a "self-exile," as opposed to a figure like Joseph Losey, who was driven out of the United States for political reasons. It also seems to me that Kubrick isn't the same sort of American abroad as Orson Welles. Jonathan Rosenbaum has pointed out that Kubrick and Welles "ended up making all the films they completed after the 1950s in exile, which surely says something about the creative possibilities of American commercial filmmaking over the past four decades" (*Essential Cinema*, 267–68). The basic point here is valid and important, but it's also important to note that Welles was persona non grata in Hollywood during the late 1940s and became a peripatetic citizen of the world, whereas Kubrick established a settled existence, remaining close to American production facilities but far enough away from Hollywood to protect his art. In Sklar's words, Kubrick "hardly ever hesitated from playing the American film business game," much of the time "by his own rules" (114).

There was always a tension between Kubrick's artistic aims and Hollywood's conventional way of manufacturing entertainment; he disliked life in Los Angeles, but he rarely had to yield authority over his films. His ability to maintain control was due in part to his talents as a producer-businessman, and partly to the fact that when he took the first steps in his career the industry was undergoing major changes. A 1948 Supreme Court ruling had divested the major Hollywood studios of their theater chains and the popular audience was increasingly obsessed with television. Movie house attendance in the United States had declined by some forty million, but two developments in the world of exhibition created markets for independent producers: the drive-in, or "passion pit," which favored exploitation films, and the urban or college-town art theater, which specialized in foreign pictures. In the trade, the art theaters came to be known as "sure-seaters" because their audiences were loyal and their films tended to attract strong reviews from critics. The films were sometimes labeled "mature," presumably because they were enjoyed by sophisticated and discriminating viewers, but also because they were more openly sexual than Hollywood's products and could be promoted in terms of a softly pornographic sensationalism. At first few if any American filmmakers seemed aware of these new circumstances. During the early 1950s, the only American-born director who made inexpensive English-language films that found a natural home in art houses was Orson Welles; but Welles's *Othello* and *Mr. Arkadin* were European imports, without the distribution networks that would later develop for independent and off-Hollywood films.

Kubrick can claim the distinction of being the first true American independent of the art-house era. He used $53,500 of his and his relatives' money to produce, direct, photograph, and edit an extremely arty war film entitled *The Shape of Fear*, which attracted the interest of a legendary distributor of foreign pictures, Joseph Burstyn, the man who had brought *Open City*, *The Bicycle Thief*, and Renoir's *A Day in the Country* to America. "He's a genius!" the excitable Burstyn purportedly said after meeting the twenty-four-year-old Kubrick. Burstyn immediately declared *The Shape of Fear* an "American art film," changed the title to the more provocative *Fear and Desire*, and in March 1953 booked it into New York City's Guild Theater, an art house located in Rockefeller Center. It received a "B" rating from the Legion of Decency because of a sex scene involving a woman strapped to a tree, but it also enjoyed a degree of mostly favorable critical attention.

Kubrick's next film, *Killer's Kiss*, self-produced for $75,000, was distributed by United Artists and shown mainly in fleapits. His Hollywood career began shortly afterward when he met James Harris, a wealthy contemporary who shared his artistic ambitions. Their first project, distributed and partly financed by United Artists, was *The Killing* (1956). UA disliked the film's splintered narrative structure and gave it almost no promotion or chance to earn profits; nevertheless, it attracted the attention of Hollywood cognoscenti at a moment when the movie business was being driven by producers and stars who controlled their own production units. Kirk

Douglas, who was at the height of his fame during the period, was much impressed with *The Killing*, and when he saw a script for Kubrick's newest project, *Paths of Glory* (1957), he offered to take the leading role and to pressure United Artists into financing and distributing the film. The price he exacted was considerable: Harris and Kubrick had to agree to move their operation to Douglas's Bryna Productions and make five other pictures with Bryna, two of which would star Douglas. Harris and Kubrick reluctantly agreed, and *Paths of Glory* went before cameras in Munich, Germany, budgeted at approximately one million dollars, a third of which went to the star. Harris and Kubrick waived their fees and agreed to work for a percentage of the picture's profits.

The working relationship between Douglas and Kubrick was tense, and Douglas had more influence over the script of *Paths of Glory* than most critics have recognized. The film nevertheless gave Kubrick a good deal of cultural capital and the reputation of having collaborated with a major star. Moreover, his new contract led to his being hired to direct *Spartacus* (1960), produced by Bryna and Universal Pictures, which was budgeted at twelve million dollars. At the time, this was the most expensive movie ever shot chiefly inside the United States. MGM's remake of *Ben-Hur* in the previous year had been slightly more expensive, but it was produced at Cinecittà in Italy, where Hollywood companies obtained tax advantages and cheaper labor. During the 1960s the so-called "flight" from domestic production, coupled with the turn toward expensive spectacles, had become so commonplace that when *Spartacus* opened, the recently elected John F. Kennedy made a special point of attending a showing at a regular theater in Washington, D.C., thereby calling attention to Douglas's and Universal's attempt to keep U.S. money at home.

Spartacus represents the only alienated labor of Kubrick's film career and has very few moments in which one can sense his directorial personality. Anthony Mann was in charge of the opening sequences, which are as good as any of the others. Kubrick's hand seems most evident in the sexually kinky moments—the visit of Roman aristocrats and their wives to the gladiator school, and the not-so-veiled homosexual conversations between Crassus and his slave, Antoninus. He had no voice in the casting or the development of the screenplay, nor did he supervise the editing. He disliked the script, which he described to Michel Ciment as "dumb" and "rarely faithful to what is known about Spartacus" (151). (Kirk Douglas has said that in spite of such complaints Kubrick offered to take credit for the work of blacklisted screenwriter Dalton Trumbo; Douglas credited Trumbo and defied the blacklist.) To make matters worse, Kubrick had trouble with veteran director of photography Russell Metty, a skilled practitioner of crane shots who had photographed

Welles's *Touch of Evil*. As a result of Metty's intransigence, very few scenes in *Spartacus* employ the source illumination we identify with Kubrick. As Kubrick told Ciment, "If I ever needed any convincing of the limits of persuasion a director can have on a film where someone else is the producer and [the director] is merely the highest-paid member of the crew, *Spartacus* provided proof to last a lifetime" (151). *Spartacus* gave Kubrick a big payday (Douglas never profited from the film), but he asked to be released from his contract with Douglas, and Douglas consented. There was bad blood between the two, but insofar as Hollywood was concerned, the most impressive thing on Kubrick's resume was *Spartacus*, which showed that he could manage a supercolossal picture with big stars.

Another opportunity arose when Kubrick and Harris acquired the rights to Vladimir Nabokov's *Lolita* just prior to its publication. After extensive battles with censors, they made the film in England, where, under the recently enacted Eady Plan, they could enjoy substantial tax advantages if at least 80 percent of the people they employed were British citizens. This arrangement provided Kubrick with distance from Hollywood's usual ways of doing business while giving him considerable technical resources. The film, with a final budget of approximately two million dollars, was made without a distributor but was ultimately released by MGM in 1962. The least critically successful but the most profitable of the Harris-Kubrick pictures, it earned almost twice its cost in the United States alone.

After *Lolita*, Harris and Kubrick amicably dissolved their partnership and Kubrick's career entered a new phase in which he became his own producer and shot all of his films in England. His first two pictures under this arrangement, *Dr. Strangelove* and *2001*, were major box-office hits, tapping into a youth audience that would serve him well over the next decade. In 1968, *2001* was filmed for approximately 10.5 million dollars, and by 1973 it had earned approximately 28 million dollars in domestic and foreign rentals, although Kubrick received little of that money because MGM was still charging him for distribution fees and interest on the financing of the film. He was unable to acquire financing for his next project, an epic film about Napoleon for which he had done massive preparation, but his disappointment must have been ameliorated when Warner Brothers offered him a contract even better than the one Welles originally signed with RKO. In 1970, John Calley, the executive vice-president for production at Warner, signed Kubrick for a three-picture deal in which he would have a unique relationship with the studio. He could remain in England, where Warner's London office would fund the purchase, development, and production of properties for him to direct; he was guaranteed final cut of his films; and his company, Hawk Films, would receive 40 percent of the film's profits. At about the same time, Calley offered Welles a chance to make a picture at Warner, but Welles declined, in part because he was leery of big studios.

The first picture Kubrick made under the new arrangement, *A Clockwork Orange* (1971), was budgeted at two million dollars and by 1982 had earned forty million dollars, making it the most profitable production of the director's career and one of the studio's biggest hits of the decade. The profits, moreover, were achieved despite the fact that *A Clockwork Orange* was an exceptionally controversial picture with a limited distribution. British newspapers accused it of prompting a series of copycat killings, and Kubrick began to receive death threats. In response he withdrew *A Clockwork Orange* from exhibition in England for his entire lifetime—a step that no other director, then or now, has had the power to take. In the United States, Kubrick personally supervised the film's promotion campaign, targeting every student newspaper and alternative radio station in America. His success was such that Ted Ashley, the chief executive at Warner, announced that Kubrick was a genius who combined "aesthetics" with "fiscal responsibility" (Sklar, "Stanley Kubrick and the American Film Industry," 121).

Kubrick remained at Warner for the rest of his career, forming a personal bond with the CEO Steve Ross (also a friend of Steven Spielberg). His ascendancy in the early 1970s had something to do with the "New Hollywood," a phenomenon he slightly predates, which is determined by the relative independence of U.S. exhibition, the liberalization of classic-era censorship codes, and the rise of youth culture. But by the late 1970s Steven Spielberg and George Lucas were producing Hollywood blockbusters in the same British facilities Kubrick had used, and Kubrick's ability to attract sufficiently large audiences was ending. After *A Clockwork Orange* he made *Barry Lyndon* (1975), which employs many of the same themes and techniques that were planned for his aborted Napoleon project. The film, which is slightly over three hours long, cost eleven million dollars to make and barely placed in the top twenty-five grosses of the year; it eventually earned a profit, but *Variety* called it a flop.

Writers in the trade press accused Kubrick of arrogance, in part because he had kept the production of *Barry Lyndon* largely a secret. His bigger problem, however, was that the top money-maker of the year was *Jaws*, which earned 133 million dollars, almost doubling the earnings record of any previous film. From this experience the studios learned new marketing practices: saturation booking of tent-pole films across the entire country, massive TV advertising and huge promotional campaigns, prerelease payments from exhibitors, and guaranteed playing time in theaters. Soon the movie studios would once again be vertically (and horizontally) integrated, and the "New Hollywood" would become a memory.

Kubrick's initial response was a highly commercial project, *The Shining* (1980). (He had declined Warner's offer to direct *The Exorcist*, which went on to become one of the studio's most profitable investments.) *The Shining* was budgeted at 18 million dollars and earned nearly 40 million in domestic rentals—a substantial sum, but not terribly impressive in a year when Lucas's *The Empire Strikes Back* brought in 140 million. The gap between "aesthetics" and "fiscal responsibility" was growing wider, and Kubrick's inability to appeal to audiences beyond the urban centers was becoming more noticeable. Warner remained faithful to him and appreciated the fact that his late films, despite their slow production schedules, were shot with relatively small, efficient crews. Even so, the periods of silence between his films grew longer, and he made only two more pictures before his death.

As all this indicates, Welles and Kubrick left their native country for very different reasons. We might ask if they lost anything in the process. Welles, though a Midwesterner, had begun his theatrical career in Ireland and was always something of an internationalist. One of his major artistic preoccupations was the death of an old world in the face of "progress"—a theme adumbrated in *Kane*, developed in *Ambersons*, and repeated in his European films, especially in *Arkadin*, *Chimes at Midnight*, and *Don Quixote*, all three of which juxtapose medieval Spanish settings against the encroachments of modernity. In this sense, his move to Europe was consistent with his career as a whole. Most of his films on the continent were financed in crazy-quilt fashion, and yet he managed to produce two distinguished adaptations of Shakespeare, two films in modern settings that provided models for younger directors, an intriguing television drama that played theatrically, and an essay film that was far ahead of its time. He often said that what he missed most about Hollywood was its technical expertise. In Europe he had to modify his style to suit the fragmented, catch-as-catch-can nature of his productions, and in his last years he had to depend upon a kind of bricolage and the garish photography of his loyal American admirer, Gary Graver. Even so, much of his European work is filled with dazzling cinematic effects achieved with great ingenuity. What is missing, in my own view, is contact with American mores, myths, and politics. The European films, with the exception of *Arkadin*, lose touch with the topicality and leftist satire of the American work and tend to retreat into the world of literary adaptation. *The Third Man*, which Welles did not direct, was obviously about contemporary Europe, but *The Trial*, partly because of budget constraints, was about an abstract Europe. *Touch of Evil* is a better film than either of these, in part because it puts Welles back in an American milieu during the civil rights era and takes full advantage of his talents as a satirist and moralist.

Welles began with a Hollywood studio at his disposal and ended as an independent filmmaker who did nearly everything—on *The Trial*, for example, he was not only writer, actor, and director but also second unit photographer, editor, and sound designer. Kubrick, on the other hand, began as an independent filmmaker who did nearly everything and rose to command stars and big studio resources in England. Despite the fact that he never lost his Bronx accent, Kubrick had something of a European sensibility. Jonathan Rosenbaum and Tom Gunning have each pointed out to me in conversation that he can be viewed as not simply a Hollywood modernist and futurist but also the last of its Viennese auteurs. His ancestors were from Austria-Hungary and his intellect was shaped by the protomodernist, largely Jewish culture that originated in pre–World War I Vienna. In addition to Freud, he was interested in Stefan Zweig and Arthur Schnitzler, and he often stated his admiration for Max Ophüls, who was born in Saarbrücken but is often regarded as the quintessential Viennese director. The Viennese cultural nexus may not seem evident in a film like *2001*, but that film is at least distantly related to Lang's *Metropolis*, and the famous image of a shuttle docking at a revolving space station to the music of "The Blue Danube" not only makes a sly Freudian joke but also evokes memories of Ophüls's *Lola Montès* (1955).

For the most part, Kubrick used Britain for non-British subject matter. (Michael Herr, who collaborated with Kubrick on *Full Metal Jacket* [1987], wrote, "I'm not sure he even really knew he wasn't living in America all along" [46].) David Thomson has severely criticized Kubrick's *Lolita*, remarking that Nabokov's "love story to America was ruinously shot in England" (*Biographical Dictionary*, 408). It seems to me, however, that Nabokov's America is mediated by the voice of a European exile (in his own commentary on the novel, Nabokov describes his version of America as a theatrical "set" and a "fantastic and personal" world), and that in roughly analogous fashion, the British workers on *Lolita* create an intangible air of America seen lucidly through a slightly foreign lens. It might also be noted that while Kubrick's next two films involved American characters, *Dr. Strangelove* ends with the quintessential British pop tune of World War II, and the astronauts in *2001* watch television broadcasts from the BBC. The only Kubrick film that deals more or less directly with contemporary Britain is *A Clockwork Orange*, which is also his most repellant film, depicting modern society as based on nothing more than innate predatory violence and rationalized, utilitarian coercion. Kubrick jettisoned the Catholic religious message of Anthony Burgess's novel and made a film whose politics are difficult to define. *A Clockwork Orange* shares Adorno's late-romantic devotion to Beethoven, his relentlessly satiric attitude toward socialism and fascism, his disdain for bureaucrats, his derisive response to kitsch, and his despair over Enlightenment rationality. Kubrick's savage treatment of reification and alienation under modernity isn't far from what one finds in the "Culture Industry" chapter of *Dialectic of Enlightenment*, and his treatment of sex roughly corresponds to that book's chapter on the Marquis de Sade ("Enlightenment as Morality"), which argues that Sade's libertinism was merely a logical development of the liberal bourgeois subject—a disavowal of religious superstition, a "busy pursuit of pleasure," and an extension of reason, efficiency, and social organization into the realm of the senses (69–70).

Kubrick's other film about Great Britain is *Barry Lyndon*, based on Thackeray's *The Luck of Barry Lyndon* (1856), which tells the story of an eighteenth-century Irish rake who seduces his way into the British aristocracy. Kubrick's approach to the subject is exactly the opposite of Thackeray's; in place of a rollicking satire he gives us a somber tragedy of manners that ends on the eve of the French Revolution. As a Jewish-American who eventually settled into a British country house, he seems to have identified with a social outsider like Barry, whom he depicts as an unwitting and unsuccessful rebel against his times. For roughly similar reasons Kubrick had identified with the Corsican upstart Napoleon, who gained ascendancy over France's old regime and became one of the founders of the modern world. I suspect that Kubrick's reference to 1789 at the end of *Barry Lyndon* functions less as an optimistic tribute to democracy than as a portent of the Napoleonic era and a nod to a film he never made. *Barry Lyndon* nevertheless resembles the epic, unmelodramatic model that Lukács and Jameson have championed in their readings of the classic historical novel. Kubrick had intended to portray Napoleon as a tragic superman, both a dictator and a force of Enlightenment liberalism, worthy of being placed in relation to the killer ape and the star-child in *2001*. He was unable to realize that ambition, but it became a kind of structuring absence in the fictional, "middling" characterizations of *Barry Lyndon* and one of the chief reasons why that film has such beauty, strangeness, and emotional force.

At the end of their careers Welles and Kubrick were honored in America, and the separate occasions were symptomatic of their forms of exile. Welles received the American Film Institute's third Life Achievement Award in 1975 and turned the televised ceremony into an overt appeal for "end money" to complete his latest movie. He showed two clips from *The Other Side of the Wind*: the first was a satiric depiction of a Hollywood celebration in honor of a famous film director, the second a scene in which one of the director's henchmen unsuccessfully tries to obtain financing from a big studio boss modeled on Robert Evans. Welles followed these excerpts with a speech in which he described himself as a lifelong "contrarian" and a "neighborhood grocery in the age of supermarkets."

Stanley Kubrick's acceptance of an honor was in every way different but no less filled with ironies. In 1999, while editing *Eyes Wide Shut*, he was presented with the D.W. Griffith Award from the Director's Guild of America. He didn't travel to Los Angeles to accept the award. Appearing as a ghostly image on closed-circuit TV, he used his acceptance speech to confirm his faith in the big artistic ambition of Griffith. Griffith's career, he recalled, had often been compared to the Icarus myth, "but at the same time I've never been certain whether the moral of the Icarus story should only be, as is generally accepted, 'Don't try to fly too high,' or whether it might also be thought of as 'Forget the wax and feathers and do a better job on the wings.'" It might be argued that Kubrick had done a better job on the wings, but, unlike Welles, he had never flown far away from the labyrinth.

The Treasure of the Sierra Madre

It flashed through his mind that he had seen many a movie in which the hero was trapped in a situation like this. But he realized at the same time that he could not remember one single picture in which the producer had not done his utmost to help the trapped hero out again to save the girl from the clutches of a bunch of villains.
B. TRAVEN, The Treasure of the Sierra Madre

The worst ain't so bad when it finally happens. Not nearly as bad as you figure it will be before it's happened.
CURTIN, in John Huston's The Treasure of the Sierra Madre

The Treasure of the Sierra Madre, B. Traven's novel published in the United States in 1935, tells the story of three down-and-out American workingmen stuck in Mexico at the end of an oil boom. Ragged and almost hopeless, they scrape together what money they have and set out to prospect for gold in the mountains. By extraordinary good fortune they strike it rich, but mutual suspicion, the harsh desert weather, and Mexican bandits all conspire to deprive them of their treasure. There's no Hollywood-style happy ending and, as the first epigraph above indicates, the very subject of movies is sometimes used by Traven as a way of showing the disparity between life and fantasy. (At one point two of the prospectors discuss using their gold to start up a movie theater in the town of their choice; the more untrustworthy of the two plans to be the entertainment director, leaving the more mundane details of management to his partner.) Even so, in 1948 Traven's novel became a classic motion picture from Warner Brothers, subsequently winning Academy Awards for best direction, best original screenplay, and best supporting actor and New York Film Critics Circle prizes for best picture and best direction. Perhaps the prospector Curtin was right: it ain't so bad when it finally happens.

On the other hand, it's easy to see why *Treasure* should have seemed a likely project for its screenwriter and director, John Huston, who was once known as a Hollywood maverick and who drifted into the movies from a life more lucky but no less vagrant than Traven's characters. Huston's films typically end in failure, though not necessarily in absolute disaster. The people in his stories are frequently involved in a dangerous quest—a search for a jeweled falcon, a bank robbery, a journey down an African river aboard a battered steamboat, a mad chase after a white whale, or an attempt to conquer an entire country and become its king. The best of these people behave with grace under pressure, but at the last moment some ironic twist usually makes everything go wrong and they become philosophers of a sort, like losers at a roulette wheel. Thus Sam Spade, using language Huston gave him (borrowed from Shakespeare), wryly calls the phony black bird "the stuff that dreams are made of" and walks sadly offscreen. Even when the characters do succeed, there's a moment toward the end when their striving comes to nothing and they have only their respect for one another as reward—for example, in *The African Queen* (1951), when Bogart and Hepburn embrace and collapse on the deck of their riverboat in complete exhaustion, the camera rising above the high marsh grass to show the ocean they seek is only a few feet away.

As Sarah Kozloff has pointed out in a fine essay on Huston's *The Man Who Would Be King* (1975), most of the director's best pictures are classic adventure stories that retain traces of an ideology he had absorbed in his youth, when he avidly read William Bolitho's *Twelve against the Gods: The Story of Adventure* (1929). His protagonists are individualists like Huck Finn or Ahab, quasi-outlaws in flight from women and the obligations of conventional society who are sometimes motivated by nothing more than greed. They travel into dangerous territories and risk their lives, and, like Odysseus, they occasionally survive to tell their tale (Kosloff, 193–95). In his best films Huston depicts their adventures as arbitrary, absurd, and cruel, and his detached irony separates him from the usual purveyors of Hollywood melodrama and romance. Nevertheless, he's deeply typical of one strain of both classic American literature and Hollywood because he strongly admires masculine stoicism and physical courage.

This attitude may have roots in Huston's experience. He was born in 1906 in Nevada, Missouri, a town he claimed that his grandfather won in a poker game. The son of actor Walter Huston and newspaperwoman Rhea Gore, he led an unstable and rather sickly childhood. Having survived illness, he became a vagabond, taking up risk as a style. As he grew older he gambled on horses, studied painting with an avant-garde group in Los Angeles, became an amateur boxing champion, acted on the stage in New York, and was made an honorary lieutenant in the Mexican cavalry. He then began a vocation as a writer by selling a few stories to H. L. Mencken at the *American Mercury*. Shortly after his stories were published, Huston followed his father to the movie studios. After a brief period writing scripts at Universal, he made an abortive attempt at working for Gaumont-British in England, where he quarreled with his boss and was fired. On the same day he discovered that a ticket he had bought for the Irish Sweepstakes was a winner, giving him just enough money to get his sick wife back to the

States. He remained behind, living for a time a sort of Orwellian bum's existence in London, but by the late 1930s he had moved again to Hollywood, where he quickly became an important writer at Warner Brothers, working on *Jezebel* (1938), *Juarez* (1939), *Sergeant York* (1941), and *High Sierra* (1941), among others. In 1941 he persuaded Jack Warner to let him direct his own adaptation of *The Maltese Falcon*, and that film, made at virtually the same time as *Citizen Kane*, gave him a debut almost as impressive as Orson Welles's. After directing two relatively minor pictures from other people's scripts (*In This Our Life* [1942] and *Across the Pacific* [1942]), he went to work for the U.S. Army film unit, where he enhanced his reputation with three of the least conventionally patriotic wartime documentaries, *Report from the Aleutians* (1943), *The Battle of San Pietro* (1944), and *Let There Be Light* (1945). Immediately after the war he returned to Warner and began *The Treasure of the Sierra Madre*, his second feature as writer/director and the one that brought him the greatest number of personal awards. A spare, relatively uncompromised adaptation of the Traven novel, it has a good feel for life in the Mexican provinces (much of it was shot on location in the state of Durango and the city of Tampico), a distinguished performance by Walter Huston, and a vivid, chilling portrayal of the bandit Gold Hat by Alfonso Bedoya. It's arguably Huston's most representative film, in various ways recalling *The Maltese Falcon* and looking forward to *The Man Who Would Be King*.

Huston had wanted to make a film of *The Treasure of the Sierra Madre* for some time, but Warner Brothers anticipated him by beginning an adaptation before he was demobilized from the war. (B. Traven, a writer who was relatively unknown in the United States, was paid five thousand dollars for the property; by contrast, when Walter Huston signed on he was guaranteed a minimum of fifty thousand dollars for eight weeks' work.) *Treasure* wasn't an entirely unusual project for the studio, which during the 1930s had gained a reputation for "proletarian" pictures starring tough guys like Cagney and Bogart. The studio was also associated with social-problem films, and it created an infrastructure of writers and directors who were inclined to take on unglamorous subjects. According to some sources, Robert Rossen wrote an early draft of the adaptation (see Thomson, *Biographical Dictionary*, 654), but it seems fairly safe to assume that Huston worked directly from the novel, following his usual practice and motivated by his longstanding interest in Traven, with whom he shared certain temperamental and intellectual qualities. By choosing *Treasure* he was returning to the same themes he had explored in *The Maltese Falcon*. Once again he was adapting a tough, male-oriented novel about a group of characters in search of a treasure; once again the search ends in ironic failure (Walter Huston's burst of Homeric laughter at the conclusion has the same function as Sydney Greenstreet's philosophic chuckle when he discovers the black bird is made of lead); once again the quest for riches reveals a paradoxical blend of greed, ingenuity, and resilience; and once again the behavior of a small, eccentric group at the margin of ordinary society becomes the vehicle for a satire of the culture as a whole.

By selecting Dashiell Hammett and B. Traven as the basis of his first two films as writer/director, Huston was indirectly declaring his sympathy with a strain of naturalism and left-existentialism that runs through modern American literature from Stephen Crane and Theodore Dreiser to the era of the Popular Front. The special appeal of his early pictures lay not merely in their gritty anti-Hollywood "realism" and the cleverness of their acting ensembles but in the slightly muffled allegorical criticism of social life in America derived from their sources. As Steven Marcus has observed in an essay on Dashiell Hammett, the black bird in *The Maltese Falcon* acts as a symbol or synecdoche for the history of capitalism: "Originally a piece of plunder, part of what Marx called 'primitive accumulation,' when its gold encrusted with gems is painted over, it becomes a mystified object, a commodity. . . . At the same time it is another fiction, a representation or work of art—which turns out itself to be a fake" (in Hammett, xxv). The falcon also enables Hammett to dramatize what Marcus calls a "pre-Marxist" or Hobbesian view of human relations, based on universal warfare and instinctive mistrust; hence the thieves who search for the rara avis are in deadly competition with one another, and Sam Spade's cool head, natural suspiciousness, and practical ethics are the only things that save him from a folly like theirs.

In the case of B. Traven, whose Marxist ideas were more foregrounded, the argument is similar: the treasure in the mountains has behind it a long history of colonial, Roman Catholic, and capitalist exploitation of Mexico; of little direct utility, it's nevertheless something that can be refined into a commodity. In the words of one of the prospectors, the nuggets are "just crying to you to take them out of the ground and make them shine in coins and on the fingers and necks of swell dames." When the plunder accumulates, however, it provokes a basic mistrust. "As long as there's no find," the character Howard says, "the noble brotherhood will last, but when the piles begin to grow, that's when the trouble starts." As Traven puts it in his own voice, once the gold is collected, its owners have "left the proletarian class and neared that of the property holders." They've "reached the first step by which man becomes the slave of his property."

Huston was such an admirer of Traven that he became involved in correspondence with the author during the early drafts of the screenplay, a communication that was facilitated by Paul Kohner, the literary agent in California for both men. Traven had earlier written a complete, unproduced filmscript based on his book *The Bridge in the Jungle* and was, according to Huston, prone to "digress and go into the philosophy of the camera" (Pratley, 59).Like nearly everyone who had managed to correspond with the man, Huston became curious about Traven, who was even more secretive and private than such later writers as Salinger and Pynchon and nearly as paranoid as some of the characters in his novels. Under his pen name he had published anticapitalist novels in German and English during the 1920s, and with the rise of Hitler he left Germany to live in Mexico. Some people thought he was born in Chicago, others thought he was a Pole or Scandinavian whose true name was Berick Traven Torsvan, and still others thought he was a German actor and left-anarchist named Ret Marut. Little was known about him in Hollywood except that he was a best-selling writer in Europe and Latin America and claimed to be a forty-seven-year-old U.S. citizen living as a recluse in Mexico. He never revealed what the letter "B" of his pen name stood for, and he wrote angry letters to Paul Kohner when the Warner Brothers contracts identified him as "Bruno Traven."

After their long communication about the movie script, Huston arranged a meeting with Traven in Mexico City. In an interview with Gerald Pratley, he tells this story of what transpired:

> I was in my hotel room in Mexico City and I awoke early in the morning. I'm one of those people who never locks his door wherever he is. Standing at the foot of my bed was the shadowy figure of a man. He took a card out and gave it to me. I put on the light, it was still dark, and it said, "Hal Croves, Interpreter, Acapulco and San Antonio." I said, "How do you do, Mr. Croves." Then he said, "I have a letter for you from Mr. B. Traven," and he gave me the letter, which I read. It said that he himself was unable to appear but this man knew as much about his work as he himself did and knew as much about the circumstances and the country and he would represent Traven in every way. We had conversations, Croves and I, for the few days I was in Mexico City. I gave him the script, he read it, liked what he read and said he was sure Traven would like it very much. (Pratley, 59)

Naturally Huston suspected that Hal Croves was Traven incognito, but he was never able to find out for certain. He hired Croves as technical advisor while the movie company was on location in Mexico, and when the film was released *Life* magazine ran an article comparing a candid photo of Croves on the set with another photo purporting to be a 1927 likeness of Traven. Humphrey Bogart was asked to identify the man in the older picture. "Sure, pal," the *Life* reporter quoted him as saying, "I'd know him anywhere. I worked with him for ten weeks in Mexico" (February 12, 1948). Huston was less certain because he thought the personality of Croves was inconsistent with the "generous" man he had known through the letters. "To this day I have my doubts," he told Pratley in 1977 (61). Most people today, however, would say that Bogart was correct. In the years leading up to his death Croves allowed himself to be called Traven.

Whatever assistance Huston received from Traven/Croves, *The Treasure of the Sierra Madre* was a slightly more difficult book to adapt for movies than *The Maltese Falcon* had been. With Hammett's short novel, which was already cast in dramatic form, Huston made few changes, preserving the dialogue almost verbatim. Traven, however, used the adventure of the three prospectors as a starting point for a series of digressions, giving the reader several minor stories related to the central one. These secondary stories, narrated by the characters in the main plot, create a history of Mexican society and an atmosphere of economic determinism, making the three prospectors only the latest agents in a very old process. For example, Howard tells about the legendary Aqua Verde mine, which had been discovered and worked by the ancient Aztecs. He describes the Spanish conquistadors as greedy sadists who tortured the Indian miners Inquisition-style, holding out crucifixes before their victims and giving part of the treasure to the Holy Father in Rome. Indian villages were raided to work the mine, until the Indians took revenge and massacred everyone in sight, covering over the mine entrance and leaving it hidden. A party of Americans rediscovered the treasure in 1900, but they eventually had a falling out. One of the survivors of their expedition was subsequently persuaded to try and find the mine again; when he was unable to locate the spot he was tortured by his suspicious companions, and when he returned home to Kansas his house was burned down by angry, greedy neighbors.

Huston compared Traven's digressive technique to Melville and remarked that "Traven was not a man who reduced his material to the bare essentials, the bone structure, but he was always putting on flesh" (Pratley, 60). Huston's first job was to strip away the secondary stories, reducing the novel to the short fable at its heart, which was more suitable for a feature film. His script gains over the novel in intensity and dramatic unity, but it lacks historical background and Traven's vigorously anticlerical, anticapitalist commentary. Because of structural changes, it also increases the sense of doom that presides over the prospecting expedition. The bandit Gold Hat, for instance, appears only once in the novel, in a digression about a horrifying train robbery told by Lacaud (or Cody, as Huston calls him). In the film, the prospectors themselves experience an attempted train robbery, and Gold Hat appears every time they see bandits. First Dobbs (Bogart) tries to shoot him from a train window; later, when a band of desperadoes invades the mining camp, Dobbs fires a warning shot straight into their leader's yellow sombrero; finally, having stolen his partners' goods, he encounters Gold Hat a third and fatal time, the bandit having become his nemesis. The film is therefore heavy with coincidence, and in some respects has a more obvious symbolism than Traven had intended.

Although Huston was dealing with a left-wing novel that he seems to have genuinely admired, he was willing to add material at various points in keeping with Hollywood mythology. For example, Curtin (Tim Holt), a boyish prospector, tells about his plans to use his share of the gold to buy land and raise peaches—an ambition that contrasts sharply with Dobbs's vision of expensive haberdashers, "swell cafes," and sexy dames. Resting beside a campfire, he recalls what life was like in the orchards of his youth: "One summer when I was a kid I worked as a picker in a peach harvest in the San Joaquin Valley. It sure was something. Hundreds of people—old and young—whole families working together. After the day's work we used to build big bonfires and sit around 'em and sing to guitar music, till morning sometimes. You'd go to sleep, wake up and sing, and go to sleep again. Everybody had a wonderful time." This speech, backed by Max Steiner's lush music, creates a vision of contented labor completely at odds with Traven. It conforms instead to a pastoral, puritan theme that in Hollywood is at least as old as D.W. Griffith: the most decent of the characters has a dream of rustic family life, whereas Dobbs, the most untrustworthy of the group, has a libidinous yearning for big cities and flashy women.

In a similar vein, Huston invented the sentimental episode involving the death of Cody, the fourth prospector, who walks into the mining camp just before the bandit attack. In the novel this character is not at all interested in sharing the other men's discovery; he wants to work nearby in a separate mine because he's convinced that a richer lode lies undiscovered somewhere in the mountain. He helps the other three ward off a bandit attack but then goes off to prospect alone, where he's still working when the original three leave with their riches. Howard cites him as an example of what he calls an "eternal prospector": "He can stay for ten years at the same place digging and digging, convinced that he is on the right spot.... He is sure that someday he will make the big hit.... I really feel sorry for that guy.... But you can't cure these fellers, and I suppose if somebody could cure them they wouldn't like it. They prefer to stay this way. It's their whole excuse for being alive."

Huston, like Traven, makes this fourth prospector a driven man with the slightly haunted look of a compulsive gambler, but he kills off the character and uses him for different purposes than Traven had done. Cody's death helps intensify the terror of the bandits and also provides an opportunity for Curtin to read aloud a letter discovered on the dead man's body, a device frequently used in Hollywood movies about World War II. (See Allan Dwan's *The Sands of Iwo Jima* [1949] and David Miller's *Flying Tigers* [1942]; for a noncombat movie of the period that uses the same sort of dead-man's letter, see William Wellman's *The Ox-Bow Incident* [1943].) "Little Jimmy is fine," Cody's wife writes, "but he misses his daddy almost as much as I do. I've never thought any material treasure, no matter how great, is worth the pain of these long separations." The chief difference from the typical war film is that here the letter acts as a criticism of the men's struggle rather than a validation of it. In the best Hollywood tradition, it evokes a loving wife, a family, and a warm hearth left behind, and it suggests that money can't buy happiness.

As Curtin reads the letter, he comes across a passage that seems to have been written for his ears alone: "The country is especially lovely this year. It's been a perfect spring—warm rains, hardly any frost. The upper orchard looks aflame and the lower like after a snowstorm. Everybody looks forward to big crops. I do hope you are back for the harvest." B. Traven had never suggested, as this does, that the three prospectors ought to be at home rather than out prospecting; indeed, he never suggested they could be doing anything else. Traven's itinerant laborers are in Mexico to find work, and failing that they try their hands at prospecting. Like most laboring men, they're materialists pure and simple, without the luxury of an idealism that comes with the comforts of home. Huston, however, contrasted the search for gold with a supposed "real" treasure, exemplified in the movie by the natives who adopt Howard as a medicine man and the vision of ripe orchards in Texas; just beneath the surface of a hard-boiled movie about desperate work and the failed dream of riches he inserted a rather complacent morality, turning the story farther away from a satirical history of capitalism and closer to a generalized critique of materialism. Even the end of his film is slightly less sardonic and satirical than his source, providing a sort of poetic justice for the three main characters: Dobbs, the greedy and psychopathic member of the group, ends up being murdered by bandits; Howard, the wisest and eldest, becomes a healer and demigod for a society of agricultural Indians; and Curtin is last seen bound for Texas, where he might meet Cody's widow and settle down to an idyllic life among the fruit trees.

Huston (or perhaps his producers at Warner) also softened the political impact of the story by cutting several touchy speeches, drawn mainly from Traven, that were originally intended to be used in the film. An early version of the script has Dobbs and Curtin overhear two men talking about hard times in Mexico: "I'll tell you why the boom's over," one of the men says.

"The Mexican government's going to declare all oil lands the property of the nation." In the final revised shooting script this reference to U.S. exploitation of Mexican resources is even more explicit. Dobbs remarks that the Mexican bandits "don't know what mercy is," and Howard replies, "Know why? Because they've never been shown any. If our people in the States had lived in poverty under all sorts of tyrannies for hundreds of years they'd have bred a race of bandits too, every bit as cruel and bloodthirsty. Come right down to it we are bandits of a kind. What right have we got to go looting their mountain anyway? About as much right as the foreign companies that take their oil without paying for it . . . and their silver and their copper."

This speech has been dropped from the film. Also omitted is an earlier exchange of dialogue that uses the hunt for treasure to illustrate a simple theory of economics. As the three men begin to divide their gold, Dobbs complains that he should have a larger share because he put up most of the money for the expedition. "In civilized places the biggest investor always gets the biggest return," he says. "That's one thing in favor of the wilds," Howard comments, adding, "I think you're wise not to put things on a strictly money basis, partner. Curtin might take it into his head he was a capitalist instead of a guy with a shovel and just sit back and take things easy and let you and me do all the work. He'd stand to realize a tidy sum on his investment without so much as turning his hand over. If anybody's to get more, I reckon it ought to be the one who does the most work." In the film, we have Dobbs's complaint that his share ought to be bigger, but Howard's comparison of capitalism and socialism has been cut.

All of this is not to say that *The Treasure of the Sierra Madre* is an orthodox film. Huston's ending is close enough to what Traven had written and the picture as a whole is one of the most resolutely unglamorous features produced during the heyday of the Hollywood studio system. It has practically no sex, no expressionist charm, and none of the *nostalgie de la boue* that had made *The Maltese Falcon* such a romantic pleasure to watch. *Treasure* is the story of gold before it has been mystified into objects and before it provokes the more subtle villainies of urban civilization and film noir. It's one of the few movies of the 1940s about hard labor, its most "civilized" moment occurring when two of the characters order expensive whiskey in a Mexican dive. And for a movie that takes place outdoors, it has an oddly claustrophobic effect; there's no attempt to compose an attractive landscape for the camera, the major part of the story being told through close-ups of sweaty, unshaven faces. As in *Falcon*, Huston seems more interested in the physiognomy of his players and in tight three-figure compositions than in the environment around them. One occasionally glimpses a wide vista, but only when it's absolutely necessary to the narrative, as when the three prospectors look down from their mountain and make out a group of bandits moving toward them across a scrubby desert. Half the action is shot at night, around a tiny studio-manufactured campsite, and in daylight there's nothing to look at but rocks, cactus plants, and a lonely Gila monster. Even the gold isn't pretty—in fact, much to the surprise of Dobbs and Curtin, in its natural state it is the color of mud.

The film is all the more unusual because it doesn't fit into any of the familiar Hollywood genres. Warner Brothers' advertising campaign for the original release, based on standard marketing procedures, stands in ironic relationship to the actual picture. Theater posters featured an artist's rendering of the three leading players, behind them a montage of colorful scenes purporting to be from the movie: a band of sombreroed horsemen at full gallop, their leader astride a white charger; a handsome mustachioed rider in the act of rescuing or perhaps capturing a dark-haired, big-breasted woman in a low-cut blouse. The ads vaguely suggest a western, except that Bogart wears a fedora instead of a cowboy hat and scowls out at the viewer like Duke Mantee. Elsewhere the theme of treasure was strongly emphasized, with exhibitors being advised to promote the picture through newspaper contests and "treasure hunts" for free passes. The Warner press book even suggested that theater owners could visit local banks and negotiate a display of bullion or gold coins.

Humphrey Bogart was one of Warner's major selling points; in fact, he was *Treasure*'s only major star, and without his strong backing Huston might never have been able to make the picture. In what were called the "tie-up" ads used to promote the opening of the film, he was featured in various store window displays endorsing a line of men's clothing; slickly lit photos showed him modeling topcoats, sport shirts, tuxedos, hats, and pipes—attire that could not be further from that of Fred C. Dobbs. The problem for the studio was that Bogart, who portrayed the insecure and ultimately paranoid prospector who deserts one of his companions and almost murders the other, provided no material for attractive publicity. In effect he was returning to the sort of part he was identified with in the 1930s, when he was usually cast as a cowardly heavy. In *Black Legion* (1936), for example, he plays a working-class family man, frustrated and envious of his fellow workers, who joins a Klan-style organization in order to live out his fantasies of power. Dobbs's inauthentic swagger, sour discontent, and almost childlike conversations with himself all seem to derive from this earlier character, which had been one of Bogart's most effective if least appealing roles.

But then Bogart's screen persona had always suggested the possibility that the Dobbs in him might surface at any moment. As a leading player after 1941, the year Huston helped make him a star in *The Maltese Falcon*, he usually appeared in two different guises that stood in mirror-image relation to one another. One was the heroic figure of *Casablanca* and *Key Largo*—an idealist turned momentarily cynical, an embittered loner cultivating his selfish instincts, who ends up sacrificing his own interests for the good of a community. The other was the unstable character in *Treasure* and later in *The Caine Mutiny*, a Nixonesque fellow who was generated by an exact reversal of the heroic pattern; outwardly a dedicated member of a community, a would-be idealist, he betrays the group out of selfishness, fear, and neurosis. Both character types were potentially sociopathic, but in his heroic appearances Bogart overcame anger and isolation, while in his more villainous or untrustworthy roles he was overcome by them.

In *Treasure*, Bogart is quite good at suggesting the desperation and bitterness of a man who has no job and whose hard luck is at least partly the result of his own instability. In fact, he's so unstable that James Agee described him as a distracting, potentially weak element in the story. "It is impossible to demonstrate or even to hint at the real depth of the problem, with him on hand," Agee wrote in his admiring review of the film for *The Nation*. "It is too easy to feel that if only a reasonably restrained and unsuspicious man were in his place, everything would be all right; we wouldn't even have wars" (*Agee on Film*, Vol. 1, 293). To Bogart's credit, however, both he and Huston had tried to make the character into as much a victim as a villain. The entire opening section of the film is devoted to showing the brutal determinants of his psychology and the humiliations of his typical day. He eyes a cigarette butt in the street but loses it to a Mexican boy who struts offscreen puffing smoke and holding his head cocked high. Several times he panhandles money from an American in a white suit, but he is so ashamed that he can't look his mark in the eye and doesn't realize that he's repeatedly approaching the same man (a cameo played by John Huston). First he uses the money for food and smokes, and in a cafe he encounters a ragged Mexican boy (Robert Blake) selling lottery tickets. Irritable and resentful that Mexican children have any kind of work when he doesn't, he tosses a glass of water in the boy's face; but when the boy persists with the sales talk, he relieves his guilt by buying a ticket. Later he bums enough money for a shave and a haircut, emerging with comically greased-down hair and powdered cheeks. Strolling down the street, he eyes a prostitute (some sources claim that Ann Sheridan makes a cameo appearance in this role, but a close look at the scene proves otherwise) and bums more money from the man in the white suit, who tells him, "Go occasionally elsewhere." Dobbs's constant need of cash and the resentment and pressure he feels without it are a prelude to his difficulties in the remainder of the film, where his emotional state can swing instantaneously from friendliness to distrust, from braggadocio to fear, from optimism to despair. He's always on the edge of something, and Bogart's brittle, even fragile physique and rather wild eyes suggest that he might break down at any moment.

Whatever the moral failings of this character, the film makes a persuasive case that such men exist; furthermore, Huston has tried to preserve and amplify Traven's notion that there's a bit of Dobbs in all of us. Howard, the mouthpiece for the author, repeatedly emphasizes that when money is at stake no one is to be trusted, and in an early episode of the movie we see his maxim illustrated when Dobbs and Curtin are hoodwinked by their employer, whom they are forced to fight for their wages. It's a dirty, expertly staged battle, initiated when the burly, straw-hatted boss (Barton MacLane) smashes Curtin on the head with a whiskey bottle and punches Dobbs to the floor, kicking him in the face. The two smaller men keep stumbling back into the fight, grabbing at the boss's heels and swinging often enough to start connecting, until they begin wearing their opponent down and at last empty his wallet. Later, when Dobbs wins money from the lottery and joins forces with Curtin and Howard on the gold hunt, he tries to assert his superiority over this dog-eat-dog behavior and makes a huge display of comradeship: "So put 'er there ... partner," he says to Curtin. As the two shake hands, the camera closes in on Howard, looking up at Dobbs with the knowledge of what gold can do to brotherly feeling.

After the gold has been discovered in the mountains, Huston adds a scene that's not in the novel, emphasizing the temptation confronting all three men: Dobbs is working in a mineshaft when a roof collapses; Curtin sees that his partner is trapped, but he hesitates for a moment before his better instincts prompt him to dig Dobbs out. This brief hesitation isn't mentioned in the final shooting script and is apparently one of the revisions Huston made during filming. We're probably supposed to remember it when, toward the end of the movie, Curtin denounces Dobbs for shooting him and leaving him to die. Huston gives Howard the last word: "I reckon we can't blame him too much. . . . I mean he's not a real killer as killers go. I think he's as honest as the next fellow—or almost. The mistake was in leaving you two alone in the depths of the wilderness with more'n a hundred thousand between you. . . . I'd have been tempted too." This belief in the pervasiveness of greed is ironically hinted at during the scene in which the bandits kill Dobbs. There are three bandits, just as there have been three prospectors, and the quarrel over the dead man's belongings serves to parody the action of the film as a whole: "Give me that shoe, you dirty cheat," one bandit cries in Spanish as he strips the body. "It's mine. I saw them first." "What difference is it to me who went for them first?" asks the other bandit. "I threw the stone that laid him out." Once again the acquisition of property turns men into enemies, and once again bickering over who deserves what share of the goods leads to trouble; as the bandits argue among themselves, Dobbs's pack mules almost escape.

As Howard, the grizzly prospector who controls his potential bad instincts and carries the burden of the film's message, Walter Huston has an acting problem opposite to Bogart's: he has to make the character seem authentic and believable while always being right about everything. If Dobbs is "fantastically undisciplined and troublesome," as Agee contended, then Howard is in danger of seeming impossibly wise and windy. John Huston seems to have recognized this problem, because in the early drafts of the script he marked several of Howard's speeches with the marginal notation "too long." Nevertheless, most of these speeches have been retained, and Walter Huston has dealt with them by removing his false teeth and speaking with extreme speed through his nose. Some of his longer monologues are thrown away so rapidly that it takes a couple of viewings of the film to hear them properly. But despite his underplaying he becomes the most interesting presence in the movie, a smart, spry, unpretentious old geezer whose performance is all the more remarkable considering that it could easily have degenerated into a Gabby Hayes sort of cuteness.

Notice also that while Howard is supposed to be a disarmingly wise, honest fellow, he has a rather clever theatrical sense that suggests another side to his character; this is evident in the way he gathers an audience in the Oso Negro flophouse with his tales of gold, or in the way he "cures" an Indian child who has nearly drowned. John Huston has staged this latter scene in an area that resembles a Greek theater, a dramatically lit stage surrounded by ranks of Indian men and women shown in Eisensteinian montage. When Howard lifts the child in his toughened old hands, which are his most expressive feature, it's easy to see how the Indians could worship and adopt him as their medicine man. In the corresponding scene in the novel, Traven comments that Howard "admitted to himself that the boy if left entirely alone might, perhaps, have come to just as well," and in the film it becomes clear that the old prospector enjoys his pretense of power. His reward—the most one could expect, even with piles of gold—is shown by a few witty, idyllic images: We see him reclining on a hammock, cooled by shade trees while behind him naked children dive and splash in a forest pool. He munches a watermelon, spitting the seeds into a girl's hand, and takes a sip of tequila. The natives bring him gifts, including a caged bird and a squealing baby pig. A pretty girl lights his cigarette and rubs his beard affectionately. He's an early version of Peachy and Danny in *The Man Who*

Would Be King, except that his pleasure in being worshiped by the colonized tribes is never allowed to develop into tragic hubris.

The minor roles in the film are also vividly and skillfully portrayed, even if they make up an improbable, neatly contrasting set of types. At one point Warner Brothers intended to cast Burgess Meredith and Ronald Reagan as Curtin and Cody, but Tim Holt and Bruce Bennett are better choices, the one suggesting a burly farm boy and the other a likable and intelligent but obsessed man with tragic undertones to his character. Of all the secondary players, however, Alfonso Bedoya in the role of Gold Hat is the most important. Bedoya had appeared in two of the best Mexican movies of the 1940s, *Doña Bárbara* (Fernando de Fuentes, 1943) and *La perla* (*The Pearl*, Emilio Fernández, 1945), and Huston was no doubt familiar with his work. He has a thick accent and a slight awkwardness that gives a feeling of authenticity to Gold Hat, who is a simple-minded and childlike but cunning fellow, able to switch mercurially from a con man's charm to a primal ruthlessness. Playing a man who is in one sense a bad actor, Bedoya always lets us know that he might drop his grin at any moment, revealing violence underneath a pretended calm. Huston reportedly coached him very little, leaving him confused and insecure, and this anxiety seems to have made him all the more contradictory and frightening; the expression on his chubby, slightly grotesque face never quite matches his nervous eyes or the tone of his speech, which is alternately fawning, honey-sweet, and psychotic. Photographer Ted McCord's close-ups of Bedoya are uniformly excellent. Consider the big, low-angle shot when the outlaw leader discovers Dobbs alone and unprotected near a water hole, a sleepy smile spreading across his face and light filtering through the holes in his sombrero like flashing gold. Later, when the Federales toss him in jail prior to his execution, he tries to snarl and spit through the bars of his prison, but his eyes seem as dazed and fearful as those of a maddened animal. On top of everything else, he gives a memorable reading of one of the most famous (and often misquoted) lines in Hollywood history: "I don't have to show you any stinking badges!"

By all accounts Huston's method of dealing with most of his actors was almost nondirective. He was skilled at the art of casting (Sterling Hayden and Louis Calhern as a safecracker and his fence in *The Asphalt Jungle* [1950], Audie Murphy as the boy soldier in *The Red Badge of Courage* [1951], and everybody in *The Maltese Falcon*), and when he had chosen the players well the characterizations seemed to evolve without much intervention. He often let the actors block their own movements. One of the pleasures of watching his movies comes from the body language of the actors, who often form little tableaux, always telegraphing their function by the way they walk, stand, or sit. James Agee was fascinated with the way the three prospectors in *Treasure* behave when they discover the body of Cody after the bandit attack: Bogart, the would-be tough guy, cocks one foot up on a rock and tries to look at the corpse as casually as if it were fresh-killed game. Tim Holt, the essentially decent young man, comes behind him and, innocently and unaware of it, clasps his hands in the respectful manner of a boy who used to go to church. Walter Huston, the experienced old man, steps quietly behind both, leans to the dead man as professionally as a doctor to a patient, and gently rifles him for papers.

There are other examples of this sort of choreography throughout the film, as when Cody first walks into the campsite: Bruce Bennett has a calm but slightly weary intensity, squatting on his haunches in an unthreatening position that allows freedom of movement should any trouble develop; Tim Holt and Walter Huston sit by the campfire, Huston facing the newcomer with his hands on show, affecting total casualness; and Bogart paces nervously in a semicircle just outside the group, uncertain what to do but hankering after violence. The most effective instance of group behavior comes near the end, in the frightening scene when the three bandits discover Bogart alone with the gold. While Bedoya questions Bogart the other two killers look him up and down, scurrying about like curious monkeys. One of them puts on Bogart's hat and lifts his pants leg to examine his shoes; the other slides rump first down a slope, stopping at his quarry's feet and sitting there, looking up and waiting for the kill.

Although Huston is generally regarded as an unobtrusive, almost styleless director, images like these show that he had a fondness for formal, rather static groupings that create simple visual statements. The groupings may have been achieved without obvious coaching, but they are tightly framed and arise inevitably out of the kinds of stories Huston liked to tell, which are fables with clearly defined functions for the characters. He said that he thought of the camera as another actor on the set, but in *Treasure* this actor is more observer than agent, more auditor than narrator. Huston frequently shows violent action obliquely, as when the Mexican bandits are hidden from view by a wall when they line up before a firing squad. It's a mistake, however, to regard this indirection or self-effacement as an "invisible" style because it has a studied casualness and a clearly expressive purpose.

The special look of Huston's films seems to me to come from his fondness for authentic locales, offbeat and unglamorous faces, and rather tightly composed shots of heads and bodies in conversation. Hence Ted McCord's sharp deep-focus photography in *Treasure* is seldom used to create dynamic spaces or long takes; Huston was more interested in slightly documentary-style close-ups that record the lines on an actor's face or the tatters in a costume. He evokes a Mexican town, a sleepy cantina, and an Indian village without using complex establishing shots or sweeping camera movements, relying instead on natural lighting and carefully selected extras to lend the images believability. Despite the conservative way he shoots and edits, there remains in his work an unusually strong ethnographic quality, putting him more in the tradition of Flaherty, Eisenstein, and the neorealists than in the line of classic Hollywood directors. Although some of his best films (*The Maltese Falcon, The Asphalt Jungle*) were made almost entirely inside a studio, he obviously enjoyed primitive or faraway locations, and he embraced Hollywood's postwar movement away from back-lot settings; *Treasure* was, in fact, one of the first Hollywood features shot in large part on location in a foreign country.

The sense of a particular place in *Treasure* struck many of the contemporary reviewers as the film's most conspicuous virtue. Bosley Crowther's review in the *New York Times* said that Huston had "resolutely applied the same sort of ruthless realism that was evident in his documentaries of war" (January 24, 1948). James Agee, who wrote the best-known accounts of the film for *Time, Life,* and *The Nation,* repeatedly stressed the artistry of McCord's camera and the truthfulness of the settings. At the other extreme were the trade journals like *Daily Variety,* which tried to assess the picture according to its box-office potential, categorizing it in generic terms as "action stuff with heavy masculine appeal" (January 15, 1948). In retrospect, the truth seems to lie somewhere between these opposing views. *Treasure* is unorthodox by some standards, traditional by others. Huston was a director who found expressive, sometimes even Hollywoodish, material outside the studio, and, despite the relaxed air he assumed on the set and in interviews, he was neither a casual witness to the acting nor a pure "realist" (whatever that term signifies). Instead he was a somewhat didactic storyteller, many of whose films are stamped with his implied personality. Within the limits of his taste and technique he could be powerfully effective. The strengths of his best work—unpretentious intelligence, economy, and witty observation of a basically cruel society—can be seen throughout *The Treasure of the Sierra Madre,* a film that shows how good he could be when he had respect for his source, a reluctance to compromise too much, and the same mixture of luck, courage, and tenacity that can be found in some of his characters.

The Return of *The Dead*

My chief concern here is John Huston's 1987 film adaptation of James Joyce's "The Dead," but I can't resist approaching the topic somewhat indirectly, by means of a trivia quiz about Joyce and the movies. Here are three questions and their respective answers:

1. What famous Hollywood gangster film contains a couple of heavies named Buck Mulligan and Blazes Boylan, two of the most unsympathetic characters in *Ulysses*?

Answer: Josef von Sternberg's *Underworld* (1927), an Academy Award–winning silent picture scripted by Ben Hecht, who was an admirer of Joyce.

2. When Darryl F. Zanuck briefly contemplated a movie version of *Ulysses* in the 1940s, whom did he propose as the director?

Answer: John Ford, who was authentically Irish and had made poetic-realist films based on Eugene O'Neill, John Steinbeck, and Graham Greene. It's difficult to imagine, however, what Ford would have made of the novel.

3. What celebrated director besides John Huston made a movie inspired by "The Dead"?

Answer: Roberto Rossellini, who filmed *Voyage to Italy* in 1953. Several distinguished filmmakers and critics, among them Eric Rohmer, Paul Schrader, and Robin Wood, have named this film as one of the ten best of all time, although none of them calls attention to its many literary allusions. The connection between *Voyage to Italy* and Joyce's "The Dead" has been pointed out by Luciana Bohne in "Rossellini's *Viaggio in Italia:* A Variation on a Theme by Joyce." In interviews Rossellini never mentioned the allusions to "The Dead," and Bohne speculates that he may have been ignorant of them. She attributes the obvious Joycean parallels to Vitaliano Brancati, Rossellini's co-scriptwriter.

The answer to the third trivia question deserves a bit of elaboration and comment. *Voyage to Italy* tells the story of a British couple named Mr. and Mrs. Joyce (George Sanders and Ingrid Bergman), who visit Italy to settle the estate of a dead uncle named Homer. The Joyce's marriage has serious problems, which are exacerbated by the heat and strangeness of Naples. Mrs. Joyce explores museums and the ruins at Pompeii, as if drawn to the Neapolitan cult of the dead. At one point, seated on a veranda in the sunlight, she turns to her husband and begins telling him a story about an unconsummated love affair she once had with a young poet:

SHE: He read [his poetry] to me. I even copied some. "Temple of the spirit, / No longer body but pure ascetic images, / Compared to which mere thought seems flesh, heavy, dim." He wrote them in Italy during the war.

HE: I never knew you were such great friends.

SHE: I knew him before I met you.

HE: Were you in love with him?

SHE: No, but we got on very well together. I saw a great deal of him. Then he got desperately ill. I couldn't even visit him. For almost a year I didn't see him, until the eve of our wedding, the night before I left for London. I was packing my bags when I heard the sound of pebbles on my window. The rain was so heavy I couldn't see anyone outside. So I ran out into the garden just as I was. And there he stood. He was shivering with cold. He was so strange and romantic. Maybe he wanted to prove to me that in spite of the high fever he had braved the rain to see me. Or maybe he wanted to die.

HE: How very poetic. Much more poetic than his verses.

Anyone who knows "The Dead" will recognize strong similarities between this scene and a crucially important conversation between Gabriel and Gretta Conroy near the end of Joyce's story; but *Voyage to Italy* isn't an adaptation—it's probably best described as a loose, partial appropriation of certain themes in Joyce. (It originated not with "The Dead" but with Rossellini's attempt to adapt *Duo*, a novel by Colette for which he was unable to obtain the screen rights.) Nevertheless, it's in some ways a more fundamentally modernist and Joycean project than John Huston's respectful, nearly straightforward adaptation. It uses Joyce in much the same way as Joyce himself used Homer, Dante, and Shakespeare: it seems to have been made by cunning, strategically silent artists who acknowledge their sources through sly allusions, planting clues for the cognoscenti and then going on to fashion an "autonomous" work. Like Joyce, they're somewhat cryptic and invisible storytellers. *Voyage to Italy* ends with a Joycean epiphany (staged against the background of a religious procession), but it's a relatively plotless and in some ways enigmatic film; even in its most lyrical moments it remains untendentious, disinterested, as if it were leaving the significance of events up to us.

In contrast, Huston announces his source and offers a sensitive, unfailingly intelligent translation of Joyce into visual and dramatic form. Most of the dialogue in his film is taken directly from Joyce's text, and whenever new speeches are invented—particularly in the first ten or fifteen minutes, when a crowd of characters assembles for the Misses Morkans' annual dinner and dance—it's difficult to detect where Joyce's words leave off and the adaptation begins. The cast of largely Irish actors inhabits its roles with conviction, and the mise-en-scène conveys an appropriate mixture of slightly down-at-heels gentility and impending death. At one point the film departs considerably from the story, creating a new character named Mr. Grace (Sean McClory), who recites a Celtic revival poem called "The Grief of a Young Girl's Heart," translated from the Gaelic by Lady Gregory, a writer whom Joyce particularly disliked. The recitation, however, is entirely in keeping with the themes and milieu of Joyce's story, and Huston uses it effectively, cutting to the different reactions of several people in the audience and then showing the Morkans' young housekeeper, Lilly, standing unobtrusively in the background during the last verses

And yet the Huston film is almost more Dickensian than Joycean in the vividly legible quality of its story and characterizations. In this version, the protagonist Gabriel Conroy (Donal McCann) is the very model of solicitude and bourgeois reserve, living a life of well-meaning but fatal compromise; Gretta Conroy (Anjelica Huston) is a passionate woman committed to a dull marriage, constantly and visibly preoccupied by distant music; Freddy Malins (Donal Donnelly) is a sad but somewhat flamboyant drunkard, his role expanded to lend moments of comic relief; and Aunt Julia Morkan (Cathleen Delany) is a dreadfully bad singer who elicits egregiously hypocritical applause from her guests. These and all the other characters, whom Joyce presented in much more ambiguous terms, are as "readable" as the actors in a good melodrama. At the same time, things that Joyce left unsaid or open to conjecture are fully explained. For example, near the beginning of the film one of the arriving guests informs us that the Morkans' party takes place on the Feast of the Epiphany—even though Joyce scholars themselves didn't realize this possibility until 1965, when Florence Walzl pointed it out in an essay published in *PMLA*. As a result of such clarifications, additions, and emendations, a masterpiece of high modernism is turned into something more immediately accessible (though by no means contemptible), like a well-made movie.

The differences between the story and the film were partly the result of John Huston's own stylistic choices, but they were also determined by his and Tony Huston's attempt to achieve a straightforward adaptation. Ironically, any effort at rendering Joyce in another medium entails a series of assumptions and procedures that are fundamentally un-Joycean. The problem is exacerbated by the canonical status of the original story, which weighs heavily on an adaptation, forcing it to move toward clarity and literalism. (As Geoffrey Nowell-Smith has observed in another context, the culture industry may not kill off high art, but it often embalms high-art corpses ["On Kiri Te Kanawa, Judy Garland, and the Culture Industry," 70–79].) Joyce's *Dubliners*, the collection of stories that ends with "The Dead," is on required reading lists for countless undergraduate English classes; given such a ticket-buying constituency, a reverent adaptation is necessary.

Some of the difficulties and constraints encountered by Huston's project have been suggested in Joyce scholar Clive Hart's useful and elegantly written *Joyce, Huston, and the Making of "The Dead,"* a pamphlet consisting of a critical commentary and three appendices: a chart illustrating Hart's conception of how the stories in *Dubliners* are organized; selected passages from the third draft of Tony and John Huston's screenplay; and the full text of Lady Gregory's 1901 translation of "The Grief of a Girl's Heart," the poem read by Mr. Grace in the film. Hart's discussion of Joyce and Huston is itself divided into two parts: in the first, Hart comments on the important relationship between "The Dead" and the other stories in Dubliners, arguing that the book can be read as "a kind of Bildungsroman" (7); in the second, he describes his own work as academic advisor to Huston's production company, offering a balanced assessment of the completed picture.

Hart is the author of an important early book on *Finnegans Wake* and of numerous essays and anthologies on Joyce's other writings; he's credited in the film as the official representative of the James Joyce Estate (a notoriously protective and obstructive entity where scholarship is concerned) and as a literary consultant for John and Tony Huston. His job, as he explains it, was "to ensure that this film prove worthy of Joyce in general and that it should not, in particular, so misrepresent the tone and spirit of the story that Joyce's name could not be associated with it" (10–11). Despite his official role as guardian of Joyce's reputation, however, he didn't attempt to police every aspect of the production. He wasn't allowed to comment after the third draft of the screenplay, and he views the finished product more like an interested bystander than a participant. He is, in fact, representative of an influential sector of the film's audience: this adaptation of "The Dead" wants to be received as a kind of translation or accurate representation, and it solicits the attention of those literary critics who might be inclined to make judgments about Huston's performance as an interpreter of a known and respected text.

How well does Huston perform? The question is likely to provoke a variety of responses, depending on the values and impressions of individual viewers; it's nevertheless a question worth asking because it requires us to focus on details. We might begin by observing that Joyce wrote a good deal of vivid dialogue, and in that respect at least his stories can be scripted with relative ease. (Irish television once dramatized some stories from *Dubliners*, and the results were impressive.) But as Hart observes, Huston needed to take certain liberties; he was addressing a relatively broad public, unfamiliar with Dublin in the period, and in any case transformation of prose fiction into another medium is impossible without "fresh and substantial artistic endeavor" (11).

To appreciate some of the problems Huston faced, we need only consider Joyce's first sentence: "Lilly, the caretaker's daughter, was literally swept off her feet." Two linguistic games have been insinuated into this plain-looking statement. The first involves a kind of controlled polysemy, akin to punning: Lilly, the Morkans' housemaid, has the same name as the flower of death, and because her name occurs at the opening of a piece called "The Dead," it makes the next important word, "caretaker," suggest "undertaker." The second game is rather like parody or pastiche and can be seen in the deliberate misuse of "literally." (If the maid were literally swept off her feet, she would be lying on the floor, or perhaps dead.) The usage here, which belongs to the kind of language Lilly herself would use, is an instance of what Hugh Kenner in *Joyce's Voices* (1978) has described as the "Uncle Charles principle," or the tendency of Joyce's third-person narration to take on the ambiance of character, as if it were oscillating between objective commentary and subjective monologue.

Huston's film never attempts a play of meanings at the level of the cinema; it simply ignores the problem, finding ways to reproduce the story's more conventional symbolism. And on this symbolic or expressive level, the film is often brilliantly successful. Without resorting to clichés of gothic or Germanic lighting, production designers Stephen Grimes and Dennis Washington and photographer Fred Murphy give the festive occasion in the Morkan sisters' household a slightly funereal aura. (Their work is enhanced by the fact that the party in the film is smaller than the one in Joyce's story, with no young people in attendance.) The warmly crowded rooms contain polished hardwood floors, lace tablecloths, and fine Victorian furnishings; even so, they look somewhat bare and decayed, precisely registering the economic condition of the Morkan sisters and imposing a stiff, circumspect gaiety on the proceedings. Huston also has at least one distinct advantage over Joyce: he can directly present the public speeches and various forms of music that are so important to the emotional effect of the story. In the film, Gabriel Conroy's florid after-dinner rhetoric is enhanced by a lyrical Irish accent, and Mary Jane Morkan's performance of her "Academy piece" has exactly the right degree of deadly virtuosity. On the other hand, Aunt Julia's rendition of "Arrayed for the Bridal" shouldn't have been made to sound so much like a strangled cat. To his credit, Huston softens the effect by having the camera discreetly exit the performance and drift upstairs to Julia's bedroom, where we see a montage of souvenirs from her youth. The counterpoint between the song and the various objects is as close as the film comes to the complex, free-associative imagery typical of Joyce's inner monologues, and it skillfully blends sentiment with intimations of death.

Unfortunately, on several other occasions the film is unable to capture the full effect of what might seem the story's most impressive visual details. Here, for instance, is the scene in which Gabriel Conroy watches Gretta listening to a voice upstairs singing "The Lass of Aughrim":

> He stood still in the gloom of the hall, trying to catch the air that the voice was singing and gazing up at his wife. There was grace and mystery in her attitude as if she were a symbol of something. He asked himself what is a woman standing on the stairs in the shadow, listening to distant music, a symbol of. If he were a painter he would paint her in that attitude. Her blue felt hat would show off the bronze of her hair against the darkness and the dark panels of her skirt would show off the light ones. *Distant Music* he would call the picture if he were a painter.

Anjelica Huston's performance as Gretta is one of the glories of *The Dead;* nevertheless, the film's version of the scene on the stairway is relatively pedestrian. Although we see the beautiful Gretta from Gabriel's perspective, we don't enter fully into his psychology and share his aestheticized vision, his tendency to see his wife as a decorative object or "symbol" in the somewhat kitschy, late-Victorian genre painting he would no doubt specialize in if only he were a painter. We also never sense the "keen pang of lust" that overcomes him shortly afterward, and as a result the climax of the film lacks a proper feeling of tumescence lapsing into detumescence and dramatic crisis.

Without pervasive offscreen commentary, any filming of "The Dead" is likely to seem more about Gretta than about Gabriel; partly for that reason, as Hart notes, the picture seems "more engaged than the story, more immediately poignant, more concerned with realism" (16). But these qualities can also be attributed to John Huston's personal attitudes and temperament. Although he directed a variety of successful literary adaptations, he almost inevitably transformed his films into ironic fables with clearly defined characters. He can be described as a realist in part because he adhered to the patterns of classical narrative and in part because he liked authentic locales and offbeat, unglamorous faces; but what I've elsewhere described as his quasi-documentary or ethnographic style often serves a didactic purpose. As an example in *The Dead,* notice the brightly lit dinner scene when Mr. Browne (Daniel O'Herlihy) becomes drunk, when Gabriel makes his bombastic speech honoring the "Three Graces of the Dublin musical world," and when a whole range of social and religious tensions threaten to surface. Huston's close-ups and tight framings of little groups during this sequence achieve a sort of compassionate harshness, as if he were revealing the dark underside of a social comedy and exposing the skull beneath each character's skin.

The only point at which I would disagree substantially with Clive Hart's judgment of the adaptation is when he interprets the relationship between "The Dead" and the other stories in *Dubliners.* Hart claims that the volume has "two main structural patterns, one linear, the other cyclic," and that "the linear sequence goes some way beyond the four famous stages Joyce enunciated in a letter: childhood, adolescence, maturity, public life." The book as a whole, he argues, resembles "a novel of personal development, in which the main character frequently changes name and sex" (7). I'm skeptical of this reading. Admittedly, Joyce's work in this period is poised somewhere between a fin-de-siècle romanticism and a radical modernism, and it's quite possible to find a pattern of "growth" in the movement of the stories in *Dubliners* from youth to maturity, from private to public, from celibacy to heterosexual marriage. Nevertheless, Hart's stress on the Bildungsroman seems to me to impose a traditional master plot on a book that has a variety of thematic relationships and structural possibilities. In my view, his reading has more in common with Huston than with Joyce, even though his interpretation of "The Dead" is different from the one offered by the film.

Narrative realism seeks to give us a feeling of centeredness, progress, and meaningful closure. Hart finds all these qualities in *Dubliners,* which he analyzes like a single story leading up to a relatively "positive" conclusion. In order to substantiate his analysis, he searches for linearity and circularity—a pattern of forward movement and return that enables us to compare the ending of the volume with the beginning, noting any changes that have occurred. He finds this novelistic pattern in the first and last paragraphs, where a boy's fear of paralysis ("the name of some maleficent and sinful being") is echoed in Gabriel Conroy's fear of Michael Furey ("some impalpable and vindictive being"). At the very end of "The Dead," he claims, "the sense of sinfulness and of its weaker echo, vindictiveness, is purged away, to leave only a mysterious receptivity." The result is a sense of "equanimity" and a story of "the growth of love through a transcending of the self" (10).

Hart's interpretation of the story is no less realistic in style than Huston's. Huston, too, was insistent on achieving a sense of narrative unity by asserting an ultimate meaning, although he was concerned with only a single story and he chose to place the emphasis on a different theme. He believed that "The Dead" was about "love, marriage, passion, and death," and he was more critical than Hart was of Gabriel Conroy's failings (Vestron Pictures press kit, 2). A committed romantic, Huston was on the side of the passionate Gretta Conroy and Michael Furey; unlike Joyce, he was also highly sympathetic toward the provincial west of Ireland and the Irish nationalism of Molly Ivors (Maria McDermottroe), who teases and disconcerts Gabriel during the party. He seems to have agreed with Gabriel's troubled perception that it's better to "pass boldly into that other world, in the full glory of some passion" than to "fade and wither dismally with age," and he acted out that belief in the very making of the film, which was his last.

Huston's film therefore depends on a special form of what might be called romantic-realist intertextuality, different from either Rossellini's *Voyage to Italy* or Joyce's short story. *The Dead* is a careful adaptation, grounded in an attempt to find a faithful match between words and images; it was heavily marketed to college audiences, and its American distributors sent out a press release to educators in English departments around the country announcing that it would "assume a prominent position in the curriculum of Literature into Film" (Vestron Pictures press kit, 1). But the adaptation also points toward a narrative about Huston himself, whose family collaborated in the production as a tribute to him, and whose autobiography was emphasized in reviews and publicity. Reviewers of the film repeatedly stressed Huston's long residence in Ireland, his encounter with Joyce's writings at an early age, his distinguished career as an adapter of literary texts, and his impending death. As an adaptation and as the work of an auteur, the film is designed as a kind of memorial. As such, it aims to create a strong feeling of closure, very close in spirit if not in moral tone to Hart's view of Joyce.

Huston's romantic realism has virtues. Certainly no major Hollywood director has ever devised a more remarkable ending to his career, and I find myself continually moved by the sense of love that permeates *The Dead*—not only the love for Joyce's fiction, but also the familial love shared among John, Tony, and Anjelica Huston. Even so, I'm disappointed by the film's closing moments. Clive Hart believes that the images of snow should have been more effective, less like "an amateur photographer's shots shown to neighbors" (18). For my own part, I think Huston should have found a more unorthodox, cinematic equivalent to the story. In the early drafts of the screenplay Tony Huston had suggested an impressionistic or subjective technique in which we would have seen images of Michael Furey standing in the rain. Perhaps a better idea would have been to follow Joyce's stage directions, showing Gabriel lying down in bed beside Gretta with his head by her feet, slowly drifting off to sleep in the pose of a graveyard sculpture. An even more important touch, however, would have been to allow Gabriel's inner monologue to evolve into a less familiar kind of voice. I miss the eerie tapping upon the window that calls Gabriel on his "journey westward." Most of all, I miss the great beauty and strange linguistic effects of Joyce's last paragraphs, which depart from the usual techniques of realist fiction and create something quite different from the spatial and temporal logic of ordinary cinema:

> His own identity was fading out into a grey impalpable world: the solid world itself, which these dead had one time reared and lived in, was dissolving and dwindling. Yes, the newspapers were right: snow was general all over Ireland. It was falling on every part of the dark central plain, on the treeless hills, falling softly on the Bog of Allen and, farther westward, softly falling into the dark mutinous Shannon waves. It was falling, too, upon every part of the lonely churchyard on the hill where Michael Furey lay buried. It lay thickly drifted on the crooked crosses and headstones, on the spears of the little gate, on the barren thorns. His soul swooned slowly as he heard the snow falling faintly through the universe and faintly falling, like the descent of their last end, upon all the living and the dead.

Here we might echo a question that Erich Auerbach once asked about narration in Virginia Woolf's *To the Lighthouse:* exactly who speaks these lines? We can't give a completely satisfactory answer to the question. Joyce's language (which the film transforms into a Hamlet-like internal monologue, spoken by Gabriel) was designed to frustrate the reader's attempts to find a clear source or point of view; it combines the "Uncle Charles principle" with isolated motifs gathered from elsewhere in the story and sometimes repeats or alludes to statements that were made earlier by characters other than Gabriel, as in "the newspapers were right: snow was general all over Ireland." In other words, it hovers between an evocation of Gabriel's consciousness and a more decentered effect representing a collective voice, or nobody's voice.

Where Clive Hart finds transcendence in this passage, I find dissolution, anticipating the "nat language" of *Finnegans Wake*. I agree with T.J. Clark, who, in a commentary on modern painting, observes that the modernist project as a whole was marked by a kind of death of signification: "The practice in question is extraordinary and desperate: it presents itself as a work of interminable and absolute decomposition, a work which is always pushing 'medium' to its limits—to its ending—to the point where it breaks or evaporates or turns back into mere unworked material" (184). The conclusion to "The Dead" has exactly those qualities. Balanced amazingly between lyricism and deconstruction, it frustrates our attempt to find a totalizing meaning, and in that sense is quite different from Huston's impressive but conventional adaptation. Although, having registered this complaint, let me add that we're unlikely ever to have a better film based on "The Dead." Huston saved one of his most ambitious and daunting undertakings for the very last, and with characteristic intelligence he passed boldly into that other world.

PART III

In Defense of Criticism

· · · · ·

In its Winter 1961/62 issue, *Film Quarterly* invited five eminent figures—Pauline Kael, Stanley Kauffmann, Gavin Lambert, Dwight Macdonald, and Jonas Mekas—to comment on their choices of films of the year. The five were writing at a significant moment: the *nouvelle vague* had recently hit the shores of San Francisco and a seismic shift was rumbling beneath U.S. culture. Hollywood was losing some of its popularity, not only among sophisticated urban audiences, who were infatuated with European art cinema, but also among ostensibly ordinary viewers in small towns, who had turned en masse toward what FCC chairman Newton Minow, in a much-publicized speech of 1961, called the "vast wasteland" of network television. Of all the films shown in the United States during that year, the ones that received the most praise from *Film Quarterly*'s quintet of judges were foreign productions. By far the favorite was Michelangelo Antonioni's *L'Avventura*, with Federico Fellini's *La Dolce Vita* and Jean-Luc Godard's *Breathless* tied for a distant second. Among the pictures receiving at least one vote were Luis Buñuel's *The Young One* and *Viridiana*, John Cassavetes's *Shadows*, Shirley Clarke's *The Connection*, John Huston's *The Misfits*, Nicholas Ray's *King of Kings*, Karel Reisz's *Saturday Night and Sunday Morning*, Robert Rossen's *The Hustler*, François Truffaut's *Shoot the Piano Player*, and Robert Wise's *West Side Story*. There was no mention of three of my own favorites—Samuel Fuller's *Underworld, U.S.A.*, Marlon Brando's *One-Eyed Jacks*, and Jerry Lewis's *The Ladies Man*—but you can't have everything.

I believe that discussion of the best films of the year was a good idea in 1961 and is still a good idea today. So in 2007, when Rob White, then editor of *Film Quarterly*, invited me to write a "Films of the Year" column in which I could list and comment on my ten favorite films, I accepted with alacrity. I wrote the column for four years and might still be doing it today except for a need to attend to other projects. It perhaps seems quaint for an academic like myself to undertake such a job because today's university teachers have grown suspicious of canons and any attempt to educate taste; to behave otherwise runs the risk of being called a cultural gatekeeper or worse. I acknowledge that my judgments, like everyone else's, are always provisional and subjective, often undergoing modifications or radical changes as time passes. I also belong to a particular demographic, or what, in academic jargon, is termed a "user group," and it's a safe bet that my list of favorite films in any given year isn't the same as yours. But I very much support criticism written in the spirit of what Rob White has called "advocacy," and I'm convinced that to rid the discourse on art of critical evaluation is also to rid it of politics—or at least to act as if aesthetics had no political valence. I agree with Peter Wollen that evaluative criteria shouldn't be regarded as fixed, timeless, and universal; but I also agree with him that "to go to the cinema, to read books or to listen to music is to be a partisan" (*Signs and Meaning*, rev. ed., 172).

Good criticism, like good art, isn't necessarily about politics but always has broadly political implications. Criticism certainly hasn't disappeared from today's academic world (I've referenced many of its writers throughout this book), but its importance in the film studies curriculum is waning. This is a glaring irony, because the humanities today usually defend themselves against the encroachment of professional schools by arguing that humanistic disciplines are uniquely qualified to teach "critical thinking." The term is uncomfortably reminiscent of the Victorian philosopher Jeremy Bentham, a utilitarian whose ideas ruled the first great age of industrial capitalism and still rule business schools, corporations, and the increasingly corporate administrations of universities. I worry about the resurgence of such thinking and about the death of humanism. Since the 1980s, most state-supported institutions of higher education in the United States (without which I wouldn't have been educated) have steadily lost government support and become largely dependent on private endowments; they spend most of their money supplementing inadequate government funding for practical science in hopes that somebody on their faculty will invent or discover something that brings in royalties. Meanwhile, the humanities, which cost much less to teach than the sciences, are under increasing pressure from administrations to be more cost-effective and practically relevant. University departments of humanities were more secure in the days of liberal humanism, which, for all its unquestionable limitations, provided an ideologically coherent justification for teaching art and criticism and proposed an alternative set of values to the world of getting and spending.

Today the humanities are in danger of losing their soul. Academic film studies has tended to focus on formal systems, industrial history, fandom, and identity politics—essential topics without which good criticism can't be written, but topics that don't engage directly with questions of art and artists. In one sense this development is understandable, even apart from the administrative turn away from the humanities. Academics have long cultivated a disinterested approach to the organization of knowledge, and where the teaching of formal poetics is concerned, it's often best to keep judgment in abeyance, concentrating on the workings of artistic systems and techniques rather than quarrels about the politics or merits of particular cases. I nevertheless think that evaluative criticism needs to be encouraged more, and I miss the days before the full-scale development of film studies, when film was made exciting and relevant by virtue of critical writing and debates over value.

In the academic world of the English-speaking countries, the best representatives of the kind of writing I have in mind were Robin Wood and Raymond Durgnat. Wood was indebted to Cambridge critic and teacher F.R. Leavis, an imposing figure who developed methods of practical literary criticism and voiced moralistic, and sometimes intimidatingly severe, opinions, demoting certain authors and championing others (Milton and Shelley were down, Eliot and Lawrence were up). An advocate of the highest literary standards, Leavis was contemptuous of movies and might seem an odd master for Wood to follow. But Leavis can also be viewed as a distant ancestor of the cultural studies movement in the contemporary academy. Popular-culture critic Richard Hoggart, literary critic Raymond Williams, and film critics Andrew Britton and Robin Wood all belonged to a "left-Leavisite" strand of British thinking that was against industrial standardization or "Americanization," but *for* close analysis and discriminating judgment of popular fiction, movies, and television.

The influence of Leavis's style can be seen everywhere in Wood, who combined ideological critique with a strong auteurist bent. In comparison, Durgnat, who taught for a while in an art school, was less moralistic, more aligned with the taste of the French critics at *Positif,* more interested in social class, and more attracted to anarchic comedy, surrealist eroticism, and pop culture. Durgnat wrote penetrating analyses of Buñuel and Vidor, and his uncondescending study of the low-budget sci-fi picture *This Island Earth* (1955), collected in his book *Films and Feelings,* belongs in my pantheon of the greatest essays on film. He also wrote a nearly comprehensive, unfortunately out-of-print volume on Hitchcock that makes good counterarguments to Wood's better-known book on the director.

Criticism of this kind is somewhat rare in contemporary academics, and it is also becoming rare in print journalism, where a handful of movie reviewers once had importance as public intellectuals. Such reviewers weren't in the business of providing quotes for advertisements: they brought historical perspective and literary skill to their work; they were interested in covering small films as well as big ones; and they didn't believe that entertainment and art are necessarily opposed. Critical voices of their kind still exist, but today's media environment makes it relatively difficult for them to be widely heard. As Manohla Dargis has pointed out, mainstream print media pay even less attention to serious films than they did in the past: "It's hard to imagine the kind of passionate debate about films like *Last Year at Marienbad* and even *Blue Velvet* going on for movies like *Once upon a Time in Anatolia* except in the more rarefied reaches of the blogosphere, which is good (sometimes) if also an index of the marginalization of serious cinema and the discussion about it" (*New York Times*, January 20, 2012).

Good critical discussion can of course be found in print journals such as *Film Quarterly, Cineaste,* and *Cinema Scope,* which also belong to the margins of the culture. (As consolation, it's worth remembering that major modern critical movements have often grown from minority culture and little magazines: F. R. Leavis's *Scrutiny,* arguably the most influential journal of literary criticism in British history, had a print run of 750 to 1,400; and *Cahiers du cinéma* and *Movie* had much smaller circulations than their eventual influence would suggest.) But the great American journalistic movie critics have sometimes enjoyed larger audiences. They contributed greatly to my knowledge of cinema history and my desire to write about cinema, and they belong to the intellectual biography of my generation. Some are still at work and have moved partly to the web (see Dave Kehr and Jonathan Rosenbaum), where intelligent commentary (see Girish Shambu and David Bordwell) mingles with a good deal of uninteresting chatter. In the following pages I pay tribute to the four—James Agee, Manny Farber, Andrew Sarris, and Jonathan Rosenbaum—who had the greatest influence on the development of my taste. More are worth consideration: I was never a fan of Pauline Kael but I'm an admirer of a number of contemporary writers, including Manohla Dargis, David Edelstein, Molly Haskell, and J. Hoberman. The death of Roger Ebert as I was writing this introduction forcefully reminded me of his importance as a popular journalist and champion of movies; he will be irreplaceable. I had to stop somewhere, however, and most would agree that the four I've chosen to discuss have written criticism of lasting value and should be part of any comprehensive history of U.S. film culture. I'm not in their class, but I've added a sample of my own work as a critic of new cinema for *Film Quarterly* because I want to practice what I preach, and believe the pictures I discussed there are worth more attention than they've received.

James Agee

James Agee is the only major American film reviewer with a significant literary reputation. (Some might say that Vachel Lindsay has the same status, but he wasn't a reviewer.) As a literary figure, Agee is sometimes compared with Thomas Wolfe: both were southerners (in Agee's case a border-state southerner) who wrote semiautobiographical novels about provincial childhood; both were influenced by Joyce's *A Portrait of the Artist as a Young Man*; both produced huge, unruly manuscripts; and both died at an early age. Of the two, however, Agee was by far the superior stylist, and his major literary achievement apart from the posthumous, unfinished *A Death in the Family* (1955) wasn't fiction but *Let Us Now Praise Famous Men* (1941), an account of the effects of the Great Depression on Alabama tenant farmers, which grew out of his job at *Fortune* magazine and could be described as a merger of radical journalism, lyrical prose, and avant-garde art.

It's been said that Agee wasted his talent on magazine work. Certainly he had moments of frustration at the Luce organization, but a more convincing argument can be made that *Time, Life, Fortune, The Nation*, and other journals helped him discover and develop his particular gifts. An above-average novelist and poet (except in poetic prose, in which he excelled—see "Knoxville: Summer of 1915"), Agee was a superb writer of essays that make nonsense of the distinction between journalism and literature. He was constrained by the Luce magazines, especially in unsigned movie reviews conforming to *Time*-speak, and was sometimes contemptuous of his job; but at *The Nation*, where he was paid fifty dollars a month, he had the freedom to champion an art and space to establish an identity. W.H. Auden wasn't entirely wrong in his fan letter to the journal saying that Agee's column "is of such profound interest, expressed with such extraordinary wit and felicity, and so transcends its ostensible—to me, rather unimportant—subject, that his articles belong in that very select class . . . of newspaper work which has permanent literary value." (Despite Auden's snobbery about movies, he contributed to Britain's G.P.O. documentary film unit in the 1930s at roughly the same moment when he was arguing that the artist "must be more than a bit like a working journalist" [Auden, 138].)

Far from transcending his subject, Agee reveals its importance. Auden is correct, however, when he says that the *Nation* reviews have "literary value." They're exactly what Victorian theologian John Henry Newman had in mind in "Literature and Style" (1899), which distinguishes between the objective, uniform language of science and the subjective, infinitely variable language of literature. Literary language, Newman argues, is addressed more to the ear than the eye, and the writer "subjects it withal to his own purposes, and moulds it according to his peculiarities . . . his views of external things, his judgments upon life, manners, and history, the exercises of his wit, of his humor, of his depth, of his sagacity, the very pulsation and throbbing of his intellect." As a result, it becomes "the faithful expression of [an] intense personality" (220–21).

Whether or not we agree with the romantic idea that "style is the man," Agee's work for *The Nation*, which makes considerable use of the first person, has "intense personality" (perhaps better described as a "persona," as long as the term doesn't imply duplicity). He's erudite, introspective, occasionally self-critical, attuned to the social class of his readers, considerate yet forceful, and passionate about the "poetic" qualities of cinema. Many of these attributes are evident at the outset (December 26, 1942), when he states his aims and defends his practice: "I would like to use this column about moving pictures as to honor and discriminate the subject through interesting and serving you who are reading it." The tone is politely formal and subtly flattering to *Nation* subscribers, conveying respect and even an undercurrent of biblical reverence for the task ahead. Two verbs and two participles—honor and discriminate, interesting and serving—secure the effect, producing a stately rhythm and creating an air of gravitas tinged with humility. Agee next elicits consent by putting himself on the same level as his audience: "It is my business to conduct one end of a conversation, as an amateur critic among amateur critics. And I will be of use and interest only in so far as my amateur judgment is sound, stimulating, or illuminating" (Vol. 1, 22). Again we have rhythmic repetition—"amateur critic among amateur critics," "sound, stimulating, or illuminating"—and a politely formal suggestion of high purpose.

Agee knows his reviews aren't conversation, but like any good essayist he writes as if they were. Anticipating typical objections (This is just your opinion isn't it? You're an amateur, so why should I take you seriously?), he argues that amateurs can have an advantage over professionals, who are often preoccupied with technical matters and box office returns. In a nice if rather high-toned use of the subjunctive, he adds that even though he respects John Ford, "I might regret ninety-nine feet in every hundred of *The Grapes of Wrath*, and be able to specify my regret; and it would be entirely a question of the maturity of my judgment, and not in the least of my professional or amateur standing, whether I was right or wrong" (Vol. 1, 23).

The reference to Ford's 1940 adaptation of John Steinbeck's novel about dust bowl farmers is significant. *Let Us Now Praise Famous Men*, which could never have been adapted in a straightforward way but might have inspired a new kind of cinema, was published one year after the Ford film, to meager sales and baffled reviews. In hinting at a comparison between himself and Ford, Agee points us toward what will emerge in the reviews as his fundamental aesthetic and social concerns—a belief in a specific kind of poetic realism, an empathy with people on the margins of industrial modernity, and a resentment of what Hollywood cinema had become in the 1940s.

Before exploring such matters, a bit more should be said about Agee's style, which is highly adjectival or adverbial and attentive to the effects of rhythm. His sentences often have a bell-like quality achieved with triple or quadruple modifiers. Pauline Kael made fun of these strings of adjectives and Manny Farber called them "pet multiplications" (*Farber on Film*, 498), but they perform work at the level of judgment and give rhythmic force to Agee's arguments—for instance, when he says that the West Times Square viewers of Val Lewton's B movies are "a specialized audience, unobstreperous, poor, metropolitan and deeply experienced" (Vol. 1, 86). Prose rhythm also depends on punctuation, paragraph breaks, and the variation of short and long clauses or sentences, which create a variety of subtle or strong pauses. Agee was a master of the technique, especially in acrobatically sustained periods such as his witty *Life* magazine description of a sequence in Keaton's *Sherlock Jr.*: "Boiling along on the handlebars of a motorcycle quite unaware that he has lost his driver, Keaton whips through city traffic, breaks up a tug-of-war, gets a shovelful of dirt in the face from a long line of Rockette-timed ditch-diggers, approaches a log at high speed which is hinged open by dynamite precisely soon enough to let him through and, hitting an obstruction, leaves the handlebars like an arrow leaving a bow, whams through the window of a shack in which the heroine is about to be violated, and hits the heavy feet first, knocking him through the opposite wall" (Vol. 1, 16). This is impressively accurate given that it was written long before anyone had the ability to study sequences on a DVD player (Agee forgets or leaves out the moment when Keaton discovers he has no driver, the moment when he narrowly misses a freight train, and the moment when, crossing a bridge with a huge gap in it, he scoots across the top of a truck that happens to pass under the bridge), and the extended string of verbs and participles punctuated by commas amusingly mimics the pace and cutting rhythm of the film. It's criticism of a high order in which description becomes meaning.

Agee belonged to the late phase of high modernism, when the scandalous and difficult art of the 1920s had achieved middlebrow respectability. In *Time* he was able to write brief but perceptive reviews of William Faulkner's *The Hamlet*, Gertrude Stein's *Ida*, Virginia Woolf's *Between the Acts*, and Harry Levin's critical book on James Joyce. But modernist culture wasn't monolithic. In 1919 Eliot had famously argued that "Poetry [and by implication any form of art] is not a turning loose of emotion, but an escape from emotion; it is not the expression of personality but the escape from personality." Agee, a romantic, could never have agreed with such ideas. He regarded Beethoven as a deity, he wrote confessional and autobiographical poetry and prose, and he was one of the first American movie reviewers to bring personality to the fore alongside commentary on industry, politics, and propaganda.

Agee's social concerns were especially apparent during the first half of his short career at *The Nation*, when World War II was being fought. He had opposed U.S. entry into the war and privately asked his employers at *Time* to help prevent him from being drafted. His politics, like his religious views, are difficult to categorize. He abandoned the church but maintained close ties with Father Flye, an Anglican priest who was his youthful mentor, and his writing is suffused with religious themes. No white intellectual of his day wrote more eloquently against racism, and none spoke more pointedly about the right-wing persecution of Charles Chaplin, yet Agee was too much of an individualist to be described as a liberal or socialist. While at *Time* he formed a bond with Whittaker Chambers. I suspect he was what he imagined John Huston to be: "a natural-born antiauthoritarian individualistic libertarian anarchist" (Vol. 1, 325). This would explain his excited and apt 1947 response to Jean Vigo's *Zero for Conduct* (1933): "I happen to share a good deal of Vigo's particular kind of obsession for liberty and against authority.... So the spirit of this film, its fierceness and gaiety, the total absence of well-constructed 'constructive' diagnosis and prescription, the enormous liberating force of its quasi-nihilism, its humor, directness, kindliness, criminality, and guile, form for me as satisfying a revolutionary expression as I know" (Vol. 1, 263).

Whatever might be Agee's politics, he was antifascist and an admirer of principled and humane forms of physical courage. The war pictures appearing every week when he began at *The Nation* provoked his anger over Hollywood's crude propaganda and his shame over his own absence from combat. Shame, a slightly different emotion from guilt, was an important element in much of his work. In *Let Us Now Praise Famous Men* it colors nearly all his interactions with tenant farmers, as when he and Evans listen to a black family's singing performance arranged by a local landlord: "I had been sick in the knowledge that they felt they were at our demand, mine and Walker's, and that I could communicate nothing otherwise; and now, in a perversion of self-torture, I played my part through. I gave their leader fifty cents, trying at the same time, through my eyes, to communicate much more . . . and he thanked me for them in a dead voice, not looking me in the eye" (31).

By openly confessing shame, Agee invites us to share in it. A clear example is the 1943 essay "America, Look at Your Shame!," which was discovered in Agee's poetry manuscripts and appeared posthumously in the January/February 2003 issue of *Oxford American*. This essay begins by describing a story Agee saw in *PM* about the Detroit race riots, accompanied by a photograph of two young white men holding up a bleeding black man and looking at the camera with "a terrific, accidental look of bearing testimony." The photograph made him ashamed because "I had to wonder whether, in such a situation, I would have been capable of that self-forgetfulness and courage." The answer came on the same day. He was riding on a New York bus when a group of U.S. sailors and soldiers, like him from the South, began bullying and shouting racist slurs at the black passengers. Agee did nothing. The only person to speak up was an old black woman who confronted one of the sailors: "She was talking very little, and crying a little, and telling [the sailor], and the whole bus, that he ought to be ashamed, talking that way. . . . Just might bout's well be Hitluh, as a white man from the South. Wearing a sailor's uniform. Fighting for your country. Ought to be ashamed." (The only flaw in this essay is Agee's phonetic spelling of the woman's dialect, which has a condescending effect.) While the woman was speaking, Agee says, "I remembered the photograph in *PM*, and looked sternly at the floor, with my cheek twitching." That evening he told this story to a group of friends, and the telling of it "embarrassed me a good deal, but not as painfully as I wish it might have, and I found their agreement that they would have done the same almost as revolting as my own performance in the doing of it, and in the telling. So now I am telling you."

In *On Shame* (2008), philosopher Michael L. Morgan discusses how Agee's essay tries to convert personal shame into an ethical "community of shame": "There is a movement, in Agee's reactions, from a personal sense of self-reproach to a sense of collective self-criticism, a multiplication of shame upon shame that focuses in the end to a charge to his readers, to feel that same shame about racism in America and America's failure of courage when confronted with it" (57). Something similar happens in Agee's film reviews when he sees pictures from the war. From the start he recognizes there might be "sinister" postwar effects because the United States (beginning with himself) is far less directly involved in the conflict than Europe: "Their experience of war is unprecedented in immediacy and unanimity. Ours, even in the fraction that has the experience at all, is essentially specialized, lonely, bitter, and sterile; our great majority will emerge from the war almost as if it had never taken place; and not all the lip-service in the world about internationalism will make that different" (Vol. 1, 55).

The problem was especially apparent in studio-manufactured combat movies aimed at the home front. John Farrow's *Wake Island* (1942), the first Hollywood fiction picture about combat, was a huge popular and critical success, but Agee's review in *Time* emphasized its dishonest representation of violence and death. Readers accused him of a lack of patriotism, but he wrote an even more negative review of Farrow's *Commandos Strike at Dawn* (1943). His strongest invective, however, was reserved for Victor Fleming's *A Guy Named Joe* (1944), a sentimental film about a dead pilot who comes back from heaven to help his wife find a new mate: "The makers ... had courage, if a moral idiot has it; I doubt whether taste and honesty entered into it at all" (Vol. 1, 90).

The war films Agee liked best were documentaries. War resulted in handheld newsreel footage of unprecedented immediacy, plus a series of intelligent, near-feature-length documentaries that helped foster a postwar appetite for neorealism. Agee admired the British *Desert Victory* (1942), but he gave special praise to Huston's *The Battle of San Pietro* (1945), which he described as close to "the essence of the power of moving pictures ... the fact that they can give you things to look at, free of urging or comment, and so ordered that they are radiant with illimitable suggestions of meaning and mystery" (Vol. 1, 164). Nevertheless, as the war progressed he began to feel uneasy watching scenes of violence. Reviewing the Paramount and Fox newsreels about the American capture of Iwo Jima (1945), he was both fascinated and worried: "I am beginning to believe that, for all that may be said in favor of our seeing these terrible records of war, we have no business seeing this sort of experience except through our presence and participation. . . . If at an incurable distance from participation, hopelessly incapable of reactions adequate to the event, we watch men killing each other, we may be quite as profoundly degrading ourselves" (Vol. 1, 152).

Agee's reviews of the war films are consistent with his critical opinions as a whole. He believes the Hollywood studios in the 1940s have made the movies prettified, blandly respectable, and utterly decadent. A case in point is the award-winning *The Song of Bernadette* (1943), which suffers from "middle-class twentieth-century genteelism, a fungus which by now all but chokes the life out of any hope from Hollywood and which threatens any vivid appetite in Hollywood's audience" (Vol. 1, 73). Movies that later became canonical are also found wanting. *The Miracle of Morgan's Creek* (1944), despite its many virtues, is symptomatic of a "terrible softening, solemnity, and idealization which ... has all but put an end to the output and intake of good motion pictures in this country" (Vol. 1, 75). *Meet Me in St. Louis* (1944), which also has virtues, is flawed by tunes sung in "up-to-date chromium and glucose style" and sets and costumes that are "too perfectly waxen" (Vol. 1, 126). Although Agee respects the talent of individual actors, he laments the main tradition of Hollywood acting, especially when "there is any pretense of portraying 'real' people" (Vol. 1, 31). He admires postwar documentaries that have "a general good taste which knows better than to use any rhetoric of image, word, or sound" and dislikes those in which "the prevailing quality has been that of American commercial romanticism, as taught, for example, by the *Life* school" (Vol. 1, 88, 65). Russian documentaries are even worse because of their "staged and falsified and rhetorical" photography and "posterish, opportunistic, and anti-human" editing, which is "derived, and degraded, from Dziga Vertov or Eisenstein" (Vol. 1, 65).

In contrast, Agee writes with pleasure about silent-era comics, Griffith, Eisenstein, Dovzhenko, and B movies such as William Castle's *When Strangers Marry* (1945), which has an off-Hollywood quality. Where contemporary Hollywood directors are concerned, he thinks Orson Welles is talented but overrated. He respects Hitchcock and Lubitsch, although he thinks their current films inferior to their work in the 1930s. In *Time* he describes Howard Hawks as one of "the real artists of picture-making" (*Film Writing and Selected Journalism*, 527). With the striking exception of Jacques Tourneur's *Out of the Past* (1947), which he utterly dismisses, he enjoys nearly all of what we now call film noir, "for it crawls with American types; and their mannerisms and affectations, and their chief preoccupations—blackmail and what's-in-it-for-me—all seem to reflect, however coolly, things that are deeply characteristic of this civilization" (Vol. 1, 203). He's blind to what were called women's pictures. The Hollywood directors who most impress him are William Wellman, William Wyler, and John Huston, whose best films in the 1940s—*The Story of G.I. Joe* (1946), *The Best Years of Our Lives* (1946), and *The Treasure of the Sierra Madre* (1948)—are male-centered and realist in style.

For Agee, realism is a major criterion of value, though it is by no means the most important criterion. He's impressed by the Italian neorealists and in a less enthusiastic way by the postwar Hollywood films produced by Louis de Rochemont, which were shot almost completely on location. But the highest accolade he can bestow upon a film is to say that it has "poetry," an idealistic term suggesting formal skill and a quasi-spiritual, emotionally charged aura, a truth or beauty that isn't synonymous with realist photography but sometimes mingles with it. One key to "poetry" is an absence of industrialized kitsch, as when he describes Chaplin's *Monsieur Verdoux* (1947) as "a manifesto against a kind of vulgarity in which Hollywood is drowned—the attempt to disguise emptiness with sumptuousness. It looks hand-made, not machine-turned . . . it is poetic, not naturalistic, though naturalistic elements are used poetically" (Vol. 1, 254). Griffith, too, for all his indebtedness to nineteenth-century melodrama, has what Agee calls "poetic" gifts: "In epic and visual and lyrical and narrative visual poetry, I can think of nobody who has surpassed him. . . . As a primitive tribal poet, combining something of the bard and the seer, he is beyond even Dovzhenko" (Vol. I, 316).

Given the dominance of studio cinema in the years when Agee was writing, poetic qualities were fleeting and usually grounded in realist photography—as in the closing scene of *The Story of G.I. Joe*, which he describes as "a war poem as great and beautiful as any of Whitman's" (Vol. 1, 173). But in all its manifestations, Agee's cinematic poetry is quite different from what the French in the 1930s called "poetic realism"—despite the fact that he uses that term in his review of *Open City* (1946) when he speaks of "the poetic-realistic root of attitude from which the grand trunk of movies at their best would have to grow" (Vol. 1, 195). Here and elsewhere he has more in common with André Bazin, who was his approximate contemporary (Agee died in 1955 and Bazin in 1958). Both writers are fine commentators on Wyler's *Best Years of Our Lives*, Chaplin's *Verdoux*, and the Italian neorealists, and both feel a kind of holy reverence for the ability of the camera to capture an imprint of the world in relatively unmediated ways. For Agee, the essence of at least one kind of cinematic poetry could be found in an absence of rhetorical embellishment and a respect for the evidence in front of the camera—a quality similar to what we see in Walker Evans, or to what Agee found in Huston's *San Pietro:* "things to look at, free of urging or comment, and so ordered that they are radiant with illimitable suggestions of meaning and mystery." But notice that the images need to be "ordered." Unlike Bazin, Agee has nothing to say about the long takes that were becoming increasingly apparent in Welles, Wyler, and much of 1940s Hollywood. His favored director is Huston, whom he praises for shifting between "passive" and "active" uses of the camera, for arranging each shot so that it "contains no more than is absolutely necessary to make the point and is cut off sharp at that instant," and for an editing style that has "the rhythm of good prose rather than of good verse" (Vol. 1, 329).

Agee not only had a strong literary reputation but also a short-lived career as a contributor to films. His work in that respect is consistent with his values as a critic and of such high quality that it deserves comment.

Writing in *The Nation* in 1945, Agee declared that "most though not all good films get much of their vitality and resonance by being designed for a broad mixed audience, whether or not they turn out to satisfy such an audience." He also argued that "if good movies are to be made any more at all, in this country, anyhow, they will have to be made on shoestrings, far outside the industry, and very likely by amateurs or semi-professionals" (Vol. 1, 150). At that moment he was engaged in demonstrating his thesis. *In the Street*, a sixteen-minute documentary instigated by Agee, was shot in Spanish Harlem with a borrowed 16mm camera operated by Agee, the painter Janice Loeb, and the gifted New York street photographer Helen Levitt (a friend of both Agee and Walker Evans and later the sister-in-law of Loeb). The footage dates from 1945 and 1946, but the film wasn't edited by Levitt until 1952. A small masterpiece, it consists of nothing more than a silent montage of quotidian life in a poor urban neighborhood, backed with Gershwin-like musical score by pianist Arthur Kleiner and introduced with a title card by Agee: "The streets of the poor quarters of great cities are, above all, a theater and a battleground. There, unaware and unnoticed, every human being is a poet, a masker, a warrior, a dancer; and in his innocent artistry he projects, against the turmoil of the street, an image of human existence."

The camera was equipped with a right-angle viewfinder, so that subjects were unaware they were being photographed. (Footage shot by Agee contains a few scenes of black kids looking into the camera, waving and showing off.) Tough, racially polyglot, and working-class, Spanish Harlem looks impoverished but more communal than the poor urban spaces of today. Bent old women gossip on the sidewalk or walk their scruffy dogs, a little boy and girl play a sweetly flirtatious game with gypsy beads, a child stuck indoors wistfully presses his or her nose and tongue against a windowpane, and kids frolic under water hydrants. Images of children predominate, no doubt because Levitt specialized in candid photos of children's culture, which she later published in a book titled *In the Street*. Several of the scenes were shot during Halloween: children scamper up and down the busy sidewalk in surreal homemade masks and costumes, and rowdy boys fill old socks or handkerchiefs with flour, pelting one another with white dust and threatening to scatter it on girls. A few adults are also singled out: a dapper, incongruous man in a fedora who might be a pimp; a pretty young woman in a stylish dress who attracts glances as she walks past; another young woman who shouts up at a friend leaning out a third-story window; and a portly lady in a fox fur and gaudy hat who picks her teeth before donning a pair of gloves.

In the Street is the finest cinematic manifestation of New York School street photography; but Levitt, who had worked briefly with Luis Buñuel at MoMA during World War II, was also an admirer of the street scenes in Vertov's *Man with a Movie Camera* and (like her friend Agee) the children's games in Vigo's *Zero for Conduct*. One never feels that *In the Street* is merely still photography transposed to cinema. It attends to facial and bodily shapes but also to a range of movement—the walking or running styles of weary old figures and swift youth, the furtive gestures and wary turns of people on a crowded sidewalk, and the changes of pace at different seasons or times of day. Most of the people are grotesque, but they aren't viewed as cartoons or human specimens. One of the film's admirers was Siegfried Kracauer, who described it as "reportage pure and simple," but reportage "done with unconcealed compassion for the people depicted: the camera dwells on them tenderly; they are not meant to stand for anything but themselves" (203; see also Deane Williams, "Helen Levitt," sensesofcinema.com/2012/cteg/helen-levitt). Not surprisingly, *In the Street*'s guerrilla-style production and untendentious simplicity also had an important impact on a later generation of the American avant-garde: Stan Brakhage listed it as one of the greatest films of all time, and Ken Jacobs credited it with persuading him that he, too, could make films.

In the same year Agee collaborated on an Academy Award–nominated semidocumentary, *The Quiet One* (1948), photographed and edited by Levitt and Loeb, directed by Sidney Meyers, and produced by Arthur Meyer and Joseph Burstyn, who were responsible for bringing the first wave of Italian neorealism to the United States. This film uses nonprofessional actors and location photography to tell the story of a potentially dangerous black boy from a broken family in Harlem who is sent to the Wiltwyck School for troubled youth in the New York countryside. We see how teachers and psychologists try to save wounded children, and how the silent, sullen boy, raised by an unloving grandmother, is slowly brought into healthy contact with others. Parts of the film are acted, and much of it is told through a voice-over narration representing the ruminations of a school psychologist. The narration was written and originally spoken by Agee, who tries to avoid an overly analytical tone. At one point, for example, we see a teacher refusing to exert control over a classroom in which hyperrestless boys play around while others merely sit, looking bored or disengaged. The narrator comments, "Children are much more deeply ashamed of being stupid than most of us realize. They are stupefied by shame. They've failed so often they're afraid even to try any more. Before they can begin to trust their intelligence, they have to be sure they're liked. . . . Before they know they're liked, they can't like you. Until they like you, they can't even begin to learn."

This style of narration owes something to social documentaries of the 1930s, but in making the narrator a character *The Quiet One* prefigures a semidocumentary like Kent MacKenzie's *The Exiles* (1961)—a more interesting film largely because its multiple narrators are also its subjects. Unfortunately, school officials and *The Quiet One*'s producers believed they could reach a larger audience if a well-known actor played the narrator, so they created a new soundtrack with actor Gary Merrill reading Agee's words. The result is stentorian, too much like a newsreel of the period or the voice of a stereotypically wise movie psychologist. The imagery, however, never disappoints, even in the poor-quality DVD now on the market. Levitt and Loeb are sensitive observers of children's improvised games. Their film is pointedly composed and briskly edited, but it often creates the realist effect Agee most admired, giving us "things to look at, free of urging and comment."

In 1939 Agee wrote a screen treatment of André Malraux's *Man's Fate* for Jay Leyda's journal *Films;* and in the late 1940s, chiefly because of his not-too-hagiographic profile of John Huston in *Life* magazine, he began to find opportunities in Hollywood, most of them involving literary adaptation and most of them made possible by Huston. This was a moment when independent productions were taking on new importance. In 1948, thanks to Huston, Agee was contracted by independent producer Huntington Hartford to write the screenplay for *The Blue Hotel*, an adaptation of a short story by Stephen Crane (at the time, Huston was on the verge of filming his adaptation of Crane's *The Red Badge of Courage*). According to biographer Laurence Bergreen, Agee completed a manuscript of more than a hundred pages in only three days. It has excellent dialogue but also lengthy instructions for editing, sound, photography, and the composition of images, written in Agee's characteristically lyric prose. The description of the opening shot takes up three pages in *Agee on Film, Vol. 2*, indicating the exact height of the camera, the number of seconds in which a totally black sky should occupy three-quarters of the frame above the horizon, and subtle changes of light (assisted with "infra-red, if need be") as a train passes and dawn breaks over a snowy landscape. A few moments later a group of men eat a meal in a prairie-town hotel and Agee spends four pages explaining their individual eating styles. Still later these characters gather for a game of poker. It's snowing outside and dusk is falling, so one of them lights a lamp: "As he finishes with the lamp and leaves the shot, HOLD a moment on the lamp, its light tender and magical in the fading day, and disclosing their faces, still bemused in the ambiguous lightings of the last daylight and of lamplight on in daylight. There is a soft, strange point of light in each eye" (Vol. 2, 414).

Agee obviously wants to direct. You can see a completed film in this screenplay, which is composed rather like a novel with cinematic properties. It's so specific that a real director probably wouldn't touch it, and in fact it was never filmed, although a shortened, "adapted" version was shown on ABC TV's *Omnibus* in 1956.

Agee also worked on another unfilmed project, a sixty-three-page screenplay entitled *Scientists and Tramps* for a film in which Chaplin's Little Tramp survives nuclear holocaust and becomes a member of a primitive utopian commune. (For a full discussion of this screenplay, see John Wranovic, *Chaplin and Agee*.) He set it aside, probably because he couldn't solve the problem of how the Tramp would function in a perfect world, but also because a more secure opportunity arrived. After accepting for the first time the representation of a literary agent (Paul Kohner, who also worked for Huston), he was hired to collaborate on the screenplay of *The African Queen* (1951). He about wrote half of the film, including the memorable scene in which Humphrey Bogart's stomach growls as he sits down to high tea with African missionaries, which is a gag Agee swiped from Chaplin's *Modern Times*. It earned him an Academy Award nomination and future work, but he suffered a heart attack while trying to keep up with Huston on the tennis court and was unable to finish the assignment. From then on, his smoking, drinking, and nonstop writing kept his life in jeopardy.

Agee again worked for Huntington Hartford, for whom he had little respect, on a screen version of the Stephen Crane short story "The Bride Comes to Yellow Sky," directed by Bretaigne Windust and released as the second part of a two-episode film, *Face to Face* (1953). It's a charming cowboy comedy in which Agee plays a bit role as a drunk named Gudger (a family name in *Let Us Now Praise Famous Men*) who is barely visible in the upstairs window of a jailhouse, but it would have been an even better film if it exactly followed the screenplay. During this same period Agee also wrote English-language narration for Manuel Conde's Philippine epic *Genghis Khan* (1950, recently given a digital restoration) and Albert Lamorisse's *White Mane* (1942), a forty-seven-minute picture about a boy and a wild horse in the Camargue region of France. More importantly, his former Harvard classmate Robert Saudek, who was in charge of CBS TV's *Omnibus*, offered him a project close to his heart: *Abraham Lincoln, the*

Early Years (1952), a two-and-a-half-hour, five-episode film written by Agee, produced by Richard de Rochemont, and mostly directed by Norman Lloyd.

Abraham Lincoln (now available on DVD) is arguably the best film on the subject. It was shot on location in Kentucky, Indiana, and Illinois in neorealist style (one of the photographers was the young Stanley Kubrick) employing a good many nonprofessional actors. It opens with an unforgettable montage of Lincoln's funeral train traveling across America, while on the soundtrack, timed to the rhythm of the train, the voice of Norman Lloyd reads Whitman's "When Lilacs Last in the Dooryard Bloom'd." At the end of the journey an aged black woman places a flower on the dead president's casket; we then flash back to witness Lincoln's boyhood and young manhood.

Agee's chief historical source was Carl Sandburg's *Abraham Lincoln: The Prairie Years*, and, like Sandburg, he views Lincoln as a mythical figure. He introduces a fictional character named Jack Kelso, an alcoholic friend of Lincoln who repeatedly quotes Shakespeare, and Agee plays the role himself. He also devotes a good deal of attention to what historians have called the mythical romance between Lincoln and Ann Rutledge. (Lincoln is played by the lanky, relatively homely Royal Dano, who had impressed Agee with his performance in Huston's *Red Badge of Courage*, and Ann is played by the then-unknown Joanne Woodward.) Agee seems to have believed that when legend becomes fact, you should print the legend, but in other ways *Abraham Lincoln, the Early Years* is quite different from a John Ford movie. It has the same antithetical relation to Ford's *Young Mr. Lincoln* (1939) as *Let Us Now Praise Famous Men* has to *The Grapes of Wrath:* slowly paced, free of pictorialism and sentimentality, it's convincingly true to backwoods life in the American heartland during the nineteenth century. Historian Frank Thompson, who has written a book-length study of twentieth-century depictions of Lincoln, describes it as "a remarkable, evocative song of Lincoln's youth, not bound by history but infused with a sense of authenticity." Thompson argues that "there is more insight here on what kind of people the Lincolns were, and what their lives must have been like, than in any other Lincoln film ever made" (quoted in Phillips and Hill, 258).

As he was working on the Lincoln project Agee was approached by director-producer David Bradley, who was seeking a writer for a low-budget film about Paul Gauguin. Bradley had come to Hollywood on the strength of a 16mm adaptation of Shakespeare's *Julius Caesar*, which he filmed in Chicago (the film's major claim to fame is that it stars Northwestern University theater student Charlton Heston); and at MGM in 1952, he had directed *Talk about a Stranger*, a noir thriller photographed in the orange-growing country of Southern California by the legendary John Alton. He had been told by Gavin Lambert of the British Film Institute that Agee might be a good candidate for the Gauguin picture. His plan, as he explained it to Agee, was to make a small film on location in Tahiti with a budget similar to that of *The Quiet One*.

Attracted to the idea of a film about a romantic artist, Agee responded warmly and agreed to a relatively modest remuneration. But agent Paul Kohner, the success of John Huston's *Moulin Rouge* (1952), and Agee's own ambition helped transform the modest project into a big picture. Items appeared in the trade press announcing that Agee was writing a biopic about Gauguin entitled *Noa Noa*. Zoltan Korda, who was living in Hollywood, told Bradley that his brother Alexander was interested in coproducing. Before long Agee and Bradley were making plans to photograph *Noa Noa* in Paris, Tahiti, and the Marquesas Islands using a new color process (and perhaps also 3-D) and starring a name actor.

Because of his commitment to Bradley and because *Noa Noa* was a project on which he could wield more than his usual influence, Agee turned down John Huston's offer to collaborate on the screenplay for *Moby Dick* (1956). On February 18, 1952, he wrote an excited letter to Bradley: "You asked if I would like to go along on the shooting. Christ yes; both out of the fascination of the journey and because I feel strongly that location shooting (all the more, when one is working originally with color and a new dimension) is bound to present problems, and opportunities for improvement, in which the writer of the script can be of great use." At the same time he noted impediments: "It may well be that by summer, some friends of mine (who made *The Quiet One*) will be ready to shoot a film which I will direct; and I care even more to direct films than to write them. . . . I'm meanwhile so deeply involved in the cutting down of the Lincoln films to a feature-length picture, and in working out the basic outlines of the original story I'm sooner or later going to direct" (David Bradley archive, Lilly Library).

"I am concerned to avoid seeming to ride on the coattails of the, to me, visually brilliant *Moulin Rouge*," Agee told Bradley (Bradley archive). But that was exactly what he was doing, just as Vincente Minnelli would do a few years later when he made *Lust for Life* (1956). On April 7, 1953, Agee reported on his progress. The epic film would have two parts. (Agee wanted to open with a title that swoops across the screen in the manner of *Gone with the Wind*.) It would tell the story chronologically, "comparable with the story told in the Stations of the Cross." We would see Gauguin successively abandoning a prosperous business, a family, and the brotherhood of artists envisioned by Van Gogh. A radical individualist, he would naïvely try to escape modernity by visiting Tahiti, where he would contract syphilis and encounter a cynical native population corrupted by Europeans. After a brief return to the decadent art market in Paris, he would venture deeper into Oceania, settling at last in the somber Marquesas. Near death, he would arrive at "what Beethoven came to in his late work; pure energy, and pure religion" (Bradley archive).

By "pure religion" Agee means the religion of art, with Christianity hovering in the background. His screenplay repeatedly compares Gauguin with Christ, and in the opening scene Agee gives instructions for an elaborate camera movement over the dead artist's body, inscribing the sign of the cross. A Protestant pastor named Vernier (to be played by Agee, probably in tribute to Father Flye) has agreed to atheist Gauguin's wish for a civil burial ceremony and tells a resistant Catholic bishop that the dead Gauguin, like Christ, has the look of "a man who has endured great suffering, with great courage, for a great purpose; and who has won a great victory" (Vol. 2, 6). We flash back to tell the story of Gauguin's life, and at the end of the film we see his burial on a hill opposite the peak of Temetiu. The camera pans from his simple grave to a wooden statuary of the crucifixion standing nearby. The weathered Christ figure is partly split open and bees have nested inside, producing honey that drips from the feet. In the last shot the camera pans up the "bee-dwelt, honey-swollen body of Christ, culminating in the head."

Noa Noa offers the possibility of a rich display of Gauguin's work and any number of scenic wonders, including a pearl-diving sequence in which Gauguin dives for treasure. Just how much Agee wanted to oversee the production becomes apparent when he gives instructions for an Eisenstein-like sequence depicting the burial of Pōmare V, the last Tahitian king: "The funeral sequence is to be cut rigidly to the music of Chopin's Funeral March. I will indicate the cuts and shots exactly.... The scoring, and performance, should be those of a French deep provincial military band of the period: rather shrill and squeaky, and not very well played; yet with genuine solemnity." There follows a list of sixty shots, most of them keyed to beats and half beats of the music. After the music and the Christian ceremony end in a moment of dead silence, we hear "an unimaginably alien and powerful and ancient native dirge" sung by Tahitians. Gauguin, deeply stirred, mutters, "If Beethoven could hear it!" (Vol. 2, 60–64).

The chief problem with the screenplay is that Agee overidentifies with his protagonist and to an embarrassing degree writes an idealized self-portrait: the religious apostate who becomes a whiskey priest of art, the sensitive soul who feels rapport with nonwhites, the husband who abandons a wife and child to follow a high calling (except Agee's calling was Hollywood). His version of Gauguin is always sympathetic, even in the long section dealing with Van Gogh at Arles, which makes an interesting contrast with *Lust for Life*. Minnelli's Gauguin is a swaggering womanizer, slightly jealous of Van Gogh but also contemptuous of Van Gogh's neediness and sentimentality. Agee's Gauguin misses his wife and family, and although he recoils from Van Gogh's religious ardor and mental instability, he feels a mixture of pity and admiration for his fellow artist.

To find an actor to play this saintly figure, Bradley and Agee circulated the screenplay to what seemed like half the leading men in the Western world, among them Charlton Heston, Marlon Brando, Jack Palance, Gregory Peck, Jeff Chandler, Jeff Morrow, Vittorio Gassman, Gérard Philipe, Gilbert Roland, Kirk Douglas, and Anthony Quinn (ironically, the last two would play Van Gogh and Gauguin in *Lust for Life*). Agee favored Gassman or Roland, but his choice was irrelevant because no actor expressed interest. Meanwhile, Zoltan Korda confessed that his brother Alexander hadn't looked at the screenplay and had never really been keen on the idea of coproducing the film. Agee lost confidence and withdrew, pressing Bradley for money that was owed to him.

The *Noa Noa* debacle was the low point of Agee's career as a screenwriter. His health was fragile, he was sinking deeper into alcoholism, and only two of his screenplays had been shown in theaters. Then came *Night of the Hunter* (1955), the most important picture with which his name would be connected. For many years it was believed that he had little to do with this film, even though he was given sole credit as screenwriter. It was said that he turned in an unfilmable manuscript consisting of dialogue from Davis Grubb's novel plus lengthy digressions into Depression-era social problems, and that Charles Laughton wrote the script that was published in *Agee on Film, Vol. 2*. There can be little doubt that the greatness of the film is due chiefly to Laughton, but both Simon Callow and Jeffrey Couchman, who have written books about *Night of the Hunter*, have shown that Agee's contribution was significant. Laughton wanted Agee to follow the novel closely, and Agee did so; his first draft was twice as long as an ordinary picture, but only because, as usual, he wrote long, beautifully descriptive passages and detailed ideas for how to shoot the film. He also expanded minor characters from the novel and introduced new ones, including a black family that John and Pearl encounter during their journey down the river. These inventions were vividly conceived and true to the spirit of the novel, but they impeded the narrative and were cut, either by Agee or Laughton. Throughout the process Laughton was an intelligent and helpful critic, guiding and trimming the final screenplay. In the end Agee wrote a letter to producer Paul Gregory asking that Laughton share the writing credit, but Laughton declined. As Jeffrey Couchman has observed, whatever part

Laughton may have played in the writing, he was undoubtedly the sort of collaborator that Dwight Macdonald, speaking in reference to *A Death in the Family*, thought Agee had never found: "What Agee needed was a sympathetically severe editor who would prune him as Maxwell Perkins pruned Thomas Wolfe" (quoted in Couchman, 91).

In some ways *Night of the Hunter* might seem the film that least represents the values Agee espoused as a critic. An expressionist fairy tale, it was shot mainly on Hollywood sets, and even though it has subject matter we associate with realism, it employs movie stars who break nearly every rule of naturalistic performance. Agee was nonetheless an excellent choice as screenwriter and the film is pervaded with his personality. He had intimate knowledge of the world depicted in Davis Grubb's novel, and at one point, at Robert Mitchum's request, he visited the set to assist with American regional accents. He knew firsthand the effects of the Depression on rural life and had worked previously on films about poor children. He must have responded instinctively to the mythic or psychological aspects of the film, which concerns a boy who travels from a loving father to a murderously evil father and from an ignorant mother to a wise and protective mother. Together, Laughton and Agee watched Griffith's major films at the Museum of Modern Art, and Laughton's borrowings from Griffith, especially the casting of Lillian Gish, excited Agee a good deal. No doubt the story's religious themes, and in particular the contrasts between biblical hate and biblical love, also appealed to him. "Hot dog! Love's a-winnin!" the Preacher cries when he illustrates the age-old struggle between right hand and left hand. *Night of the Hunter* is a powerful expression of the victory of a love that the Christian Bible calls "charity." It can also be described with the words Agee used for Chaplin's *Verdoux:* "It looks hand-made, not machine-turned ... it is poetic, not naturalistic, though naturalistic elements are used poetically." Agee was fortunate at the end of his life. No other film on which he worked so completely exemplifies what he thought of as the medium's highest virtues.

Manny Farber

FROM MODERNISM TO POP

James Agee came to film criticism by way of journalism and literature, but Manny Farber came by way of skilled carpentry and painting (with college experience as a sports reporter). Despite their different backgrounds, the two men were friends and their careers as reviewers partly overlapped. Farber became an art and film critic for *The New Republic* in 1942, replacing Otis Ferguson; with the help of Agee, he moved to *The Nation* in 1949 and also briefly reviewed for *Time*. In 1952, he reviewed the Agee-Levitt-Loeb *In the Street*, which at that point had no title, naming it, along with Hollywood's *Red River* (1948), *He Walked by Night* (1948), and *Act of Violence* (1949), as one of the "top pictures made in the last five years" (*Farber on Film*, 382; all quotes are from this source unless otherwise noted). In 1966, Helen Levitt, Agee's collaborator on *In the Street*, introduced Farber to his second wife and late-life writing partner, Patricia Patterson.

During the period when he and Agee were both reviewing films, Farber was less prone to effusive praise, more attuned to visual surfaces, and more inclined to support genre movies (not only male action pictures but also—surprisingly, given his masculine persona—a couple of Bette Davis melodramas and *Love Letters* [1945]) over art films. Both men were admirers of Hawks and Val Lewton, and both wrote glowing reviews of William Wellman's *The Ox-Bow Incident* (1943) and *The Story of G.I. Joe*. (In 1977, Farber told Richard Jameson that he had given too much praise to the former film; the review was entitled "Let Us Now Praise Movies."). Both had relatively few good things to say about Ford, both thought Lubitsch and Hitchcock did their best work in the 1930s, and both were somewhat ambivalent about Sturges (although in later years Farber became an unqualified Sturges fan). Except in the case of *The Stranger* (1946), they both had reservations about Welles; indeed, Farber wrote what was probably the most savage review *The Magnificent Ambersons* has ever received, dubbing it "Orson Welles's latest I-did-it." (Many years later he told Jonathan Rosenbaum, "I missed the boat on that one.") They were equally excited by Noel Coward's *In Which We Serve* (1942), the British Film Unit's *Desert Victory*, and John Huston's thirty-minute *The Battle of San Pietro*—but Farber was critical of the Huston film's excessive narration, much of which runs against the grain of the images.

Huston is the figure who brings out the strongest differences between the two critics. At roughly the same moment as Agee's *Life* profile of Huston, Farber wrote an essay on the director for *The Nation*, describing him as "a smooth blend of iconoclast and sheep" with "an Eisenstein-lubricated brain" (317). Huston's style, he argues, is "so tony it should embarrass his threadbare subjects" (318). Farber thought the postwar Huston films too static and pictorial, too prone to big close-ups, and lacking the virtues of classic Hollywood, "which, from Sennett to Wellman, has visualized stories by means of the unbroken action sequence . . . where terrain and individual are blended together and the whole effect is scenic rather than portraiture" (318). In *The Treasure of the Sierra Madre*, "the first shot of a brawl shows a modest Tampico saloon, the second expands the saloon into a skating rink." During the mining operation in that same film, "huge men seem nailed in front of mountains" (318–19). Farber later described *The Asphalt Jungle* (1950) as full of "tricky hucksterish flash that earlier Huston doesn't have," and a "freakishness that isn't far from Camp" (319). There were things he admired in Huston—the attention to details in the robbery sequence in *The Asphalt Jungle*, the color photography and design of the musical sequences in *Moulin Rouge*—but these didn't compensate for what he viewed as self-conscious artiness. His 1951 review of *The Red Badge of Courage* is typical: "a thin study, overdirected and underwritten . . . and, in the pure sense, one of the most uncompromisingly artistic films ever made in this country. (In my opinion, this is not especially to its credit.)" (370).

The problem Farber sees in Huston—an artful quality that appeals to middlebrows—is similar to what he describes in his 1958 review of *Agee on Film*, originally titled "Stargazing for Middlebrows" and later anthologized as "Nearer My Agee to Thee." This essay is a good example of Farber's celebrated late style, which is so rich with puns, allusions, contradictory adjectives, and jazzy shifts of diction that you're never sure whether he likes or dislikes the things he's discussing (in his case, not necessarily a flaw, and arguably a virtue). It praises Agee as "the most intriguing star-gazer in the middle-brow era of Hollywood" and is irreverent about Agee's "deep-dish" reviews in *The Nation* (499). Farber prefers the "flawless" *Time* reviews—an odd compliment, since *Time* subjected its writers to so much editorial revision and conformity that Farber refused to republish his own reviews for that magazine. He especially admires Agee's ability to put aesthetics above knee-jerk political opinion: "his Tol'able Jim classic, *Let Us Now Praise Famous Men*, disclosed that he was an unorthodox, unsure left-fielder," and yet "even at his worst, in reviews where he was nice, thoughtful, and guilty until he seemed an 'intellectual' hatched in Mack Sennett's brain, Agee was a fine antidote to the paralyzing plot-sociologists who hit the jackpot in the 1940s" (497). Agee's skill with language, Farber observes, also enabled him to build "a Jim-Dandy fan club almost the equal of Dylan Thomas's," but even though he "modified and showboated until the reader had the Jim-jams, the style was exciting in its pea-soup density." What may have gone unnoticed in all the excitement, Farber says, is that "Agee's appreciations stick pretty close to what the middle-brow wants to hear" (498).

Farber may not have been middlebrow, but his judgments of films in the 1940s are much the same as Agee's, and he, too, has a showboating style. Despite the ordinary-Joe lingo he occasionally uses in reviews for *The New Republic* and *The Nation*, he can string adjectives together with the best of them. He also has a lively ability to pin down and condense meaning through unorthodox verbs or verbal constructions. Speaking of *The Blue Dahlia* (1946), he tells you a good deal of what you need to know about Raymond Chandler by describing his fiction as an "Adrian-izing of Dashiell Hammett" (273; Adrian was the costume designer at MGM). Farber is also very good at similes: the exhilarating music in *The Third Man* (1949) "sounds like a trio and hits one's consciousness like a cloudburst of sewing needles" (332); and in *The Men* (1950), Marlon Brando "commands a GI troop into battle like a slow, doped traffic cop wagging cars through an intersection" (341). Nobody has excelled him in vivid and amusing description of actors in movement, as when he says the female victims of a psychotic sharpshooter in *The Sniper* (1952) "go into a cyclonic version of Leon Errol's rubber-legged walk before smashing into a brick wall or table" (387).

Farber's frequent jokes help to keep critical pretentiousness or snobbishness at bay. His 1942 review of *Mrs. Miniver*, for example, imitates the style of a bored journalist holding his chin in one hand and typing with the other: "Probably 'Mrs. Miniver' will be called the best picture of 1942. It has all the things that win Academy awards. 'The Great Ziegfeld' and 'GWTW' were miles long and Miniver is so long it gets lost. Also it has Morality. So it is in the way of being an epic and I can't remember an epic that didn't win something, or why do they make them?" (13). But the jokes never conceal the fact that Farber thought deeply about the total culture of film. One of the valuable aspects of his work for *The New Republic* and *The Nation* was his habit of writing columns about general issues, among them authorship, exhibition practices, studio production values, the changing representations of heroes, newsreels, wartime movies, and theatricality in film. These essays would make a useful small book, showing off Farber's talents as both a film theorist and a humorist. His commentary on exhibition is a salutary reminder that the experience of watching movies with audiences in the so-called good old days could be pretty horrible, just as it is today; and I especially like the piece entitled "Up from Slavery," which provides numerous suggestions for the ideal Hollywood Dadaist film: "I have always thought that the best way to film a famous novel would be to let the audience read it word for word off the screen; at the end of each chapter a list of suitable questions could be asked to see if the audience is getting it.... And then there would be an Orson Welles movie in which the camera mucked around on a dark stairway for two hours looking for Welles" (159).

The long-form essay, or what Farber called the "long-position article," became his specialty in later years, when he published in *Commentary, Commonweal, Film Culture,* and various small magazines. His most famous writings—"Underground Films," "White Elephant Art vs. Termite Art," the essays on Hawks and Sturges, and the pieces on European art films by Buñuel, Godard, Fassbinder, Herzog, Straub, and Duras—belong to this period and were eventually collected in *Negative Space* (1971), the book that in large part accounts for his enduring reputation as a critic. In speaking of these later essays, Robert Polito, editor of the Library of America's *Farber on Film* (2009), makes the important observation that "Farber is perhaps the only American critic of modernism to write as a modernist." Polito nicely describes Farber's language as a "topographical prose that aspired, termite-fashion, through fragmentation, parody, allusions, multiple focus, and clashing dictions to engage the formal spaces of the new films." It was a prose that had the effect of "a kind of back-door poetry" (xix). Jonathan Rosenbaum's description of the style is also excellent and would apply equally well to Farber's late paintings: "Farber's most characteristic method is to pile [his] observations on top of one another, or juxtapose them in a disordered heap on the flat surface of a page, not string them together into linear narratives or arguments. To say that they go nowhere would miss the point; in point of fact they go everywhere, creating a busy and unwieldy sprawl that spills beyond the frame of whatever he happens to be discussing" (*Placing Movies,* 60).

A typical example is Farber's short, aggressively hip 1969 article on Samuel Fuller, which is almost completely devoted to marshaling lowbrow and highbrow taste against the dreaded middlebrow. Funny and observant, the piece is written with exploding-fireworks prose and shotgun allusiveness. In the space of about four pages, Farber compares Fuller with Chester Gould, Fats Waller, John Foster Dulles, Milton Caniff, Robert Bresson, Pieter Brueghel, Ford Madox Ford, and Jean-Luc Godard—meanwhile contrasting him with Hollywood prestige directors George Stevens and Frank Capra, who would supposedly consider his movies "hopelessly drab" (669). In Farber's view, Fuller's films are to be admired for their bold, sometimes nutty surfaces and simple force:

> Apart from the madness for Oriental art work that has an undressed look and has been dropped onto an unlikely spot by a helicopter (after being constructed overnight by a blind carpenter), the craziness of these propagandist films [*The Steel Helmet* and *China Gate*] is that the white hero is such trash: unprincipled, stupid, loud-mouthed, mean, thinking nothing about mauling women or any man a foot shorter. Zack, who starts *The Steel Helmet* as a helmet with a hole in it, a bit like a turtle until the helmet rises an inch off the stubbled field to show these meager, nasty eyes, slowly shifting back and forth, casing the area, is like someone born on Torment Street between Malicious and Crude. (669)

China Gate is even more demented, yet lovable for Farber, "so absurd that it becomes an enchantment to the camp taste" (671).

As a critic Farber appears to have started as a modernist like Agee and remained one on some level, but he evolved with the times, and his later essays and paintings reflect new cultural developments. In his 1977 interview with Richard Thompson, he said that his late painting, which makes reference to such things as old movies and candy wrappers, has "nothing to do with Pop" because "I think it's sinful to give the audience material it knows already" (*Negative Space*, 354). Perhaps so, but the Fuller article is symptomatic of certain tendencies in pop-art criticism. Its giddy pleasure in what it mistakenly takes to be Fuller's primitive vulgarity, its fascination with surfaces, its praise of apparent kitsch, its generous reference to camp—all this is fully in keeping with Susan Sontag's *Against Interpretation* and signals an emergent, virtually regnant postmodernism.

SPACE

I've always admired the cool-sounding title *Negative Space*, but for many years I didn't realize that it's a well-known term in art criticism. In a 1953 discussion of 3-D, Farber defined the term as "the spaces in a composition that are more or less unfilled" (444). In the introduction to *Negative Space*, he defines it more globally and vaguely, as "the command of experience which an artist can set resonating within a film . . . a sense of terrain created partly by the audience's imagination and partly by the camera-actors-director" (9). Whatever he means, Farber's entire approach to film criticism is guided by spatial concepts—he speaks of screen space, psychological space, acting space, geographic space, allegorical space, and so forth. "Time" is a less important word in his lexicon. He's less interested the manipulations of plot and editing than in the considerations that arise when space determines time, as it often does in painting, sculpture, architecture, stage design, or games like baseball, football, or chess.

Farber wants us to think of the screen not as a frame or a mask for the unfolding of narrative or argument but as a movable playing field for visual strategies, a territory or geometry that controls everything else. For him, the temporal register is largely a matter of a) bodily movement within a space—which explains why Farber was such a great writer about actors—and b) camera or eye movement across and through a setting. This spatialization of motion, together with Farber's tough-guy, very American prose style, which combines a sports reporter's masculine, no-nonsense tone with an almost baroque vocabulary and syntax, is what gives his criticism much of its originality and power.

The simplest and most helpful definition of negative space I've encountered uses a cartoon by Chuck Jones, one of Farber's favorite artists, as an illustration. When Wile E. Coyote drops a half mile off a cliff and lands spread-eagle on the ground, he leaves a cavity in the shape of his body, which is the positive space. The negative space is everything around the positive space—the dirt and rock and color that make up the ground for the shape of the figure. To develop an eye for negative space you need to look outside the lines, at the periphery; you need to cultivate a sort of reverse-priority gaze (as in a photographic negative) that appreciates how marginal elements function in relation to the whole, or even on their own. This mode of viewing accounts for Farber's practice as both a painter and a critic. His painting entitled "Sherlock, Jr.," for example, consists of a dominant ground—a slightly skewed circle with narrow railroad tracks cutting across its diagonal and horizontal diameters, with a tiny train out of *The General* running along one of them. It looks like a sort of wheel or pie-shaped tabletop divided into four quadrants of different colors, within which, apparently at random, are scattered a painted collage of small objects of different sizes and perspectives—a candy bar called "Look," a Civil War canon, a park bench, a book of receipts, some tiny houses with red roofs. It's a visual flea market with occasional allusions to Keaton. The viewer's eye tends to jump or skitter around the composition, always aware of the ground but pausing to focus on details; and unlike montage or realist representation, the scattered collage allows each small element to retain relative autonomy and charm.

Compare this to Farber's famous description of John Wayne in *The Man Who Shot Liberty Valance* (1962), which draws our attention to both the ground and the peripheral detail: "In an Arizona town that is too placid, where the cactus was planted last night and nostalgically cast actors do a generalized drunkenness, cowardice, voraciousness, Wayne is the termite actor focusing only on a tiny present area, nibbling at it with engaging professionalism and a hipster sense of how to sit in a chair leaned against the wall, eye flogging an over-actor (Lee Marvin)" (535). The termite eye looks for what Farber elsewhere called "the flash-bomb vitality that one scene, actor, or technician injects across the grain of a film," and what he described in his own paintings as "not centered portraiture but a composition which uses the field of the painting as a performing stage for deployments, paths [that are] dispersed, like a throw of the dice" (*Negative Space*, 354). No wonder Farber admired Preston Sturges, whose films were crowded with vivid types boiling around in a comic carnival; and no wonder one of his favorite pictures was Michael Snow's *Wavelength* (1967), a forty-five-minute camera journey across a loft apartment toward a picture on a far wall, during which various items, including what appears to be a dead body, become momentarily visible at the periphery of the screen.

In Farber's view, the de-centered details in a good film or painting need to be governed by an overall spatial design—a composition that for him seems more important than plot or politics. Thus Farber ignores what Patricia Patterson rightly calls the "Marxism with a silver spoon in your mouth" of Marguerite Duras's *India Song* and instead praises the way the film deploys action within a space: "As in late Snow, Altman, Rivette, everything has been pushed to the periphery, characters constantly entering and exiting a movie that is mostly at the edge of the frame" (*Negative Space*, 359). It's not that everything in a film has to be peripheral, only that space has to have an interesting activity or purpose. Consider his description of *Touch of Evil*, which, despite a few inaccuracies, has never been improved upon; it goes to the heart of the picture's thematic concerns ("an American blonde marries a Mexican attorney, and all her fears about Mexicans come true") but gives most of its attention to faces, bodies, and movements within a generalized space: "an aggressive-dynamic-robust-excessive-silly universe with Welles's inevitable effort with space—to make it prismatic and a quagmire at the same time." This "allegorical space" also gives us "endless bits of excruciating black humor," as when a "deaf mute grocery clerk [actually she's blind] squints in the foreground, while Charlton

Heston on the phone, embarrassed by his wife's eroticism from a motel bed, tries to suggest nonchalance" (694).

Farber's criticism sometimes has the romantic habit of valuing the fragment over the whole, and with important qualifications he can be bracketed among film writers who believe the essence of the medium lies in fetishized detail—the surrealists, for example, or the French theorists of *photogènie*, or the contemporary school of academic cinephiles represented by Robert Ray and Christian Keathley. The difference is that Farber isn't interested in Freud or free association, and he gives space priority over time. He also reveals that space can have ideological implications. He prefers Mann over Ford, for example, because Ford thinks of space in "mythical" terms and is always sending out freighted, iconic messages. "In a Ford movie," Farber says, "the star of the movie is always in the center of the scene telling you what the point of the scene is, the camera's always upshooting." Ford doesn't really care about landscape, Farber argues, and therefore always uses the same Monument Valley as a backdrop. Mann, on the other hand, is keenly aware of the background and "is able to get the character off the center, somewhat peripheral, toward the edge of the screen" (*Negative Space*, 377), thus upsetting the usual visual hierarchies of tendentious art.

STYLE AND CULTURAL POLITICS

Having mentioned ideology, I should say more about Farber's politics. Robert Polito tells us that as a carpenter in San Francisco during the 1930s, Farber tried to join the Communist Party. At some point in the 1940s, however, he seemed to become conservative or libertarian. He was certainly no "insecure left-fielder," as he said of Agee. His World War II–era reviews are vigorously critical of American racism (even though he frequently refers to "Japs" in Hollywood war movies), and one of his last acts was to vote for Barack Obama in 2008.

Polito also reminds us that one of Farber's major aims during most of his career "was specifically dethroning the vulgarities and hypocrisy of liberal New Deal Hollywood" (xxviii). Along with this agenda came his attacks on the liberalism of so-called middlebrow art. Farber had grown up during the Depression and was shaped by the New York intellectual environment of the 1940s and '50s, when Clement Greenberg was the ruling art theorist, when American abstract expressionism (which Farber initially practiced) was the last gesture of modernist painting against the onslaught of reified modernity, and when most intellectual discourse, whether left-wing or right-wing, consisted of attacks on the middle-class aspirations of the commercial and academic culture industries. In this environment, Farber's criticism was idiosyncratic but resolutely American in taste, discriminating in regard to popular movies but suspicious of both liberal Hollywood and what he regarded as pretentious Greenwich Village aestheticism. In 1946, his tough-guy attitude took on a nasty tone when he described Maya Deren as "lesbianish" and "pansyish . . . totally lacking in sensuousness, humor and love. . . . She seems to petrify the subject until it takes on the character of a museum piece. . . . She has no feeling for light and dark and is as unable to spot a cliché as a Tin Pan Alley hack" (292). Later in his career he sought to preserve an austere and in some ways populist aestheticism by elevating certain members of the cinematic avant-garde (especially Straub-Huillet and Michael Snow) and the supposedly disreputable male action directors (who were not quite so underground as he claimed) over liberals such as Huston, Wyler, and above all the early Orson Welles.

Citizen Kane became for Farber the original sin of liberal Hollywood, the snake in the garden of the classic system, a film that not only made the clichés of psychoanalysis seem profound but also destroyed the free-flowing middle-distance camera work of earlier periods. "The Gimp," his brilliant 1952 analysis of the postwar influence of *Kane*, pays tribute to Welles and Toland's "exciting, if hammy" picture, but correctly notes that it showed less talented yet ambitious directors—especially Kazan, Wilder, Wyler, Stevens, and Huston—how to inject overstated philosophy, psychoanalysis, and vulgarized liberalism into both the plots and visual style of movies. Slyly alluding to Marx and Engels, Farber argues, "The ghost of *Citizen Kane* stalks a monstrous-looking screen. The entire physical structure of movies has been slowed down and brought closer to the front plane of the screen [through wide-angle, deep-focus photography] so that eccentric effects can be deeply felt" (397). A key example of the kind of overstated eccentricity he hates is the scene in Wilder's *Sunset Boulevard* when the camera zeros in on a huge, sharply focused close-up of a smarmy clerk in an expensive men's store as he whispers, "After all, if the lady is paying . . ." into the ear of a wincing William Holden. The shot, Farber writes, has "all the freshness of an old tire-patch, consisting . . . of naïve moral gibberish that no adult in his right mind would mouth" (389). Perhaps significantly, this very shot had been singled out for praise by James Agee in his *Sight and Sound* review of the film. Farber was almost equally contemptuous of Huston's *African Queen*, scripted by Huston and Agee, which "was shot entirely in the Belgian Congo, but the characters [brought near to the front plane of the screen] do almost nothing that couldn't have been done on one studio set with the aid of some library shots" (393).

Another case of the visual overstatement he hates is *Sweet Smell of Success* (1957), which Farber used as a key example in his famous essay

"Hard-Sell Cinema." Farber had an extremely sensitive nose for anything that gave off the odor of an arty social-problem picture. *Sweet Smell*, he writes, is "all clever, racy surface and mean-spirited liberalism," which he equates with a school of "hard working mediocrities"—including Dave Brubeck, Stan Getz, J.D. Salinger, Saul Bellow, Franz Kline, Larry Rivers, Sidney Lumet, Paddy Chayefsky, Budd Schulberg, Rod Serling, and John Frankenheimer—whose work gives the feeling of "a high-powered salesman using empty tricks" (477). Of Tony Curtis's performance, he says only that it "breaks the Olympic record for fast acting," leaving the viewer with a feeling that "the jingle-jangle of hard-sell cinema is a long way from the complicated art of simple picture-making, as it has been practiced by the unrecognized Hawks, Walsh, Anthony Mann, and John Farrow" (484–85).

Farber finds the same hard sell in other liberal movies of the period—*Twelve Angry Men*, *Marty*, *A Face in the Crowd*, and *The Strange One*—and attributes it to the rise of a "business mind" that had begun to influence "American creativity" (478). "If you are wondering what happened to the tough, impersonal, against-the-grain innovator in our times," he writes, "the type of artist who has the anonymous strength of a Walker Evans, the natural grace of a James Agee, the geographic sense of an Anthony Mann, the bitingly exact earthiness of a J.R. Williams, the suavely fluid humanism of a Howard Hawks—he has been hidden by a fantastic army of commercial fine-artists, little locustlike creatures who have the dedication of a Sammy Glick" (486).

I've always had respect for *Sweet Smell of Success* (and to a lesser extent for *The Strange One*), and, contra Farber, I would defend it as a gutsy act of revenge by members of the Hollywood left who had suffered under McCarthyism and were attacking the no less business-obsessed but dying media environment of the classic studio system and old-style publicists like Walter Winchell. (Participants in the film whose careers had been directly impacted by the far more mean-spirited Red scare of the early 1950s included Harold Hecht, Burt Lancaster, Clifford Odets, Elmer Bernstein, and Sam Levine.) As for Tony Curtis's impressive performance, it derives from a tradition of fast-talking newspaper pictures and is certainly no speedier or louder than Rosalind Russell or Cary Grant in Hawks's *His Girl Friday*. The only difference is that it's played for black humor and not-so-quiet desperation, which the direction and James Wong Howe's photography emphasize. Curtis plays a Sammy Glick type, but that doesn't mean he was one. (Glick, we should recall, originated in Budd Schulberg's 1941 novel *What Makes Sammy Run?*, but he didn't appear on-screen until a 1959 TV adaptation that followed close on the heels of *Sweet Smell*.) The Hecht-Hill-Lancaster production company was no doubt interested in making money, just as Farber says (they had just made a bundle off of *Marty, Vera Cruz*, and *Trapeze*), but no matter how hard they tried to sell this picture, it was hardly the sort of thing that could have become a hit. *Sweet Smell* was such a dark drama that audiences hated it; it lost so much at the box office that it nearly wrecked the production company and director Alexander Mackendrick's career.

I say all this partly in order to emphasize that one doesn't have to agree with Farber or any critic in order to appreciate their work. Farber's critical writing is grounded in a serious, coherent, and wide-ranging argument about the culture, and whenever I disagree with him I feel a need to justify my opinions. I reread him with pleasure, not just for his unique style but also for the attitudes embodied in the style. He's the scourge of "deep-dish" Hollywood, but also the poet of unpretentious action and radical cinematic form.

Andrew Sarris

Andrew Sarris was such a profound influence on my writing about movies that I can't hope to do him justice in a short space. To alleviate the problem, I've fallen back on a set of notes (revised and expanded from an earlier published set) that I hope will be true to the spirit of concision in Sarris's *The American Cinema* (1968), his reviews in the *Village Voice*, and some of his other writings. I've arranged my thoughts as alphabetical entries in a sort of dictionary made up of key words, titles, or names. Some letters of the alphabet are more important than others, and in these cases I've allowed myself to list more than one word. In other cases, I've whimsically combined two or three letters in a single entry. The result is an "ABC" of reading Andrew Sarris.

AUTEURISM, AMERICAN, ACADEMIC, AMATEUR, ART

As I've indicated earlier in this volume, auteurism is best described as a movement originating in Parisian film culture of the 1950s and 1960s that took on slightly different implications as it entered other national contexts. One of Sarris's major achievements was to reinterpret this movement for America. Like Truffaut, he launched a polemical attack against a "tradition of quality" made up chiefly of literary adaptations and social-problem dramas; his specific targets, however, were not Autant-Lara, Carné, and Delannoy, but Huston, Wyler, and Kazan. Along similar lines, he challenged intellectual opinion by arguing that Hollywood, not Europe, had the most artistically important cinema in the world. Meanwhile, he stressed the academic importance of auteurism. Because he was a teacher at Columbia and other schools rather than a would-be director, Sarris used the auteurist debates to write a full-scale history of American movies. One of his explicit aims in *The American Cinema* was to make film historiography more evaluative and less of an amateur calling, an effort that required both scholarly commitment and discriminating intelligence. He placed an emphasis on personal style and was contemptuous of both the sociologists and the nonprofessional hobbyists. But what gave Sarris's writing special force was his ability to remain an amateur in the etymological sense of the passionate lover while also functioning as a critic and a scholar. Unlike the typical academic, Sarris addressed his remarks to a civilized common viewer. He was able to do so because he believed in art—the most crucial term in his vocabulary.

BAZIN, ANDRÉ

Bazin was a true theorist and a major influence on the New Wave directors who wrote for *Cahiers du cinéma* in the 1950s. But, again as I've previously indicated in this book, he wasn't an auteurist. He praised the "genius of the system"; he was skeptical of Hitchcock; he wrote about literary adaptations; and he put Wyler, who was initially demoted by the auteurists, on nearly the same level as Welles. His importance to the younger generation lay not in his critical policy but in his existential humanism, which reached an almost mystical level in his writings on photography and cinematic space. Bazin's commentaries on Renoir, Rossellini, and Welles are not only major contributions to the poetics of film but also subtle essays about the ethical/ideological implications of the camera's encounter with the world. They influenced Sarris at many points in *The American Cinema*, especially in the entries on Chaplin, Flaherty, and Murnau, but also in his writing elsewhere.

CINEPHILIA, CANONS

Auteurism in the United States was nourished by revival theaters, film societies, museums, and the increasing presence of old movies on TV. Above all, it grew out of cinephilia in New York during the 1950s and '60s. Cinephila is still very much with us, especially in the world of DVD collectors and the Internet, but now as then it needs to be tempered by discriminating criticism. This is a point Molly Haskell makes indirectly in her finely observed and finely written memoir, *Love and Other Infectious Diseases*, where she describes New York film culture in the years when she met Sarris and emphasizes his desire not simply to know film history but to distinguish the good from the bad.

> In those days [the 1960s], before there were film courses . . . one caught old movies wherever one could. It was in the byways and back alleys of cinema [in rooms where 16mm was shown] that I first met members of

that strange underground species, the film buff.... As a group, they were almost entirely male—probably because voyeurism is essentially a male activity, as is complete surrender to fantasy.... These were men who lived without women, without wives or girlfriends to hold the mirror up to them, make them eat decent food, get fresh air, spend a few hours away from a movie theater.... Yet Andrew, though resembling them in some outward respects, wasn't quite one of them. For one thing, he was more interested in good movies than obscure ones. Once there was a choice between seeing Hitchcock's *Shadow of a Doubt* and a rural B picture called *The Girl of the Limberlost*, and Andrew's was the only hand raised in favor of the former, the latter—"better" for being unseen—was the near unanimous choice. (101–2)

Auteurism in all its forms was relentlessly evaluative, and as a result it produced canons. Part of the significance of Sarris's work in *The American Cinema* lies precisely in his attempt to build a canon by naming, in what he called a tentative or provisional fashion, the most important directors and films. Ironically, just at the point when his work was absorbed into the American academy, it encountered theories bent on destroying both cinephilia and canons. Even so, the High Theorists kept returning to the "texts" Sarris and his colleagues had established. We're now at a point where we need more canon building and less theorizing about the latest blockbusters. The monuments erected by such activity aren't engraved and they don't necessarily honor Dead White Men. Without serious attempts to create provisional canons, Hollywood wins; we're left with only historical data, box-office statistics, audience research, and quasi-scientific explanations of formal systems. Film study would be greatly enlivened if we had another book like *The American Cinema*, devoted to naming and providing justification for the best Hollywood directors and pictures of the past thirty years. This book would need to be written by someone as talented and educated as Sarris—someone who knows TV as well as movies, and who is willing to put her values on the line.

DIRECTORS; DEMILLE, CECIL B.

French auteurism centered on directors partly because many of the people involved wanted to become directors in a new French art cinema. Sarris was more scholarly and academic in his ambitions, and therefore more of a systematic historian of the classic studio system, which was almost dead by the time *The American Cinema* was written. In his book Sarris argues quite plausibly that the studios gave directors more freedom than writers, especially in genre projects. Even so, the overwhelming majority of artists in Sarris's pantheon were also producers or independents, working slightly apart from studio bosses or middle-management executives (names include Griffith, Chaplin, Keaton, Ford, Hawks, Hitchcock, and Welles). There's nothing especially unusual about a book that praises such figures. Like some of the French, Sarris is most unorthodox and challenging not when he argues on behalf of Chaplin or Welles but when he defends certain of their movies, such as *Limelight* (1952) or *The Lady from Shanghai* (1948). He's also challenging when he shows admiration for women's soap operas in addition to male action pictures, and when he places an intellectually unfashionable producer-director like Cecil B. DeMille (the very symbol of Hollywood vulgarity and right-wing bombast) on "The Far Side of Paradise."

EPIGRAMMATIC STYLE

The American Cinema is a model of critical economy, written in a style that aspires to the condition of epigrammatic wit. The entry on DeMille is a good example: "He may ... have been the last Victorian, although the late George Orwell would probably have held out for Salvador Dali" (*American Cinema*, 91; unless otherwise noted, quotes are from this source). The one-sentence contrast between Welles and Hitchcock is even better: "Wellesian cinema is as much the cinema of the exhibitionist as Hitchcockian cinema is the cinema of the voyeur" (80).

Here and in his other writings, Sarris's style is based on well-rounded, highly quotable sentences rather than ruminative paragraphs; in a modern fashion, he resembles neoclassicists such as Samuel Johnson or Alexander Pope, who condensed arguments into a phrase or a heroic couplet. One of his ways of achieving this effect is through symmetrically balanced syntactic oppositions that state a kind of deep-structural rule: "The idea of the actor has always contradicted the idea of the masses, just as the close-up has always distorted the long view of history" (41). Another way of achieving the effect is through alliteration, which is one of the most distinctive features of his style: "In [Will] Rogers, iconoclasm wrestles an often losing battle with philistinism, and, not infrequently, populism is smothered in the pieties of the plutocrat" (*John Ford Movie Mystery*, 52).

FORD, JOHN; GRIFFITH, D. W; HAWKS, HOWARD

Three directors, alphabetically adjacent to one another in the Sarris pantheon. Of the three, Hawks is the most "modern" or closest in spirit to the pragmatic efficiency of industrialized America. Ford is equally efficient as a craftsman, equally committed to "invisible" editing and "invisible" camera movement, and equally good when the plot pauses to make room for grace notes of characterization; but in most other ways Ford is Hawks's dialectical opposite. Sarris wrote a great deal about both directors (his excellent early book, *The John Ford Movie Mystery,* is sadly out of print), and the classically balanced quality of his prose style pays huge dividends when he puts two equally compelling figures side by side. In his book on Ford, for example, he points out that although Ford's *Air Mail* (1932) and Hawks's *Ceiling Zero* (1936) were both written by Frank Wead and have virtually the same plot, "Ford's is the view from long shot, submerging the squabbling egos of the pilots in cameraman Karl Freund's luminous contemplation of the plane itself as the communal vehicle of all the hopes and fears of the characters. By contrast, Hawks' celebrated eye-level viewpoint concentrates on the aerial/Ariel aspirations of the fliers themselves, and reduces the planes to bird-like appendages of the presumptuous groundlings" (47).

In the background of these contrasts stands the paternal Griffith, who embodies certain qualities of both Hawks and Ford yet transcends them. Griffith's work, Sarris remarks, may look dated because the world he represented is no longer ours, but there is no such thing as progress in art, only differing visions. Griffith, Sarris argues, was a pragmatic technician who "managed to synthesize the dramatic and documentary elements of the modern feature film" and whose style became more deceptively simple or invisible in order to achieve "psychological penetration of the dramatic issues that concerned him" (51). Like Ford, Griffith was a pictorialist of landscape; but Ford's landscapes served as monumental symbols of historical struggles and collective hopes and fears, while Griffith's landscapes "expressed metaphorically the emotional life of his heroines" (51). Griffith was not only a master of wide shots and Hawksian eye-level medium shots, but also of close-ups that "shifted characters from the republic of prose to the kingdom of poetry" (52).

ICONOCLASM

Sarris was so influential in shaping our tastes that in some ways he no longer seems iconoclastic. It might help to recall that Bosley Crowther was still the chief movie critic at the *New York Times* when Sarris became a reviewer, and that Crowther dismissed many of the pictures Sarris praised. With the exception of Mamoulian, Milestone, and Wellman, all of the directors in the "Less Than Meets the Eye" or "Strained Seriousness" categories of *The American Cinema* were quite active, and most of them were regarded by American critics as the leading artists in Hollywood. Most American film historians thought that the aging Ford's greatest picture was *The Informer* (1935), and figures like Sirk, Fuller, and Mann, all of whom

Sarris placed in his second-highest category, "The Far Side of Paradise," had nothing like their present reputations. Sarris thought—rightly—that Ford's career was far from over and that his best pictures of 1935 had been two comedies: *The Whole Town's Talking* and *Steamboat Round the Bend*. And perhaps because of his good luck in having the equally fine critic Molly Haskell as a wife and companion, or simply because of his love of women, Sarris was much less susceptible to the overwhelmingly masculine critical values of his day. His *Village Voice* review of David Lean's much-praised *Lawrence of Arabia* (1962) is a case in point:

> José Ferrer plays a coughing Turkish pederast to the hilt as he literally unveils his blond captive and fondles his breast.... Let a man be stripped and flogged, and we are supposed to be impressed with the seriousness of the theme. Perhaps *Lawrence of Arabia* is one brutal queer film too many. Perhaps I am a little weary of people telling me about the silliness of the heterosexual action in *The Lovers* and about the profundity of the sadism in *Billy Budd*. Perhaps I am just plain tired of all these "serious" moral films with no women in the cast. There is a calculating sickness at work here, an Anglo-American syndrome of abstract morality for men only that sickens me as a recurringly acclaimed theme of the cinema. By all means, let's bring on the girls. (*Confessions*, 67)

Sarris's against-the-grain judgments made him slightly controversial, but his true rebelliousness lay in his straightforward assertion of art as personal expression. The idea that the best films usually have something to do with a director's worldview is almost as embattled today. Its opponents are in one sense justified, because the discourse on personal expression (as on anything else) can have pernicious effects; it can easily degenerate into celebrity cultism, romantic escapism, or bourgeois ideology. Individual artists are nevertheless as much a material fact as the studio system or the budgets. To take them seriously, to make intelligent comments on their attitudes and stylistic choices, can be an unorthodox, socially powerful, and critically resistant thing to do.

JOHNNY GUITAR, *KISS ME DEADLY*

Two films of the mid-1950s, relatively ignored by the American critical establishment, that became touchstones of auteurist taste. Both were indecorous if not downright delirious in their treatment of genre conventions, and, in an indirect way, they probably inspired the French to make pictures like *Breathless*. In *The American Cinema*, Sarris names *Johnny Guitar* as the fifth best movie of 1954 (after films by Hitchcock, Ford, Renoir, Rossellini, and Buñuel) and *Kiss Me Deadly* as the sixth best of 1955 (after films by Rossellini, Hitchcock, Sirk, Welles, and Ford). In both cases he stresses the anarchic-romantic temperament of the director: *Johnny Guitar* is Nicholas Ray's "most bizarre film, and probably his most personal" (108); and *Kiss Me Deadly* is "a testament to [Robert] Aldrich's anarchic spirit" (84). I saw both films in my early adolescence, long before reading Sarris, and they made no special impression on me at the time. They certainly do now, perhaps because of the impressive critical readings that have been generated by them. I don't know how personal they were, but I can't watch them today without being aware of how much I originally missed and without feeling gratitude toward Sarris and other auteurists who championed Ray and Aldrich.

LISTS

The American Cinema is a book of evaluative lists. Sarris lists his favorite directors alphabetically in hierarchical categories; he lists each director's films chronologically, italicizing the best ones, and, at the end of the book, he lists the best films of each year from 1915 onward (after their directors' names), italicizing the true masterpieces. His technique is once again borrowed from the French New Wave, who repeatedly used ten-best lists as a shock tactic. Sarris expanded this strategy into a large-scale history, producing both a complex reference work and a guide to his personal tastes. We need not ask if his judgments were correct; his lists are provocations, stimulating debate and making us want to look more closely at certain pictures. More critics ought to follow his example. We have too many "Ten Worst Movies of All Time" and too many lists of last week's box-office results.

MODERNITY, MONTAGE, MEMORY, NATURE, NOSTALGIA

Sarris can be considered a "modern" because he's a strong advocate of the twentieth century's most influential art form. He also has a few things in common with the twentieth-century avant-garde: a fondness for lists and manifestos; a declared affiliation with a "theory" or "ism"; and a preference for certain lowbrow movies over respectable middlebrow dramas. In many important ways, however, he's critical of both industrial and artistic modernity. *The American Cinema* repeatedly argues that there is no such thing as progress in the arts; it supports the romantic belief that individual artists can transcend Hollywood, protecting certain values against the encroachments of capitalism and industrial rationality; and, like Bazin, it's skeptical of montage, which was central to modernist aesthetics in all the arts. Despite the montage-like quality of Sarris's own book, he favors continuity and long takes. He's also fond of what might be called the cinema of memory, and of directors who evoke the nineteenth century or the preindustrial past. This is what makes his commentaries on figures such as Griffith, Chaplin, Ford, and Welles particularly effective. The cinema of memory is inevitably the cinema of nostalgia, often producing a complex longing for nature or for the myth of an organically unified world. Sarris is aware of this myth and is quite good at showing how it operates in certain directors; in Robert Flaherty, for example, whose cinema, as Sarris observes, offers us "one of the last testaments of the 'cult of nature,' and, as such, is infinitely precious" (43).

OPHÜLS, MAX

One of the directors in the Sarris pantheon, about whom Sarris planned to write a book. The short entry on Ophüls in *The American Cinema* is especially good, showing how meaning arises out of visual style, evoking the exact feel of the films, and answering every possible objection to the director's work. Notice that Ophüls is in many ways quite different from Ford, whom Sarris equally admires. A European sophisticate and a director of "women's" pictures, Ophüls specialized in tragic love stories, and his style depended upon elegant camera movements keyed to the rhythms of fashionable walks up winding stairways or across ballrooms and town squares. But Ophüls, like Ford, was also a director who dealt in nostalgia. For Sarris, the meaning of Ophülsian camera movement is that "time has no stop." Unlike montage, which tends to operate "in a limbo of abstract images," Ophüls's moving camera "records inexorably the passage of time" and shows the characters' "imprisonment in time" (72). This theme is basic to the cinema of memory and to romanticism in general. (See, for example, the poems of Wordsworth or Yeats.) It gives a kind of poignancy to Ophüls, but also to Sarris's own writing.

PLEASURE, PERFORMANCE, PARADOX

Like all the auteurists, Sarris conveys his great pleasure in many of the things he discusses. He's also aware that one of the basic pleasures of movies comes from watching the stars. Hence, despite his commitment to directors, he makes numerous interesting observations about acting. He's relatively unenthusiastic about the modern performances in Antonioni or the Method-inspired directors; he prefers the classic Hollywood style and is especially good at commenting on the relation between old-fashioned male directors and their female stars. He also devotes an entire section of *The American Cinema* to comic performers, who are usually far more important than their directors to the overall effect of their films. Above all he admires the "torrents and torrents of classical acting" in Griffith. "Lillian Gish is an infinitely greater actress than Monica Vitti," he writes, because Griffith's cinema demands "a rediscovery of behavioral reality" and a sense of "psychological harmony with nature" (52).

This sort of pleasure is paradoxical because the "behavioral reality," even in a presumptive realist like Griffith, is mediated through theatrical conventions, costuming, makeup, and a photographic apparatus. *The American Cinema* is equally paradoxical in the way it uses a theory of individual expression to explain an industrial art, and in the way it inverts the usual critical values, dissolving the boundaries between highbrow and lowbrow. Even its basic conception of the movie director is founded on a paradox: "The director," Sarris says, "is both the least necessary and most important component of film-making. . . . He *[sic]* would not be worth bothering with if he were not capable now and then of a sublimity of expression almost miraculously extracted from his money-oriented environment" (37).

THE QUIET AMERICAN, RED LINE 7000

Sarris was never a slavish imitator of French fashion; as he put it, "no self-respecting American film historian should ever accept Paris as the final authority on the American cinema" (28). One of Godard's favorite directors in the 1950s and 1960s was Joseph L. Mankiewicz, whom Sarris placed in the "Less Than Meets the Eye" category of the 1968 edition of *The American Cinema*. In 1958, an *annus mirabilis* of the New Wave, Godard ranked Mankiewicz's *The Quiet American* as the best film of the year, putting it a whopping six places above Welles's *Touch of Evil;* a decade later Sarris listed *Touch of Evil* as the second best film of 1958 (after *Vertigo*) and wrote that Mankiewicz was "unable to cope" with the Graham Greene novel on which his picture was based (162). In 1966, French critic Jean Narboni, writing in *Cahiers,* claimed that Howard Hawks's *Red Line 7000* was "a masterly presentation of various ways of twisting convention—an epitome of and treatise on deconstruction" (Hillier, *"Cahiers du Cinéma": The 1960s,* 218). Sarris greatly admired Hawks, but he wrote in the *Village Voice* that *Red Line 7000* was a disappointment and little more than a "self-parody" (*Confessions,* 301).

By the mid-1960s French theory and French cinema—or at least the cinema as represented by Godard—were becoming more radical, foreshadowing the Parisian "events" of May 1968. In this period Sarris and the French seemed to grow further apart. Consider Sarris's April 1968 column in the *Village Voice,* where he reviewed Godard's *La Chinoise* alongside Don

Siegel's *Madigan*. Sarris admired both films. He praised Godard as "the only contemporary director with the ability to express through graceful cinema what young people are feeling at this time in world history" (*Confessions*, 350), but he argued that in the years leading up to *La Chinoise* Godard had been "exploiting the most provincial prejudices of the Idiot Left." Long ago, he recalled, "I had loved Godard's criticism for its open-mindedness. The movies were everything, Godard had insisted, from Hitchcock to Rossellini, from Eisenstein to Flaherty. Now suddenly the movies were only what Godard and his cronies permitted them to be" (*Confessions*, 349). *La Chinoise*, in Sarris's view, was a return to Godard at his best, but the Siegel film, which was at another pole of cinema, was almost as good, displaying "the often forgotten virtues of classical editing" and, by virtue of the no-longer-blacklisted screenwriter Abraham Polonsky's moral ambiguities, bestowing "seriousness" on a genre picture (*Confessions*, 352).

STYLE

In Sarris, the term *style* seldom refers to an abstract system of formal rules, as in "the Hollywood style." He usually employs the word in its expressive sense, describing individual styles. A famous linguist once explained this usage by analogy with a tennis match (one of Sarris's favorite sports): style is the way an individual player copes with the rules of the game, managing to get the ball over the net. Because of the relatively formulaic genre system and the industrialized nature of classic Hollywood, the rules of the movie game were almost as consistent as those of tennis, making it possible to notice individual ways of dealing with them. As Sarris puts it, "The classical cinema was more functional than the modern cinema. It knew its audience and their expectations, but it often provided something extra. That something extra is the concern of the auteur theory" (32). Of course it's also possible to recognize "something extra" in the personalities of producers, writers, actors, or photographers. Sarris acknowledged this and even commented on it from time to time, but he placed emphasis on the director in order to counteract the literary/theatrical bias of much earlier criticism; the director, he argued, was the figure most often responsible for making production choices that determine cinematic style, and for imbuing those choices with meaning.

THUNDERBALL AND *TOPAZ*

Thunderball (1965), based on an Ian Fleming novel and directed by low-budget British auteur Terence Young, was the longest and most expensive

James Bond movie up to that point in time. A box-office smash, it featured Oscar-winning special effects, super-wide-screen views of tourist locations in the Bahamas, and numerous bikini-clad young women, some of whom had appeared in even less clothing in *Playboy*. *Topaz* (1969), based on a Leon Uris novel, was one of Alfred Hitchcock's last and least successful pictures. Expensively mounted and quite lengthy (the original ending and several other scenes were cut by the studio), it dealt with historical events in France leading up to the Cuban missile crisis. It had no stars, its female cast members were relatively unappealing, and its leading actor, Frederick Stafford, who resembled Sean Connery, lacked what Sarris described as "even the bare minimum of emotional expressiveness" (*Primal Screen*, 183).

Sarris was puzzled by the success of *Thunderball*, which he argued was a "triumph of merchandising and advertising" (*Primal Screen*, 180). Somehow the film was popular despite overlong underwater sequences, rampant chauvinism, lame jokes, and almost indistinguishable bikinied women. Sean Connery, who had recently acted for Hitchcock, wasn't an especially big box-office attraction outside the Bond series, the plot of the picture was as old and improbable as Fu Manchu, and the Bond character was a relatively stupid and clumsy detective. "Still," Sarris wrote, "the Bonds are not the worst bonanza I can imagine. There is no cant in them and very little solemnity." Unfortunately their only beauty lay in scenes of orgiastic violence. "Bond obviously derives more ecstasy from strangling a man than embracing a woman" (*Primal Screen*, 182).

Hitchcock had long been associated with amusing spy thrillers, and in a sense *North by Northwest* (1959) had paved the way for Bond. But *Topaz*, a realistic film, was a departure from what audiences expected from the Master of Suspense and appeared politically old-fashioned. Sarris observed, "If the Bond series had any moral at all, it was that the Cold War was over, and we all had to band together against international criminals" (*Primal Screen*, 184). When French reporters, having read the right-wing Uris novel on which *Topaz* was based (the film itself was banned in France), asked Hitchcock if he regarded himself as a liberal, he replied, "I think I am in every sense of the term. I was recently asked whether I was a Democrat. I answered that I was a Democrat, but in respect to my money I am a Republican" (quoted in *Hitchcock*, 331). In Sarris's view, *Topaz* was filled with "blemishes and drawbacks," but he praised it for rewriting Uris, for some of "the most deliriously obsessed camera movements since *Psycho*," and for moments when Hitchcock's style transcended the basic material, offering pessimistic commentary on both "picayune Cold War politics and the cerebral irrationality of French manners and institutions" (*Primal Screen*, 184).

These two reviews hint at some of the complex relations between aesthetics and politics in Sarris's writings. He was wary of liberal message pictures and critical of both right-wing and left-wing pieties. He loved intelligent, artistically sophisticated popular cinema, but he wasn't a champion of pop culture. In some ways he resembled George Orwell, a writer he greatly admired—not the Orwell of *1984*, but the Orwell of *Homage to Catalonia* and *The Road to Wigan Pier*, books that blamed the sorry state of Europe in the 1930s on both jackbooted fascists and naïve socialist intellectuals. One of the most impressive reviews Sarris wrote for the *Village Voice* was not of a movie but of Orwell's essays and collected journalism. He admired Orwell's acute perceptions of class and power relationships (including those in the world of the literary intelligentsia), his coherent view of world literature, and his ability to recognize that artistic talent need not be judged in terms of morality and ideology. Sarris observed that even though Orwell wrote brilliant sociological essays on Donald McGill's postcards, boys' weeklies, and popular crime fiction, he despised "most of what passed for mass culture, particularly in its emphasis on mindless violence and power-worshipping 'realism'" (*Primal Screen*, 297). Sarris also noted, "What sustained Orwell as a relatively affirmative political activist was a belief in a modest form of Socialism dissociated from Utopianism" (*Primal Screen*, 291). It was the kind of politics that didn't try to make the world perfect but wanted to make it better.

ULMER, EDGAR G.

If Edgar G. Ulmer had not existed, the auteurists would need to invent him. Happily, he did exist, and he is the surest single proof that an artistic temperament can transcend pulp formulas and impossible working conditions. One of the many reasons Sarris deserves praise is that he helped call attention to Ulmer's work. "That a personal style could emerge from the lowest depths of Poverty Row," Sarris wrote, "is a tribute to a director without alibis" (143).

VON STERNBERG, JOSEF

Another member of Sarris's pantheon, and another director about whom Sarris wrote a book. No filmmaker in Hollywood was more out of tune with the tough-guy and cultural front ethos of the 1930s and 1940s (see John Dos Passos's cruel, thinly veiled portrait of Sternberg in *The Big Money*), and no filmmaker was more "against nature" or associated with screen glamour. Surprisingly, despite the last of these qualities, Sarris responds powerfully to Sternberg's films. He's more interested in their "autobiographical" quality than in their overt perversity, and he appropriately describes them with a series of paradoxes: surface becomes essence; trivia becomes profundity; absurdity becomes lyricism; stillness becomes violence; and all the characters behave like aestheticized Hemingway types, showing "poise under pressure," "style under stress," and "stoic calm" (*Films of Josef von Sternberg*, 8). Sarris also admires the photographic qualities of the Sternberg films, which have more in common with Murnau than with Eisenstein: "Sternberg entered the cinema through the camera rather than the cutting room and thus became a lyricist of light and shadow rather than a master of montage. . . . He concentrated on the spatial integrity of his images rather than their metaphorical juxtaposition" (*Films of Joseph von Sternberg*, 6).

WILDE, OSCAR

In introducing Wilde's name I should perhaps make clear that I'm not suggesting a latent homosexuality in Sarris or the auteurists, as Pauline Kael once did. I'm aware that Andrew and Oscar were separated by a hundred years and were quite different on many levels: Sarris was a heterosexual American movie critic of Greek descent, whereas Wilde was an Anglo-Irish literary dandy with Hellenic aspirations. But consider what the two have in common: both are iconoclastic, both are fond of epigrams and paradoxes, and both validate the pleasures of performance. Two of Sarris's favorite directors— Ophüls and Sternberg—are among the cinema's greatest aesthetes and might have been admired by Wilde. The key difference, it seems to me, lies in Sarris's implicit belief in nature or a world not made by art (even if a world of the director's emotions). Notice also that Sarris was resolutely opposed to camp interpretation. Another key theme of *The American Cinema* is that old Hollywood movies, especially the ones directed by Sternberg, should be appreciated with a mostly straight face and not with the "giddy rationalizations of pop, camp, and trivia" (29).

XANADU

David Thomson, another auteurist, has said that he once thought of calling his biographical encyclopedia of films *The Xanadu Inventory*. That title would apply just as well to Sarris's *The American Cinema*. Like an ideal investigator of Kane's estate, Sarris provides us with an immensely useful map to the bewildering and bizarre maze of American movies, separating the junk from the treasures and making sure that nobody tosses a Rosebud into the furnace. He also writes impressively about Orson Welles and is right to see *Citizen Kane* as the work of an auteur rather than a studio.

YOUTH

The French auteurists were sometimes known as "young Turks," and their unfettered romanticism makes them seem youthful even today. Unlike critics such as Wilde, however, they never made a cult of youth. Even in their salad days, part of their charm lay in their respect for old directors and for quiet, meditative, unspectacular films. Sarris in particular was never taken in by razzle-dazzle. He was keenly sensitive to pictures such as Ford's *The Sun Shines Bright* (1954) and Benton's *Nobody's Fool* (1994), which have an elegiac tone and a leisurely pace that seems anathema in Hollywood.

ZINNEMANN, FRED

One of the least admired figures in *The American Cinema*, whom Sarris relegates to the "Less Than Meets the Eye" category. In Sarris's hierarchy, Zinnemann represents the dull director of realistic projects who never stooped to entertainment. "In cinema, as in all art," Sarris wrote of Zinnemann, "only those who risk the ridiculous have a real shot at the sublime" (169). I wouldn't radically challenge this view, but when Zinnemann died I was reminded that he was one of the artists, along with Robert Siodmak, Billy Wilder, and Edgar Ulmer, who made *People on Sunday* (1929). I also remembered how much I admire *Act of Violence* (1948), *The Search* (1950), and *Day of the Jackal* (1973). Zinnemann may be a pygmy compared to Orson Welles, but he's a giant compared to Renny Harlin and many others one could name. One of the beauties of *The American Cinema* and of Sarris's journalism is that his incessant comparison of one director with another makes us want to introduce new comparisons, reexamining the major and minor directors together with the actors, writers, and photographers. It gives a human face to Hollywood and invites us to compare notes with the author. Sarris himself modified many of his opinions over the years (he retracted his negative judgment of Kubrick, Mankiewicz, Wilder, and Wyler, for example), and there's no reason why we can't disagree with his opinions and still find him invigorating. In the last analysis, he knew that many of the great movies had relatively little to do with their directors. His value is that he encourages a thoughtful cinephilia, challenging historians to see more.

Jonathan Rosenbaum

In the interest of transparency I should make clear that Jonathan Rosenbaum, whom I'll be referring to most of the time as "Rosenbaum," has been a good friend of mine for over two decades. We have many things in common. We're almost exact contemporaries (he's two years younger), we're both southerners (he was born into a Jewish family and I into a tribe of Baptists), and we have virtually the same politics. We're both jazz fans, though he can play it and has written a good deal of jazz criticism (for a bibliography of his writing on the subject, see Ehsan Khoshbakht's jazz blog at http://ehsankhoshbakht.blogspot.com/2013/02/jr.html). We both were college English majors, we're Orson Wellesians, and in our younger years we were strongly influenced by Andrew Sarris's *The American Cinema* and Noël Burch's *Theory of Film Practice*. We both think that Jacques Tourneur's *Stars in My Crown* (1950) is one of the best American movies and that Erich Auerbach's *Mimesis* is the greatest book of literary history and criticism. We don't see eye to eye about everything: he likes Altman more than I do, and I like *Police, Adjective* (2009) more than he does; he places Proust above Joyce, and I place Joyce above everybody (but Jonathan's essay on Godard's *Histoire(s) du cinéma*, first published in a 1997 issue of *Trafic* and expanded for *Goodbye Cinema, Hello Cinephilia* [2010], shows deep appreciation of what Joyce is up to in *Finnegans Wake*.) We've worked together several times and given one another professional help: we collaborated on a couple of DVD commentaries, I've written blurbs for some of his books, and at his invitation I participated in a "conversation" with Adrian Martin for *Movie Mutations: The Changing Face of World Cinephilia* (2003), an anthology that Jonathan and Adrian coedited; for his part, Jonathan has written a review of one of my books and forwards for the Chinese translations of two others, and he and Mehrnaz Saeed-Vafa are the authors of *Abbas Kiarostami* (2003), one of the first volumes in a book series that I used to edit with the University of Illinois Press.

A brief biographical note: Rosenbaum is descended from a family of movie-theater owners who started exhibiting pictures in 1915, at roughly the time when Griffith was shooting *Birth of a Nation*. He went to college in the 1960s with the ambition of becoming a novelist, but he soon began reading periodical literature about cinema and working as a film journalist in Paris and London. After a period as an assistant editor of *Monthly Film Bulletin*, a staff writer for *Sight and Sound*, and a regular contributor to *Film Comment* and the *Village Voice*, he was hired sight unseen by Manny Farber, who knew his writings, for a teaching stint at the University of California, San Diego (His account of working with Farber—a lovely blend of autobiography and critical analysis entitled "They Drive by Night: The Criticism of Manny Farber"—can be found in his book *Placing Movies: The Practice of Film Criticism* [1995]). In 1987 he became the chief reviewer for the *Chicago Reader*. He retired from that paper in 2008 but developed a website (www.jonathanrosenbaum.com) and continues to write both online and in print. His early life and career are described in an unusual memoir, *Moving Places* (1980), and most of his reviews and essays are available in a series of books published by university presses or on his website.

As a critic, Rosenbaum has written more and discussed a greater variety of things than the other three figures I've discussed. I'm obviously not a neutral observer, but I regard him as one of the world's most important writers on movies. I have interrelated reasons for making this claim, all based on his response to his historical situation.

More than any of the critics I've been discussing and more than most academics I know, Rosenbaum is an internationalist. Agee wrote in a period before a postwar art cinema boom that would bring increasing numbers of foreign pictures to the United States; Farber in his late career wrote influential pieces not only on older Hollywood but also on Akerman, Godard, Straub-Huillet, Herzog, and Fassbinder; Sarris was chiefly interested in Hollywood, although (more often than Pauline Kael) he took respectful sidelong glances at Europe. But Rosenbaum, writing from the American Midwest in the late twentieth and early twenty-first centuries, has regularly contributed to European publications and consistently made U.S. readers aware of cinema from around the world. He's done so, moreover, in the face of Reagan-Bush jingoism and a U.S. media industry that tries everything within its power to keep audiences ignorant of foreign offerings.

Rosenbaum has had the advantage of working for an "alternative" newspaper that allowed him more space and freedom (but less money) than the *New York Times* or the *New Yorker*, and he benefits from a late-twentieth-century proliferation of international film festivals. But he also brings to his work cosmopolitan instincts, wide learning, and a talent for unpretentious, highly readable interpretation of difficult or unfamiliar material. He's the best English-language commentator not only on Godard's late films, but also on such rarely screened items as Kira Muratova's *The Asthenic Syndrome* (1989), Béla Tarr's *Sátántangó* (1994), and Raúl Ruiz's *Time Regained* (2000). By the same token, he's written many pieces about revivals of important, relatively little-known older films that seldom get attention from the press. His lengthy, educational, and closely analytic review for the *Chicago Reader* of the 1998 color restoration of Jacques Tati's *Jour de fête* (originally released in 1949 in black and white) concludes by pointing out that the film's U.S. distributor, Miramax, brought it to the country reluctantly, with no ads and only a few bookings—unlike their treatment that same year of an English-language literary adaptation with known actors: "It is much more serious these days to spit on the grave of Henry James with a slimy soft-core travelogue like *Wings of the Dove*. . . . Because of the money and muscle Miramax expended [on that] cheesy factory product, it hasn't had any trouble gaining the recognition and (in most cases) reverence of *Time*, *Newsweek*, *The New Yorker*, the *New York Times*, the *New York Review of Books*, the TV reviewers and numerous other media players, none of which has shown a flicker of interest in the color *Jour de fête*" (*Essential Cinema*, 24). His equally long review of a 2002 Alexander Dovzhenko retrospective at Chicago's Gene Siskel Film Center makes a similar point, meanwhile giving us a somewhat better explanation than James Agee and others have done for why Dovzhenko's films are called "poetic": "Conceivably the most neglected major filmmaker of the twentieth century, the Ukrainian writer-director has never come close to receiving his due . . . in large part because his fervent, pantheistic, folkloric films develop more like lyric poems, moving from one stanza to the next, than they do like narratives, proceeding by way of paragraphs or chapters. . . . One calls this poetry in part because it comprises a paean to sheer existence, singing about rather than recounting what it sees. But if satire is what closes in New Haven, we all know that lyric poetry doesn't even open" (*Essential Cinema*, 399).

As the above quotes may suggest, Rosenbaum is a strong critic not only of the movies as art but also of the production, distribution, and marketing that supports them. His passionate defense of foreign films and revivals is linked to his outrage over the system of power relations controlling how films are distributed and received in the United States. His most extended analysis of that system can be found not in his reviews but in his 2000 book

Movie Wars: How Hollywood and the Media Limit What Films We Can See, much of which should be required reading for students of U.S. film. In his introduction to the book, Rosenbaum challenges the long-standing argument that Hollywood gives audiences what they want. According to the current version of the argument, which must be familiar to anyone with even a mildly serious interest in movies, the dumbing-down of U.S. culture is caused not by capitalist businessmen but by teenage consumers with too much money and semiliterates who have an aversion to subtitles. Rosenbaum doesn't dismiss such factors, but he asks whether Hollywood might also be responsible, and indeed might be "spearheading as well as defining this decline." Given the uncritical newspaper and TV promotion of the major studio releases, he observes, "one might even posit that the press, in order to justify its own priorities, maintains a vested interest in viewing the audience as brain-dead" (2).

Public opinion surveys, market research, and test screenings have long been used to determine how movies are made and distributed; but Rosenbaum reminds us that data from such undertakings is unreliable in the cultural sphere and can be manipulated to justify industry opinion. He cites a December 17, 1993, report in the *Wall Street Journal* concerning roughly two dozen former employees of National Research Group, Inc., which at the time handled most Hollywood test marketing; the employees, who ranged from hourly workers to senior officials, stated that National Research sometimes manipulated audience data to please their paying clients, boosting the approval ratings for such films as *Teen Wolf* (1985), *The Godfather III* (1990), and *L.A. Story* (1991). He also points to contradictions in the way the industry responds to market research. For example, we're told that U.S. audiences don't like subtitles; but *Dances with Wolves* (1990) and *Schindler's List* (1993), both of which make considerable use of subtitles, were hits. Rosenbaum concludes, "A more accurate mantra might be 'Americans hate subtitles—except when they don't.'" He goes on, "If one bears in mind both the crippling refusal of most producers to invest in black-and-white pictures and the extensive use of black-and-white videos on MTV, one might hazard the statement, 'Teenagers hate to watch anything in black-and-white—except when they don't'" (*Movie Wars*, 9).

The current situation is especially exasperating given the fact that we have so much historical evidence of important movies spoiled by test screenings that are used to justify what producers already think (one need only recall the major cuts and revisions to *The Magnificent Ambersons* in 1942). Focusing on recent years, Rosenbaum gives the example of Peter Bogdanovich's *The Thing Called Love* (1993), a film about country-music hopefuls that was test-marketed to an audience of country-music fans ("a move that seems about as logical as previewing *One Flew over the Cuckoo's Nest* in a mental institution" [*Movie Wars*, 6]). He's particularly incensed by the sad case of James L. Brooks's *I'll Do Anything* (1994), which was shot as a musical but, as a result of test screenings, had its musical numbers cut. And test marketing isn't the only means by which "the industry and its propaganda machine routinely mask their operations" (*Movie Wars*, 11). Rosenbaum extends his *j'accuse* to the MPPA, a supposedly neutral censorship agency run by Hollywood, which is consistently more lenient toward studio productions than toward foreign and independent releases. Hollywood even manipulates the term "independent," giving us the impression that the market is relatively free and that a writer-director like Quentin Tarantino is in complete charge of his films. Rosenbaum notes that Tarantino works for Miramax and is in a very different position from true independents like Jim Jarmusch and Rob Tregenza, who have final cut but never receive the auteur publicity that follows Tarantino's every move.

For me as for Rosenbaum, one of the most depressing symptoms of U.S. film culture today is the regularity with which newspapers, magazines, and TV shows report on box-office receipts, as if profit had something to do with quality. If memory serves, this phenomenon began in the Reagan 1980s, which was also the moment when *People* magazine began to appear, eclipsing news magazines like *Time*. I can recall my shock roughly a decade later, in 1989, when TV's network evening news chose to devote part of its very limited time to a report on the opening of *Batman*. Rosenbaum, whose father was the manager of a movie theater, remarks that if a newspaper "in the thirties, forties, fifties, sixties, or even seventies had started to list the top ten grossers every week, its readers would have supposed that the editor had rocks in his head" (*Movie Wars*, 15). Why is it, he asks, that newspapers don't report the ten best-selling soft drinks, fast-food restaurants, or automobiles, detailing their weekly gross receipts, as with movies? Some readers of the reports probably think that if lots of people are paying ten dollars to see a film, it must be good, even though movie revenue is significantly related to the power of a studio to control the number of screens on which a picture is booked during its first week.

The rise in information about box-office returns has been accompanied by a decline in the attention given to foreign films on the part of U.S. critics, and by a tendency among academics to resist the formation of artistic canons. Rosenbaum is justifiably critical of both camps. The press, he argues, has abnegated any commitment to the public "beyond serving privileged business interests," and academic film study has failed "to engage meaningfully with American film culture as a whole" (*Movie Wars*, 16–17). The result is a lowering of critical standards, a critical focus on big-budget productions in wide release, and a feeling that anybody is qualified to express opinions about movies as long as they've seen a few. (As we know, Walter Benjamin predicted that mechanical reproduction would eliminate the cult of expertise; but Benjamin's technological determinism blinded him to the ways in which the absence of informed opinion can be useful to business interests and even encouraged by them.) Rosenbaum finds symptoms of decadence in several prominent places: the *New York Times* and the *New York Review of Books* sometimes assign their few reviews of film books to writers who have relatively little knowledge of film; the 1999 edition of *The Best American Movie Writing* overlooked several of the most original, knowledgeable, and readable academic critics in the United States and excluded the better academic film journals from its bibliography; and in 1998–99 the American Film Institute, its government funding drastically cut, stopped projecting movies and joined forces with Hollywood to produce a couple of prime-time CBS-TV broadcasts, showcasing a list of the one hundred greatest American movies and a list of the one hundred greatest movie-star "legends." The list of films included such everlasting masterpieces as *Butch Cassidy and the Sundance Kid, Guess Who's Coming to Dinner, To Kill a Mockingbird,* and *Dances with Wolves,* rivaling the Academy Awards for irrelevance.

In response to the AFI's list of the hundred best films, which he describes as a "brute commercial ploy . . . to repackage familiar goods" (*Movie Wars*, 91), Rosenbaum proposes his own one hundred U.S. films, adhering to a personal but conservative standard of judgment and deliberately avoiding the twenty-seven titles on the AFI list that most viewers with a good knowledge of film history would consider legitimate contenders (*Movie Wars*, 103–6). He admits that he could easily have nominated another hundred films, because the United States has incomparably the richest national cinema; he also points out that he favors the 1950s, which is the decade of his youth, and that an older critic like Manny Farber might have given more weight to the 1930s, just as younger cinephiles might have named more titles from the 1970s or '80s. His list, arranged alphabetically, contains offbeat choices of pictures by famous directors (Preston Sturges's *Christmas in July* [1940] and Lewis Milestone's *Hallelujah, I'm a Bum* [1933]) and ranges from big studio productions (Vincente Minnelli's *Meet Me in St. Louis* [1944] and Ernst Lubitsch's *Trouble in Paradise* [1932]) to little-seen, truly independent films (Thom Andersen's *Eadweard Muybridge, Zoopraxographer* [1974] and Barbara Loden's *Wanda* [1971]). Its purpose is not to legislate but to "defend the breadth, richness, and intelligence of the American cinema against its self-appointed custodians, who seem to want to lock us into an eternity of Oscar nights" (*Movie Wars*, 94). It also performs an educational function, trying to achieve what in Rosenbaum's school days, when there were hardly any academic courses on film, "was the best or at least the most typical way of acquiring some knowledge about what an art form had to offer" (*Movie Wars*, 83).

If the mass media have promoted a list of "great" movies based on commercial instincts and a low estimation of the popular audience, the universities have exacerbated the problem by avoiding not only lists of required viewing but also most kinds of artistic value judgments. As Rosenbaum puts it, "the mainstream continued to go about its promotional business in elevating certain films as aesthetic objects," while academic film study "became mainly passive and complicitous, in spite of its better impulses" (*Movie Wars*, 86). The complicity has taken a couple of decades to form. In the 1970s the auteurist canon in emerging film departments came under partly justified criticism and gave way to another sort of canon, made up of European high theorists and "counter cinemas." By the end of the century, when Rosenbaum wrote *Movie Wars*, High Theory was also unfashionable. Most academic programs specializing in film were evolving into "media" departments that offered courses not only on film but also on TV, video gaming, and the Internet. These departments were typically made up of industry historians, sociologists, and theorists rather than aesthetically inclined critics and close readers. There was no longer a generally agreed upon canon because the very process of canonization had become suspect: scholars could study the history of taste in the manner of sociologists or anthropologists, but they had no business shaping taste; formal aesthetics and the history of film form could be studied, but relatively little energy was spent on the question of why one film might be more artistically interesting than another. At the same time, there was growing institutional pressure to make departments prove their worth by the size of their enrollments. In such an environment, the taste of undergraduates, which in part is created by the movie industry, rules the curriculum: introductory film courses are dumbed down; the study of older films, foreign films, unknown films, and nongeneric films gives way to the study of *Star Wars*; and sociology tries to compensate for the devaluation of aesthetics.

There are many U.S. teachers of media history and film art that do valuable research, heighten their students' knowledge and appreciation of the medium, and encourage political critique of the culture. But for all of academic film study's sophisticated formalism, widening conception of movie history (which now acknowledges nontheatrical cinema), and political activism, the study of film at the beginning of the twenty-first century is ironically similar to literary study at the beginning of the twentieth century, when English departments were dominated by history and philology and had not yet been reformed by the New Criticism. Rosenbaum is an important writer at this moment because he's a critic with literary gifts who is conversant with academic research and theory, and who laments "the absolute rift that exists [in the United States] between journalism and academia, and in most cases between cinema and other academic subjects within universities" (*Goodbye Cinema*, 296).

A good deal of Rosenbaum's work could be understood as an attempt to repair rifts of one kind or another. His early memoir, *Moving Places*, for example, is an autobiographical experiment attempting to bridge the psychological distance between his Alabama childhood and his career in New York, Paris, London, and San Diego; at the same time, this book tries to conquer the divide between Rosenbaum's literary ambition and his work as a critic. Avowedly Proustian in structure, it opens with a discussion of two Hollywood films, *Bird of Paradise* (1951) and *On Moonlight Bay* (1951), which he saw on TV in the late 1970s and which brought back memories of his childhood. His fascination with the two films leads him into detailed research, much of it conducted in his hometown of Florence, Alabama, and to a recovery of lost time—an examination of his family, his upbringing, and what he elsewhere describes as "all the circumstantial, personal, historical, and ideological aspects of experiencing movies that criticism generally factors out" (*Placing Movies*, 1).

Rosenbaum has been disappointed by the book's reception: "As a writing project it was literary and personal/historical rather than critical in any conventional sense, and I naively hoped at the time that such a book could pave my way out of film criticism and into a literary career." Unfortunately, it was reviewed mostly as a book about movies and became what Rosenbaum describes as a "cult item" for film lovers; meanwhile, at the critical and scholarly levels, it has never been recognized "as a book with any status in relation to sociology, social history, film history, or film exhibition" (*Placing Movies*, 2). This is a shame, because *Moving Places*, like many things that can't be slotted into known categories, is a real achievement, a remarkable blend of imagination, critical insight, and social and personal history that aspires to what Rosenbaum, in an essay on Orson Welles's essay films, describes as "collapsing, combining, and/or juxtaposing fiction and nonfiction in order to facilitate and broaden a . . . grasp on a subject in the interests of truth" (*Placing Movies*, 171). It can be appreciated both for its literary values and for what it tells us about watching movies.

Moving Places belongs in company with Rosenbaum's other work because he's a highly autobiographical critic, far more than Farber or Sarris, and in a less romantic, more objectively self-critical fashion than Agee. He repeatedly moves between the personal and the public, trying to contextualize his experience of seeing films. He also mentions his friends or other writers in his reviews, creating a sense of community that's unusual in the world of U.S. criticism. He tends to "place" his opinions, revealing his biases and larger values, and trying in indirect ways to reconcile the divisions in his history: the small-town southerner who lives in the northern metropole; the U.S. citizen who has experienced more community abroad; the literary artist who has become a critic; the movie reviewer who is also a scholar. He's a dialectical writer, not least in the way he tries to synthesize the divided selfhood we all experience.

One of the places where this dialectical quality is most apparent is in Rosenbaum's synthesis of critical opinion and historical fact. He has written that "one of the most underrated elements in criticism is quite simply information—relevant facts deriving from research—and how this is imparted to the reader in relation to other elements. Thanks to the prestige of theory in academia and the equally valued role played by rhetoric in journalism, facts often seem to be held in relatively low esteem in critical writing . . . , but as long as criticism aspires to be a vehicle for discovery, it seems to me that research should play a much larger role than it normally does" (*Placing Movies*, 77). At this level Rosenbaum has much to contribute to scholarship and teaching as he does to criticism.

It isn't unusual for journalistic critics to teach in universities. Farber taught at UCSD; Sarris taught for many years at Columbia; and Rosenbaum has taught at UCSD, NYU, the School of Visual Arts in New York, U.C. Berkeley, the School of the Art Institute of Chicago, and Virginia Commonwealth. But unlike the earlier journalistic critics, Rosenbaum's movie reviews and writings engage in a dialogue with academics fairly directly. His reviews often give credit to the writings of professors, or even make jokes about them, as in his 1977 essay on the neglected French critic and filmmaker Luc Moullet: "suggested title for a hypothetical article in *Screen* about LM: 'Suture/Self' . . . A special dividend: this pun would be comprehensible only to those who pronounce *suture* the English way, thus leaving the Francophiles out in the cold for a change" (*Goodbye Cinema*, 40).

He has also made many contributions to film scholarship, perhaps chief among them his extremely useful appendices to the Bogdanovich-Welles interviews in *This Is Orson Welles* (1992), which provide a detailed chronology of Welles's career and a critically informed reconstruction of the original *Magnificent Ambersons;* and his role in the "reconstruction" of *Touch of Evil*. But I would argue that his major intervention where academic debates are concerned is the appendix to *Essential Cinema: On the Necessity of Film Canons* (2004), which lists one thousand of his favorite films from the years 1895 to 2003, one hundred of them marked with an asterisk to indicate what for Rosenbaum "currently represents la crème de la crème" (408). By my count the periods that receive the most entries are 1928–32 and 1948–60. The undertaking as a whole constitutes a response to what Rosenbaum calls a "fundamental distrust of art, often unacknowledged as such," which has led to the "unraveling" of film canons in the twenty-first-century academy (*Essential Cinema,* xiii). Unlike Harold Bloom's often-criticized literary canon, Rosenbaum's canon isn't confined to the Western world and isn't shaped by purely aesthetic considerations. It's an active attempt to combat market forces that limit knowledge of movies, and it doesn't regard stylized art and documentary information as separate categories. Admittedly personal, it's offered in the spirit of "a critical manifesto that can be debated" (*Essential Cinema,* xx). But for anyone who tracks down all the films it names, it also provides a kind of liberal education and a thousand nights of pleasure.

Another division that Rosenbaum seeks to repair is the debate over film versus DVDs. He's one of the few cinephiles of my generation to make peace with the digital revolution and to voice optimism about certain of its possibilities. His position seems to have changed since 2000, when he took academics to task for not learning from the late French critic and theorist Serge Daney's writings about watching films on television. At that point Rosenbaum called for "a theoretical and practical guide for coping with the differences between film and video" and speculated that "the relative disfavor in recent years of aesthetics in film study . . . coincides precisely with some of the conditions of watching films on video" (*Movie Wars,* 89). A number of U.S. academics, among them David Bordwell, Mary Ann Doane, and Stephen Prince, have in recent years thought seriously about the phenomenology and aesthetics of film versus digital formats, though perhaps not in the ways Rosenbaum had in mind (in addition, see the essays in Scott Balcerzak and Jason Sperb, eds., *Cinephilia in the Age of Digital Reproduction* [2009]). Classroom technology has also advanced into the world of HDTV and Blu-ray. Whether or not for these reasons, Rosenbaum feels relatively sanguine about the current environment. In his introduction to the essays in *Goodbye Cinema, Hello Cinephilia: Film Culture in Transition* (2010), he tells us that he has certain things in common with his twentysomething friends, many of whom believe that both cinema and cinema criticism are undergoing a "resurgence and renaissance" (ix).

In keeping with these interests, Rosenbaum writes a regular column entitled "Global Discoveries on DVD" for *Cinema Scope,* and is, along with Dave Kehr, who covers domestic DVD releases in the *New York Times,* our most valuable guide to the multitude of films now available in digital form. He speaks of "a new kind of cinephilia in which cinema in the old sense doesn't exactly disappear but becomes reconfigured" (*Goodbye Cinema*, 5–6), and he imagines a digital utopia in which present-day equivalents of the old-fashioned cine-clubs will proliferate, meeting in small groups to see and discuss DVDs. He recommends (and I strongly concur) that anyone who has an interest in movies should purchase a relatively inexpensive multiregional Blu-ray player. He rightly praises both the aesthetic and pedagogic achievements of the best DVDs, which often exceed what was available with celluloid: "Today, for instance, it's possible to see the beautiful colors of the second part of *Ivan the Terrible*, accompanied by superb historical documentation . . . [on] the Criterion edition of the DVD, with commentaries by Yuri Tsivian and Joan Neuberger. Admittedly, this isn't the same thing as seeing a 35mm print of the film with incorrect colors and with less comprehensive documentation in Paris or New York thirty years ago, but can we really say with assurance that we're necessarily less fortunate today?" (*Goodbye Cinema*, 6).

There are, as Rosenbaum knows, many boring DVD commentaries or "extras," some of them filled with misinformation; but, as he shows in his lengthy *Cineaste* review of the European boxed set "Chaplin Collection," the digital format is capable of giving us extraordinary viewing pleasure and edification. The set is rich with commentaries by a variety of directors, but it also enables Rosenbaum to observe the films more closely. How many of us have noticed (as James Agee, who beautifully described the scene, did not, but as Rosenbaum does) that the famous shot/reverse shot of the Tramp and the flower girl at the end of *City Lights* is mismatched, and that the mismatch doesn't spoil anything? Rosenbaum argues that this exchange of looks "should be shown and described to every film student who has ever believed that eyeline matches count for very much outside of routine filmmaking" (*Goodbye Cinema*, 90).

Rosenbaum writes equally well and with similar enthusiasm about the potential value of film criticism on the web, which has a more international character than print journalism. "Speaking as someone who currently feels that he lives on the Internet more than he lives in Chicago," he says, "I consider this distinction vital to the ways that I function as a writer" (*Goodbye Cinema*, 281). He recognizes that the Internet can seem a tower of Babel, but he feels that we've entered "a transitional period where enormous paradigmatic shifts should be engendering new concepts, new terms, and new kinds of analysis . . . not to mention new kinds of political and social formations, as well as new forms of etiquette" (280). We seem a long way from achieving these things, but in *Goodbye Cinema* Rosenbaum at least provides us with the names of some of the more important e-zines, among them *Rouge* and *Senses of Cinema* (I would add *La Furia Umana* and the annual poll of best film moments published by the Museum of the Moving Image). He pays tribute to critics' blogs devoted to Serge Daney and Raymond Durgnat (the latter was removed for a time but has been restored) and recommends other blogs maintained by Fred Camper, Steve Erickson, Chris Fujiwara, and Dave Kehr.

One of the things that has most pleased Rosenbaum in recent years, he tells us, occurred when he visited the Mar del Plata International Film Festival in Argentina. There he encountered a schoolteacher named Roger Alan Koza who had established DVD cine-clubs in several towns and was showing some of the more esoteric films Rosenbaum had praised in his writings. One of these was Forough Farrokhzad's *The House Is Black* (1962), which Rosenbaum places at or near the top of his favorites (see his essay on the film in *Goodbye Cinema*, 260–65). "[Koza] told me the combined audiences of such screenings for each film was somewhere between 700 and 800 people. Considering how unlikely it would be to fill a single auditorium of that size in most major cities of the world for such films, I realized that the shifting paradigms of today might also transform what we normally regard as a minority taste" (*Goodbye Cinema*, 284). Whatever transformations might occur, the Argentine cine-clubs have benefited from a critic of integrity who gives us some hope for cinema in the digital age.

I took advantage of my friendship with Jonathan Rosenbaum to interview him by email about the practical concerns or realpolitik of working as a film reviewer. His replies give us insight into at least one corner of the world of critical journalism:

> JN: As a weekly film reviewer for the *Chicago Reader*, were you given the word length you needed for reviews? Was there any pressure, however subtle, to review big commercial films over art films and revivals? Any censorship of politics or judgment? Would the situation be different for reviewers at the *Tribune*, the *New Yorker*, or the *New York Times*?
>
> JR: For most of my twenty years at the *Reader* I had virtually unlimited space. Eventually, I had to limit the length of my capsule reviews and also (a practice that continues to this day) condense earlier ones that were being reprinted; and after roughly seventeen years, my long reviews had to become much shorter. During much of this time, my editors would sometimes complain about my not reviewing the big commercial films more frequently, but I can't recall them ever putting their foot down about this. Even better, for most of this period they allowed me to write at length about some commercial releases weeks or even months after they opened, as long as they were still playing somewhere in Chicago. This freedom was eventually withdrawn so that my reviews had to come out the same week

as the films. As far as I know, none of these freedoms, when they existed, ever existed at the *Tribune,* the *New Yorker,* or the *Times*—although I hasten to add I've only written once for any of these publications, when I was commissioned to write an op-ed piece for the *Times* after Ingmar Bergman died. This had to be rewritten several times, and in retrospect my agreeing to accept their invitation was tantamount to signing a pact with the devil—giving up much of my freedom and autonomy in exchange for mainstream exposure.

I was always edited at the *Reader,* usually by excellent editors, and the main freedom I lacked was the ability to choose the titles of my longer pieces—a freedom I've rarely had elsewhere with any consistency. There was never any interference about my judgments, and instances of political censorship were infrequent. I can recall only two, both of them sore points. Significantly, neither came from my most frequent copy editor at the time—who was far more conservative than me (even though the *Reader* was basically a leftist paper, especially on local issues), leading to many heated quarrels—but from the main editor, who didn't believe she was censoring me and thought she was simply holding me to certain journalistic standards. In one case she objected to me citing the claim that Bush and Cheney had hopes of finding a way to invade Iraq before 9/11, which she considered a paranoid fantasy; in the other case, she objected to me claiming, after a visit to Tehran, that Iran was as ethnically and racially multicultural as the United States, without offering anything she regarded as evidence. (It was only much later, alas, that I discovered that figures on the CIA's website would have furnished this evidence.) In both cases I felt these deletions were censorship because of how selective she was being about what claims of mine required evidence—and because she wasn't even allowing me to cite an opinion that others could claim was wrong.

It's important to add that during this same twenty-year period what were formerly called "alternative" newspapers stopped being alternative, especially in their outlook. Not long after the *Reader* went online, it started listings of "what the *Reader* is reading," and these tended to be exclusively items in the mainstream press. More generally, "alternate" newspapers showed an increasing desire to duplicate mainstream publications, which struck me as suicidal—one reason why I decided to go freelance after twenty years, a decision I haven't regretted. If any "alternative" journalism survives today, it's clearly on the Internet, but by and large I believe the whole concept of "alternative" outlets has been replaced by the concept of niche markets, which I tend to find more congenial. Another way of putting this is to say that I enjoy being a cult writer, which can bring more intensity to one's engagement with readers. The few times I've written for big mainstream publications with millions of readers the responses have been far less satisfying even when they're intense—

in part because it's hard to sort out how much they're responding to the institutional aura of those publications.

JN: How large was your readership, and how did you imagine your typical reader? How did you conceive the public role of a film critic? Did you get much positive or negative mail from readers?

JR: To cite some figures from pages 262–63 of my collection *Placing Movies:* "On the basis of a detailed survey about its readership carried out a few years ago, the *Reader* . . . has a circulation of 137,000 and an estimated readership of about 412,000. . . . The movie listings and capsule reviews [were] the most widely read or 'looked at' featured in the paper," while the long reviews came in third, "with front-cover articles in second place and cartoons in fourth." Most of the paper's highly targeted readership was single (77 percent) and white (77 percent), with a median age of thirty-one and a median annual household income of $39,500, which was quite close to my salary at the time. By contrast, over the past month (writing on January 8, 2013), over 67,000 visits have been paid to my website by 52,000 people. But whereas my readers at the *Reader* were almost exclusively Chicagoans, those at my website live in 165 separate countries, with over 26,000 of these based in the United States (2,258 of them are in New York, the highest concentration in a single city, and roughly half that number are in Chicago), approximately a tenth as many in France, and 249 each in Croatia and Egypt, to cite a few more random figures.

For me, the film critic's principal role is to assist in the public discussion of films—a discussion that usually starts before the critic arrives and continues long after the review is read. Godard once said to me in an interview that he wanted to be regarded as an airplane rather than an airport, and this is an aspiration I share—meaning, to some extent, that people should take me to get wherever they want to go and then step off. At the *Reader*, I would say that the mail I received was both relatively sparse and more positive than negative, except for when I wrote an attack on something like *Star Wars* or *No Country for Old Men*, when it became voluminous and mainly negative. Today, based on what I access via emails, Twitter, Facebook, and blogs, most of the feedback I get is highly supportive and positive—except for when I sound off against something like *Inglourious Basterds*, when it's mainly dismissive and negative.

JN: How much time usually went by between seeing a film and turning in a review? Did you ever feel that the pressure of deadlines was causing you to make snap judgments or give insufficient attention to films? Did you ever want to take back what you wrote?

JR: My lead times usually varied a lot, because sometimes films get press-shown well in advance of their openings. Most often, when I wanted to see a film more than once before writing my review, I was able to, but I'm sure there were occasions when more time and/or further research would have altered my positions or sharpened my insights. When *Basic Instinct* came out in 1992 my long review was sarcastic and gave it no stars, but at some point afterward I became a big Verhoeven fan and I now regard it as one of his best movies. More recently, in my post-*Reader* phase, I called *Margaret* a "brilliant mess" until another viewing persuaded me that it wasn't a mess at all. One thing I like about my website, over which I have complete editorial control, is the possibility of critiquing some of my earlier pieces, explaining how or why my mind got changed, and in a few cases, when I'm not happy with the way I was originally edited, making corresponding adjustments. In one of my more recent books, *Discovering Orson Welles*, I go out of my way to retain original errors of fact or judgment and then signal these flaws, for pedagogical purposes, to help demonstrate how shaky some Welles scholarship often turns out to be. The only long pieces of mine that I regret enough to exclude from my website (in contrast to several others that I now simply disagree with or dislike for other reasons, and include) are an over-the-top attack on Donald Richie's book on Ozu that I published in *Sight and Sound* and my dissenting piece about Bergman in the *Times* (which also drew a lot of negative mail), although in the second case I did post my original draft.

JN: In *Goodbye Cinema, Hello Cinephilia*, you've said that the digital revolution has led to "paradigmatic changes," not only in the way we view movies, but also in the way we "think and write about them" (xv). Is good film criticism on the web different from good criticism in print? Are we experiencing a decline of good print criticism, and if so does that matter?

JR: This is a tougher question to answer than the others. As for changes in how we view movies, there are so many variations nowadays in the qualities of film prints and digital copies and the ways they get shown and seen that it's hard to make any qualitative generalizations, just as one can't really deal adequately with globalization simply by calling it "good" or "bad." There are certainly important differences, but these vary a great deal in separate situations.

By and large, I think there's more good stuff than ever and more bad stuff than ever on the Internet, and one of the most striking paradigmatic changes from the past and print culture is how quickly one can get feedback to whatever one writes online. After seeing a Bresson film in the early '60s, you might have to wait a few weeks or months before reading about it in a film magazine, and sometimes wait as long or even longer before finding someone with whom you could discuss it. After seeing a Pedro Costa film today, you don't have to wait for a social or communal response to either the film or your own written response to it if you post something about it—with the advantage of immediate feedback and the possibilities of international exchanges and the disadvantage of less time for reflection. (On Facebook and diverse blogs, it's often disturbing to see how many people can post before thinking, and I'm sometimes guilty of this myself.)

We're obviously experiencing a decline in reviews that appear on paper, but I disagree with those who think there's much of a decline in what's known as "professional" reviewing, because, as you know, I'm highly dubious about most of the criteria used in both academia and journalism for defining professionalism. And in book publishing, could one really argue that the BFI Film Classics, which we've both contributed volumes to, are any sort of downgrade from the monographs about directors that proliferated in France several decades ago? One could also maintain that even though *Sight and Sound* has been diminished nowadays by its more formulaic consumerist orientation, *Film Quarterly* and *Cineaste* have gotten livelier, and online journals such as *Rouge* and its semi-successor, *Lola,* are in many ways superior to almost all of the film magazines in English that appeared on paper in the so-called Golden Age of Criticism (i.e., the '60s and '70s). At the same time, even if one justifiably laments, in French criticism on paper, the depletion of energy and innovation in *Cahiers du cinéma,* the thirteen issues of *Cinéma* edited by Bernard Eisenschitz in 2002–7, most of which included DVDs of rare and precious archival material, and the eighty-four issues of *Trafic* that have appeared since Serge Daney founded it in 1991 are hardly signs of decline.

Four Years as a Critic

2007–2010

Writing about what one regards as the best pictures of the year is a much easier job than reviewing movies on a regular basis, if only because it's always more pleasant to praise or defend films than to attack or dismiss them. Nevertheless, anyone who proposes a list of best pictures in a given year is confronted with two practical problems. The first is that no critic, not even one who makes a living by reviewing for the daily press, can possibly see everything. The second has to do with the dating of films. Old productions are found and made available on DVD, new films are given different release dates in different countries, and some films go direct to video stores, while others open in select U.S. cities at the end of December or the beginning of January. Charles Burnett's *Killer of Sheep* and Florian Henckel von Donnersmarck's *The Lives of Others* appeared on several ten-best lists of 2007 in the United States, but by my reckoning the first of these was originally exhibited in the 1970s and the second had a U.S. screening in 2006. By the same token, Cristian Mungiu's *4 Months, 3 Weeks, and 2 Days*, which also appeared on some 2007 lists, didn't open officially in the United States until 2008. To put reasonable limits on the choices I made for my "Films of the Year" in *Film Quarterly*, I tried to restrict myself to feature-length pictures of any date that, as far as I could determine, had their first U.S. big-screen showing, not counting film festivals, during the year in question (in once case I included a TV series, *Mad Men*, first broadcast in that year). What follows are six of the pictures I discussed during the years in question, followed by my lists of the best films of each year. Even if you disagree with the rankings, these lists give evidence of the continuing importance and considerable achievement of cinema in the twenty-first century.

2007: COLOSSAL YOUTH

The most impressive film I saw in 2007 was the 2006 Portuguese/French/Swiss production of Pedro Costa's *Colossal Youth* (*Juventude em Marcha*, properly translated as "Youth on the March"), which played at a dozen or so museum or art-cinema venues across the United States. This is the third in a trilogy of films Costa has made among the poorest slum dwellers of the Fontainhas area in Lisbon, most of whom are immigrants from the rocky, volcanic Cape Verde Islands, a former Portuguese colony established to serve the African slave trade. In 1994, Costa traveled to Cape Verde to make an excellent wide-screen fiction film, *Down to Earth* (*Casa de Lava*, or "House of Lava"), and upon returning he brought gifts to people in Fontainhas from their relatives who had worked in the film. Soon he began shooting in the Lisbon favelas, using the residents as actors in a series of improvised "stories" derived from their own experience. His first effort, *Bones* (*Ossos*, 1997), concerns a desperately poor teenaged couple and their baby; the second, *In Vanda's Room* (*No Quarto da Vanda*, 2000), takes place almost entirely within a tiny room where Vanda Duarte, a drug addict who appeared in *Bones*, snorts crack cocaine, shoots heroin, and talks with friends. *Colossal Youth* also features Vanda, now clean and taking state-supplied methadone, but the focus has shifted to a black man named Ventura, who also appeared briefly in *Bones*.

At the point when the film begins, Fontainhas has been virtually demolished by city planners and its inhabitants are being moved to a public housing project in Amador on the outskirts of the city. Ventura's wife, fed up with the life he has given her, brandishes a knife and throws him out of their slum dwelling. The seventy-five-year-old Ventura, a tall, slender, haunted figure in a dark suit and a white shirt, wanders about like a lost soul, dreading the clean, well-lighted, but empty rooms the city has assigned him, passing the time by visiting friends and various "children." (He has a damaged memory and so many possible offspring from his history of falling drunkenly into strange beds that neither he nor we can be sure if any of the people he visits are actually his relations; he seems never to have been a legal or emotional father in the strict sense, although his "children" accept him as one of their own.) During his wanderings we occasionally flash back to the period of the 1974 Portuguese revolution, when he and his friend Lento were guest workers assigned to building projects in Lisbon. Baffled and terrified by the social upheaval around them, they huddle together in a tiny shack, where Ventura composes and ceaselessly repeats a love poem, urging Lento to memorize it for his wife in Cape Verde. The poem is made up partly from lines appropriated from French surrealist Robert Desnos and partly from lines composed by Ventura himself. Unfortunately, Lento dies in an accident outside the shack and never learns the poem.

A good deal of the contextual information I've just supplied, such as the source of the poem, derives from program notes for *Colossal Youth* or from published interviews with Costa. The film itself is mysterious, beautiful, and elliptical, so intimately related to its characters that it refuses exposition and leaves us to find our bearings as best we can. Costa's politics will probably not be fully evident to most U.S. viewers; it helps to know that in his youth he enthusiastically celebrated the fall of the fascist dictatorship in Portugal, but he later discovered that black workers like Ventura, who had labored to construct Lisbon's museums, schools, and middle-class residences, were completely abandoned by the "democratic" revolution and even persecuted by the Portuguese military. (Useful background on the politics of the film can be found at http://chainedtothecinematheque.blogspot.com.)

Like many important films and an equal number of bad or unethical ones, *Colossal Youth* troubles the distinction between documentary and fiction; its most distinctive attribute, however, is that in stylistic terms it works completely against the grain of neorealism, giving us no sense of grainy, jerky "immediacy." Costa shot the picture without a crew, using only a lightweight digital camera, DAT for sound, and a couple of microphones and tripods; there was no lighting equipment other than mirrors and Styrofoam reflectors, and in some locations there was no electricity. Nevertheless, *Colossal Youth* has a superbly disciplined feeling for composition and color. The images, which have been compared to Vermeer, seem to rise out of a dialectical conflict between painterly stillness, appropriate to a world where the characters live outside capitalist time, and motion pictures, appropriate to the modernity that surrounds and determines the characters. No wonder the brilliant art photographer Jeff Wall, who is equally sensitive to color, texture, and staged "documentary," is among Costa's admirers.

In a lecture for a group of young filmmakers in Tokyo, published in the online journal *Rouge*, Costa speaks of the way he "resists" the comfortable versatility of the digital camera, refusing to do what "the managers of Panasonic in the skyscrapers of Tokyo" want him to do. "They want me to move it around a lot, and I don't want to move it." His camera usually stands at a respectful distance from the actors, who are treated with discretion, dignity, and patient attention. Each actor in *Colossal Youth* contributed her or his own story, which was modified during rehearsal, and the production took fifteen months of all-day shooting for six days a week, with up to twenty or thirty takes per shot. The finished product consists mainly of lengthy sequence shots exquisitely framed by an unmoving camera, with relatively little figure movement within the frame. (There is a single ostentatious camera movement—a leisurely 180-degree pan along a pastoral stream outside Lisbon's Gulbenkian Museum, looking toward street traffic in the distance.) The atmosphere is hushed, formal, with characters walking in or out of frame in stately, almost ghostly fashion.

Many viewers will become impatient because nothing dramatic happens; in one sequence we listen to an entire record that Ventura plays for Lento ("Labanda Breco," a song in praise of Amílcar Cabral, the leader of the Cape Verdean independence movement), and in another we watch three characters silently eating a meal. But each direct cut to the opening of a new sequence is visually stunning. The most startling is when Costa suddenly cuts to the interior of the Gulbenkian museum, an edifice that Ventura helped to build when he was a construction worker, and where he goes to visit one of his "sons," a museum caretaker. The sequence begins with a distant shot of a small painting by Rubens, almost aglow in a shadowy corner (Costa repeatedly uses a single touch of color to transform monochrome environments); then we cut to a large painting by Van Dyck; and then to Ventura, innocently sitting on one of the art objects, a seventeenth-century French settee upholstered by Gobelins, posed with all the lanky grace of the young Henry Fonda in *My Darling Clementine*.

Other sequences have moments of extraordinary intimacy, although the film is never sensational. Ventura's several visits with Vanda, who lives in one of the new high-rise buildings and works as a maid, are especially memorable. A motormouth and a fascinatingly natural performer, Vanda sits on her bed and spins out long, druggy-sounding monologues. She suffers from a head cold and occasionally leans over to spit in a wastebasket. Now and then she pauses to glance at her television set, which is always on, or she looks down at a beautiful, dark-eyed baby girl playing on the floor and encourages the girl to dance to the television music ("Dança, bebê, dança!"). An equally striking scene occurs toward the end of the film, when Ventura visits one of his "daughters" in a battered hovel in Fontainhas; the two have a quiet, dreamy conversation and begin playing a game of finding shapes of people or objects in the ragged scars on the wall, much as one would find shapes in the clouds. The young woman observes that the housing project where they will soon be moved is covered with white paint; in the new environment, their very imaginations will be impoverished.

Costa has been compared with Bresson, partly because of the unemotional quality of his actors and partly because of his "empty" shots in which we see a room or a wall after a character has left the frame. He tends to compare himself with Hollywood directors: with Chaplin, who made street films about the immigrant ghetto; with Ford, who had a "stock company" and a favorite location; and above all with Jacques Tourneur, who was a poetic realist working at the lower levels of the industry. (He also admires Danièle Huillet and Jean-Marie Straub, about whom he has made an extraordinary documentary, *Where Does Your Hidden Smile Lie?* [*Onde Jaz o Teu Sorriso?*, 2001].) Ultimately, however, he is unique. He risks being charged with aestheticizing poverty, but I agree when he says, borrowing a phrase from Brecht, that he wants only to make "jewels for the poor."

2008: *24 CITY*

In recent years director Jia Zhangke has been making part fictional, part documentary films about China's turbulent transition from a planned to a market economy. He prefers HDV for these pictures, he says, because changes to the nation are so rapid they require flexible, relatively lightweight equipment to record them. His latest film, *24 City*, is microcosmic in approach, focusing entirely on the demolition of a factory in Chengdu, the ancient capital of Sichuan province—a city that in the past two decades has become best known for its digital communications industry and its research institute for the study of pandas. (The movie was shot before the 2008 earthquake on the outskirts of Chengdu and before the crisis of global capitalism.) Established in 1958, Factory 420 was a semisecret government facility employing nearly thirty thousand workers for the manufacture and repair of military aircraft engines. After the Vietnam War, however, demand for its product diminished. It was downsized and retooled to make refrigerators and other consumer products, and then a few years ago its land was sold to a private company for a real estate development called 24 City. The name of the development sounds appropriate for a science-fiction movie, but it actually comes from an ancient Chinese poem: "The cherished hibiscus of 24 city in full bloom / Chengdu shone and prospered."

Brecht once said that you can't understand a factory (and by extension a city) by taking its picture. In *24 City*, which has unusual formal properties, Jia gives us many stunning pictures of the rusted factory being torn down to make room for high-rise condominiums and a five-star hotel. Near the beginning we see a wave of blue-uniformed workers exiting the factory gates—an allusion to *Workers Leaving the Lumière Factory*—followed by beautiful color HDV images photographed by Yu Lik-wai and Wang Yu showing the remaining laborers on the factory floor using tongs and hammers to manipulate glowing steel ingots. The film documents the factory's subsequent demolition and takes us through the immediate environs—dormitories, streets, and recreation halls where the workers live and play. Occasionally it gives us nearly still compositions from within the empty buildings (a butterfly on a windowsill, rain dripping on a broken pane of glass), inserts of historical artifacts (an identity card from the 1960s, an old food-ration coupon), and workers looking straight at the camera as if posing for a Walker Evans photo (these last images play on the effect of stillness versus motion: a woman poses near a fan that blows her hair; a worker stands with his arm around a pal's shoulder, looking somber, and then lifts his hand to tickle his pal's ear). But despite the mesmerizing beauty of the imagery and the absence of narration, *24 City* gains much of its dramatic force, historical depth, and analytic complexity from words—sometimes from quoted poetry, but more often from the oral testimony of individual workers who share their memories of the factory.

The poetry has an ironic and poignant effect. At one point, for example, the words of William Butler Yeats's "The Coming of Wisdom with Time" are shown against a black screen: "Though leaves are many, the root is one;/Through all the lying days of my youth/I swayed my leaves and flowers in the sun;/Now I may wither into the truth." Fade into a group of barren trees against the sky; then the camera cranes up to reveal that the trees have been painted on a wall, on the other side of which is the demolished factory. Most of the oral testimonies are also poignant. Jia interviewed more than 130 workers or their descendants and distilled their testimony down to filmed interviews with nine people representing five generations. Almost half of these are played by actors—a strategy the film jokes about when Joan Chen says that in her youth the men at the factory thought she resembled Joan Chen. Some of the interview subjects are shown in dramatized scenes at home or in social encounters, but the interviews themselves, punctuated with intermittent fades to black, tend to be conducted in static long takes against intriguing deep-focus backgrounds, with the subjects speaking to an offscreen, barely heard questioner (there are no shot/reverse shots in Jia's cinema). Nearly all the interviews have carefully composed minimalist settings, and they usually lead to weeping disclosures that are crafted like dramatic monologues or short stories (the film was cowritten by Jia and Zhai Yongming, a celebrated female poet who specializes in confessional verse).

It would be wrong to conclude from all this that *24 City* is a metafilm designed to comment on the paradoxical relation between documentary and fiction. Its larger purpose is to maintain documentary authenticity while using words, performance signs, and narrative structure to give meaning to fifty years of history. We meet an array of characters, beginning with a machinist who recalls how workers once made their own tools and passed them down to the next generation: "This small thing," said his mentor, "has come into our hands through those of many others. It can still be used." A woman remembers leaving the countryside to work in the factory for fourteen years, then being laid off. "I'd never come late," she says, "and always did my best," but at the age of forty-one, with a child in school, she was reduced to selling flowers in the street. Another woman tells of a boat journey she and her family took to join the factory, during which she briefly went ashore and lost her child in a crowd; out of patriotic fervor and the need to maintain solidarity with her coworkers, she reboarded the boat and left the child behind. The tone here and throughout seems more resigned, sad, or acquiescent than angry.

In the course of the interviews we learn that Factory 420 was once a privileged enclave containing shops, a cinema, and recreational facilities; its workers were fed better than other residents of Chengdu and even had their own bottling plant for soft drinks. When the economy changed, they became poor and marginalized. The culture is now different: a snippet of Chinese opera and a mass singing of "The Internationale" give way to the disco beat of "The World Outside," a pop hit of 1990. A young television announcer, representative of the rising bourgeoisie, tells us that he once tried to work in Factory 420 but the job was so alienating that "something snaps in your mind." The film ends when a "personal shopper" (Zhao Tao, one of Jia's favorite actors) stands high atop the 24 City project and tells us that as a child she wasn't studious and disliked Factory 420; she feels guilty about following a path different from her family and is tearful over their present condition. She's purchased a shiny new car "for credibility" and hopes to make lots of money so that she can give her parents an apartment in 24 City. "I can do it," she says. "I'm the daughter of a worker." At these words the camera pans away from her and looks out across the immense city of Chengdu, population over eleven million, which we see for the first time, looking gray, amazingly dense, and shrouded in smog. The film has completed its movement from an age of industrialization and mass conformity to an age of individualism and consumerism. Both periods have been treated with tenderness and a sharply critical eye.

2009: *POLICE, ADJECTIVE*

Corneliu Porumboiu's *Police, Adjective*, the story of a law officer who has a guilty conscience about one of his investigations, could be described as an anti–police procedural containing a great deal of gray humor. Even so, many elements of the *policier* are on display. The detective protagonist, Christi (Dragos Buçur), doggedly shadows a suspect, writes daily reports in a battered squad room, gathers evidence from the scene of a crime, stakes out the suspect's house, interviews an informant, searches automotive and criminal records, and so forth. We also see moments of "human interest" typical of police films, showing the detective's domestic life and quotidian activity in the squad room. (One of Christi's colleagues wants to lose weight by joining a group that plays "foot tennis." Like me, you probably don't know what that is, but we later see Christi playing it during his off-hours.) The film is more significant for what is missing. No chase scene, no sex, no violence. The setting is Vaslui, a drab Romanian city (Porumboiu's hometown) where the streets are half deserted and winter is coming on; the justice system is populated by a feckless, irritable staff and their pompous supervisors; the home life of the newly married detective is troubled; his hard work is completely ignored by the city prosecutor and police chief; and the unseen arrest of the culprit—a teenager with no previous record who will likely spend three years in jail for smoking hash—is little more than a reflexive exercise in bureaucratic authority.

Police, Adjective is also a film about language. The characters discuss the meaning of words, the camera lingers over Christi's handwritten reports of his activity ("The suspect did not meet anyone, did not use his mobile phone, and smoked a single cigarette, which I checked and which is not relevant to this case."), and in the powerful climactic scene we are given a dictionary definition of the title: the adjectival form of "police," we are told, can be used to describe a police officer, a police novel or film involving "mysterious happenings that are resolved in the end by the ingenuity of a police officer or detective," and "police states or regimes which are supported by the police and which exercise control through repressive methods." ("Ridiculous!" the detective's boss declares when he hears the last example. "All states depend upon the police!") Three other terms are defined: "law," "moral" (one meaning of which is "conclusion contained in a text, especially in a fable"), and "conscience."

Porumboiu has said that in the long scenes of Christi's stakeout, which contain the only POV shots of the film, he was thinking of Antonioni's *Blow-Up*. We watch ordinary comings and goings, their details too far away to become fetishized, until the virtually empty street and its ambient sounds (the bark of a dog, the squeak of a bicycle, a car engine, the wind, the chirping of birds) take on a blank quality. This is a world in which meaning is imposed upon nothing by the raw authority of the state. At dinner one evening, Christi's wife, a high-school language teacher, patronizingly tells him that he made a spelling mistake in one of the reports he left lying about the house: as of two years ago, the Romanian Academy has decided that "not any" is a "negative pronominal adjective" and should be written as one word. His boss later informs him in the tones of a self-righteous intellectual that "conscience" is an outdated concept; once backed by the authority of the Bible, it now has various interpretations. Today, he points out, what is good or bad is determined by "law," which is written by civil officials. The police have a duty to enforce law, not to follow the vagaries of individual conscience.

The entire film is rendered "objectively," in sequence shots or long takes viewed from a distance and filled with dead time. This style has become a hallmark of the Romanian new wave, but too little has been written about the different rhythms and moods it can sustain. In the case of *Police, Adjective*, the undramatic, dialogue-less sequences—in which Christi follows suspects on foot, walks down hallways, eats three complete meals, and waits to be admitted to his boss's office—eventually create a wry, humorous effect that Porumboiu has called "absurd time" while also eliciting our admiration for Christi's literal-minded professionalism, simple integrity, and graceful movement. Dragoş Bucur, whose performance has no large close-ups and only the subtlest changes of posture and expression, usually enters slightly after a scene begins, opening a door or emerging from around a corner, his head slightly bowed, his dark eyes peering ahead like a hunter. His movements were modeled to some extent on Bresson's *Pickpocket* (1959), but Bucur also contributes a sad, patient face. He is as important to this film as Delphine Seyrig is to Chantal Akerman's *Jeanne Dielman* (1975), which uses dead time in more painterly fashion and with more disturbing results.

One of the most elaborate and slyly amusing scenes in the film, an eleven-minute sequence shot during which we hear an entire song maddeningly repeated three times, is played almost deadpan. It shows Christi returning home after a long day and engaging in a discussion of language with his wife. The camera is positioned in the foyer of a small apartment, panning occasionally to look into the open doorways of different rooms. The wife (Irina Saulescu), who resents Christi's absences, sits at a computer, making restless movements in a swivel chair and watching a YouTube clip of a Eurotrash pop tune, its volume turned up full blast: "I won't leave you, love, for a moment of illusion. I won't leave your side if you will be with me. What would the sea be without the sun? What would the field be without the flower? What would today be without tomorrow? What would life be without you?" She barely acknowledges Christi, telling him that dinner is in the kitchen. He goes into the tiny kitchen and through the doorframe we watch him solemnly eat the meal. The song comes to an end, starts up again, ends, and starts again. "This food is good," Christi shouts, turning in his chair to take a beer from the refrigerator. He finishes his meal, goes into the living room, slouches on a couch near his wife, toys with a TV remote, and puts his beer atop the computer tower. The wife moves the beer to her desk and continues to watch the screen. "This song doesn't make any sense," Christi says. The wife says she hasn't thought much about the lyrics, which are "like images." She explicates, "'I won't leave you love.' So it's an anaphora, a rhetorical device. . . . It tries to define this ideal love by associating it with symbols." "Are they images or symbols?" Christi asks, playing dumb. The wife points out that he has been drinking too much, shuts down the computer, and prepares for bed. Christi goes into the bathroom to brush his teeth. "It's like, 'what would toothpaste be without a toothbrush,'" he says innocently. His wife smirks and shakes her head.

A more important and affectively complex sequence occurs near the end, when Christi and his colleague, a big-bellied, slow-witted fellow with a stone face, are summoned to meet with their chief (Vlad Ivanov, who played the abortionist in Cristian Mungiu's *4 Months, 3 Weeks and 2 Days*). They wait interminably in an outer office where a secretary types documents into a computer. The colleague tries to find a newspaper to read: "I've read the *Times*, I've read the *Journal*; let's see what the *Truth* has to say." Eventually admitted to the chief, the two men sit facing one another at either side of the screen like schoolchildren meeting with the principal, while their boss sits between them in a slightly elevated position behind his desk. The camera angle barely changes but the mood shifts from comic to sinister. The chief glowers at Christi, tells him he's made a spelling mistake in one of his reports, and quietly orders him to mount a sting operation and arrest the kid he has been following. Christi argues that the boy is a harmless hash smoker whose so-called friend has "squealed" on him. "Denounced," the chief corrects, and repeats his order. Christi refuses: "I don't want to have that kid on my conscience." The chief asks him to define "conscience" and begins to conduct an elaborate, increasingly humiliating school lesson. First he orders the fat colleague to write Christi's definition on a blackboard ("Conscience is something within me that stops me from doing something bad that afterwards I'd regret") and then has the secretary find a Romanian dictionary. He leans back in pleasure: "Lads, you know what we're doing here? Dialectics!" When at last the dictionary arrives, he orders Christi to look up words and read the definitions aloud (an insert shows the printed pages). "You no longer know what you are," he concludes, and explains that Christi must decide "if you're going to be a police officer and enforce the law or if you're going to follow this moral law of yours and leave the police."

Porumboiu depicts a society barely emerged from autocratic rule—a still Kafkaesque state that subordinates fear of doing harm to others (the dictates of conscience and morality) to fear of transgression and punishment (the dictates of law). But *Police, Adjective* also raises philosophical and ethical issues about modernity in general. Christi is hemmed in by the politics of language, the rule of law, and the government filing system. He suffers from what in English during the Middle Ages was aptly called the "agenbite of inwit" (the modernized spelling is by James Joyce), which might be defined as "the repeated biting of inner knowledge," but he must repress or ignore this biting if he wishes to remain a dutiful instrument of near-universal bureaucracy.

2009: SHIRIN

Abbas Kiarostami's films are usually situated on the boundary between fiction and documentary, but *Shirin* belongs in a zone somewhere between fiction and museum installation. It consists entirely of close-ups of women sitting in a movie theater as they watch an Iranian popular film. The women are played by 112 of Iran's professional actresses, plus Juliette Binoche, who happened to be working with Kiarostami on another project and was nearby. The film they supposedly watch is a fanciful, sentimental melodrama entitled *Shirin*, based on Nizami Ganjavi's *Khosrow and Shirin*, a celebrated epic poem of the late twelfth or early thirteenth century. But in fact, this film doesn't exist. Kiarostami constructed a "theater" in his living room, directing his actors to react to a spot on the wall behind the camera. Afterward, he invented an offscreen soundtrack made up of formalized dialogue, horses galloping, water splashing, swords clashing, and stirring music by four contemporary Iranian composers. The result is a metafilm of considerable richness, giving us the opportunity to "see" a movie in our minds as we watch the play of emotion across women's faces and become conscious of our own role as cinematic spectators.

For critical insight and useful cultural background on *Shirin*, I recommend a conversation between Jonathan Rosenbaum and Mehrnaz Saeed-Vafa, published on Rosenbaum's website, www.JonathanRosenbaum.net. (I also strongly recommend Saeed-Vafa and Rosenbaum's earlier book on Kiarostami [*Abbas Kiarostami*, 2003]). My own remarks will be concerned mainly with close-ups and film acting. As we know, Kuleshov theorized that the meaning of facial expressions in close-ups is determined in the last instance by editing, and his colleague Pudovkin praised actors who could simply think for the camera in "gestureless moments." Kiarostami's film partly confirms such notions: we read the women's faces in relation to the sounds we hear from offscreen; there are no reverse angles, but the post-synchronized soundtrack sutures the close-ups into an imaginary world and motivates the women's reactions. This account, however, is inadequate, in part because the actors perform essential work. Kiarostami surely told them what kind of movie they were watching and directed them to react to its different moods. Significantly, his previous films have made considerable use of nonprofessional actors, whereas here all the players are professional. I very much doubt that *Shirin* could achieve its effects without their ability to convey meaning with minimal resources. To appreciate what they contribute, we might do better to recall Béla Balázs's rhapsodic praise of the unique power of silent film close-ups to turn faces into windows to the inner life; the isolated face in movies, he writes, can "radiate a tender human attitude in the contemplation of hidden things," reveal to us "what is really happening under the surface of appearances," and speak to us in "silent soliloquy" (274–77).

The women of *Shirin* are viewed in standard-size close-ups that bring their shoulders into view and allow them to use their hands as expressive instruments; they appear to be seated at different places in the auditorium, gazing at the screen from slightly different angles, and are cleverly lit, ostensibly by the soft, flickering light of the screen but also by a subtle backlighting. Each covers her hair and frames her face with a scarf. Some are old and some are young, and they appear to represent slightly different social classes. Some are in a black limbo, others in a position that enables us to see men and women behind them. All have lovely, lived-in faces; indeed, one of the pleasures of the film is a growing appreciation of the variety of faces and the empathy that comes from looking at them—a phenomenon that needs a philosopher such as Emmanuel Levinas to fully explore.

One might also enlist the help of the social scientists, ranging from Charles Darwin to Paul Ekman, who have tried to codify facial expressions. The women actors in *Shirin* produce a variety of tiny but eloquent expressive signs keyed to the changing moods of the film they watch. We inevitably assign meanings to some of these signs: pensive concentration, casual relaxation, rapt engagement, tearful identification, concern, fear, and so forth. Occasionally we see a slight smile, a frown, a slow chewing of gum, a surprised widening of the eyes. One woman attentively "reads" the film, her eyes moving back and forth across an imaginary screen. During a violent scene a woman flinches and looks away and another closes her eyes, lowering her head in a kind of grief. Hands are as important as faces—adjusting a scarf, biting a nail, posing thoughtfully with a finger touching a chin, staving off sobs by covering the mouth with a hand. But these modern performance signs resist neat codification; they belong to the idiolect of performers who suggest "inner" meanings beyond the reach of full articulation. One of the remarkable qualities of the women in *Shirin* is their ability to create the impression of fully embodied persons with emotional lives beyond the movie theater—lives we can sense but never know. The overwhelming emotion they generate is one of sadness over both the film and the world.

Given that *Shirin* is a film about women watching a melodrama, Kiarostami runs the risk of falling into sexist clichés; but it's difficult to watch the film without thinking about the situation of women in Iran. In her conversation with Jonathan Rosenbaum, Mehrnaz Saeed-Vafa has pointed out that because all the women wear scarves, they can't be disassociated with the present political and social moment in their country: "When you see these women crying, you can't help but think of martyrdom. At the beginning, we even hear Shirin addressing other women, 'Listen to me, my sisters,' ... and then at the end, she says to them, 'I'm so tired, my sad sisters,' asking them whether they're crying for her or for their own, inner Shirins." It should also be noted that *Shirin* prevents us from being completely detached observers. As David Bordwell notes on his website, this is a film that watches us. *Shirin* makes us aware of our own faces, and in the process enlists us in a human community.

2010: *UNCLE BOONMEE WHO CAN RECALL HIS PAST LIVES*

Thai filmmaker Apichatpong Weerasethakul was educated at the School of the Art Institute in Chicago, where a collection of "exquisite corpse" drawings by the French surrealists gave him the idea for one of his early films, *Mysterious Object at Noon* (2000). His subsequent work, consisting of museum installations as well as films, has many things in common with surrealism, including a desublimation of ordinary experience, a disregard for the coherence of realist narrative, a love of the fantastic, and an oscillation of tone between the poetic and the playful. All of this is evident in *Uncle Boonmee Who Can Recall His Past Lives*, which tells the story of a Thai farmer dying of kidney failure (Apichatpong's father, a medical doctor, died of the same condition) and his mysterious encounter with past and future lives.

But *Uncle Boonmee* can't be explained simply as a form of surrealism or, despite Apichatpong's admiration for Gabriel García Márquez, as "magic realism." The film was inspired by a book by Phra Sripariyattiweti, a Tibetan Buddhist monk, and the finished product, though secular, retains an aura of Buddhist spirituality. *Boonmee* is also related to *The Primitive* (2009), Apichatpong's museum installation about the violent history of the Renu Nakhon district of northeastern Thailand, where he was born and where the film is set. This region was occupied by the Thai army during the Vietnam War, and many of its inhabitants, who were accused of being communists, were raped, tortured, and murdered. (According to Human Rights Watch, the Thai military continues a policy of political repression and "disappearances" throughout the country.) *Boonmee* therefore offers indirect political commentary alongside its haunting meditation on death, transmigration of souls, and cinema.

In stylistic terms, *Boonmee* is "slow cinema," sparing of close-ups and reverse-field editing, respectful of stillness, acted in an almost deadpan manner. Not much happens: nearing death, Uncle Boonmee (Thanapat Saisaymar) is visited by his sister-in-law Jen (Jenjira Pongpas) and her son Tong (Sakda Kaewbuadee), who live in the city. Tong nurses Boonmee, helping to drain his ailing kidney, and Boonmee shows Jen around his farm, where he raises tamarind, maize, and bees. Jen is suspicious of the illegal Chinese immigrants and "smelly" Laotians who work the farm, but as she limps around the sunny fields (her right leg is shorter than her left), she becomes friendly with one of them. At one point Boonmee tells her that his illness might be the result of bad karma: "I killed too many communists," he explains. "I killed bugs, too."

At night the world is different, populated by spirits with stories of their own. The opening of the film prepares us for these nocturnal presences. First we see an epigraph: "Facing the jungle, the hills and vales, my past lives as an animal and other beings rise up before me." Next, the silhouetted, moonlit image of a huge water buffalo, who looks toward the jungle and seems to hear something in the susurrus of insects and animals; uttering a short, painful cry, the beast breaks free of its tether and runs off through rice fields into the dense foliage. Later, when night falls over Boonmee's house, stranger things occur. During an evening meal, Boonmee's long-dead wife Huay appears at one end of the dinner table. The living characters are momentarily disconcerted, but they settle into matter-of-fact conversation with the ghostly figure, who gradually takes solid form. In the midst of their conversation, the night air is filled with a minatory, pulsing noise (the film's sound design is as impressive as its imagery), and a dark figure who looks like a B-movie actor in an ape suit, eyes glowing like E.T.'s fingertips, enters from downstairs, sits at the table, and identifies himself as Boonmee's lost son who is presumed dead. "Why did you let your hair grow so long?" Auntie Jen asks in comic amazement. "There are many beings outside," the son says to his father, "spirits and hungry animals like me. They sense your illness." He explains that as a young man he experimented with the art of photography and became fascinated by the apelike creatures his developed pictures revealed in the trees beyond the farm. He wandered away to a forgotten "old world" and mated with one of the "monkey ghosts" who roam in the night.

Perhaps it should be noted that ghosts in Buddhism are different from the ones we know in the West: they can be dead spirits who visit the living, or "hungry ghosts" who occupy a liminal state between life and death. The "monkey ghosts" in *Uncle Boonmee* seem to belong more to the latter category, and it may be significant that both of the spirit characters appear during a meal. In any case, the family's gentle acceptance of the ghostly visitors makes them seem less uncanny than marvelous. Still later that evening, with hardly any motivation, we cut away from the farm to witness a self-contained episode from the folkloric past, perhaps from one of Boonmee's previous lives, which provides another illustration of the intercourse between spirits, animals, and humans. A Thai princess, her beautiful eyes visible above a veil, travels through the nighttime jungle in a regal litter borne by her male servants. She reaches out and caresses the hair and arm of one of the handsome bearers, who looks up and secretly touches her hand. Soon she arrives at a moonlit pool beside a waterfall (the scene is shot day-for-night, its eeriness enhanced by a blue-green filter), where she removes her veil, revealing a homely, scarred face. The reflection she sees in the pool, however, is that of a lovely woman. The handsome young servant approaches and tries to make love to her, but she sends him away because she doubts his sincerity and doesn't trust the reflection. Alone, she kneels and weeps. A large catfish raises his head above the water and speaks: "Princess, don't waste your tears," he says, and begins describing her beauty in seductive tones. When he swims away, she wades into the pool, removing her jeweled necklaces, offering them as a gift for his return. Swooning, she extends her body and floats on her back, her legs spread. Suddenly she experiences a series of orgasmic jolts and spasms. The fish's giant tail flaps and splashes between her legs. Down below, under the murky water, a necklace drifts away in a cloud of bubbles and a pair of catfish swim around, their long tendrils swaying in the current.

This is one of the most arresting cinematic moments I've witnessed in years, a surreal blend of the marvelous and the erotic, merging animal with human and carnal with sublime. The remainder of the film is less vividly supernatural but no less strange. As Boonmee's death approaches, his dead wife leads his family group through the forest and into a hillside cave, where they glimpse phosphorescent rocks, pools of albino fish, and cave drawings. "This cave," Boonmee says, "it's like a womb, isn't it? I was born here, I don't know if as a woman or man." Then the film briefly becomes a sort of *photo-roman* accompanied by Boonmee's narration: "Last night I dreamed of the future, ruled by an authority able to make people disappear. . . . I was afraid because I had friends in this future." We see still photos of teenage soldiers in camouflage, capturing ape-men and posing for the camera—images derived from Apichatpong's earlier museum installation about Thai military repression and the disappeared or forgotten history of political violence. Back in the cave, Boonmee's wife opens the tube leading into his kidney and lets it drain onto the ground.

Boonmee's funeral is held in the city, where Jen counts up gifts of money from mourners. Tong, we discover, is a Buddhist monk, but after the funeral he wants to change out of his robes and visit a 7-Eleven convenience store or a café. (Apichatpong has previously been censored by Thai authorities for portraying monks in this lightly satiric fashion.) As he and Jen prepare to leave, one of the film's rare instances of shot/reverse shot editing gives them pause: they look offscreen and see themselves watching TV in the same spot they occupied a few moments before. The film ends in a karaoke café where they sit in silence, perhaps thinking of the temporal displacement they've experienced and remembering the old world they left behind.

Some of Apichatpong's aims in the film can be inferred from his evocative essay "Ghosts in the Darkness," which is both a theory of cinema and a commentary on his key images and themes (available in English in James Quandt, ed., *Apichatpong Weerasethakul*). "If you notice the people around you while watching a film," he writes, "you will see that their behavior is like that of ghosts, lifting up their heads to see the moving images.... The moving images on the screen are camera records of events that have already taken place; they are remains of the past, strung together and called a film. In this hall of darkness, ghosts are watching ghosts." But the situation isn't as morbid as it may sound. "Just as we like to look at ghosts," Apichatpong explains, "we seem instinctively to want to enter dark halls ... like returning to our mother's womb, fleeing there for safety, like the time during the war in Laos, when people living on the Ho Chi Minh Trail ... were attacked by phosphorous bombs during an air raid and took refuge in a cave.... The cave is probably still full of bones, ranging from small children to adults. If you went to see it now you might see real ghosts there—you wouldn't need a film." A more striking example from the same period, he observes, was the Quan Y cave on Cat Ba Island in Vietnam, which served not only as a hidden hospital but also as a recreation area and a cinema. "You come to the conclusion that we watch films instinctively, as therapy for mental and emotional pain. Tens of thousands of years ago, when our ancestors were living in caves, they often drew on the walls of the cave, showing us how they lived their lives.... Looking at it like this, you could say that cinemas, whether inside or outside department stores, are our modern day caves."

In an influential essay of 1975, "The Apparatus: Metapsychological Approaches to the Impression of Reality in the Cinema," French theorist Jean-Louis Baudry compared cinema to the lights flickering on the back wall of Plato's cave, an illusory shadow show from which we need to liberate ourselves. Apichatpong thinks exactly otherwise. His cinema-cave is dedicated to recovering repressed history, healing pain, and connecting our spirits with others.

2010: *MYSTERIES OF LISBON*

I've never read the prolific Portuguese author Camilo Castelo Branco (1825–90), but two of his novels have been adapted by major directors—

Manoel de Oliveira's *Doomed Love* (1978) and Raúl Ruiz's *Mysteries of Lisbon* (2010)—and based on this evidence it seems clear what sort of writer he was, at least in some of his work. The novels in question, dated 1862 and 1854 respectively, were influenced by the romantic tradition of Chateaubriand and Hugo; they give us passionate individuals in conflict with oppressive aristocrats, clashes of tragic and grotesque emotion, swirling melodramatic action, and sympathetic portrayals of characters who are orphaned, illegitimate, or victims of the ruling patriarchy (in real life Castelo Branco was all three). They were probably composed at great speed because Castelo Branco was the first Portuguese writer to live entirely by his pen. He became a master of the feuilleton and the multivolume novel and was a talented practitioner of the nineteenth-century version of pulp fiction or soap opera.

The Oliveira and Ruiz films are interesting to compare and contrast. Each is approximately four and a half hours long, intended to be shown as a TV miniseries. Working from a short novel, Oliveira is radically literal; instead of condensing his source by converting novelistic description into spectacle, as films normally do, he preserves virtually all of Castelo Branco's language, emphasizing telling rather than showing. The paradoxical result, as Randal Johnson has pointed out in his *Manoel de Oliveira*, is the transformation of a theatrical, emotional, melodramatic text into an austere experiment in cinematic modernism. Ruiz's approach is just the opposite, though in some ways no less modernist. His screenwriter, Carlos Saboga, has condensed a triple-decker novel into four and a half hours, somehow retaining its plot and leaving enough room for Ruiz to add embellishments of his own; HD photographer André Szankowski and art director Isabel Branco create a gorgeous period-film spectacle filled with scenic locations; and Ruiz, who began his career in Chile making soap operas, keeps the large cast and the convoluted strands of the narrative moving at a swift pace.

In an interview publicizing the film, Ruiz said that *Mysteries of Lisbon* has a "gliding" and "labyrinthine" form. In keeping the first of these qualities—and with what many describe as the baroque theatricality of the novel—he employs long takes, sinuous camera movements, 360-degree pans, lateral tracking shots that slide past the walls of rooms, and complex, graceful blocking. He often frames scenes through doorways, windows, or parted curtains, sometimes using the technique to show us contrasting levels of action. (One of the most amusing sequence shots has two frames within the frame: a priest disembarks from a closed carriage, looks down the street at a violent quarrel, and gets back in the carriage; through the vehicle's near window we see him reading from a Bible as the action on the street boils past the window beyond him.) Occasionally he places a servant on one side of a doorway or behind a wall, overhearing a private conversation in the distance. Several of his compositions are reminiscent of Welles and Toland in *Citizen Kane:* wide-angle, floor-level views and deep-focus arrangements in which a giant head—at one point the head of a parrot—occupies the extreme foreground while action occurs in the far background. Now and then he experiments with antique behavior and old-fashioned theatricality: characters who faint upon hearing shocking news are framed in wide shot, flopping to the floor like rag dolls.

The labyrinthine plot defies description and contains many surprises. In somewhat Dickensian fashion, it begins when the orphan Pedro da Silva (played as a child by João Luís Arrais and as an adult by Alfonso Pimentel), with the help of a kindly priest (Adriano Luz), discovers that he's the love child of a Portuguese countess who was forced to abandon him. Soon, however, everything veers off into stories within the story, told in flashback by multiple narrators. I kept losing track of where it all started, but I was never disappointed. Pedro intermittently returns, and several episodes are introduced by inserts of a small, beautifully decorated cardboard theater given to him by his mother. At the end we discover that he's been narrating everything from his deathbed in Brazil. By the time we reach this point, we've also learned that nearly all the important characters have hidden identities and secrets that undermine the assumptions we initially made about them.

The major theme of the film could be described as the instability of human identity, which is always constructed out of individual memories, internalized narratives, and social performances, and which, under certain conditions, is subject to fluctuation and change. The characters in *Mysteries of Lisbon* inhabit a world of immutable aristocracy and Catholic hierarchy, governed by unalterably established institutions. But that world is decadent, beginning to resemble a Gothic novel in which things aren't necessarily as they appear. Significantly, one of the characters has been reading Ann Radcliffe, who was among the inventors of gothic fiction. It's a world in which outlaws become priests, mothers become nuns, and hired killers become aristocrats. The shape-shifting characters, together with the classically realist plot that goes in so many directions it seems to have no goal, make this film and the old novel on which it's based seem not only romantically fun and fascinatingly mysterious, but also very modern.

BEST FILMS, 2007–2010

2007

1. *Colossal Youth* (Pedro Costa, 2006)
2. *Cuadecuc-Vampir* (Pere Portabella, 1970)

3. *Bamako* (Abderrahmane Sissako, 2006)
4. *Ratatouille* (Brad Bird and Jan Pinkava)
5. *Once* (John Carney)
6. *No End in Sight* (Charles Ferguson)
7. *Away from Her* (Sarah Polley)
8. *Black Book* (Paul Verhoeven)
9. *The Assassination of Jesse James by the Coward Robert Ford* (Andrew Dominik)
10. *Mad Men* (Matthew Weiner)

Honorable mention (alphabetical): *Before the Devil Knows You're Dead* (Sidney Lumet), *Brand upon the Brain!* (Guy Maddin), *Alice's House* (*Casa de Alice,* Chico Teixeira), *The Darjeeling Limited* (Wes Anderson), *Eastern Promises* (David Cronenberg), *Gone Baby Gone* (Ben Affleck), *Helvetica* (Gary Hustwit), *The Host* (Bong Joon-Ho), *I'm Not There* (Todd Haynes), *Inland Empire* (David Lynch), *In the Valley of Elah* (Paul Haggis), *Lions for Lambs* (Robert Redford), *Michael Clayton* (Tony Gilroy), *No Country for Old Men* (Joel and Ethan Coen), *Redacted* (Brian De Palma), *There Will Be Blood* (Paul Thomas Anderson), *The Wind That Shakes the Barley* (Ken Loach), *Zodiac* (David Fincher)

2008

1. *24 City* (Jia Zhangke)
2. *My Winnipeg* (Guy Maddin)
3. *Of Time and the City* (Terence Davies)
4. *The Exiles* (Kent Mackenzie, 1961)
5. *Wendy and Lucy* (Kelly Reichardt)
6. *Happy-Go-Lucky* (Mike Leigh)
7. *Let the Right One In* (Tomas Alfredson)
8. *The Duchess of Langeais* (Jacques Rivette)
9. *Flight of the Red Balloon* (Hou Hsiao-hsien)
10. *The Band's Visit* (Eran Kolirin)

Honorable mention (alphabetical): *Che, Parts I & II* (Steven Soderbergh), *The Dark Knight* (Christopher Nolan), *The Edge of Heaven* (Fatih Akin), *Elite Squad* (José Padilha), *Gran Torino* (Clint Eastwood), *The Last Mistress* (Catherine Breillat), *Milk* (Gus Van Sant), *My Mexican Shivah* (Alejandro

Springall), *Native Dancer* (Gulshat Omarova), *Nights and Weekends* (Joe Swanberg and Greta Gerwig), *The Order of Myths* (Margaret Brown), *Profit Motive and the Whispering Wind* (John Gianvito), *A Secret* (Claude Miller), *Vicky Cristina Barcelona* (Woody Allen), *The Visitor* (Thomas McCarthy), *WALL-E* (Andrew Stanton)

2009

1. *Police, Adjective* (Corneliu Porumboiu)
2. *Shirin* (Abbas Kiarostami)
3. *Tulpan* (Sergey Dvortsevoy)
4. *Henri-Georges Clouzot's Inferno* (Serge Bromberg and Ruxandra Medrea)
5. *35 Shots of Rum* (Claire Denis)
6. *The Hurt Locker* (Kathryn Bigelow)
7. *Sita Sings the Blues* (Nina Paley)
8. *Me and Orson Welles* (Richard Linklater)
9. *Summer Hours* (Olivier Assayas)
10. *Eccentricities of a Blond-Haired Girl* (Manoel de Oliveira)

Honorable mention (alphabetical): *The Beaches of Agnès* (Agnès Varda), *Bright Star* (Jane Campion), *District 9* (Neill Blomkamp), *An Education* (Lone Scherfig), *Fantastic Mr. Fox* (Wes Anderson), *Goodbye Solo* (Ramin Bahrani), *The Headless Woman* (Lucrecia Martel), *The Informant!* (Steven Soderbergh), *Loren Cass* (Chris Fuller), *Lorna's Silence* (Jean-Pierre and Luc Dardenne), *The Maid* (Sebastián Silva), *Ne Change Rien* (Pedro Costa), *Séraphine* (Martin Provost), *Sugar* (Anna Boden and Ryan Fleck), *Where the Wild Things Are* (Spike Jonze)

2010

1. *Uncle Boonmee Who Can Recall His Past Lives* (Apichatpong Weerasethakul)
2. *Mysteries of Lisbon* (Raúl Ruiz)
3. *Carlos* (Olivier Assayas)
4. *The Strange Case of Angelica* (Manoel de Oliveira)
5. *Everyone Else* (Maren Ade)
6. *Vincere* (Marco Bellocchio)

7. *Winter's Bone* (Debra Granik)
8. *I Am Love* (Luca Guadagnino)
9. *Sweetgrass* (Lucien Castaing-Taylor and Ilisa Barbash)
10. *Inside Job* (Charles Ferguson)

Honorable mention (alphabetical): *Alice in Wonderland* (Tim Burton), *The Art of the Steal* (Don Argott), *Black Swan* (Darren Aronofsky), *Certified Copy* (Abbas Kiarostami), *Fair Game* (Doug Liman), *The Ghost Writer* (Roman Polanski), *If I Want to Whistle, I Whistle* (Florin Serban), *Hitler in Hollywood* (Frédéric Sojcher), *The Kids Are All Right* (Lisa Cholodenko), *La Danse: The Paris Opera Ballet* (Frederick Wiseman), *Let It Rain* (Agnès Jaoui), *Poetry* (Lee Chang-dong), *White Material* (Claire Denis), *The Social Network* (David Fincher), *The Square* (Nash Edgerton), *Toy Story 3* (Lee Unkrich)

Works Cited

Abrams, M.H. *The Mirror and the Lamp.* New York: Oxford, 1971.
Adorno, Theodor W. "On the Fetish Character of Music and the Regression of Listening." In *The Essential Frankfurt School Reader,* ed. Andrew Arato and Eike Gebhardt, 270–99. New York: Continuum, 1987.
———. *Prisms.* Trans. Samuel and Shierry Weber. Cambridge, MA: MIT Press, 1990.
Agee, James. *Agee on Film,* Vol. 1. New York: McDowell, Obolensky, 1958.
———. *Agee on Film,* Vol. 2. New York: McDowell, Obolensky, 1960.
———. *Agee: Film Writing and Selected Journalism.* Ed. Michael Sragow. New York: Library of America, 2005.
———. *Let Us Now Praise Famous Men.* New York: Houghton Mifflin Company, 1960.
Allen, Richard, and S. Ishii Gonzales, eds. *Alfred Hitchcock Centenary Essays.* London: BFI, 1999.
Althusser, Louis. *Lenin and Philosophy.* Trans. Ben Brewster. New York: Monthly Review Press, 1971.
Altman, Rick. *The Hollywood Film Musical.* Bloomington: Indiana University Press, 1987.
Anderegg, Michael. "Orson Welles as Performer." *Persistence of Vision* 7 (1989): 73.
———. *Orson Welles, Shakespeare, and Popular Culture.* New York: Columbia University Press, 1999.
Andrew, Dudley. "Adaptation." In *Film Adaptation,* ed. Naremore, 28–37.
———. "The Unauthorized Auteur Today." In *Film Theory Goes to the Movies,* ed. Jim Collins, Hillary Radner, and Ava Preacher Collins, 77–85. New York: Routledge.
Auden, W..H. *Prose and Travel Books in Prose and Verse,* vol. 1. Ed. Edward Mendelson. Princeton, NJ: Princeton University Press, 1996.
Ayfre, Amedee. "Neo-Realism and Phenomenology." In *"Cahiers du Cinéma": The 1950s,* ed. Jim Hillier, 182–91.
Baecque, Antoine de. "Que reste-t-il de la politique des auteurs?" *Cahiers du cinéma* 518 (November 1997): 22–25.
Bakhtin, Mikhail. *The Dialogic Imagination.* Ed. Michael Holquist. Austin: University of Texas Press, 1981.

Balázs, Béla. "From *Theory of Film.*" In *Film Theory and Criticism* (7th edition), ed. Leo Braudy and Marshall Cohen, 273–281. New York: Oxford University Press, 2009.

Balcerzak, Scott and Jason Sperb. *Cinephilia in the Age of Digital Reproduction.* London: Wallflower Press, 2009.

Barthes, Roland. *A Barthes Reader.* Ed. Susan Sontag. New York: Hill and Wang, 1982.

Baudry, Jean-Louis. "The Apparatus: Metapsychological Approaches to the Impression of Reality in Cinema." In *Film Theory and Criticism* (7th edition), ed. Leo Braudy and Marshall Cohen, 171–188. New York: Oxford University Press, 2009.

Bazin, André. "Adaptation, or the Cinema as Digest." In *Film Adaptation,* ed. Naremore, 28–37.

———. "The Death of Humphrey Bogart." In *"Cahiers du Cinéma": The 1950s,* ed. Hillier, 98–101.

———. "Hitchcock vs. Hitchcock." In *Focus on Hitchcock,* ed. LaValley, 60–69.

———. *What Is Cinema?* Trans. Timothy Bernard. Montreal: Caboose, 2009.

Behlmer, Rudy. *Inside Warner Bros.: 1935–1951.* New York: Simon & Schuster, 1985.

Bellour, Raymond. "The Obvious and the Code." In *The Analysis of Film,* ed. Constance Penley, 69–76. Bloomington: Indiana University Press, 2001.

Bender, John, and David Wellbery. "Rhetoricality: On the Modernist Return of Rhetoric." In Bender and Wellbery, eds., *The Ends of Rhetoric: History, Theory, Practice,* 3–39. Stanford, CA: Stanford University Press, 1990.

Benjamin, Walter. "The Work of Art in the Age of Mechanical Reproduction." In *Illuminations.* New York: Schocken Books, 1969.

Benstock, Bernard. "The Dead." In *James Joyce's Dubliners,* ed. Clive Hart, 153–69. New York: Viking Press, 1969.

Bergreen, Laurence. *James Agee: A Life.* New York: E. P. Dutton, 1984.

Bluestone, George. *Novels into Film: The Metamorphosis of Fiction into Cinema.* Berkeley: University of California Press, 1973.

Bogle, Donald. *Toms, Coons, Mulattoes, Mammies, and Bucks: An Interpretive History of Blacks in American Films.* New York: Continuum, 1991.

Bohne, Luciana. "Rossellini's *Viaggio in Italia*: A Variation on a Theme by Joyce." *Film Criticism* 3, no. 2 (Winter 1979): 43–52.

Booth, Wayne. *The Rhetoric of Fiction.* Chicago: University of Chicago Press, 1961.

Borde, Raymond, and Etienne Chaumeton. *A Panorama of American Film Noir, 1941–1953.* Trans. Paul Hammond. San Francisco: City Lights, 2002.

Bordwell, David. *Figures Traced in Light: On Cinematic Staging.* Berkeley: University of California Press, 2005.

———. *Narration in Fiction Film.* Madison: University of Wisconsin Press, 1985.

Bordwell, David, Janet Staiger, and Kristin Thompson. *The Classical Hollywood Cinema: Film Style and Mode of Production to 1960.* New York: Columbia University Press, 1985.

Bordwell, David, and Kristin Thompson. *Film Art,* 10th edition. New York: McGraw-Hill, 2012.

Brady, John. *The Craft of the Screenwriter.* New York: Touchstone Books, 1982.

Brantlinger, Patrick. "*Heart of Darkness:* Anti-Imperialism, Racism, or

Impressionism?" In *Heart of Darkness*, ed. Ross C. Murfin, 277–98. New York: St. Martin's Press, 1996.
Braudy, Leo. *Native Informant*. New York: Oxford University Press, 1991.
———. *The World in a Frame: What We See in Films*. Garden City, NY: Anchor Books, 1977.
Brecht, Bertolt. *Brecht on Theater*. Trans. John Willet. New York: Hill and Wang, 1964.
Breton, André, ed. *Anthology of Black Humor*. Trans. Mark Polizzotti. San Francisco: City Lights Books, 1997.
Brill, Lesley. *The Hitchcock Romance: Love and Irony in Hitchcock's Films*. Princeton, NJ: Princeton University Press, 1988.
———. "Redemptive Comedy in the Films of Alfred Hitchcock and Preston Sturges: 'Are Snakes Necessary?'" In *Alfred Hitchcock Centenary Essays*, ed. Richard Allen and S. Ishii Gonzales, 205–20. London: BFI, 1999.
Brion, Patrick. *Le film noir*. Paris: Editions de La Martinière, 1992.
Britton, Andrew. *Cary Grant: Comedy and Male Desire*. Newcastle upon Tyne: Tyneside Cinema, 1987.
Brooks, Louise. *Lulu in Hollywood*. New York: Knopf, 1983.
Browne, Nick. *The Rhetoric of Filmic Narration*. Ann Arbor, MI: University Microfilms International, n.d.
Bruno, Giuliana. *Streetwalking on a Ruined Map*. Princeton, NJ: Princeton University Press, 1993.
Buck-Morss, Susan. *The Dialectics of Seeing: Walter Benjamin and the Arcades Project*. Cambridge, MA: MIT Press, 1989.
Burke, Peter. "The 'Discovery' of Popular Culture." In *People's History and Socialist Theory*, ed. Raphael Samuel, 215–22. London: Routledge & Kegan Paul, 1983.
Cahill, James. " . . . and Afterwards? Martin Arnold's Phantom Cinema." *Spectator* 27. Supplement: Deaths of Cinema, Special Graduate Conference Issue (2007): 19–25.
Calinescu, Matei. *Five Faces of Modernity*. Durham, NC: Duke University Press, 1987.
Callow, Simon. *Night of the Hunter*. London: British Film Institute, 2000.
Carringer, Robert. *The Making of* Citizen Kane. Berkeley: University of California Press, 1985.
Cavell, Stanley. "North by Northwest." In *A Hitchcock Reader*, ed. Marshall Deutelbaum and Leland Poague. 249–61. Ames: Iowa State University Press, 1986.
Chandler, Raymond. *Raymond Chandler: Later Novels and Other Writings*. New York: Library of America, 1995.
———. *Raymond Chandler: Stories and Early Novels*. New York: Library of America, 1995.
———. *Selected Letters of Raymond Chandler*. Ed. Frank MacShane. New York: Delta, 1981.
Chatman, Seymour. *Coming to Terms: The Rhetoric of Narrative in Fiction and Film*. Ithaca, NY: Cornell University Press, 1990.
———. "What Novels Can Do That Films Can't (and Vice Versa)." In *On Narrative*, ed. W. J. T. Mitchell, 117–36. Chicago: University of Chicago Press, 1981.
Ciment, Michael. *Kubrick: The Definitive Edition*. New York: Faber and Faber, 2001.

Clark, T.J. "More on the Differences between Comrade Greenberg and Ourselves." In *Modernism and Modernity: The Vancouver Conference Papers*, ed. Benjamin Buchloh, Serge Guilbaut, and David Solkin, 184–94. Nova Scotia: The Press of Nova Scotia College of Art and Design, 1983.

Cobos, Juan, Miguel Rubio, and J.A. Pruneda. "A Trip to Don Quixoteland: Conversations with Orson Welles." In Ronald Gottesman, ed., *Focus on "Citizen Kane,"* 7–24. Englewood Cliffs, NJ: Prentice-Hall, 1971.

Cohen, Keith. *Film and Fiction: The Dynamics of Exchange.* New Haven, CT: Yale University Press, 1979.

Cole, Toby, and Helen Krich Chinoy, eds. *Actors on Acting.* New York: Crown, 1970.

Cook, David A. *A History of Narrative Film.* New York: Norton, 1990.

Corrigan, Timothy. *Cinema without Walls.* New Brunswick, NJ: Rutgers University Press, 1991.

Couchman, Jeffrey. *The Night of the Hunter: A Biography of a Film.* Evanston, IL: Northwestern University Press, 2009.

Crafton, Donald. *Shadow of a Mouse: Performance, Belief, and World-Making in Animation.* Berkeley: University of California Press, 2012.

Cripps, Thomas. *Black Film as Genre.* Bloomington: Indiana University Press, 1979.

Culler, Jonathan. *The Pursuit of Signs: Semiotics, Literature, and Deconstruction.* Ithaca, NY: Cornell University Press, 1981.

Davis, Mike. *City of Quartz.* New York: Vintage Books, 1992.

DeBona, Guerric. *Film Adaptation in the Hollywood Studio Era.* Urbana: University of Illinois Press, 2010.

Deleuze, Gilles. "Qu'est-ce que l'acte de création?" *Trafic* 27 (Autumn 1998): 133–42.

Denby, David. *Do the Movies Have a Future?* New York: Simon and Schuster, 2012.

Denning, Michael. *Cover Stories: Narrative and Ideology in the British Spy Thriller.* London: Routledge & Kegan Paul, 1987.

———. *The Cultural Front: The Laboring of American Culture in the Twentieth Century.* London: Verso, 1996.

Diawara, Manthia. "Black Spectatorship: Problems of Identification and Resistance." *Screen* 29, no. 4 (Autumn 1988): 66–79.

Doherty, Thomas. "To Catch a Filmmaker: *The Girl*, Hitchcock, and Hitchcock." *Cineaste* 37, no. 2 (2013): 4–7.

Domarchi, Jean, and Jean Douchet. "Entretien avec Alfred Hitchcock." *Cahiers du cinéma* 102 (December 1959): 19–31.

Durgnat, Raymond. *Films and Feelings.* Cambridge, MA: MIT Press, 1971.

———. *The Strange Case of Alfred Hitchcock.* Cambridge, MA: MIT Press, 1974.

Durgnat, Raymond, and Scott Simmon. *King Vidor: American.* Berkeley: University of California Press, 1989.

Dyer, Richard. "Entertainment and Utopia." In *Genre: The Musical*, ed. Rick Altman, 175–89. London: Routledge & Kegan Paul, 1981.

———. "Postscript: Queers and Women in Film Noir." In *Women in Film Noir*, ed. E. Ann Kaplan, 123–29. London: BFI, 1998.

———. *Stars.* Revised edition. London: BFI, 1998.

Eagleton, Terry. *Literary Theory: An Introduction.* Minneapolis: University of Minnesota Press, 1983.

Eliot, T.S. *Selected Prose.* Harmondsworth: Penguin, 1953.

Farber, Manny. *Farber on Film.* Ed. Robert Polito. New York: Library of America, 2009.

———. *Negative Space: Manny Farber on the Movies.* Expanded edition. New York: Da Capo Press, 1998.

Fassbinder, Rainer Werner. "Preliminary Remarks on *Querelle.*" Trans. Krishna Winston. In *The Anarchy of the Imagination,* ed. Michael Töteberg and Leo A. Lensing, 167–69. Baltimore, MD: Johns Hopkins University Press, 1992.

Feuer, Jane. *The Hollywood Musical.* Bloomington: Indiana University Press, 1982.

Fleishman, Avrom. *Narrated Films: Storytelling Situations in Cinema History.* Baltimore, MD: Johns Hopkins University Press, 1992.

Flitterman-Lewis, Sandy. "To Desire Differently: Feminism and the French Cinema." In *Film and Theory,* ed. Robert Stam and Toby Miller, 16–19. Malden, MA: Blackwell, 2000.

Fordin, Hugh. *The Movies' Greatest Musicals.* New York: Frederick Ungar, 1984.

Frampton, Hollis. "The Invention without a Future." *October* 109 (Summer 2004): 64–75.

Frank, Nino. "Un nouveau genre 'policier': L'aventure criminelle." *L'Écran français* 61 (1946): 8–9, 14.

Freud, Sigmund. *Jokes and Their Relation to the Unconscious.* Trans. James Strachey. New York: Norton, 1960.

———. *Standard Edition of the Complete Works of Sigmund Freud.* Vol. 20. Trans. James Strachey. London: Hogarth Press, 1953.

Friedman, Lester D., ed. *Unspeakable Images: Ethnicity and the American Cinema.* Urbana: University of Illinois Press, 1991.

Frye, Northrup. *Anatomy of Criticism: Four Essays.* Princeton, NJ: Princeton University Press, 1957.

Gates, Henry Louis, Jr. "The Trope of the New Negro and the Reconstruction of the Image of the Black." *Representations* 24 (Fall 1988): 129–55.

Genette, Gérard. *Narrative Discourse: An Essay in Method.* Trans. Jane E. Lewin. Ithaca, NY: Cornell University Press, 1980.

Giddins, Gary. *Natural Selection.* New York: Oxford University Press, 2008.

Gilling, Ted. "Interview with George Colouris." *Sight and Sound* (Summer 1973): 42–43.

Girard, René. *Mimesis and Theory: Essays on Literature and Criticism, 1953–2005.* Ed. Robert Doran. Stanford, CA: Stanford University Press, 2008.

Godard, Jean-Luc. *Godard on Godard.* Ed. Jean Narboni and Tom Milne. New York: Viking Press. 1972.

Gottlieb, Sidney. *Hitchcock on Hitchcock.* Berkeley: University of California Press, 1995.

Greenberg, Clement. *Pollock and After.* New York: Harper and Row, 1985.

Greene, Graham. *Graham Greene: Collected Essays.* Harmondsworth: Penguin, 1970.

Grusin, Richard, and Jay David Bolter. *Remediation: Understanding New Media.* Cambridge, MA: MIT Press, 2000.

Gunning, Tom. *The Films of Fritz Lang: Allegories of Vision and Modernity.* London: BFI, 2000.

Hammett, Dashiell. *The Continental Op.* Ed. Stephen Marcus. London: Macmillan, 1975.

Hammond, Paul. *The Shadow and Its Shadow: Surrealist Writings on the Cinema.* 3rd ed. Ed. and trans. Paul Hammond. San Francisco: City Lights Books, 2000.
Hart, Clive. *Joyce, Huston, and the Making of* The Dead. Buckinghamshire, England: Colin Smythe Ltd., 1988.
Harvey, Stephen. *Directed by Vincente Minnelli.* New York: Harper and Row, 1989.
Harvey, Sylvia. *May '68 and Film Culture.* London: BFI, 1978.
Haskell, Molly. *Love and Other Infectious Diseases.* New York: William Morrow, 1990.
Herr, Michael. *Kubrick.* New York: Grove Press, 2000.
Hiller, Jim, ed. *"Cahiers du Cinéma": The 1950s.* Cambridge, MA: Harvard University Press, 1985.
———, ed. *"Cahiers du Cinéma": The 1960s.* Cambridge, MA: Harvard University Press, 1986.
Hirsh, Foster. *Film Noir: The Dark Side of the Screen.* New York: A. S. Barnes, 1981.
Hitchcock. Supplement to *Sight and Sound.* London: BFI, 1999.
Hoberman, J. *Film after Film: Or, What Became of 21st Century Cinema.* London: Verso, 2012.
Horkheimer, Max, and Theodor W. Adorno. *Dialectic of Enlightenment.* New York: Seabury, 1972.
Houseman, John. *Run-Through: A Memoir.* New York: Simon & Schuster, 1972.
Hughes, Langston. *Five Plays.* Ed. Webster Smalley. Bloomington: Indiana University Press, 1968.
Hutcheon, Linda. *A Theory of Adaptation.* New York: Routledge, 2006.
Huyssen, Andreas. *After the Great Divide.* Bloomington: Indiana University Press, 1986.
Jameson, Fredric. *The Political Unconscious.* Ithaca, NY: Cornell University Press, 1981.
———. *Postmodernism, or, the Cultural Logic of Late Capitalism.* Durham, NC: Duke University Press, 1991.
———. *Signatures of the Visible.* New York: Routledge, 1990.
Johnson, Randal. *Manoel de Oliveira.* Urbana: University of Illinois Press, 2007.
Kant, Immanuel. *Critique of Judgment.* Trans. J. H. Bernard. New York: Harper, 1951.
Kapsis, Robert. *Hitchcock: The Making of a Reputation.* Chicago: University of Chicago Press, 1992.
Kehr, Dave. *When Movies Mattered.* Chicago: University of Chicago Press, 2012.
Kenner, Hugh. *Joyce's Voices.* Berkeley: University of California Press, 1978.
King, Homay. *Lost in Translation: Orientalism, Cinema, and the Enigmatic Signifier.* Durham, NC: Duke University Press, 2010.
Kozloff, Sarah. *Invisible Storytellers: Voice-Over Narration in American Film.* Berkeley: University of California Press, 1988.
———. "Taking Us Along on *The Man Who Would Be King.*" In *Perspectives on John Huston*, ed. Stephen Cooper, 188–97. Boston: G. K. Hall, 1994.
Kracauer, Siegfried. *The Theory of Film: The Redemption of Physical Reality.* New York: Oxford University Press, 1960.
Kroeber, Karl. *Make Believe in Film and Fiction.* New York: Palgrave, 2006.
LaValley, Albert J., ed. *Focus on Hitchcock.* Englewood Cliffs, NJ: Prentice-Hall, 1972.

Lawrence, D.H. *Selected Literary Criticism*, ed. Anthony Beal. New York: Viking Press, 1966.

Leavis, F.R. *The Great Tradition: George Eliot, Henry James, Joseph Conrad.* New edition. Harmondsworth: Penguin Books, 1993.

Lehmann, Courtney. "Kenneth Branagh at the Quilting Point." *Post Script* 17 (Fall 1997): 6–27.

Leitch, Thomas M. *Film Adaptation and Its Discontents: From 'Gone with the Wind' to 'Passion of the Christ.'* Baltimore, MD: Johns Hopkins University Press, 2007.

———. *Find the Director and Other Hitchcock Games.* Athens: University of Georgia Press, 1991.

———. "The Outer Circle: Hitchcock on Television." In *Alfred Hitchcock Centenary Essays*, ed. Richard Allen and S. Ishii Gonzales, 59–71. London: BFI, 1999.

Lichtenstein, Jacqueline. *The Eloquence of Color.* Trans. Emily McVarish. Berkeley: University of California Press, 1993.

Locke, Alain. "The New Negro." In *Black Voices*, ed. Abraham Chapman, 512–23. New York: Mentor Books, 1968.

Magny, Claude-Edmonde. *The Age of the American Novel: The Film Aesthetic of Fiction between the Two Wars.* Trans. Eleanor Hochman. New York: Ungar, 1972.

Maltby, Richard. "The Politics of the Maladjusted Text." In *The Book of Film Noir*, ed. Ian Cameron, 39–48. New York: Continuum, 1993.

———. "'To Prevent the Prevalent Type of Book': Censorship and Adaptation in Hollywood, 1924–34." In *Film Adaptation*, ed. Naremore, 79–105.

Marchetti, Gina. "Ethnicity, the Cinema and Cultural Studies." In *Unspeakable Images: Ethnicity and the American Cinema*, ed. Lester D. Friedman, 277–307. Urbana: University of Illinois Press, 1991.

McCabe, Colin, Kathleen Murray, and Rick Warner, eds. *True to the Spirit: Film Adaptation and the Question of Fidelity.* New York: Oxford University Press, 2011.

McCarthy, Todd. *Howard Hawks: The Grey Fox of Hollywood.* New York: Grove Press, 1997.

McFarlane, Brian. *Novel to Film: An Introduction to the Theory of Adaptation.* Oxford: Clarendon Press, 1996.

McGilligan, Patrick. *Alfred Hitchcock: A Life in Darkness and Light.* New York: ReganBooks, 2003.

McNeil, Alex. *Total Television.* 3rd edition. New York: Penguin Books, 1996.

Minnelli, Vincente, with Hector Acre. *I Remember It Well.* Garden City, NJ: Doubleday, 1974.

Modleski, Tania. *The Women Who Knew Too Much: Hitchcock and Feminist Theory.* New York: Methuen, 1988.

Mordden, Ethan. *The Hollywood Studios.* New York: Simon & Schuster, 1989.

Morgan, Michael. *On Shame.* New York: Routledge, 2008.

Mulvey, Laura. *Visual and Other Pleasures.* Bloomington: Indiana University Press, 1989.

Naremore, James. *Acting in the Cinema.* Berkeley: University of California Press, 1998.

———. "The Trial: The FBI vs. Orson Welles." *Film Comment* (January–February 1991): 22–27.

———, ed. *Film Adaptation*. New Brunswick, NJ: Rutgers University Press, 2000.
Newman, John Henry Cardinal. *The Essential Newman*, ed. Vincent Ferrer Blehl. New York: Mentor Books, 1963.
Nichols, Bill. "Film and the Uses of Rhetoric." Society for Cinema Studies Conference, San Diego, CA, 1998.
Nowell-Smith, Geoffrey. "On Kiri Te Kanawa, Judy Garland, and the Culture Industry." In *Modernity and Mass Culture*, ed. James Naremore and Patrick Brantlinger, 70–79. Bloomington: Indiana University Press, 1991.
Palmer, R. Barton, and David Boyd, eds. *Hitchcock at the Source: The Auteur as Adapter*. Albany: State University of New York Press, 2011.
Paul, William. *Laughing Screaming: Modern Hollywood Horror and Comedy*. New York: Columbia University Press, 1994.
Perez, Gilberto. *The Material Ghost: Films and their Medium*. Baltimore, MD: Johns Hopkins University Press, 1988.
Peucker, Brigitte. "The Cut of Representation: Painting and Sculpture in Hitchcock." In *Alfred Hitchcock Centenary Essays*, ed. Richard Allen and S. Ishii Gonzales, 141–56. London: BFI, 1999.
Phillips, Gene D. and Rodney Hill, eds. *The Encyclopedia of Stanley Kubrick*. New York: Checkmark Books, 2002.
Polan, Dana. "The Light Side of Genius: Hitchcock's *Mr. and Mrs. Smith* in the Screwball Tradition." In *Comedy/Cinema/Theory*, ed. Andrew S. Horton, 136–43. Berkeley: University of California Press, 1991.
Pratley, Gerald. *The Cinema of John Huston*. New York: A. S. Barnes, 1997.
Pudovkin, Vsevolod. *Film Technique and Film Acting: The Cinema Writings of V. I. Pudovkin*. Trans. Ivor Montague. New York: Bonanza Books, 1949.
Quandt, James, ed. *Apichatpong Weerasethakul* Vienna: Austrian Film Museum, 2009.
Ray, Robert B. *A Certain Tendency of the Hollywood Cinema, 1930–1980*. Princeton, NJ: Princeton University Press, 1985.
———. "The Field of 'Literature and Film.'" In *Film Adaptation*, ed. Naremore, 38–53.
Rodowick, D. N. *The Virtual Life of Film*. Cambridge, MA: Harvard University Press, 2007.
Rosenbaum, Jonathan. *Discovering Orson Welles*. Berkeley: University of California Press, 2007.
———. *Essential Cinema: On the Necessity of Film Canons*. Baltimore, MD: Johns Hopkins University Press, 2004.
———. *Goodbye Cinema, Hello Cinephilia: Film Culture in Transition*. Chicago: University of Chicago Press, 2010.
———. *Movie Wars: How Hollywood and the Media Limit What Films We Can See*. Chicago: A Cappella Books, 2000.
———. *Movies as Politics*. Berkeley: University of California Press, 1997.
———. *Moving Places: A Life in Film*. Berkeley: University of California Press, 1995.
———. *Placing Movies: The Practice of Film Criticism*. Berkeley: University of California Press, 1995.
Rosenbaum, Jonathan, and Mehrnaz Saeed-Vafa. *Abbas Kiarostami*. Urbana: University of Illinois Press, 2003.
Salecl, Renata. "The Right Man and the Wrong Woman." In *Everything You Always Wanted to Ask Lacan (But Were Afraid to Ask Hitchcock)*, ed. Slavoj Žižek, 185–94. New York: Verso, 1992.

Sarris, Andrew. *The American Cinema: Directors and Directions.* New York: E.P. Dutton, 1968.
———. *Confessions of a Cultist: On the Cinema, 1955–1969.* New York: Simon and Schuster, 1970.
———. *The Films of Josef von Sternberg.* Garden City, NY: Doubleday & Co., 1966.
———. *The John Ford Movie Mystery.* Bloomington: Indiana University Press, 1975.
———. *The Primal Screen: Essays on Film and Related Subjects.* New York: Simon and Schuster, 1973.
Scholes, Robert, and Robert Kellogg. *The Nature of Narrative.* New York: Oxford University Press, 1979.
Schrader, Paul. "Notes on Film Noir." In *Film Noir Reader,* ed. Alain Silver and James Ursini, 53–64. New York: Limelight Editions, 1996.
Sconce, Jeffrey. "Narrative Authority and Social Narrativity: The Cinematic Reconstruction of Bronte's *Jane Eyre.*" In *The Studio System,* ed. Janet Staiger, 140–62. New Brunswick, NJ: Rutgers University Press, 1995.
Shohat, Ella. "Ethnicities-in-Relation: Toward a Multicultural Reading of American Cinema." In *Unspeakable Images: Ethnicity in the American Cinema,* ed. Lester D. Friedman, 215–50. Urbana: University of Illinois Press, 1991.
Shrank, Joseph, and Marc Connelly. *Cabin in the Sky.* Mimeograph filmscript, September-October 1942. Lilly Library, Bloomington, Indiana.
Silver, Alain, and Elizabeth Ward, eds. *Film Noir: An Encyclopedic Reference to the American Style.* Revised edition. Woodstock: Overlook Press, 1992.
Silverman, Kaja. "The Acoustic Mirror: The Female Voice in Psychoanalysis and Cinema." Bloomington: Indiana University Press, 1998.
Sklar, Robert. "Capote." *Cineaste* 31, no. 1 (Winter 2005): 57–58.
———. "Stanley Kubrick and the American Film Industry." *Current Research in Film Audience, Economics, and Law* 4 (1988): 112–18.
Spiegel, Alan. *Fiction and the Camera Eye: Visual Consciousness in Film and the Modern Novel.* Charlottesville: University Press of Virginia, 1976.
Spoto, Donald. *The Dark Side of Genius: The Life of Alfred Hitchcock.* New York: Random House, 1983.
Stallabrass, Julian. "The Idea of the Primitive: British Art and Anthropology, 1918–1930." *New Left Review* 183 (1990): 95–115.
Stam, Robert. "Bakhtin, Polyphony and Ethnic/Racial Representation." In *Unspeakable Images: Ethnicity and the American Cinema,* ed. Lester D. Friedman, 251–76. Urbana: University of Illinois Press, 1991.
———. "Beyond Fidelity: The Dialogics of Adaptation." In *Film Adaptation,* ed. Naremore, 54–76.
———. *Literature through Film: Realism, Magic, and the Art of Adaptation.* Malden, MA: Blackwell, 2005.
Stam, Robert, and Alessandra Raengo, eds. *A Companion to Literature and Film.* Malden, MA: Blackwell, 2005.
———. *Literature and Film: A Guide to the Theory and Practice of Adaptation.* Malden, MA: Blackwell, 2005.
Stead, C.K. *Pound, Yeats, Eliot and the Modernist Movement.* New Brunswick, NJ: Rutgers University Press, 1986.
Steinberg, Cobbett. *Reel Facts.* New York: Vintage Books, 1978.

Suarez, Juan. *Bike Boys, Drag Queens, and Superstars: Avant-Garde, Mass Culture, and Gay Identities in 1960s Underground Cinema.* Bloomington: Indiana University Press, 1996.

Thomas, François. "La Signature effacée: Welles et la notion d'auteur." *Positif* 449/450.

Thompson, Kristin. *Breaking the Glass Armor: Neoformalist Film Analysis.* Princeton, NJ: Princeton University Press, 1988.

Thomson, David. *The Big Sleep.* London: BFI, 1997.

———. *A Biographical Dictionary of Film*, 3rd edition. New York: Knopf, 1994.

Torgovnick, Marianna. *Gone Primitive: Savage Intellects, Modern Lives.* Chicago: University of Chicago Press, 1990.

Truffaut, François. *Hitchcock/Truffaut.* Revised edition. New York: Simon and Schuster, 1985.

———. *The Films of My Life.* Trans. Leonard Mayhew. New York : Simon and Schuster, 1978.

Uricchio, William, and Roberta E. Peterson. *Reframing Culture.* Princeton, NJ: Princeton University Press, 1993.

Walzl, Florence. "The Liturgy of the Epiphany Season and the Epiphanies of Joyce." *PMLA* (September 1965): 449.

Welles, Orson, and Peter Bogdanovich. *This Is Orson Welles.* Ed. Jonathan Rosenbaum. New York: Harper Collins, 1992.

Wexman, Virginia. "The Critic as Consumer: Film Study in the University, *Vertigo*, and the Film Canon." *Film Quarterly* 39, no. 2 (Spring 1986): 32–41.

Wilde, Oscar. *The Complete Works of Oscar Wilde.* New York: Harper and Row, 1989.

Williams, Raymond. *The Country and the City.* New York: Oxford University Press, 1973.

———. *Culture.* London: Fontana, 1981.

———. *Culture and Society.* New York: Harper and Row, 1950.

Wilson, George M. *Narration in Light: Studies in Cinematic Point of View.*

Wollen, Peter. "*Rope:* Three Hypotheses." In *Alfred Hitchcock Centenary Essays*, ed. Richard Allen and S. Ishii Gonzales, 75–85. London: BFI, 1999.

———. *Signs and Meaning in the Cinema.* Bloomington: Indiana University Press, 1969.

———. *Signs and Meaning in the Cinema*, rev. ed. Bloomington: Indiana University Press, 1972.

———. *Singin' in the Rain.* London: BFI, 1992.

Wood, Bret. *Orson Welles: A Bio-Bibliography.* Westport, CT: Greenwood Press, 1990.

Wood, Robin. *Hitchcock's Films Revisited.* New York: Columbia University Press, 1989.

———. "Ideology, Genre, Auteur." In *Film Genre Reader*, ed. Barry Keith Grant, 59–73. Austin: University of Texas Press, 1986.

Wranovic, John. *Chaplin and Agee.* New York: Palgrave, 2005.

Žižek, Slavoj. "In His Bold Gaze My Ruin Is Writ Large." In *Everything You Always Wanted to Know About Lacan (But Were Afraid to Ask Hitchcock)*, ed. Slavoj Žižek, 211–72. New York: Verso, 1992.

———. *Looking Awry: An Introduction to Jacques Lacan through Popular Culture.* Cambridge, MA: MIT Press, 1991.

Index of Names and Titles

Abbott, Berenice, 205
Abraham Lincoln, the Early Years, 258–259
Abraham Lincoln: The Prairie Years, 259
Abrams, M.H., 59, 78
Achebe, Chinua, 185
Across the Pacific, 217
Act of Violence, 264, 288
Adair, Gilbert, 44
Addams, Charles, 133
Ade, Marion, 324
Adorno, Theodor, 35, 109–110, 175, 201, 212–213
Adrian, 266
Affleck, Ben, 323
The African Queen, 216, 258, 272
Against Interpretation, 268
L'Âge d'or, 131
Agee, James, 1, 2, 109–110, 111, 150, 225, 228–229, 230, 246, 247–263, 264, 265–266, 271, 272, 273, 290, 291, 296, 299
The Agony and the Ecstasy, 72
Aguirre, Wrath of God, 5
A.I. Artificial Intelligence, 56
Air Mail, 279
Akerman, Chantal, 290, 313
Akin, Fatih, 323
Aldrich, Robert, 17, 24, 199, 281
Alfred Hitchcock Presents, 133–136, 167
Alfredson, Tomas, 323
Alice in Wonderland, 325
Alice's House, 323
All about Eve, 64
Allardice, James, 134
Allen, Fred, 136
Allen, Frederick Lewis, 98, 100
Allen, Woody, 324

Almodóvar, Pedro, 30
Althusser, Louis, 28, 29, 161
Altman, Rick, 116, 117, 120–121
Altman, Robert, 51, 88, 270, 289
Alton, John, 15, 147
Ambler, Eric, 159, 162
"America, Look at Your Shame," 251
The American Cinema, 275–282, 287–288, 289
An American in Paris, 113
An American Tragedy, 37
Anderegg, Michael, 188, 195, 205
Anders, Glenn, 193, 194
Andersen, Thom, 294
Anderson, Christopher, 135–136
Anderson, Eddie, 104, 110, 114, 119, 122
Anderson, Melody, 73
Anderson, Michael, 162
Anderson, Paul Thomas, 323
Anderson, Wes, 11, 323, 324
Andrew, Dudley, 41–42, 46
Andrews, Dana, 68, 143
Animal Farm, 42
Anthologie de l'humour noir (*Anthology of Black Humor*), 131, 133, 134
Antonioni, Michelangelo, 1, 8, 21, 243, 312
Apocalypse Now, 173
Apollinaire, Guillaume, 24
The Apostle, 83
Aragon, Louis, 24
Arbus, Diane, 205
Archer, William, 59, 80
Arden, Eve, 68
Arden, Robert, 194
Argott, Don, 325
Aristotle, 58, 60, 77, 78, 80

337

Arlen, Harold, 110
Armstrong, Louis, 108, 109
Arnez, Desi, 204
Arnold, Matthew, 34, 35, 38
Aronofsky, Darren, 325
Arrais, João Luís, 322
The Art of the Steal, 325
Ashenden, 159
Ashley, Ted, 210
"As I Walked Out One Evening," 133
The Asphalt Jungle, 199, 228, 265
The Assassination of Jesse James by the Coward Robert Ford, 323
Assayas, Olivier, 324
Astaire, Fred, 51
The Asthenic Syndrome, 291
Astruc, Alexandre, 16–17, 39
At Home Abroad, 113, 120
Aubert, Charles, 52
Auden, W.H., 98, 133, 247–248
Auer, Mischa, 194
Auerbach, Erich, 15, 27, 239, 289
Austen, Jane, 173
Autant-Lara, Claude, 275
Aventure Malgache, 132
Away from Her, 323
Ayfre, Amédée, 82

Baboona, 183
Bacall, Lauren, 67, 87, 91–93, 97
Bacon, Francis, 59, 78
Bahrani, Ramin, 324
Baker, Josephine, 113
Bakhtin, Mikhaïl, 43, 106
Balázs, Béla, 316
Balcerzak, Scott, 298
Bale, Christian, 68
Ball, Lucille, 204
Bamako, 323
The Band's Visit, 323
Barbash, Ilisa, 325
The Barefoot Contessa, 67, 90
Barnard, Timothy, 47
Barry Lyndon, 210, 213
Barrymore, John, 66
Barthes, Roland, 27, 28, 29, 31, 39, 83
Basic Instinct, 154, 172, 303
Basie, Count, 108
Bass, Saul, 156, 159
Bataan, 108
Batman, 293
The Battle of San Pietro, 217, 252, 265
Baudelaire, Charles, 131, 145

Baudry, Jean-Louis, 320
Baxter, Anne, 64
Bay, Michael, 30
Bazin, André, 7, 17, 18, 22, 33, 38, 44–46, 47–48, 57, 82, 83, 90, 132, 152, 182, 200, 254, 276, 281
The Beaches of Agnès, 324
Beckett, Samuel, 198
Bedoya, Alfonso, 217, 228, 229
Beery, Wallace, 66
Beethoven, Ludwig van, 44, 250, 261
Before Midnight, 11
Before the Devil Knows You're Dead, 323
Behind the Candelabra, 74
Being Julia, 64–65
Belasco, David, 52, 166, 188
Bel Geddes, Barbara, 136
Bell, Daniel, 29
Bellocchio, Marco, 324
Bellour, Raymond, 91
Bellow, Saul, 273
Belmondo, Jean-Paul, 24
Benchley, Robert, 113
Bender, John, 78, 84
Ben Hur, 208
Bening, Annette, 64–65
Benjamin, Walter, 2, 25, 29, 44, 294
Bennett, Bruce, 228, 229
Benny, Jack, 134
Bentham, Jeremy, 244
Benton, Robert, 288
Benveniste, Émile, 27
Bergman, Andrew, 126
Bergman, Ingmar, 1, 8, 17, 301, 303
Bergman, Ingrid, 89, 184, 232
Bergreen, Laurence, 257
Berkeley, Busby, 10, 15, 118
Berlin Alexanderplatz, 38
Bernie, 11
Bernstein, Elmer, 273
Best American Movie Writing, 1999, 294
The Best Years of Our Lives, 253, 254
Bethel, Jean, 91
Between the Acts, 250
Beyond the Sea, 70
Bicentennial Man, 56
The Bicycle Thief, 207
The Big Clock, 141
Bigelow, Kathryn, 324
The Big Money, 286
The Big Sleep (film), 67, 87–103, 145, 146
The Big Sleep (novel), 87–103
Bill, Leo, 75

Billy Budd, 280
Binoche, Juliette, 315
Bird, Brad, 323
Bird of Paradise, 296
The Birds, 39, 72, 88, 127, 137
Birth of a Nation, 36, 80, 81, 290
Bismarck, Otto von, 177
Black Book, 323
Black Legion, 224
Blackmail, 129, 157
Black Mask, 149
Black Swan, 325
Blade Runner, 56
Blake, Robert, 225
Blanchett, Cate, 68–69
Blitzstein, Marc, 190
Blomkamp, Neill, 324
Blonde Venus, 112
The Blood of Jesus, 117, 118, 120, *121*
Bloom, Harold, 298
Blow-Up, 312
The Blue Dahlia, 141, 266
The Blue Hotel, 257–258
Blue Steel, 172
Bluestone, George, 37–38, 39, 40
Blue Velvet, 246
Boden, Anna, 324
Body Double, 154
Boetticher, Budd, 24
Bogart, Humphrey, 67–68, 87–96, 143, 150, 216, 217, 219–220, 224–226, 229, 258
Bogdanovich, Peter, 24, 176, 180, 191–192, 292, 297
Bogle, Donald, 110
Bohne, Luciana, 231
Bolaño, Roberto, 11
Bolitho, William, 216
Bolter, Jay David, 3
Bones, 306
Bong, Joon-Ho, 323
Bon Voyage, 132
Booth, Wayne, 77, 79
Borde, Raymond, 101, 140–141, 146
Bordwell, David, 5, 35, 39, 53, 146, 246, 298, 317
Bourdieu, Pierre, 29, 175
Boyd, David, 46
Boyle, Robert, 156
Brackett, Leigh, 92, 99
Bradley, David, 259–262
Brakhage, Stan, 256
Branagh, Kenneth, 74, 76
Brancati, Vitaliano, 231

Branco, Isabel, 321
Brando, Marlon, 51, 53–54, 68, 243, 262, 266
Brand upon the Brain!, 323
Brantlinger, Patrick, 185
Braudy, Leo, 22–23, 70
Breathless, 24, 243, 280
Brecht, Bertolt, 54–55, 58, 125, 189, 190, 195, 196, 199, 309
Breillat, Catherine, 323
Bresson, Robert, 22, 38, 55, 60–61, 76, 82, 187, 268, 303, 308, 313
Breton, André, 19, 131, 132, 134
"The Bride Comes to Yellow Sky," 258
The Bridge in the Jungle, 219
The Bridge on the River Kwai, 22
Bridges, Harry, 201
Bright Star, 324
Brill, Lesley, 125, 127, 151, 171
Bringing Up Baby, 97
Brion, Patrick, 139
Britton, Andrew, 158, 245
Brokeback Mountain, 51
Bromberg, Serge, 324
Brooks, James L., 293
Brooks, Louise, 67, 89, 90
Brooks, Mel, 5
Brooks, Peter, 204
Brown, Margaret, 324
Browne, Nick, 77
Brubeck, Dave, 273
Brueghel, Pieter, the Elder, 268
Bruno, Giuliana, 31
Buchan, John, 39, 159, 160, 163–164, 166
Büchner, Georg, 183
Buçur, Dragos, 311, 313
Buñuel, Luis, 82, 131, 243, 245, 256, 267, 280
Burch, Noel, 289
Burgess, Anthony, 212
Burke, Peter, 107
Burks, Robert, 156
Burnett, Charles, 305
Burstyn, Joseph, 207, 256
Burton, Tim, 325
Bush, George H.W., 290
Bush, George W., 290, 301
Butch Cassidy and the Sundance Kid, 294
Byron, George Gordon Noel, 175, 185

The Cabinet of Dr. Caligari, 52, 199
Cabin in the Sky, 8, 104–123, *115*, *118*, *122*
Cabral, Amílcar, 308

Index

Cagney, James, 68, 107, 192, 217
Cahill, James, 2
Cain, James M., 43, 149
The Caine Mutiny, 225
Calhern, Louis, 144, 228
Calley, John, 209–210
Call Northside 777, 145
Callow, Simon, 262
Cameron, James, 30
Camper, Fred, 300
Campion, Jane, 40, 324
Caniff, Milton, 268
A Canterbury Tale, 7
Cape Fear, 41
Capote, 71–72
Capra, Frank, 30, 31, 268
Carax, Leos, 11
Cardullo, Bert, 33
Carlos, 324
Carmen Jones, 104
Carné, Marcel, 275
Carney, John, 323
Carringer, Robert, 174, 181
Carroll, Leo G., 144, 163
Carruth, Shane, 11
Carter, Jack, 174, 178
Casablanca, 88, 90, 108, 117, 225
Casparay, Vera, 34
Cassavetes, John, 243
Castaing-Taylor, Lucian, 325
Castelo Branco, Camilo, 320–322
The Castle, 133
Castle, William, 253
Caught, 139
Cause for Alarm, 159
Cavell, Stanley, 125, 151, 158, 171
Ceiling Zero, 279
Certified Copy, 325
Césaire, Aimé, 112
Ceylan, Nuri Bilge, 11
Chabrol, Claude, 16, 24
Chaliapin, Feodor, 189
Chambers, Whittaker, 163, 250
Champagne, 127
Champion, Marge, 56
Chandler, Jeff, 262
Chandler, Raymond, 15, 87–103, 143, 145, 149, 173, 180, 266
Chaney, Lon, 52
Chang, 183
Chaplin, Ben, 75
Chaplin, Charles, 52, 131, 158, 198, 250, 254, 258, 263, 276, 278, 282, 299, 308

Charade, 167
Charlie's Angels, 42
Chateaubriand, François-René de, 321
Chatman, Seymour, 40, 77
Chatterton, Thomas, 44
Chaumeton, Etienne, 101, 140–141, 146
Chayefsky, Paddy, 273
Che, Parts I & II, 323
Chen, Joan, 310
Cheney, Dick, 301
Cherkasov, Nikolai, 57
Chevalier, Maurice, 62, 66
Un Chien Andalou, 131
Child, Julia, 71
Chimes at Midnight, 176, 204, 211
China Gate, 268
Chinatown, 96, 102
La Chinoise, 283
Cholodenko, Lisa, 325
Chopin, Frédéric, 261
Christie, Agatha, 149
A Christmas Carol, 42
Christmas in July, 294
Ciment, Michel, 208, 209
Cineaste, 246, 304
Cinéma, 304
Cinema Scope, 246
Citizen Kane, 23, 31, 48, 82, 142, 173, 175, 177, 182, 183, 184, 185, 189, 190, 193, 194, 196, 199–200, 201, 202, 205, 211, 217, 272, 288, 322
City Lights, 299
Clark, T. J., 239–240
Clarke, Shirley, 243
Clift, Montgomery, 60, 92, 96
Cloak and Dagger, 166
A Clockwork Orange, 210, 212–213
Close Encounters of the Third Kind, 168
Cobb, Lee J., 51
Coen, Ethan, 323
Coen, Joel, 323
Coetzee, J. M., 47
A Coffin for Dimitrios, 164
Cohen, Keith, 37
Cole, Nat King, 108
Coleman, Ronald, 144
Coleridge, Samuel Taylor, 3, 34
Colette, Sidonie-Gabrielle, 232
Collier, Constance, 152
Collins, Ray, 174, 191
Colossal Youth, 306–309, 322
"The Coming of Wisdom with Time," 310
Comingore, Dorothy, 191

Commandos Strike at Dawn, 252
Comolli, Jean-Louis, 28
Conde, Manuel, 258
Confidential Agent, 159
Congorilla, 183
The Connection, 243
Connelly, Marc, 107, 119
Connery, Sean, 285
Conrad, Joseph, 37, 39, 79, 80, 112, 159, 160, 164, 172–186, 199
Conte, Richard, 67
Contempt, 39
Cook, David, 36
Cook, Elisha, Jr., 67, 89, 91
Cooper, Gladys, 152
Cooper, James Fenimore, 92
Coote, Robert, 177, 181, 194
Coppola, Francis, 173
*Corpus Callosum, 57
Corrigan, Timothy, 29–30, 39
Cortez, Stanley, 181
Costa, Pedro, 5, 6, 303, 306–309, 322, 324
Cotten, Joseph, 75, 153, 188
Couchman, Jeffrey, 262–263
Coulouris, George, 75, 183, 191
The Count of Monte Cristo, 42
Coward, Noel, 265
The Cradle Will Rock, 190, 201
Craig, Hardin, 188
Crane, Stephen, 218, 257, 258
Crichton, Michael, 42
Crime and Punishment, 39, 203
Cripps, Thomas, 117
Cronenberg, David, 323
Crosby, Bing, 117
Crouching Beast, 183
Croves, Hal, 219–220
Crowther, Bosley, 230, 279
Cruise, Tom, 53
Cuadecuc-Vampir, 322
Culler, Jonathan, 26
Culture and Anarchy, 34
Curtis, Simon, 73
Curtis, Tony, 68–69, 273

Dabney, Ford, 116
Dafoe, Willem, 69
Dahl, Roald, 39, 133
Dalí, Salvador, 278
Dances with Wolves, 292, 294
Dandridge, Dorothy, 108
Daney, Serge, 298, 300, 304
Dano, Royal, 259

La Danse: Paris Opera Ballet, 325
Dante Alighieri, 36, 232
Danton's Death, 183
D'Arcy, James, 73
Dardenne, Jean-Pierre, 11, 324
Dardenne, Luc, 11, 324
Dargis, Manohla, 6, 83, 246
Darin, Bobby, 70
The Darjeeling Limited, 323
The Dark Frontier, 159
The Dark Knight, 323
Darrin, Sonia, 99
Darrow, Clarence, 196
Darwin, Charles, 316
Dassin, Jules, 204
David Copperfield, 42, 45
Davies, Terence, 11, 323
Davis, Bette, 15, 64, 68, 264
Davis, Mike, 101, 150
Day of the Jackal, 288
The Dead, 231–240
Dead End Kids, 68
A Death in the Family, 247
Death in Venice, 44
DeBona, Guerric, 45, 46, 174
Decasia, 4
de Certeau, Michel, 29
The Deep, 205
The Deep Blue Sea, 11
Defoe, Daniel, 47
Deighton, Len, 160
Delaney, Cathleen, 233
Delannoy, Jean, 275
Deleuze, Gilles, 83
Delsarte, François, 52, 57
Demarest, William, 67
DeMille, Cecil B., 30, 55, 143, 277–278
Demme, Jonathan, 167
Les Demoiselles d'Avignon, 112
Denby, David, 1
Denis, Claire, 324, 325
Denning, Michael, 159, 162, 174–175
De Palma, Brian, 138, 167, 323
Depp, Johnny, 50
De Quincey, Thomas, 134–135, 138
Deren, Maya, 272
de Rochement, Louis, 254
de Rochement, Richard, 259
Desert Victory, 252, 265
Desnos, Robert, 306
Detour, 142
deWilde, Brandon, 136
Dialectic of Enlightenment, 109, 213

Diary of a Country Priest, 38
Dibdin, Michael, 43
Dickens, Charles, 36, 173, 233, 322
Diderot, Denis, 58, 59, 65, 66
Disney, Walt, 56
District 9, 324
Doane, Mary Ann, 298
Doherty, Thomas, 72–73
La Dolce Vita, 243
Dolivet, Louis, 203
Dominik, Andrew, 323
Doña Bárbara, 228
Donat, Robert, 127
Donen, Stanley, 167
Donnelly, Donal, 233
Donnersmarck, Florian Henckel von, 305
D'Onofrio, Vincent, 75
Don Quixote, 42, 196, 204, 211
Doomed Love, 321
Dos Passos, John, 36, 37, 199, 286
Dostoyevsky, Fyodor, 39
Double Indemnity, 55, 141, 150, 140, 172
Douglas, Kirk, 68, 207–208, 262
Douglas, Michael, 74, 76
Dovzhenko, Alexander, 253, 254, 291
Down to Earth, 306
Drake, Herbert, 184
Dreiser, Theodore, 218
Dressler, Marie, 50, 66
Drew, John, 190
Dreyer, Carl, 82, 141
Dr. Jekyll and Mr. Hyde, 153, 178
Dr. Strangelove, 51, 198, 209, 212
Duarte, Vanda, 306, 308
Dubliners, 234, 237
The Duchess of Langeais, 323
Duke, Vernon, 110
Dulles, Alan, 163
Dulles, John Foster, 268
du Maurier, Daphne, 39, 43, 142
Dunham, Katherine, 107, 109
Duo, 232
Duras, Marguerite, 267, 270
Durgnat, Raymond, 9, 24, 127, 137, 150, 151, 171, 245, 300
Duvall, Robert, 83
Duvivier, Julien, 182
Dvortsevoy, Sergey, 324
Dwan, Allan, 222
Dyer, Richard, 54, 67, 68, 97, 105–106, 122
Dylan, Bob, 68

Eadweard Muybridge, Zoopraxographer, 294
Eagleton, Terry, 84
Eastern Promises, 323
Eastwood, Clint, 71, 323
Ebert, Roger, 246
Eccentricities of a Blond-Haired Girl, 324
Edelstein, David, 246
The Edge of Heaven, 323
Edgerton, Nash, 325
An Education, 324
Efron, Zac, 75
Egoyan, Atom, 30
Eisenschitz, Bernard, 304
Eisenstein, Sergei, 8, 15, 21, 28, 37, 39, 54, 66, 191, 230, 253, 261, 265, 284, 287
Ekman, Paul, 56, 316
Eliot, T.S., 26, 34, 69, 79, 133, 173, 245, 250
Elite Squad, 323
Elkin, Stanley, 133
Ellington, Duke, 108, 109, 111, 113, 117, 117
Elliott, Laura, 152
Ellroy, James, 42
Emery, John, 177
The Empire Strikes Back, 211
Engel, Morris, 205
Engels, Friedrich, 10, 272
Epitaph for a Spy, 159
Epstein, Philip, 93
Erickson, Steve, 300
Errol, Leon, 266
Evans, Robert, 213
Evans, Walker, 251, 254, 255, 273, 310
Everyone Else, 324
The Exiles, 257, 323
The Exorcist, 210
Eyes Wide Shut, 214

A Face in the Crowd, 273
Face to Face, 258
Faigin, Gary, 56
Fair Game, 325
The Fall of the House of Usher, 154
Fantastic Mr. Fox, 324
Farber, Manny, 25, 97, 99, 191, 246, 249, 264–274, 290, 290, 294, 296, 297
Farewell, My Lovely, 95, 96
Farrokhzad, Forough, 300
Farrow, John, 252, 273
Fassbinder, Rainer Werner, 38, 267
Faulkner, William, 24, 36, 37, 87, 92, 99, 173, 199, 250
Fear and Desire, 207

Fellini, Federico, 70, 243
Ferguson, Charles, 323, 325
Ferguson, Otis, 264
Fernández, Emilo, 228
F for Fake, 189, 195, 196, 204
Fiedler, Leslie, 20
Fields, W.C., 66
Film Quarterly, 243, 246, 304, 305
Final Analysis, 154
Final Fantasy: The Spirits Within, 56
Fincher, David, 323, 325
Finnegans Wake, 40, 234, 239, 289
Fitzgerald, F. Scott, 26, 36, 173. 199
Flaherty, Robert, 15, 230, 276, 282, 284
Flaubert, Gustave, 37, 45
Fleck, Ryan, 324
Fleishman, Avrom, 77
Fleming, Ian, 284
Fleming, Victor, 252
Flight, 11
Flight of the Red Balloon, 323
Flitterman-Lewis, Sandy, 31
Flye, Father James Harold, 250, 261
Flying Tigers, 222
Foe, 47
Fonda, Henry, 81, 308
Fontaine, Joan, 127
Ford, Ford Maddox, 79, 268
Ford, John, 23, 26, 53, 81, 143, 182, 191, 231, 249, 259, 264, 271, 278–79, 280, 281, 282, 288, 308
Forester, C.S., 42
Forster, E.M., 42
Forsythe, John, 144
Forty Guns, 20
Foucault, Michel, 28, 31
The Fountain of Youth, 195, 196, 204
Four Feathers, 183
Four Horsemen of the Apocalypse, 47
4 Months, 3 Weeks, and 2 Days, 305, 314
Foxworth, F.E., 201–202
Fragonard, Jean-Honoré, 18
Frampton, Hollis, 1–4
Frank, Nino, 140
Frank, Robert, 205
Frankenheimer, John, 273
Franklin, Marcus Carl, 68
Freed, Arthur, 110, 111, 113, 115, 117, 123
Frenzy, 138
Freud, Sigmund, 54, 112, 114, 129–131, 132, 138, 166, 199, 200, 212, 271
Friedlander, Lee, 205
The Front Page, 193–194

Fry, Roger, 112
Frye, Northrup, 126, 127–128
Fuentes, Fernando de, 228
Fuentes, Marlon, 84
The Fugitive, 42
Fujiwara, Chris, 300
Fuller, Chris, 324
Fuller, Samuel, 20, 21, 22, 24, 243, 268, 279
Full Metal Jacket, 173, 212
The Fury, 167

Gable, Clark, 68
Galileo, 190
Gambon, Michael, 65
Gance, Abel, 44
Ganjavi, Nizami, 315
Garbo, Greta, 67
García Márquez, Gabriel, 317
Gardner, Ava, 68
Garland, Judy, 120
Garner, James, 89
Garrick, David, 66
Gaslight, 153
Gassman, Vittorio, 262
Gauguin, Paul, 259–262
Gavin, John, 17
Gehr, Ernie, 83
The General, 269
Genette, Gérard, 39
Genghis Khan, 258
Gere, Richard, 68
Gershwin, George, 105, 255
Gervasi, Sacha, 73
Gerwig, Greta, 324
Getz, Stan, 273
"Ghosts in the Darkness," 320
The Ghost Writer, 325
Gianvito, John, 324
Gibson, Mel, 66
Giddins, Gary, 67
Gide, André, 131
Gielgud, John, 66
Gigi, 113
Gilda, 139
Gilroy, Tony, 323
Girard, René, 59–60
The Girl, 72
The Girl of the Limberlost, 277
Gish, Lillian, 52, 263, 283
Gobelins, 308
Godard, Jean-Luc, 2, 3, 6, 16–29, 39, 55, 82, 145, 146, 243, 267, 268, 283–284, 289, 290, 291

The Godfather, 54
The Godfather: Part II, 54
The Godfather: Part III, 292
Godmilow, Jill, 84
Goethe, Johann Wolfgang von, 36, 196
Gold Diggers of 1935, 10
The Golem, 56
Gomes, Miguel, 11
Gone Baby Gone, 323
Gone with the Wind, 43, 260, 266
Goodbye Solo, 324
Gore, Rhea, 216
Gorky, Maxim, 42
Gottlieb, Sidney, 125
Gould, Chester, 268
Gramsci, Antonio, 29
Grand Illusion, 182, 184
Granik, Debra, 325
Grant, Cary, 68, 88, 132, 144, 156, 157–159, 163, 167, 168, 169, 170, 273
Gran Torino, 323
The Grapes of Wrath (film) 34, 38, 249, 259
The Grapes of Wrath (novel), 34, 107, 249
Graver, Gary, 211
The Great Gatsby, 173
The Great Ziegfeld, 266
Greed, 37
Greenberg, Clement, 35–36, 271
Greene, Graham, 159, 160, 162, 164, 168, 231, 283
The Green Pastures (film), 104, 108, 111
The Green Pastures (play), 107
Greenstreet, Sydney, 67, 218
Gregory, Lady Isabella Augusta, 233
Gregory, Paul, 262
"The Grief of a Young Girl's Heart," 233, 234
Griffith, D.W., 15, 17, 18, 28, 36, 52, 80–81, 148, 155, 166, 185, 191, 214, 221, 253, 254, 263, 278, 279, 282, 283, 290
Griffiths, Susan, 73
Grimes, Stephen, 235
Grisham, John, 42
Une Grosse Légume, 198
Grubb, Davis, 262
Grusin, Richard, 3
Guadagnino, Luca, 324
Guazzoni, Enrico, 36
Guédiguian, Robert, 30
Guérin, Jean, 75
Guess Who's Coming to Dinner, 294
Guinness, Alec, 61–62
Gun Crazy, 21, 139

Gunning, Tom, 125, 212
A Guy Named Joe, 252
Gwenn, Edmund, 144

Haggis, Paul, 323
Hallelujah!, 104, 111, 117
Hallelujah, I'm a Bum, 294
The Hamlet, 250
Hammerstein, Oscar, 105
Hammett, Dashiell, 96, 101, 143, 149, 154, 218, 220
A Handful of Dust, 133
Hansen, Miriam, 10
Happy-Go-Lucky, 323
Harburg, E.Y., 110, 117
Hardwicke, Cedric, 144
Harlin, Renny, 288
Harris, Fred, 136
Harris, James, 207–208
Harrison, Joan, 134, 141, 162
Hart, Clive, 234–238
Hartford, Huntington, 257, 258
Harvey, Stephen, 113
Harvey, Sylvia, 27
Haskell, Molly, 92, 246, 276–277
Hatari!, 23
Hauser, Arnold, 37
Hawks, Howard, 9, 21, 23, 25, 29, 30, 53, 87–103, 127, 187, 194, 198, 253, 264, 267, 273, 278–79, 283
Hawthorne, Nathaniel, 96
Hayden, Sterling, 228
Haynes, Todd, 43, 68, 323
Hayworth, Rita, 191, 194, 203, 204
The Headless Woman, 324
Hearst, William Randolph, 201, 202
Heart of Darkness, 112, 164, 172–186, 190, 194
Hearts in Dixie, 104
Heath, Stephen, 27
Heaven Can Wait, 118
Hecht, Ben, 193, 231
Hecht, Harold, 273
Hedren, Tippi, 73, 127
Hegel, Georg Wilhelm Friedrich, 34, 131
Heisler, Stuart, 108
Helmore, Tom, 155
Helvetica, 323
Hemingway, Ernest, 37, 149
Henreid, Paul, 67
Henri-George Clouzot's Inferno, 324
Henry, O., 135
Hepburn, Katharine, 68

Herr, Michael, 212
Herrmann, Bernard, 15, 156, 159, 183
Herzog, Werner, 5
Heston, Charlton, 72, 191, 259, 262, 270–271
He Walked by Night, 264
Heydt, Louis Jean, 99
Hickox, Sid, 87
Hicks, Catherine, 73
High Noon, 126
High School Musical, 75
High Sierra, 88, 217
Highsmith, Patricia, 141
The High Window, 96
Hiller, Erwin, 7
Hiller, Jim, 21
Hilty, Megan, 74
Hirsch, Seymour, 139
His Girl Friday, 33, 97, 101, 127, 194, 273
"His Honor, the Mayor," 201
Hiss, Alger, 163
Histoire(s) du cinéma, 289
"History," 83
Hitchcock, 73
Hitchcock, Alfred, 9, 15, 21, 24, 25–26, 28, 30, 31, 34, 39, 44, 55, 72–73, 88, 124–171, 174, 245, 253, 264, 276, 278, 280, 281, 284, 285
Hitler in Hollywood, 325
Hobbes, Thomas, 59, 218
Hoberman, J., 1, 6, 246
Hobsbawm, Eric, 154
Hoffman, Philip Seymour, 71–72
Hoffmann, Deborah, 84
Hoggart, Richard, 245
Holden, William, 272
Hold That Wild Boar, 183
Holiday, Billie, 120
"The Hollow Men," 173
"Hollywood Victory Caravan," 67
Holt, Tim, 221, 228, 229
Holy Motors, 11
Homage to Catalonia, 286
Homer, 232
Hood, R.B., 203
Hoover, J. Edgar, 201
Hope, Bob, 50, 134
Hopkins, Anthony, 73
Hopper, Hedda, 201, 203
Horatio Hornblower, 42
Horkheimer, Max, 109, 175, 201
Horne, Lena, 104, 108, 111, 114, 120, 122
The Host, 323
Hou, Hsiao-hsien, 323

The House Is Black, 300
Houseman, John, 75, 102, 174, 175, 189
Howe, James Wong, 273
Hoysradt, John, 183
Hugo, Victor, 321
Huillet, Danièle, 28, 272, 290, 309
Hunter, Evan, 127
The Hurt Locker, 324
The Hustler, 243
Huston, Anjelica, 233, 236, 238
Huston, John, 9, 21, 67, 71, 215–240, 243, 250, 252, 253, 254–255, 257, 258, 259, 260, 265, 272, 275
Huston, Tony, 234, 238, 239
Huston, Walter, 216, 217, 218, 227–228, 229
Hustwit, Gary, 323
Hutcheon, Linda, 47
Huyssen, Andreas, 20, 31, 148–149

I Am Love, 324
Ibberson, D.J., 88
Ibsen, Henrik, 59
I Confess, 147
Ida, 250
If I Want to Whistle, I Whistle, 325
I'll Do Anything, 293
The Immortal Story, 196, 204
I'm Not There, 68, 323
In a Lonely Place, 90, 91, 150
In Cold Blood, 71
India Song, 270
Infamous, 71–72
The Informant!, 324
Information Please, 134
The Informer, 38, 279
Inglourious Basterds, 302
Ingram, Rex, 47, 107, 120
Inland Empire, 323
Inside Job, 325
In the Street (book), 255
In the Street (film), 255–256, 264
In the Valley of Elah, 323
In This Our Life, 108, 217
In Vanda's Room, 306
In Which We Serve, 265
The Ipcress File, 160
It's All True, 200, 202
Ivan the Terrible, 299
Ivory, James, 42
I Was a Male War Bride, 198

Jackson, Peter, 56
Jacobs, Ken, 256

Jamaica Inn, 140
James, Henry, 37, 40, 79, 159, 164, 291
Jameson, Fredric, 41, 46, 167, 172–173, 199, 200–201
Jameson, Richard, 264
Jane Eyre, 43
Jaoui, Agnès, 325
Jarmusch, Jim, 293
Jarrold, Julian, 72
Jarry, Alfred, 131
The Jazz Singer, 105
Jeanne Dielman, 313
The Jerk, 51
Jesus Christ, 69
Jet Pilot, 23
Le jeu d'Adam, 47
Jezebel, 217
Jia, Zhangke, 8, 309–311, 323
Joan of Arc, 141
Johansson, Scarlett, 73
The John Ford Movie Mystery, 279
Johnny Guitar, 280–281
Johnson, Hall, 108–109, 119
Johnson, Randal, 321
Johnson, Samuel, 278
Jolson, Al, 69–70
Jolson Sings Again, 70
The Jolson Story, 69–70
Jones, Chuck, 269
Jones, Toby, 71–72, 73
Jonze, Spike, 324
Jour de fête, 291
Journey into Fear, 142
Joyce, James, 18, 34–35, 37, 40, 45, 79, 199, 231–240, 247, 250, 289, 314
Juarez, 217
Jubilee, 113
Judd, Ashley, 73
Julian, Isaac, 84
Julie and Julia, 71
Julius Caesar (Bradley), 259
Julius Caesar (Welles), 75, 76, 174
Jung, Carl, 199
Junge, Alfred, 7
Jungle Madness, 183

Kael, Pauline, 243, 246, 249, 287, 290
Kaewbuadee, Sakda, 318
Kafka, Franz, 131, 133, 160, 199, 314
Kant, Immanuel, 34, 78
Kauffman, Stanley, 150, 243
Kazan, Elia, 187, 272, 275
Keathley, Christian, 271

Keaton, Buster, 54, 249–250, 269, 278
Keener, Catherine, 72
Kehr, Dave, 1, 6, 246, 298, 300
Kelly, Grace, 132, 144
Kennedy, John Fitzgerald, 205, 208
Kenner, Hugh, 79, 235
Kent, Amalia, 181
Kern, Jerome, 105
Keyes, Evelyn, 70
Key Largo, 225
Khoshbakht, Ehsan, 289
Khosrow and Shirin, 315
Khrushchev, Nikita, 163
Kiarostami, Abbas, 8, 30, 315–317, 324, 325
Kidd, Michael, 15, 191
The Kids Are All Right, 325
The Kid with a Bike, 11
Killer of Sheep, 305
Killer's Kiss, 142, 205, 207
The Killers, 153
The Killing, 199, 207–208
King, Homay, 96
King, Stephen, 42
King Lear, 204
King of Kings, 243
Kipling, Rudyard, 159
Kiss Me Deadly, 17, 22, 146, 280–281
Kitano, Takeshi, 30
Kleiner, Arthur, 255
Kline, Franz, 273
"Knoxville: Summer of 1915," 247
Kodar, Oja, 196
Kohner, Paul, 219, 258, 260
Kolirin, Eran, 323
Korda, Alexander, 260, 262
Korda, Zoltan, 260, 262
Koza, Alan, 300
Kozloff, Sarah, 77, 216
Kracauer, Siegfried, 256
Krasna, Norman, 126
Kubrick, Stanley, 9, 51, 56, 137, 173, 198–200, 205–214, 259, 288
Kuleshov, Lev, 49, 164
Kurosawa, Akira, 21
Kwietniowski, Richard, 43–44

Laban, Rudolph, 55
Lacan, Jacques, 28, 29
Ladd, Alan, 89
Ladd, D.M., 203
The Ladies' Man, 243
The Lady and the Duke, 57

The Lady Eve, 127
The Lady from Shanghai, 96, 142, 146, 150, 183, 185, 190, 194, 195, 196, 199, 204, 278
The Lady in the Lake, 180
The Ladykillers, 61
Laine, Frankie, 117
LaMarche, Maurice, 75
Lambert, Gavin, 260
"Lamb to the Slaughter," 39, 136
Lamorisse, Albert, 258
Lancaster, Burt, 68, 273
Landau, Martin, 164
Landis, Jessie Royce, 164
The Landru Story, 198
Land without Bread, 82
Lang, Fritz, 17, 23, 51, 125, 166, 212
Langlois, André, 27
Lardner, David, 110–111
LaSalle, Martin, 60–61
The Last Mistress, 323
L.A. Story, 292
Last Year at Marienbad, 246
Latouche, John, 107, 109, 110
Laughton, Charles, 144, 151, 262–263
Laura, 34, 97, 140, 142, 143, 172
Lawrence, D. H., 92, 245
Lawrence of Arabia, 280
Lead Belly, 107
Leaming, Barbara, 190
Lean, David, 280
Leavis, F. R., 25, 31, 34, 173, 245, 246
le Carré, John, 61, 159
Lecoq, Jacques, 55
Ledger, Heath, 51, 68
Lee, Chang-dong, 325
Lee, Harper, 72
Lehman, Ernest, 156–157, 159, 163
Leigh, Janet, 73, 191
Leigh, Mike, 323
Leitch, Thomas, 46, 125, 132, 134
Leonardo da Vinci, 25
The Leopard, 200
Le Queux, William, 159
LeRoy, Mervyn, 141
Lester, Richard, 206
Let It Rain, 325
Letter from an Unknown Woman, 39
Let There Be Light, 217
Let the Right One In, 323
Let Us Now Praise Famous Men, 247, 249, 251, 258, 259, 266
Leve, Samuel, 75

Levin, Harry, 250
Levine, Sam, 273
Levitt, Helen, 255, 256, 257, 264
Lewis, Albert, 108
Lewis, Jerry, 55, 243
Lewis, Joseph H., 142
Lewis, Ramona, 111
Lewton, Val, 249, 264
Leyda, Jay, 257
Lichtenstein, Jacqueline, 78, 80
Lifeboat, 128, 132
Liman, Doug, 325
Limelight, 278
Lincoln, Abraham, 69, 258–259
Lindsay, Vachel, 247
Linklater, Richard, 11, 57, 75, 324
Lions for Lambs, 323
"Literature and Style," 248
The Little Sister, 88, 100, 103
Littlewood, Joan, 55
Litvak, Anatole, 140
Lively, Blake, 73
The Lives of Others, 305
Lloyd, Norman, 75, 134, 259
Loach, Ken, 323
Locke, Alain, 112
The Locket, 153
Loden, Barbara, 60, 73, 294
The Lodger, 134
Loeb, Janice, 255, 256, 257, 264
Lohan, Lindsay, 73
Lola, 304
Lola Montes, 212
Lolita, 44, 133, 209, 212
Lombard, Carol, 126
The Long Goodbye, 88
Loos, Anita, 15
Lord Jim, 186
Loren Cass, 324
Lorna's Silence, 324
Lorne, Marion, 152
Lorre, Peter, 49, 67
Losey, Joseph, 204, 206
Love and Death on Long Island, 43–44
Love Letters, 264
The Love Parade, 62, 66
The Lovers, 280
Lubitsch, Ernst, 62–63, 66, 118, 253, 264, 294
Lucas, George, 168, 210, 211
Luce, Henry, 247
The Luck of Barry Lyndon, 213
Lukács, Georg, 200–201

Lumet, Sidney, 273, 323
Lumière, Louis, 1–3, 19
Lunt, Alfred, 158
Lust for Life, 113, 260, 262
Luz, Adriano, 322
Lynch, David, 6, 30, 323

Macao, 96
MacArthur, Charles, 193
Macbeth, 174, 204, 205
MacCabe, Colin, 27, 46
MacDonald, Dwight, 243, 263
MacDonald, Jeanette, 62
Macfadyen, Angus, 75
Mack, Cecil, 116
MacKaye, Steele, 52
Mackendrick, Alexander, 61, 274
MacKenna, Kenneth, 157
MacKenzie, Kent, 257, 323
MacLane, Barton, 226
MacLean, Fred M., 87
MacMurray, Fred, 55
Maddin, Guy, 323
Madigan, 283–284
Mad Men, 305, 323
Madonna, 73
The Magnificent Ambersons (film), 39, 82, 142, 153, 181, 187, 192–193, 196, 199, 200–201, 211, 265, 292, 297
The Magnificent Ambersons (novel), 76
Magny, Claude-Edmonde, 37, 48
The Maid, 324
Main, Marjorie, 67
Malkovich, John, 173
Malone, Dorothy, 94, 95
Malraux, André, 47, 257
Maltby, Richard, 37
The Maltese Falcon (film), 67, 88, 90, 139, 140, 141, 217, 223, 225, 228
The Maltese Falcon (novel), 218, 220
Mamoulian, Rouben, 66, 178, 279
Mangolte, Babette, 60–61
Manhattan Transfer, 48
Mankiewicz, Joseph L., 283, 288
Mann, Anthony, 208, 271, 273, 279
Mann, Thomas, 44
Man's Fate, 48, 257
The Man Who Knew Too Much (1937), 164
The Man Who Knew Too Much (1956), 124–125, 147
"The Man Who Liked Dickens," 133
The Man Who Shot Liberty Valance, 270

The Man Who Would Be King, 216, 217, 227–228
Man with a Movie Camera, 256
Marcus, Steven, 218
Margaret, 303
Marnie, 73, 137, 147, 169
Marsan, Eddie, 75
Marshall, Herbert, 62–63
Martel, Lucrecia, 324
Martin, Adrian, 289
Martin, Dean, 196
Martin, Dewey, 92, 96
Martin, Steve, 51
Marty, 22, 273, 274
Marvin, Lee, 270
Marx, Karl, 10, 218, 270, 272
Marx Brothers, 15, 55, 66
The Mask of Dimitrios, 139
Mason, James, 144, 164
Maugham, Somerset, 64, 159, 160
Maupassant, Guy de, 40
Mayer, Louis B., 110
McCann, Donal, 233
McCarthy, Joseph, 204
McCarthy, Thomas, 324
McCarthy, Todd, 99, 100
McClory, Sean, 233
McCord, Ted, 228, 229, 230
McDermottroe, Maria, 238
McFarlane, Brian, 41
McFee, Katharine, 74
McGill, Donald, 286
McGilligan, Patrick, 135
McGuire, Matthew, 201
McKay, Christian, 75–76
McKinney, Nina Mae, 120
McQueen, Butterfly, 119
Me and Orson Welles, 75–76, 324
Medrea, Ruxandra, 324
Meet Me in St. Louis, 120, 253, 294
Meisner, Sanford, 59
Mekas, Jonas, 243
Méliès, Georges, 7
Melville, Herman, 220
The Men, 266
Mencken, H. L., 149, 216
Mendonça, Kléber Filho, 11
Merchant, Ismail, 42
The Merchant of Venice, 196
Meredith, Burgess, 228
Merrill, Gary, 257
Methot, Mayo, 91
Metropolis, 52, 56, 212

Metty, Russell, 208–209
Metz, Christian, 28
Meyer, Arthur, 256
Meyerhold, Vsevold, 54, 188
Meyers, Sidney, 256
Michael Clayton, 323
A Midsummer Night's Dream, 97
Mildred Pierce, 43
Milestone, Lewis, 279, 294
Milk, 69, 323
Milk, Harvey, 69
Milland, Ray, 144
Miller, Claude, 324
Miller, David, 222
Miller, Frank, 57
Miller, Henry, 17
Miller, Sienna, 73
Milton, John, 245
Mimesis, 289
The Ministry of Fear (film), 166
The Ministry of Fear (novel), 159, 164
Minnelli, Vincente, 9, 20, 47, 81, 113–123, 114, 143, 260, 262, 294
Minow, Newton, 243
The Miracle of Morgan's Creek, 253
Mirren, Helen, 50, 73
The Misfits, 243
Mission Impossible, 33
Miss Lonelyhearts, 149
Mitchell, Margaret, 43
Mitchum, Robert, 52, 263
Mizoguchi, Kenji, 21
Moby Dick (film), 260
Moby Dick (novel), 42, 45
Model, Lisette, 205
Modern Times, 258
Modleski, Tania, 150
The Mod Squad, 42
Mohr, Gerald, 89
Monk, Sophie, 74
Monroe, Marilyn, 50, 68, 73–74
Monsieur Verdoux, 198, 254, 263
Montague, Ivor, 164
Montgomery, Poppy, 74
Montgomery, Robert, 126, 127, 180
Moonrise Kingdom, 11
Moorehead, Agnes, 49, 191, 192–193
Morgan, Michael L., 251
Mori, Paola, 194
Morris, Errol, 84
Morrison, Bill, 4
Morrow, Jeff, 262
Moss, Carleton, 108

Moulin Rouge, 260, 265
Moullet, Luc, 297
Moving Places, 290, 296
Mozart, Wolfgang Amadeus, 82
Mr. and Mrs. Smith, 126
Mr. Arkadin, 193, 194, 196, 204, 205, 211
Mrs. Dalloway, 33
Mrs. Miniver, 266
Mule Bone, 107
Mulholland Drive, 50, 51
Mulvey, Laura, 27, 92, 151
Mungiu, Cristian, 305, 314
Muratova, Kira, 291
Murder, My Sweet, 140, 145, 172
Murder by Experts, 134
Murnau, F. W., 15, 39, 164, 276, 287
Murphy, Audie, 228
Murphy, Fred, 235
Murray, Kathleen, 46
My Darling Clementine, 81, 308
My Mexican Shiva, 323
My Name Is Julia Ross, 142
Mysteries of Lisbon, 320–322, 324
Mysterious Object at Noon, 317
My Week with Marilyn, 73
My Winnipeg, 323

Nabokov, Vladimir, 44, 79, 133, 212
Napoleon Bonaparte, 69, 209, 213
Narboni, Jean, 28, 283
Native Dancer, 324
Native Son, 174, 190, 202
Ne Change Rien, 324
Negative Space, 268–269
The Negro Soldier, 108
Neighboring Sounds, 11
Nelson, Ricky, 92
Neuberger, Joan, 299
Newman, John Henry, 248
Nichols, Bill, 84
Nicholson, Virginia, 175
Nietzsche, Friedrich, 131, 134, 149, 199
The Nigger of the Narcissus, 185
The Night of the Hunter, 52, 262–263
Nights and Weekends, 324
1984, 286
Niven, Barbara, 74
Niven, David, 158
Nixon, Richard M., 163, 225
Noa Noa, 259–262
Nobody's Fool, 288
No Country for Old Men, 302, 323
No End in Sight, 323

Nolan, Christopher, 323
North by Northwest, 126, 128, 129, 139, 156–171, 285
Nostalgia, 3
Notari, Elvira, 31
Notorious, 128, 139, 140–141, 157, 158
Nowell-Smith, Geoffrey, 113, 234

Obama, Barack, 271
Obsession, 154
O'Casey, Seán, 156
October, 39
Odets, Clifford, 273
Of Time and the City, 323
O'Herlihy, Daniel, 237
Oliveira, Manoel de, 321, 324
Oliver Twist, 36
Olivier, Laurence, 66, 73, 74, 144, 188
Omarova, Gulshat, 324
Omnibus, 258
Once, 323
Once Upon a Time in Anatolia, 11, 246
One-Eyed Jacks, 243
One Flew Over the Cuckoo's Nest, 293
One Hour with You, 62, 66
O'Neill, Eugene, 36, 231
Only Angels Have Wings, 88
On Moonlight Bay, 296
On Murder Considered as One of the Fine Arts, 134–135
On the Waterfront, 51, 54
Open City, 207, 254
Operation Cinderella, 198
Ophüls, Max, 26, 29, 39, 212, 282, 287
The Order of Myths, 324
Orlando, 33
Ormonde, Czenzi, 143
Orson Welles' Sketchbook, 195
Orwell, George, 170, 217, 278, 286
Oshima, Nagisa, 28
Osment, Haley Joel, 56
Othello, 193, 204, 207
The Other Side of the Wind, 187, 213
Out of the Past, 153, 253
The Ox-Bow Incident, 222, 264
Ozick, Cynthia, 40–41
Ozu, Yasujirō, 28, 303

Padilha, José, 323
Palance, Jack, 262
Paley, Nina, 324
Pallette, Eugene, 67
Palmer, R. Barton, 46

Panahi, Jafar, 11
Panama Hattie, 113
Pangborn, Franklin, 67
A Panorama of American Film Noir, 1941–1953, 140–141
The Paradine Case, 140, 141, 144, 150–151, 154
Parks, Larry, 69–70
Parlo, Dita, 184
"Une Partie de Campagne" (*A Day in the Country*), 40, 207
Pater, Walter, 25
Paths of Glory, 208
Patterson, Patricia, 264, 270
Patton, 83
Pavlov, Ivan, 164
Pearson, Roberta E., 36, 51
Peck, Gregory, 144, 262
"Pen, Pencil, and Poison," 135
Penn, Sean, 69
People on Sunday, 288
Pépé le Moko, 182
Perez, Gilberto, 81
Perkins, Anthony, 73, 136, 188
Perkins, Maxwell, 263
Perkins, Victor, 24
La perla (*The Pearl*), 228
Phantom Lady, 141
Philipe, Gérard, 262
Picasso, Pablo, 112, 189
Pickpocket, 60–61, 313
Pick-Up, 40
Pimentel, Alfonso, 322
Pinkava, Jan, 323
Pinter, Harold, 199
The Pirate, 119
Piscator, Erwin, 196
Le Plaisir, 17, 19
Plato, 60, 78, 80
Plautus, 126
Poe, Edgar Allan, 131, 154
Poetry, 325
Polan, Dana, 126, 127
Polanski, Roman, 102, 325
Police, Adjective, 289, 311–315, 324
Polito, Robert, 267, 271
Polley, Sarah, 11, 323
Polonsky, Abraham, 284
Pōmare V, 261
Pongpas, Jenjira, 318
Pope, Alexander, 278
Porgy and Bess, 105, 107, 116
Portabella, Pere, 322

Porter, Cole, 113
Porter, Edwin, 28
A Portrait of a Lady, 40
Portrait of Jennie, 154
A Portrait of the Artist as a Young Man, 34–35, 247
Porumboiu, Corneliu, 311–315, 324
Potter, Sally, 30
Powell, Dick, 89
Powell, Jane, 120
Powell, Michael, 7
The Power and the Glory, 48
Preminger, Otto, 24, 142
Presley, Elvis, 54
Pressburger, Emeric, 7
The Primitive, 317
Prince, Stephen, 298
The Prince and the Showgirl, 73, 74
Profit Motive and the Whispering Wind, 324
Proust, Marcel, 37, 199, 289, 296
Provost, Martin, 324
Psycho, 39, 44, 73, 132, 133–134, 142, 144, 145, 147, 154, 167, 168, 285
Pudovkin, V. I., 51, 59, 62, 315
Pulver, Liselotte, 17
Purcell, Eric, 75
Pursued, 139
Pushover, 141
Pynchon, Thomas, 11, 219

The Queen, 50
Queen Christina, 67
Querelle, 38
The Quiet American, 283
The Quiet One, 256–257, 260
Quinn, Anthony, 262
Quo Vadis?, 36

Radcliffe, Ann, 322
Raengo, Alessandra, 46
Rafferty, Tom, 89, 96
Raiders of the Lost Ark, 168
Rains, Claude, 144
Random Harvest, 41
Ratatouille, 323
Ray, Nicholas, 17, 21, 199, 243, 281
Ray, Robert B., 33, 271
Reagan, Ronald, 228
Rear Window, 127, 133
Rebecca, 43, 127, 132, 139, 140, 142, 150, 152, 154
Rebello, Stephen, 73
Redacted, 323
The Red Badge of Courage, 228, 257, 259, 265
Redford, Robert, 323
Red Line 7000, 23, 283
Red River, 92, 264
Reed, Carol, 188
Reed, Oliver, 55
Regan, Ronald, 29, 290, 293
Reichardt, Kelly, 323
Reign of Terror, 139
Reisz, Karel, 243
Remarque, Erich Maria, 17, 19
Rembrandt, 44
Renoir, Jean, 21, 22, 24, 26, 40, 42, 82, 182, 207, 276, 280
Report from the Aleutians, 217
Resnais, Alain, 8, 21, 30
Reville, Alma, 73, 150
Reynolds, Debbie, 120
Rice, Elmer, 110
Rich and Strange, 127
Richie, Donald, 303
Ridgely, John, 89
Riggs, Marlon, 84
Rilke, Rainer Maria, 24
Rimbaud, Arthur, 131
Rio Bravo, 92, 126
Ritter, Thelma, 64, 67
Rivers, Larry, 273
Rivette, Jacques, 16, 270, 323
The Road to Wigan Pier, 286
Robert-Houdin, Jean-Eugène, 189
Robeson, Paul, 109
Robinson, Bruce, 125
Robinson, Edgar G., 68
Robinson Crusoe, 47
Robocop, 57
Rockefeller, Nelson, 163
Rodowick, D. N., 4
Rodriguez, Robert, 57
Roeg, Nicholas, 173
Rogers, Will, 50, 81, 278
Rohmer, Éric, 16, 24, 57, 231
Roland, Gilbert, 262
Rooney, Mickey, 49, 66
Roosevelt, Franklin D., 94, 112, 200, 201, 203, 205
Root, Lynn, 107
Rope, 135, 140, 141, 152
Rosenbaum, Jonathan, 1–2, 174, 178, 179, 180, 196, 206, 212, 246, 265, 267, 289–290, 315, 317

Ross, Steve, 210
Rossellini, Roberto, 21, 22, 231–233, 238, 276, 280, 281, 284
Rossen, Robert, 217, 243
Roth, Tim, 173
Rouge, 304, 307
Rousseau, Jean Jacques, 185
Rowe, Misty, 74
Rubens, Peter Paul, 308
Ruiz, Raúl, 8, 291, 320–322, 324
Russell, Rosalind, 273
Rutledge, Ann, 259

Saboga, Carlos, 321
Sabotage, 39, 129, 133, 140, 160
Saboteur, 157
Sabrina, 90
Sade, Marquis de, 131, 213
Sadoul, Georges, 100
Saecl, Renata, 145–146
Saeed-Vafa, Mehrnaz, 289, 315, 317
Sahara, 108
Saint, Eva Marie, 164, 167, 170
Saisaymar, Thanaput, 318
Salinger, J.D., 219, 273
Sandberg, Carl, 259
Sanders, George, 144, 232
Sanders of the River, 183
Sandoe, James, 100
The Sands of Iwo Jima, 222
Sanford, Erskine, 183
Sarris, Andrew, 9, 25, 246, 275–288, 290, 296, 297
Sartre, Jean-Paul, 139
Sátántangó, 291
Saturday Night and Sunday Morning, 243
Saudek, Robert, 258
Saulescu, Irina, 313
Saussure, Ferdinand de, 29
Sayers, Dorothy, 149
The Scarlet Letter, 96
Schatz, Thomas, 18
Scherfig, Lone, 324
Schiller, Friedrich, 34
Schilling, Gus, 183
Schindler's List, 292
Schnitzler, Arthur, 212
Schrader, Paul, 24, 153, 231
Schrank, Joseph, 110, 119
Schreck, Max, 69
Schreiber, Liev, 75
Schulberg, Budd, 273
Schwarzenegger, Arnold, 56

Scientists and Tramps, 258
Scorsese, Martin, 41
Scott, George C., 83
Scrutiny, 246
The Search, 288
The Searchers, 25
Seberg, Jean, 24
A Secret, 324
The Secret Agent (film), 160, 168
The Secret Agent (novel), 160
Sellers, Peter, 55
Selznick, David O., 15, 43, 45, 107, 132, 142, 144, 151, 154
Sennett, Mack, 54, 131, 265, 266
Séraphine, 324
Serban, Florin, 325
Serena Blandish, 113, *114*
Sergeant York, 217
Serkis, Andy, 56
Serling, Rod, 273
The Set Up, 33
Seyrig, Delphine, 313
Shadow of a Doubt, 88, 139, 140, 141, 142, 144, 145, 150, 152–153, 168, 172, 277
Shadows, 243
Shaftesbury, Edmund, 52
Shakespeare, William, 24, 36, 44, 45, 59, 66, 174, 175, 189, 191, 198, 211, 216, 232, 259
Shambu, Girish, 246
The Shanghai Gesture, 96
The Shape of Fear, 207
Shelley, Percy Bysshe, 245
Shenar, Paul, 75
Sheridan, Ann, 225
Sherlock Jr., (film) 249–250
"Sherlock Jr." (painting), 269
The Shining, 210
Shirin, 315–317, 324
Shoot the Piano Player, 243
Show Boat, 105
Siegel, Don, 283–284
Sienkiewicz, Henryk, 36
Silva, Sebastián, 324
Silver, Alain, 139
The Simple Art of Murder, 100
Sin City, 57
Siodmak, Robert, 141, 288
Sirk, Douglas, 17–18, 29, 279, 281
Sissako, Abderrahmane, 8, 323
Sita Sings the Blues, 324
Sklar, Robert, 72, 206
Slesar, Henry, 133

Sloane, Everett, 183, 193, 194
The Smart Set, 149
Smash, 74
The Snake Pit, 140
The Sniper, 266
Snow, Michael, 3, 57, 83, 270, 272
Sobchack, Vivian, 153
Social Network, 325
Soderbergh, Steven, 74, 323, 324
Sojcher, Frédéric, 325
Sokoloff, Vladimir, 183
Some Came Running, 20, 22, 81
Some Like It Hot, 68
Something Wild, 167
The Song of Bernadette, 253
Song of the South, 104
The Son of Kong, 183
Sontag, Susan, 20, 268
Sophocles, 126
"The Sorcerer's Apprentice," 136
The Sorrows of Young Werther, 36
Sorvino, Mira, 74
Spacey, Kevin, 70
Spartacus, 208–209
Spellbound, 128, 140, 147
Spencer, Kenneth, 120
Sperb, Jason, 298
Spiegel, Alan, 37
Spielberg, Steven, 30, 56, 168, 210
The Spiral Staircase, 153–154
Spitzer, Leo, 27
Spoto, Donald, 73
Springall, Alejandro, 323–324
The Square, 325
Sripariyattiweti, Phra, 317
Stafford, Frederick, 285
Stagecoach, 182
Stage Fright, 144, 147
Stam, Robert, 43, 46
Stanislavsky, Konstantin, 51, 52, 53–54, 57, 59, 80, 188, 189, 190
Stanton, Andrew, 324
Stars in My Crown, 289
Star Wars, 295, 302
Steamboat Round the Bend, 280
Steele, Bob, 89
The Steel Helmet, 268
Stein, Gertrude, 250
Steinbeck, John, 34, 104, 231, 249
Steiner, Max, 15, 87, 221
Stern, Howard, 42
Sternberg, Josef von, 23, 112, 231, 286–287
Stevens, George, 268

Stevenson, Robert, 133
Stewart, James, 68, 124, 155
Stories We Tell, 11
Stormy Weather, 104, 108
The Story of G.I. Joe, 253, 254, 264
The Strange Case of Angelica, 324
The Strange One, 273
The Stranger, 142, 195, 265
Strangers on a Train, 128, 129, 139, 141, 142, 147, 148, 172
Strasberg, Lee, 53, 54, 58
Straub, Jean-Marie, 28, 267, 272, 290, 309
Streep, Meryl, 71
A Streetcar Named Desire, 54
Strike, 66
Stroheim, Erich von, 37
Sturges, Preston, 67, 127, 264–265, 267, 270, 294
Suarez, Juan A., 36
Sublett, John Bubbles, 116–117
Suez, 183
Sugar, 324
Sullivan, Charlotte, 74
Sullivan's Travels, 127
Summer Hours, 324
Sunrise, 39
Sunset Blvd., 52, 272
The Sun Shines Bright, 23, 288
Suspense, 134
Suspicion, 139, 140, 154, 158
Swanberg, Joe, 5, 324
Swanson, Gloria, 52
Sweetgrass, 325
Sweet Smell of Success, 139, 272–274
Swift, Jonathan, 131
Szankowski, André, 321

Tabu, 11
Tales of Manhattan, 104
Talk about a Stranger, 259
Tamiroff, Akim, 67, 193, 194
Tarantino, Quentin, 293
Tarkington, Booth, 76
Tarr, Béla, 11, 291
Tashlin, Frank, 23
Tati, Jacques, 291
Taylor, Rod, 127
Taymor, Julie, 55
Teen Wolf, 292
Teixeira, Chico, 323
Temple, Shirley, 50
The Terminator, 56
Thackeray, William Makepeace, 213

Thatcher, Margaret, 29
Theatre (Maugham), 64
Theory of Film Practice, 289
There Will Be Blood, 323
They Live by Night, 17
They Won't Forget, 141
The Thing Called Love, 292–293
The Third Man, 173, 187, 188–189, 204, 211, 266
35 Shots of Rum, 324
The 39 Steps (film), 39, 127, 132, 140, 156, 157, 169
The Thirty-Nine Steps (novel), 142, 160–161
This Island Earth, 245
This Is Not a Film, 11
Thomas, Dylan, 266
Thomas, François, 194
Thompson, Frank, 259
Thompson, Jim, 137
Thompson, Kristin, 35, 39
Thompson, Sunny, 74
Thomson, David, 24, 95, 98, 100, 212, 287
The Thousand Eyes of Dr. Mabuse, 23
Thunderball, 284–285
Thurman, Uma, 74
Time Regained, 291
A Time to Love and a Time to Die, 17–19, 23, 25
Tinker, Tailor, Soldier, Spy, 61
Tobin, Genevieve, 62
To Catch a Thief, 132, 152
Togliatti, Palmiro, 204
To Have and Have Not, 88, 92, 93
To Kill a Mockingbird, 72, 294
Toland, Gregg, 182, 272, 322
Tolson, Clyde, 203
Tolstoy, Leo, 42
Toomey, Regis, 89
Topaz, 285
Torn Curtain, 138, 166
Totem and Taboo, 112
To the Lighthouse, 239
Touch of Evil, 142, 191, 193, 204, 209, 211, 270, 283, 297
Tourneur, Jacques, 253, 289, 308–309
Toy Story 3, 325
Trafic, 304
Trapeze, 274
Traven, B., 215, 217–223
The Treasure of the Sierra Madre (novel), 215, 217–223
The Treasure of the Sierra Madre (film), 215–230, 253, 265

Tregenza, Rob, 293
The Trial, 133, 142, 176, 185, 196, 204, 211, 212
Trilling, Lionel, 9, 26
Trouble in Paradise, 62–62, 294
The Trouble with Harry, 132
Truffaut, François, 16, 17, 20, 22, 23, 24, 34, 38, 39, 136, 146, 147, 151–152, 156, 161, 168, 169, 195, 243, 275
Trumbo, Dalton, 208
Tsivian, Yuri, 299
Tulpan, 324
Tupper, James, 75
The Turin Horse, 11
Twain, Mark, 45, 130
Twelve against the Gods: The Story of Adventure, 216
Twelve Angry Men, 273
Twelve Monkeys, 33
24 City, 309–311, 323
Two or Three Things I Know about Her, 55
2001: A Space Odyssey, 51, 209, 212, 213
The Two Towers, 56
Two Weeks with Love, 120
Typhoon, 184

Ulmer, Edgar G., 142, 286, 288
Ulysses, 18, 34–35, 231
Uncle Boonmee Who Can Recall His Past Lives, 317–320, 324
Under Capricorn, 132, 141
Underworld, 231
Underworld, U.S.A., 243
Unkrich, Lee, 325
The Unthinking Lobster, 198
Upstream Color, 11
Uricchio, William, 36
Uris, Leon, 285

Vaché, Jacques, 131
Valli, Alida, 151
Van Dyck, Anthony, 308
Van Gogh, Vincent, 262
Van Sant, Gus, 323
Varda, Agnès, 324
Veidt, Conrad, 52
Ventura, 306–309
Venturi, Robert, 20
Vera Cruz, 274
Verboten!, 22
Verhoeven, Paul, 303, 323
Vermeer, Jan, 307

Vertigo, 22, 132, 139, 142, 154–155, 168, 169, 283
Vertov, Dziga, 27, 28, 253, 256
Vickers, Jon, 5
Vickers, Martha, 93
Vicky Cristina Barcelona, 324
Vidor, King, 111, 117, 245
Vigo, Jean, 250, 256
Vincere, 324
Viridiana, 243
Visconti, Luchino, 200
The Visitor, 324
Vitti, Monica, 283
Vlady, Marina, 55
Voyage to Italy, 231–233, 238

Wainewright, Thomas, 135
Wake Island, 252
Waking Life, 57
Walburn, Raymond, 67
Walken, Christopher, 68
Wall, Jeff, 307
Wallace, David Foster, 11
Wallace, Henry, 203
WALL-E, 324
Waller, Fats, 268
Walsh, Raoul, 24, 29, 273
Walzl, Florence, 233
Wanda, 60, 294
Wang, Yu, 309
Wanger, Walter, 107
Ward, Elizabeth, 139
Warhol, Andy, 11, 20
Warner, Jack, 97, 217
Warner, Rick, 46
War of the Worlds, 174
Washington, Dennis, 235
Wasserman, Lew, 167
The Waste Land, 37, 79, 133
Waters, Ethel, 104, 111, 113, 114, 116, 120, 122
Watts, Naomi, 50, 51
Waugh, Evelyn, 133
Wavelength, 270
Wayne, John, 50, 68, 270
Wead, Frank, 279
Weaver, Dennis, 191
Webb, Clifton, 143
Weber, Max, 110
Weegee, 205
Weerasethakul, Apichatpong, 8, 317–320, 324
Weiner, Matthew, 323

Wellbery, David, 78, 84
Weller, Peter, 57
Welles, Orson, 8, 9, 11, 22, 28, 30, 31, 39, 51, 75–76, 82, 136, 141, 142, 147, 150, 153, 172–205, 206, 207, 211–212, 213–214, 217, 253, 254, 265, 267, 270, 272, 276, 278, 281, 282, 283, 289, 296, 297, 322
Wellman, William, 222, 253, 264, 265, 279
Wendy and Lucy, 323
West, Nathaniel, 149
West Side Story, 243
Wexman, Virginia, 169
Whale, James, 145
What Makes Sammy Run?, 273
"When Lilacs Last in the Dooryard Bloom'd," 259
When Strangers Marry, 253
Where Does Your Hidden Smile Lie?, 309
Where the Wild Things Are, 324
Whistler, James McNeill, 89
White, Rob, 243, 244
White, Walter, 107–108
White Hunter, Black Heart, 71
White Mane, 258
White Material, 325
Whitman, Walt, 254, 259
The Whole Town's Talking, 280
Wilde, Oscar, 25, 135, 163, 287, 288
Wilder, Billy, 23, 90, 132, 272, 288
The Wild One, 54
Willeford, Charles, 40
Williams, J.R., 273
Williams, John, 144
Williams, Michelle, 74, 76
Williams, Raymond, 7, 16, 59, 245
Williams, Spencer, 117, 120, *121*
Willis, Gordon, 15
Willkie, Wendell, 107, 111
Wilson, Dooley, 110
Wilson, Edmund, 149
Wilson, George M., 77
Winchell, Walter, 273
The Wind That Shakes the Barley, 323
Windust, Bretaigne, 258
The Wings of the Dove, 291
Winters, Shelly, 54
Winter's Bone, 325
Wise, Naomi, 92
Wise, Robert, 243
Wiseman, Frederick, 325
The Wizard of Oz, 110
Wolfe, Thomas, 247

Wollen, Peter, 24, 26, 28, 92, 135, 244
Wood, Robin, 9, 24–26, 28, 31, 92, 137, 151, 171, 231, 245
Woodward, Joanne, 259
Woolf, Virginia, 9, 37, 239, 250
Wordsworth, William, 282
Workers Leaving the Lumière Factory, 309
The Wreck of the Mary Deare, 157, 162
Wright, Richard, 190, 202
The Wrong Man, 126, 129, 133, 139, 144, 145–146, 147, 170
Wuthering Heights, 38
Wyler, William, 22, 253, 254, 272, 275, 276, 288
Wyman, Jane, 144
Wynn, Ed, 62

Yeats, William Butler, 77, 282, 310
Yolanda and the Thief, 119
You and Me, 125
Young, Terence, 284
Young Mr. Lincoln, 259
The Young One, 243
You Only Live Once, 17
Yu, Lik-wai, 309

Zanuck, Darryl, 15, 107, 231
Zemeckis, Robert, 11
Zero for Conduct, 250, 256
Zhao, Tao, 311
Ziegfield, Florenz, 118
The Ziegfield Follies of 1936, 113
Zinnemann, Fred, 288
Žižek, Slavoj, 139–140
Zodiac, 323
Zola, Émile, 42
Zweig, Stefan, 212

www.ingramcontent.com/pod-product-compliance
Lightning Source LLC
Chambersburg PA
CBHW03051823O426
43665CB00010B/673